BEING AUSTRALIAN

In memory of my mother, Anne Therese Elder.

BEING AUSTRALIAN
NARRATIVES OF NATIONAL IDENTITY

CATRIONA ELDER

ALLEN&UNWIN

First published in 2007

Allen & Unwin
83 Alexander Street
Crows Nest NSW 2065
Australia
Phone: (61 2) 8425 0100
Fax: (61 2) 9906 2218
Email: info@allenandunwin.com
Web: www.allenandunwin.com

National Library of Australia
Cataloguing-in-Publication entry:

Elder, Catriona.
    Being Australia: narratives of national identity.

    Bibliography.
    Includes index.
    ISBN 978 1 74114 928 9.

    1. National characteristic, Australian. 2. Australia –
    Social life and customs. I. Title.

305.800994

Typeset in New Baskerville 11/13 pt by Midland Typesetters, Australia.
Printed by Ligare Book Printers, Australia.

10 9 8 7 6 5 4 3 2 1

CONTENTS

Figures and Tables   *vii*
Acknowledgements   *ix*

Introduction   1

Part 1: Stories in the making

1 Imagining nations: Telling national tales   23
2 The working man is everywhere: Class and national identity   40
3 The invisible woman: Gender and nation   65
4 Populate or perish: Sexuality and nation   93
5 White Australia meets multiculturalism: Ethnicity and nation   115
6 The myth of *terra nullius*: Indigeneity and nation   147

Part 2: Ways of being Australian

7 The cultural nation: Art, cinema and music   181
8 The heart of the country: Place, space and land   212
9 The land of the long weekend: Public holidays and national events   239
10 Taking to the streets: (non) National uses of public spaces   262
11 Backyards and barracking: The everyday in Australia   287
12 Australia on display: Museums, heritage and the national capital   320

Conclusion   352

Glossary   *354*
Bibliography   *362*
Index   *381*

FIGURES AND TABLES

Figures

1.1 The Sydney Olympic Opening Ceremony began its story
of Australia with dozens of stockmen and women   33

1.2 A segment of the Indigenous tableau   35

2.1 Nowhere is egalitarianism demonstrated more clearly
than in local pubs   45

3.1 Nineteenth-century cartoon mocking the declining
Anglo–Australian birth rate   83

4.1 Brook Andrew's artwork, *Sexy and Dangerous* (1998)   102

4.2 Destiny Deacon's *Blak Like Me* (1991/2003)   103

5.1 The cartoon 'Wake Australia Wake'   121

5.2 Image from an Australian magazine in the 1890s   123

5.3 A headline of the *Sun-Herald*   125

5.4 Poster used in the 'We are all boat people' 2001 campaign   128

5.5 Hou Leong's 1995 'An Australian' image   138

6.1 A 1930s advertisement for Trans-Australian Railway   152

6.2 Advertisement by the Australian National Travel
Association   153

6.3 Travel advertisement from the early twentieth century   154

6.4 Advertisement for the main resort at Uluru   161

6.5 Gordon Bennett's *Self Portrait (But I Always Wanted
to be One of the Good Guys)*   171

7.1 *Shearing the Rams* (1888–90) by Tom Roberts   185

7.2 Frederick McCubbin's three-panelled work   186

8.1 Percy Trompf poster advertising travel to central
Australia in the 1930s   218

8.2 A 1997 advertisement for travel to the Northern
     Territory   219
8.3 Jan Sensberg's painting *Borchgevinck's Foot* (1987–88)   229
8.4 The famous Peter Dombrovski photograph   236
10.1 Flashmobbers taking part in an 'action'   271
10.2 MEMORIAL, part of the 1997 Sydney Gay and
     Lesbian Mardi Gras   279
11.1 St Kilda player Nicky Winmar   296
11.2 James Mellon's *Gene @ Home* (2003)   300
11.3 A young Australian, with an Australian flag worn
     as a cape   305
11.4 Cartoon from Canada's *Globe and Mail*   306
12.1 *The Aboriginal Memorial* (1987–88) by Ramingining
     Artists   333
12.2 The Parliamentary 'triangle' in Canberra   341
12.3 The view down Anzac Parade to the Australian War
     Memorial and Mount Ainslie   343
12.4 Advertisement for Canberra   345
12.5 Poster for the Australian War Memorial's travelling
     exhibition   346

Tables

3.1 Gender Profile of Victim and Person of Interest (POI)   76
3.2 Mean Weekly Earnings ($) of Australian Men and
     Women   81
5.1 Top 10 Countries of Origin of Migrants to Australia   130

ACKNOWLEDGEMENTS

THIS BOOK HAS taken me some time to put together and it was a real pleasure to close my eyes and remember all those who helped me with it, because, as I have recently learned, being helped is wonderful. I would like to thank Alison Bashford who first suggested I write this book. To my editor, Elizabeth Weiss, thanks for pulling my proposal out of the pile and saying yes. I am grateful to the anonymous Allen & Unwin readers, who had so many thoughtful suggestions on how to make this book better. Editors Karen Gee, Sue Jarvis and Joanne Holliman put in an enormous effort working on the manuscript and I thank them for their input. Thank you to Jessica Ainscow and Kate Huppatz for research assistance. Alison Bashford, Cath Styles, Ben Maddison, Emma Partridge, Sarah Maddison, Murray Pratt, Cath Ellis and Adrian Vickers all read draft chapters. Your responses were invaluable and your time, patience and insight was appreciated.

In 2002 Professor David Goodman at the Institute for International Studies, University of Technology, Sydney provided me with a Visiting Fellowship which is much appreciated. Thank you also to the School of Society Culture and Performance at the University of Sydney who granted funding to undertake work on the book in 2004. In 2006 I received a Writing Fellowship from the Research Institute of Humanities and Social Sciences at the University of Sydney for which I am grateful. I have worked jointly with Cath Ellis, Angela Pratt and Aunty Barbara Nicholson on reconciliation in Australia. Sections of this book draw on the many conversations and considerable research we did together. I have acknowledged our published work in the text, but I would like to acknowledge everything this co-work gave me here. To the students, on whom I have tried out so many of these ideas, your responses helped me to rethink issues. To Professor Marilyn Lake—who rekindled my interest in Australian scholarship—I owe you a scholarly debt.

This book was written in the shadow of my mother's death. My love and gratitude is extended to all those who knew this and helped me along the way: Alison, Cath and Yoli, Emma and Sarah, Murray, Ben, Mark and Marisa (I love your constant care, which seems to be available at all times), Rebecca, and Amanda and Edith (who even missed the Beasts of Bourbon for this book). To Dad and Cathie, thank you for asking how it was going and for having faith. To my family, my love and thanks, always.

My mother died before I had really contributed much to the world. I hope this book in some small way adds to what is good in my community and makes real my mother's faith in me.

Catriona Elder

The author would like to thank the following artists for permission to quote from their lyrics: Kev Carmody, 'Bloodlines' (© Song Cycles Pty Ltd); Paul Kelly and Kev Carmody, 'From Little Things Big Things Grow' (© Universal Music Publishing P/L and Song Cycles P/L, all rights reserved); Bruce Dawe, 'The Family Man' from *Sometimes Gladness: Collected Poems 1955–1997*, 6th edition (© Bruce Dawe, published by Pearson Education Australia); Anita Heiss, 'Deprived of Culture' from *Token Koori* (© Anita Heiss, published by Curringa Communications); Rob Hirst, Jim Moginie and Peter Garrett, 'Beds Are Burning' (© 1986 Midnight Oil / Sony Music Australia); Neil Murray, 'My Island Home' (Neil Murray / © Rondor Music Australia Pty Ltd. All Rights Reserved. International Copyright Secured.); Lyrics from the 'Many Rhymes, One Rhythm' project (used with the permission of the National Museum of Australia); South West Syndicate 'Definition of Danger' (© South West Syndicate, written by Munkimuk [Mark Ross]); Yothu Yindi, Paul Kelly, Midnight Oil, 'Treaty' (© 1996 Yothu Yindi Music Pty Ltd, 1996 Mushroom Records International).

INTRODUCTION

In October 2005, the wife of Prince Frederik, the heir apparent to the Danish throne, gave birth to a baby boy—a future king. The mother of the baby was Mary Donaldson, a former citizen of Australia. Donaldson, a Tasmanian, was working as a real estate agent in Sydney when she met Prince Frederik at a Sydney pub during the 2000 Olympics. The pair fell in love and became engaged to be married. Part of the preparation for the wedding involved Mary learning etiquette and deportment, taking lessons in Danish and giving up her Australian citizenship in favour of Danish citizenship. Yet, when Princess Mary produced the Danish heir newspapers here ran headlines such as the *Adelaide Advertiser*'s 'Hail Our Prince. True Blue Link to the Throne' (2005). Australian journalists jostled with the locals at the maternity wing of the hospital, asking the royal family and Mary's family questions about the new Australian baby. On a number of occasions, they were politely reminded by the Danes that Princess Mary and the child were Danish. It is likely that most readers of the news about the Danish royal birth would have understood the sense in which the new Danish prince was Australian, even if the child would probably never hold an Australian passport. For many Australians another set of characteristics made Princess Mary and the baby 'theirs', made them Australian, characteristics unrelated to citizenship.

A few years earlier, at a ceremony at Government House held towards the end of 2002, Australian military personnel were awarded conduct medals for their meritorious actions when on duty in

Afghanistan in the war to dislodge the Taliban and find the terrorist Osama Bin Laden. One medal recipient was asked what it was that had helped him cope in the very difficult situation where he and others had earned their awards. The soldier did not reply that his training had helped him keep a cool head. Instead, he responded that the vital ingredient was 'being Australian'. Most viewers of the ABC television news about the military medal recipients would have understood and been able to make sense of—and perhaps even identify with—the soldier's statement that being Australian explained his military survival and endeavour. In both cases 'being Australian' is a complex notion that extends well beyond concepts of citizenship and it influences aspects of life that may seem unconnected to nationality.

If being Australian is something attributed to a variety of characteristics, then so is being 'un-Australian'. In 2001, a man named Sharaz Kayani set himself on fire outside Parliament House in Canberra. He did so at the end of a long struggle to bring his family to Australia. He had a daughter with cerebral palsy, and this fact made his attempts more difficult. Philip Ruddock, the minister for immigration at the time, noted Kayani's act as 'not something we are used to or experienced with' (Birch 2001). The act was seen as alien to Australia—as un-Australian.

Being un-Australian is something Australians can do as well. In December 2005 a large group of Anglo–Australians went on a rampage at Cronulla and Maroubra beaches in south Sydney, attacking people they identified as 'Arabs' and 'Lebs' and who the newspapers the next day more politely called people of 'Middle Eastern appearance'. The crowd, some of whom were draped in Australian flags or wearing Australian flag t-shirts, chanted slogans such as 'kill the leb' as they ran looking for, and attacking, men and women they saw as different. The various government responses to this mob violence were to identify it as un-Australian. New South Wales Magistrate William Brydon described the actions as 'very' un-Australian when he refused one of the arrested men bail. The premier of New South Wales also labelled the riot and the attack that sparked the riot as un-Australian. This term un-Australian has become a way of trying to define what are seen as the limits of acceptable behaviour in the Australian nation. In the incidents at Cronulla one group of Anglo–Australians identified other Australians as acting in ways they saw as un-Australian—a beach lifesaver had been reported as beaten up by a group of non-Anglo–Australian men. The response of the Anglo–Australians was in turn understood as un-Australian as well.

Being un-Australian seems quite common in contemporary Australia. The former opposition leader Kim Beazley has in recent years condemned tax cuts for the rich and a failure to participate in politics as un-Australian. Some labour unions have argued being made to work on Christmas Day is un-Australian. The prime minister has referred to anti-globalisation protests as un-Australian and Greens Senator Bob Brown has argued that the shrinking access to quality public education is un-Australian. For some people being labelled un-Australian by their political rivals is a badge of honour. Others use the term with irony and wit—dressing up for the opera might be seen as un-Australian. But the term is often used as both an insult and a disciplining expression and it can have very real and alienating implications, as was demonstrated at Cronulla Beach.

This book explores how ideas of being Australian and of being un-Australian form. The simple phrase 'being Australian' has, as a result of decades of storytelling, myth-making, news reporting, academic pontificating, cinema production and watching, and more, become a recognisable shorthand way of expressing a certain conglomerate of desirable characteristics that are seen as unique to Australians. Here we explore the origins, meaning and effects of a variety of stories of being Australian and being un-Australian. I ask questions about how ideas of 'Australia' are produced and interrogate the ambivalence that can reside in these ideas. How are these ideas deployed to explain life within the nation? What purpose these claims of Australian-ness and un-Australian-ness serve?

It is quite common to hear discussions about whether one idea of being Australian—say, the 'ocker' bloke—should be or has been replaced by another (say, the metro-sexual). I would suggest that it is more important to think about *why* citizens need these iconic images. Why do governments, the media, the education sector, film directors and advertisers spend so much time and money discovering or creating and 'selling' these icons of Australianness? What purpose is served? (White 1981: viii) What happens when the 'ocker' image is used to encourage Australians to exercise more or water their gardens more wisely? What happens when the Indigenous athlete Cathy Freeman, wrapped in an Aboriginal flag, covers newspaper front pages all across the nation, as she did during the 1994 Commonwealth Games? The argument is that the purpose varies; however, by exploring what that purpose is, it is possible to see more clearly how different people fit in, are fitted into or are excluded from stories of being Australian.

One of the most stereotyped, out of date and yet long-lived and most popular narratives of Australian-ness is that of the 'Aussie bloke'. It was this narrative that the Australian soldier was drawing on, or reproducing, in his story on the television news. In the 1950s, historian Russel Ward outlined how he thought this narrative had come into being. His book *The Australian Legend* (1958) explored the origins of the 'myth' of the 'typical' Australian—the type known as the Aussie bloke. He put together one of the most famous descriptions of this bloke, the 'typical Australian':

> . . . a practical man, rough and ready in his manners and quick to decry any appearance of affectation in others . . . Though capable of great exertion in an emergency, he normally feels no impulse to work hard without good cause. He swears hard and consistently, gambles heavily and often, and drinks deeply on occasion . . . he is a great knocker of eminent people unless, as is in the case of his sporting heroes, they are distinguished by physical prowess. He is fiercely independent . . . above all he will stick to his mates through thick and thin, even if he thinks they may be wrong . . . He tends to be a rolling stone, highly suspect if he should chance to gather much moss. (1958: 16–17)

Today, many Australians would scoff at Ward's already ironic description, but aspects of this idea—however mocked—still circulate today when generalisations are made about Australian-being. For example, in 2002 the National Capital Authority, the body charged with overseeing the planning of the national capital—Canberra—released a set of guidelines to assist people who were seeking to have someone or something commemorated in the capital. The guidelines suggest that any commemorative spaces in the capital need to reflect national 'values and aspirations' and 'reinforce and transmit collective values' (National Capital Authority 2002b: 5). The guidelines list what these collective values are, including: 'first and foremost egalitarianism', social responsibility, freedom, civility, humour, democratic principles, civic awareness, peace, order, respect of the rule of law, mateship, diversity and tolerance, irreverence and fairness. The range in 2002 was much broader than those understood as Australian in the 1900s or 1950s. However, buried in these values is the ghost of Ward's typical Australian, and also the ideas the soldier was referring to when he spoke of his ability to cope during war.

Many Australians obviously disagree with the idea of typical Australian-ness deriving from this laconic bush bloke. Indeed, Australians tend to treat most iconic figures of Australian-ness with irony. For example when the wildlife entrepreneur Steve Irwin died unexpectedly in 2006 many Australians were sad at his early death while at the same time a bit embarrassed that Irwin was understood overseas as a typical Australian. This was also obvious in the closing ceremony of the 2000 Olympics in Sydney. The ceremony was a witty and gently mocking tribute to Australian symbols such as Kylie Minogue and the rubber thong. Yet, even amongst this self-knowing irony, what has not been given up is the idea of Australian-ness. Many Australians still relish the idea that some things, people and feelings are Australian, while other people, things and feelings are seen as foreign or 'un-Australian'. Australians still tell stories about who they are. Ward's Aussie bloke may be out of date and the process of icon-making may be self-aware, but the endeavour of creating stories about being Australian is still a central way in which being Australian is reinforced.

As the National Capital Authority guidelines suggest, the story of being Australian can be expressed through a wide variety of values. The story told by Ward and the soldier on the ABC news is just one of a myriad stories of Australian-ness. This particular story emerges from tales of the bush and war. It produces a narrative that represents Australians as natural fighters, drawing on a long heritage of independent spirit and a resourcefulness born of a life in the bush. Books such as C.E.W. Bean's history of World War I (1936); the more recent cinema and television productions about Australia's war participation (especially the film *Gallipoli* (1981)); the dotting of the landscape with cenotaphs and war memorials; government-sponsored commemorations such as *Australia Remembers*, remembering the 50th anniversary of the end of World War II, and the 75th and 90th anniversaries of the landing at Gallipoli; the media reporting of the success of the Australian INTERFET troops in East Timor; the war in Iraq, and Australian military assistance to survivors of the 2004 Boxing Day tsunami and the 2002 and 2005 Bali bombings, have all added to and emboldened this narrative.

These stories have all helped produce a legend of being an Australian that has built a picture of Australian-ness as golden youth, larrikin nonchalance and unpretentious courage. This meant that in 2002 a soldier could say it was his Australian-ness that helped him do his duty, and many Australians could make a link in their mind with the popular story about Australian-ness and masculine soldierly ability and understand his meaning. The National Capital Authority could write guidelines about what belongs in the Australian capital city and many of the values link to the bush and military story. This story of being Australian has also been attached to victorious cricket teams, weary volunteer firefighters, and farm families in times of drought. It is just one strand of the complex understanding that circulates about Australian-ness, but it is a powerful one.

This book explores a range of dominant or exemplary tales about being Australian over the twentieth century. It analyses who supported them, and how and when they changed. Such a project is not unique. It was most famously and successfully undertaken by Richard White (1981) in his book *Inventing Australia*. What *Being Australian* does is extend and rethink some of the ground covered by White. Since he wrote his book, there have been significant issues and events that have reshaped or influenced the stories of Australian-ness. Added to this are new theories for framing the issue of Australian national identity. Here, these new ideas and issues will be used to organise the argument. I will argue, as White suggested, that dominant ideas of being Australian are invented, and that these inventions have been and continue to be organised around a desire for the land, a fear of others who may claim the land and, as a result of this, a deep ambivalence about belonging to this space. These anxieties, desires and ambivalences mean that securing a strong story about non-Indigenous white belonging is an important aspect of Australian national identity narratives. These narratives privilege elements of non-Indigeneity, whiteness masculinity and heterosexuality.

Narrating the nation

When it is stated that we will explore 'stories' and 'tales' about being Australian, this does not mean the focus will simply be on the literature of Australia—the stories of Henry Lawson or Tim Winton, for example, or the poetry of Oodgeroo Noonuccal or Ania Walwicz. The terms 'stories' and 'tales' are used in a much wider and looser sense. The argument is that the way people make sense of things—their lives, nation and the world—is to construct 'narratives'. These narratives, with their beginning, middle and end, are representations of people's understandings of being Australian. Some of these stories are sad, some are happy; some include the past, others focus on the future. These narratives may be mostly true, partly true or completely false. They are not only stories that are written or spoken through literature, law or news; they also appear in physical spaces. The stories may be constructed through architecture or design; they may appear in spaces filled with people or empty of people. These narratives may be inspired by what people hoped would happen rather than what did. They may reflect fears or leave out what people are ashamed of or cannot face. The narratives that are the focus of this book are those that posit a vision of Australia, or seek to make sense of being Australian, or convey or share the pleasures or difficulties of being Australian.

Only a few people—mostly historians—write authorised national narratives and have them formally published. But all of us construct narratives. Narratives are constructed though yarning and talking with people, writing letters or posting blogs on the net. Narratives of national life are created in the school classroom in dialogues between students and teachers. They are created by politicians to encourage Australians to vote for them, or by artists who want to share their vision of the nation. Australians see and hear these narratives on television and radio, read them in magazines and books, and watch them at the cinema. Stories of being Australian appear on billboards, on posters taped to telephone poles, and on free postcards on the counters of cafes. Narratives are created and shared in Anzac Day memorial services to remember the war dead as well as the festivities and protests that mark Australia Day. Attending exhibitions and museums to see aspects of past and present cultures of Australia exposes citizens to narratives of the nation. Attending an agricultural show, a rodeo, a music festival or a sporting event may do the same thing. All these activities, texts, events and exhibitions are part of the process of narrating stories about Australia.

Space and place

As suggested above, stories about being Australian are produced in relation to place. Where a person is located in the imagined nation shapes how they are understood and perhaps how they understand themselves. Meanings of being Australian change between different spaces. A powerful example of this is that in the mid-twentieth century an Indigenous person could be classified as Indigenous in one state of Australia and as non-Indigenous in another. Some places are seen as more Australian than others—for example the beach is represented in dominant stories of the nation as more Australian than a city or its outer suburbs. The Australian-ness of spaces can change. For instance, some Australians seeing images of a suburb gripped by riots (as has been the case in Australia in recent years) express how alien the images seem. They do not identify the place as Australian. When a riot ends the place is reclaimed as Australian. Some bodies are seen as more at home in some spaces than others. For example, when the ethnic mix of a suburb changes some Australians express feelings of being more or less at home in that place.

As Melissa Butcher (2003: 133) explains issues of power are always important when thinking about space, belonging and the nation. As was demonstrated in the example of the changing status of Indigenous people in different spaces it was Anglo–Australians who had the power to define who belonged where. It is still Anglo–Australians who have the most power to monitor the boundaries of places and decide who belongs and who does not. Young non-Anglo–Australians who congregate in shopping malls or Indigenous peoples who meet in parks to socialise are often understood as not belonging in these spaces and moved on by security guards or the police. This moving on is part of a process of 'purify[ing] space' of bodies that '"do not fit the dominant classifications" or values' (Butcher 2003: 133).

Other stories

Being Australian explores not just the powerful and dominant stories of Australian-ness. It also explores stories generally perceived to be alternative and subversive as well. It analyses how different narratives relate to each other. It analyses the stories that contradict the powerful stories—that exist at the same time as a powerful story and counter or irritate that story. Though the yarn of the laconic Aussie bloke who nonchalantly ambles through a war, and in moments of seriousness focuses on the needs of his mates, may be a pleasurable and popular narrative of being Australian, there are many stories that irritate or counter this story: the stories of the men who shoot themselves in the foot rather than go back to the battle front, the stories of men who suffer mentally and emotionally as a result of the terror of war, and even the stories of soldiers committing war crimes also make up the experience of 'being Australian'. But these stories are not as powerful as others. War exacts a tremendous mental cost on many participants. Post-traumatic stress disorder is proof of this. However, in national narratives, the idea of soldiers refusing to fight or never regaining mental health is difficult to come to terms with. So the more palatable stories dominate, though the others are still there.

The process of story-making has been called 'narrating the nation' (Bhabha 1990: 1), and it is a *dynamic* process. That means when a person reads, sees or hears narratives of the nation they do not receive them passively. The narratives are open to response and perhaps change. For example, in May 1997 Prime Minister John Howard appeared at a very important community convention on reconciliation in Melbourne. In the weeks preceding this national meeting, the federal government divided the nation by refusing to apologise to the Indigenous adults who make up the 'stolen generations' for the policy that saw them removed from their families. This act of apology had been recommended by *Bringing Them Home*, the report of HREOC, the inquiry into the practices of Indigenous child removal. Many delegates at the convention disagreed with the government's refusal to apologise. This refusal made them ashamed and angry about being Australian. To express these feelings of anger or shame, some members of the audience started booing when John Howard gave his address opening the conference. Others turned their backs on the prime minister. Not everyone booed, however; some audience members listened. In response to the cat-calls, the prime minister started to speak more loudly. At one point he thumped the lectern at which he was standing. He also pointed at Indigenous leaders in the audience, saying he had allocated a 'great deal of time in trying to find a just, fair and workable outcome' following the High Court's *Wik* ruling on native title. In this example, the convention centre is a site where a narrative of the nation—that told by the prime minister about reconciliation—is challenged by another narrative (the boo-ing and back turning). Different people attending the convention responded to the official narrative of the nation in different ways. They provided counter-stories.

The people in the audience were individuals with 'agency'. To have agency is to have some capacity to respond to the circumstances of life in ways that can lead to the world better reflecting your understanding of how the world should be. So, in the Reconciliation Convention example, those who disagreed with the government actions booed, letting it be known that the present situation did not reflect their idea of being Australian. Their responses could at some point actually work to bring about change. How much power these people or the population generally have to effect change depends on their circumstances. Tens of thousands of people at a sporting event or a rally may have more chance of effecting change than a single letter-writer to the prime minister. Some citizens will have limited agency because they are poor and disenfranchised, so their ability to make an impact on the story of Australia may be limited. Others will have more power and more chance to participate in debates about being Australian.

The first part of this book considers some of the key factors that have shaped people's agency—both as individuals and as collectives—and so their capacity to intervene in discussions about what it means to be Australian. Issues of class, gender, sexuality, ethnicity and Indigeneity are all considered as factors that both shape how people experience being Australian and also shape the capacity of people to participate in formal venues where Australian-ness is produced. These five key issues are used to help readers think about how Australian-ness is played out, produced and explored in different times, places and circumstances. In the second part of the book, a series of important stories, narratives or spaces are explored. National stories that are produced through classic cultural forms such as art, film and music are analysed. Narratives that focus on the land and others that emerge in official rituals such as Australia Day and Anzac Day are also explored. Part 2 also examines unofficial gatherings and rituals—counter-narratives—such as labour strikes and demonstrations and the Sydney Gay and Lesbian Mardi Gras. Narratives of nation are also made in everyday life. So spaces such as the sporting arena, the suburbs and the country town are explored. Governments spend a lot of time and money creating over-arching historical narratives of the nation. So the book finishes with a chapter exploring public spaces, such as museums and heritage sites. Finally, the national capital is considered as a space that lays out a national story for all to see and visit.

Australia's stories

The stories that are told about being Australian come from myriad places and take many shapes. However, there are two key themes that mark many of the dominant stories. The first is that stories of being Australian are always made *in relation to* other ways of being that are marked as similar or different. The second is that stories of being Australian are underpinned by feelings of anxiety. In thinking about these themes, issues of race and ethnicity are key.

Being Australian *in relation* to others

Stories of being Australian are created in relation to groups of people and places that are understood to not be Australian or to be un-Australian. These relationships can be seen as positive or negative. For example, Australian-ness has long been produced in relation to British-ness. After the August 2005 London Underground train and bus bombings, this relationship was visible. The saturation media coverage in Australia reinforced the connections between the two nations. Some months later, when the Australian men's cricket team lost the 'Ashes', this relationship was framed slightly differently. The differences, rather than similarities, between Australian-ness and British-ness were emphasised. In both cases being Australian was made in relation to England.

Australian-ness is also produced in relation to the United States, Europe and Asia. It is defined in relation to near neighbours such as New Zealand, Papua New Guinea, Fiji and Indonesia. Historically, wars have shaped these relationships. In World War I, the New Zealand and Australian contribution to the British Imperial forces forged a link between these two nations that is still recognisable in the acronym Anzac. Australian-ness was also made in relation to England in World War I. The United States of America, an ally in World War II and the Vietnam War, and Germany and Japan, as former war enemies, are placed differently in stories of Australian-ness. Originally England was seen as the 'mother country'—a country Australia was obliged to help and which in turn would help Australia. The historical association between the two nations—part of the same empire and common-wealth—made this bond logical and powerful. There was always a tension in this relationship, as Australia also sought to assert its inde-pendence from mother England. After 1945, when the United States had come to Australia's aid in the war against the Japanese in the Pacific, this relationship of obligation shifted from England to the United States. Again, Australian governments negotiated the balance between national needs and the obligations to a 'big brother'.

Australian-ness is also created in relation to groups internal to the nation. Some citizens are seen as more Australian than others. The key group against whom ideas of Australian-ness have been made comprises the Indigenous peoples of Australia. However, being Australian is also defined in relation to newly arrived migrant groups, people with different regional affiliations (mainlanders versus Tasmanians, easterners versus those from the west) and the ubiquitous rural and urban divide.

Being White

As suggested earlier, ethnicity is a key factor in the shaping of stories of being Australian. In particular being Australian is organised around a notion of whiteness. The well-known phrase 'white Australia' highlights this. Suvendrini Perera (2005: 31) explains how whiteness works in stories of being Australian: 'The state and the bodies of its citizens were explicitly constructed in and through their relation to whiteness, establishing a hierarchy of belonging and entitlement.'

Being white was understood by the Australian state as the norm and all peoples in Australia and around Australia were measured in relation to this norm. The closer a citizen or potential citizen was to this norm the more likely they were to have access to the privileges of the state. So, for example, for most of the twentieth century a migrant from Britain could gain permanent residency status in a shorter time than a migrant from India or Indonesia.

The status of being white was complex. It was not a matter of being either white or not. There were 'a range of categories of difference' applied to people deemed not-white and their meaning changed over time, in different places and on different occasions (Perera 2005: 31). What was certain was that a particular type of person was understood as the 'sort' wanted in Australia and people who did not fit were marked as unsuitable or un-Australian.

The federation rallying cry of white Australia emphasised the desire of many Australians to be connected to other white or English-speaking nations—especially Britain and the United States. The white Australia story was also formed around a desire to exclude those who were not English speaking, especially people from the countries of Asia. Before federation, and for decades after, the Asian region was a site of anxiety for Australian governments and peoples. Though the geographical proximity of this region might suggest a closeness, Asia was not represented in terms of familial connection, but rather in terms of danger and aggression. Nikos Papastergiadis (2004) calls this an 'invasion complex'. The different countries of the Asian region were represented as having their eyes on Australia—as always, just waiting to invade or overrun the nation. This 'invasion complex' can be seen operating in the example of the Cronulla beach riots when the locals—mostly Anglo–Australians—represented the Lebanese–Australians who came to the beach from their homes in Sydney's south-western suburbs as entering a space where they did not belong.

White Australian national identity can further be understood as being shaped in relation to an outsider residing within the nation—Indigenous peoples. The notion of a white nation has implications for how Indigenous peoples are understood in dominant national stories and how they are able to live their lives in Australia. As Aileen Moreton-Robinson (1998: 12) explains:

Australia has a history of preferring and privileging those people who have White skin. Indigenous people are conscious of how White skin privilege works because we have lived within the constraints of Whiteness. Living with Whiteness means being treated as less than white; not entitled to an equal share in Australian society and consciously knowing that White culture does not respect, value or view as legitimate our knowledges and rights.

The cultural group who produced the key stories about being Australian did not consist of Indigenous peoples but the dominant non-Indigenous group—Anglo–Australians, who identified as white. As a result Indigenous peoples' views were mostly missing from the stories of Australian-ness. Where they appeared Indigenous people were 'presented as the problem' (Moreton-Robinson 1998: 12).

For most of the twentieth century, the rights and privileges granted to white people—British subjects or Australian citizens— were not extended to Indigenous peoples, just as they were not extended to residents of Australia who had come from Asia. Meaghan Morris (1998) writes about this twin fear of a threatening outsider and a threatening insider. She suggests that in both cases Anglo–Australians represent themselves as victims. Morris argues that white Australians understand themselves as victims of a harsh land that kills them—a process represented as '*de*-population'. This understanding neutralises and reverses the story of who is actually in danger in Australia. It has been Indigenous peoples whose populations have been threatened by colonisers. However, white Australians also understand themselves as victims of a potential outside threat— '*over*-population'. Here: 'Asia is posited as the threat to the new nation through invasion' (Morris 1998: 247).

A vocabulary for stories

In order to make national narratives, a vocabulary is required. Jennifer Rutherford (2000) argues that, in the process of the colonisation of Australia (the process of establishing a non-Indigenous narrative about Australia), the colonisers were faced with a world that did not fit their 'symbolic order'. That is, they were faced with a place in which their sense of the world was not matched by what they were experiencing. The process of naming and putting objects and ideas into language was not easy in the new environment. Many of the things the colonisers saw (strange animals and plants) and experienced (back-to-front seasons) were outside their conceptual framework (What do you call a kangaroo? What is a kangaroo?). However, making sense of the world was the only way the colonisers could 'own' this space: 'naming was essential to colonisation' (Rutherford 2000: 31). The alien had to be made familiar: 'Maps had to be drawn up, directions given, and landmarks seized upon to differentiate the space' (2001: 31). It was this naming, the creation of a national vocabulary, that began the process of non-Indigenous cultural formation in Australia.

Rutherford argues that, in undertaking this naming—what she calls 'bringing into signification'—the British colonisers came face to face with another system of naming—that of Indigenous peoples. Indigenous peoples had comprehensively named and mapped the Australian space. In order for the non-Indigenous narrative to be created, the original story had to be erased or the continent emptied of Indigenous accounts so the colonial story could unfold. Rutherford argues that, as a result, both the origins and ongoing creation of non-Indigenous Australian cultural narratives 'involve[s] a collective endeavour, through fantasy, idealisation, and aggression to self and Other, to keep this [original Indigenous narrative] at bay' (2000: 32). Yet this is never totally achieved. As will be explored in *Being Australian*, the original and ongoing story of Indigenous occupation and sovereignty may have been ignored, muted, violently silenced and appropriated, but it has never been totally erased. The repression of Indigenous stories is one of the anxieties built into non-Indigenous narratives of being Australian. The understanding that Australia is someone else's land is sometimes dimly realised, but mostly repressed by non-Indigenous Australians.

Global links

Though the story of Australia as an isolated 'white' nation has been prominent, the idea of Australia as part of a global community has also always existed. From the time of colonisation in the late eighteenth century, Australia has slowly been integrated into political and economic spheres that link the nation to empires, to international trading groups and to global political associations. As Anthony Moran (2005: 4) writes:

> Australians by virtue of their position in the world—in the world economy, geographically—as members of a nation formed by waves and waves of immigration—a product of the former British empire, now a highly developed minor player in world affairs—[have] always had one eye firmly fixed on the outside world.

These global links were reflected in a 2003 speech given by the now retired federal MP Mark Latham before he briefly became leader of the Australian Labor Party. In expressing his understanding of

Australian foreign policy, he said: '[It] has three pillars. Our membership of the United Nations, our alliance with the United States and comprehensive engagement with Asia' (cited in Ramsey 2004: 25). In this speech, Latham reiterates a number of times the point that he, as a leader, would always make decisions that put Australia's national interest first. He said: 'When I have a decision to make . . . I'll ask only one question: what is in Australia's national interest.' Latham was using a quite common understanding of how Australia stands in relation to the rest of the world. He reinforced the idea of the primacy of the Australian nation–state. The presumption that Australians write their own story—sovereignty—is there, but so is the presumption of connecting to the wider world. Latham frames Australia as a global nation noting the relationship that Australia has to an inter-national body—the United Nations—and then to two different regional 'partners'—the United States and the many countries of Asia.

Globalisation has intensified in the last few decades. Technological, economic and cultural globalisation are key aspects of these feeling of intensification. As Allaine Cerwonka (2004: 3) writes: 'Transnational flows of images and products . . . challenge the experience of a distinct national character of those who never leave their local community.' Advances in communication and media technologies have created international links between segments of different national popula-tions—links never possible before. Media conglomerates such as Hollywood have a global reach and make it possible for an homogenous (American) product to circulate the globe. The internet has meant that many young people in Australia can communicate with other people their same age in the United States or Sweden just as easily as they can with young Australians in Perth or Penrith.

The shape of late capitalism has meant that multinational companies are often bigger—and often more influential—economic enterprises than most nation–states. The dominance of a global economic discourse of free trade and individualism has come to Australia. In the last 30 years, the primacy of the nation–state as a special economic unit has been challenged. The development of groups such as the (expanded) European Union, NAFTA and ASEAN reflects this tendency. Ideas of being Australian are therefore produced in a global context.

Globalisation and Whiteness

The important role of immigration in the Australian story partly explains why global connections have always been important. The increasing mobility of the world's population has seen millions of people move between and through different nations in the last 200 years. Much of the immigration that shaped the Australian colonies in the first 150 years of colonisation was English, Irish and Scottish. After 1945, immigration escalated and diversified. Australia rapidly increased its non-British and non-Irish population. In the last 30 or so years, Australian governments have sought to move away from the foundational idea of Australia as a white nation. Indeed, most Australians now pride themselves on the multicultural nature of their country.

Yet many of the dominant stories of being Australian reflect a 'white diasporic loyalty', that is, many of the strongest 'cultural, political, economic and military alliances' Australia has in this globalising world are with other 'white' nations (Osuri and Banerjee, 2004: 152). So though Australia is a multicultural nation and a nation that acknowledges an Indigenous population it also produces 'transnational loyalties among populations that subscribe to the kinship of whiteness' (Osuri and Banerjee 2004: 152). Goldie Osuri and Bobby Banerjee give the example of the September 11, 2001 bombings of the World Trade Centre in New York. In the aftermath of this event the Australian commercial media and government represented the interests of (white) Western democratic Australia and the United States as linked against a non-Western extremist Islamic other. Not surprisingly this gave license to many non-Muslim Australians to harass Muslim–Australians who were conflated with the terrorist other.

Another impact of globalisation has been the circulation of different critiques of colonialism. The stories of Indigenous peoples' and colonised peoples' fights against oppression and racism became more freely available to Indigenous peoples in Australia. For example, in the 1960s Indigenous and non-Indigenous Australians drew on stories from black rights groups in the United States and used them to agitate for an end to the limited civil rights accorded Indigenous peoples in Australia. The *Racial Discrimination Act* 1975 drew on international covenants to which Australia was party. Yet the impact of international human rights laws has not completely displaced a national story of a white nation. Many non-Indigenous peoples continue to see Indigenous peoples' calls for land rights as a threat. Further, the new terrorist discourse of the 2000s has meant invasion anxieties have escalated. In the wake of the September 11, 2001 attacks in the United States and the 2002 and 2005 Bali and 2005 London bombings, the fear of an external threat has increased in Australia. In late 2005, the federal government, in tandem with all the state governments, passed draconian new anti-terrorism laws aimed at dealing with what are referred to as 'home-grown' terrorist threats. Yet again, Australia is framed as having an un-Australian internal group as well as external un-Australian enemies.

Anxiety

The second important theme to emerge from these national narratives of being Australian is the idea of anxiety. Being Australian is not simply about the pleasure of the past and the excitement of the future. It is not just about that funny feeling a citizen might get when the Australian flag is raised at the Olympics. Being Australian also encompasses feelings, ideas and emotions that vary from joy to shame, guilt to confusion, hatred to love. Yet in most national narratives these feelings of anxiety are erased or repressed in favour of the pleasurable aspects of national identity. Finding pleasure in being Australian is valuable; however, exploring and explaining the anxiety and fear that lie at the heart of the idea of being Australian is also important.

One way of explaining the anxiety felt by non-Indigenous Australians is that it emerged from a lack of familiarity the newcomers had with the land. The logic of this explanation suggests that time would create a sense of belonging and would erase the anxiety. In time non-Indigenous peoples would be as at home as Indigenous peoples. Though today the majority of Australians do see themselves as at home, anxiety continues to frame many non-Indigenous narratives of being Australian. In part this anxiety stems from the repressed or denied knowledge that Australia is someone else's place. The original 'emptying' of the space by non-Indigenous peoples for their own ends is never completely acknowledged. This anxiety also relates to the injustice built into white Australia and the exclusion of non-white peoples. David Walker in his book *Anxious Nation* (1999) explicitly identified anxiety as an aspect of the Australian state's relationship with Asia.

Alongside these various feelings of anxiety is an aggression that emerges in stories of being Australian when this repressed anxiety appears. The aggression is aimed both at groups who challenge an easy feeling of belonging and at the individual feeling the anxiety. Feelings of being Australian are obviously complicated—they are ambivalent. They are made up of feelings of pride and shame. When, how and why one might experience any of these feelings, positive or negative, in relation to Australia depends on who you are and where you fit in relation to dominant stories. Many non-Indigenous narratives of being Australian tend to focus on the 'good' aspects of Australian history, while never being able to completely erase the 'bad'. The earlier example of the 1997 Reconciliation Convention clearly demonstrates this point. Prime Minister John Howard found it very difficult to deal with the idea of non-Indigenous Australians needing to acknowledge any shame in Australia's past. He became aggressive, pointing to Indigenous leaders and thumping the podium at which he was speaking. He wanted to focus on the 'good'. The new focus on the maltreatment of Indigenous peoples made it harder to repress the story of the dispossession of Indigenous peoples. The response to the emergence of this story was aggression.

Conclusion

This book explores a range of stories about being Australian. In particular it focuses on some of the less acknowledged aspects of Australian-ness—in particular aspects of being Australian that may be anxiety inducing or uncomfortable. For example, for some migrants being Australian is understood in relation to a 'home' other than Australia. They have feelings of being at 'home' in two different places. Other migrants feel totally at home in Australia, yet these feelings are not reflected back by compatriots who tell them to 'go home'. Being Australian may be experienced differently again by Indigenous peoples. The spiritual connections associated with being Indigenous shape how it feels to live in Australia. Feelings of cultural pride may intersect with sorrow when faced with severe community disadvantage.

This book seeks to find the patterns in the stories about being Australian. It also highlights ways of being Australian that are often ignored. For example, ideas of being Australian may differ across generations. Particular ideas of being Australian that were so important to an earlier generation often seem meaningless to the next. For example, for many 'baby boomer' women, who put so much energy into feminism and changing Australian social attitudes towards women, it is mystifying to be faced with younger Australian women who see themselves as post-feminist. Similarly, the secularism of the 'genXers' has given way to a new religious fervour in many young people that seems alien to many older citizens. Yet all these multiple ways of being Australian need to be considered in any story of Australia. The task here is not finding the 'real' Australia or the 'real'

Australian amongst the country's 23 million citizens, it is exploring the ambivalences, anxieties and complexities of being Australian today in relation to Australia in the last century.

FURTHER READING

Carter, David 2005, *Dispossession, Dreams and Diversity*, Palgrave Macmillan, Sydney.

Moran, Anthony 2005, *Australia: Nation, Belonging and Globalization*, Routledge, London.

Rutherford, Jennifer 2000, *The Gauche Intruder: Freud, Lacan and the White Australian Fantasy*, Melbourne University Press, Melbourne.

Walker, David 1999, *Anxious Nation: Australia and the Rise of Asia 1850–1939*, University of Queensland Press, Brisbane.

White, Richard 1981, *Inventing Australia: Images and Identity 1688–1980*, Allen & Unwin, Sydney.

Part 1
STORIES IN THE MAKING

1

IMAGINING NATIONS

Telling national tales

NATIONS ARE RELATIVELY new ways of organising people and authority. Today the word 'nation' is used interchangeably with 'state' or 'country', but it is worth exploring the distinctions between these terms. When the idea of a nation emerged in early nineteenth-century Europe, it referred to a group of people who had a shared ethnicity, language and culture—a nation was not a political entity, but a cultural one. This contrasts with the concept of a state, defined as a sovereign political entity with set territorial boundaries that has to answer to no higher political power. Australia is obviously a state. Technically, Australia is not a nation in the way nineteenth-century thinkers understood the term. A group such as the Waradjuri nation (a coalition of Koori people from central New South Wales), however, would be understood as a nation in these terms. However, the Waradjuri are not recognised as a state. More contemporary understandings of nations define what members of a nation share as being civic values. In this sense Australia is a nation. Yet the idea of a shared ethnicity still informs many stories of the Australian nation.

Today it is common to link nation and state together to produce the hyphenated term 'nation–state'. Jointly, this suggests both a political territorial entity and the idea of shared culture and heritage. Nation–states develop initiatives, policies and legislation to reinforce or encourage the belief that the people within their territory are culturally homogenous (Shapiro 1999: 45). In these terms, the governments of the Australian nation–state work to encourage the idea of a coherent and shared identity amongst a group of people of diverse ethnicity, sexuality, religious conviction, economic status, age, cultural affiliation and geographic location. Over time, governments have passed legislation setting out what is expected of an Australian citizen, enacted policies shaping the type of Australian histories school children will be taught, and declared particular days to be holidays of national significance. All these initiatives are designed to create a feeling of national togetherness over and above any differences.

If a nation is about cultural similarity, then nationalism can be described as the feeling of attachment to the culture of that nation. Like nations, nationalism is not natural: these feelings are constructed. Nationalism is a powerful method for securing and maintaining feelings of 'unity and identity' amongst a group of people who 'share historic territory' (Smith 1996: 359). Ernest Gellner (1983) has provided an historical explanation for the emergence of nationalism in Europe. He posits that nationalism resulted from 'the organisation of human groups into large, centrally educated, culturally homogenous units' (1983: 35). Gellner argues that the new skill demands and urbanisation associated with the Industrial Revolution encouraged higher levels of education and increased geographic mobility amongst people who previously had been more settled and physically isolated. This mobility led to increasing social and economic connections between previously fragmented or separated communities. As a result, the emerging 'national' governments had to devise ways in which to control and connect the increasing number of urban-based communities distanced from their traditional affiliations. Governments placed more emphasis on the need for a common language and common values to help facilitate these connections. The newly emerging central governments also emphasised the links between themselves and the people.

Nationalism seems so simple—who would not want to love their country? Nationalism can have productive effects: a sense of shared destiny and sameness encourages citizens to act in ways that may benefit the general community, but not themselves personally (Moran 2005: 55). However, nationalism is complex in the way it structures how individuals and groups of people understand themselves in relation to states. Nationalism is an ideology: it does not simply reflect what the nation is. As cultural theorist Graeme Turner (1993: 123) puts it:

> the dominant version of Australian nationalism . . . is not dominant because most Australians 'lived it', or because it is an unmediated reflection of social conditions at any one point in time. Rather, it is

dominant because it is currently accepted as the construction . . . of nationalism in Australia.

Nationalism helps make particular stories of Australian-ness. The longevity or centrality of particular national stories does not reflect the truth of these stories or their accuracy; rather, it reflects the power of the story. Or, more importantly, it reflects the power of the story makers.

Historian Benedict Anderson (1983) argues that nations are constructed rather than given. He calls them 'imagined communities'. Anderson's argument is that in a modern nation there are too many people for citizens to feel any real connection with each other (as a person might feel for their extended family or a club where all the members are known). There are also as many differences as connections between citizens. To overcome or accommodate these gaps, the national community is imagined. Anderson suggests that what links the citizens of a nation is not the fact that everyone knows each other, but that citizens of a nation share a common imaginary— a common set of stories. Instead of meeting all the people in one's nation and thinking 'ah yes they are like me', citizens are given— through education, popular culture and political rhetoric—images and stories, sayings and histories that encourage a feeling of connection and shared values, where they might not actually exist. However, to say a nation is imagined is not to suggest the stories of the nation are just made up. National narratives are usually based on real historical events—indeed, historical stories and myths are integral parts of 'imagined communities'. The imagining is the process of encouraging citizens to identify with one set of stories that are said to have formed the nation over another.

A nationalistic narrative posits that citizens all share beliefs and values, even though the reality is that many citizens are living and experiencing different sorts of lives to the ones told in the stories. Graeme Turner (1993) calls these stories of an imagined community shared 'representational codes'. Citizens are encouraged to draw on these shared sets of understandings and feelings of what it means to be Australian. For example, if there is an international sporting event and an Australian participant or team wins, the stories that are produced tend to suggest that all Australians will feel the same joyful and proud emotions. Media headlines will declare, or politicians will say: 'All Australians feel proud today!' Sometimes connections are made by referring to historical moments that are declared important to all Australians. This can mean calling contemporary sports heroes 'diggers' or an Australian-bred horse winning the Melbourne Cup as 'preserving Anzac pride' (Thomas 2002). The outcome is to reinforce a feeling of national connection between citizens and a connection with a particular historical past. This is what nationalism is: the belief that citizens of the Australian nation will share a common understanding of being Australian, and that this understanding—seen to have historical roots—bonds them together in a common love for their shared nation. Over time, the dominant story or representational codes become naturalised and come to stand as commonsense.

National identit(ies)

The emphasis on shared values means that, within national stories, there is an emphasis on a shared identity—a national identity. Stuart Hall (1990: 226) explains what identities are: 'identities are the names we give to the different ways we are positioned by, and position ourselves within, the narratives of the past'. Overall, the process of creating national stories works to produce 'a mythic connection between nationhood and personhood in the form of a story of how the nation arises naturally from the character of its people' (Shapiro, 1999: 47). So not only is the national community presumed to be based on commonality and shared purpose, but it is often suggested that nations are made up of 'types' of people. National identity is seen to be based on what are considered to be shared character traits often deriving from history. A good Australian example is the idea of the 'Aussie bloke' and the belief that this type of person is unique to Australia.

Yet any individual will understand themselves in terms of multiple identities—for example, their gender, class, age, sexual preference, ethnic heritage and national affiliation. Given the multiple nature of individual identity, it is very hard to believe that a single or unified identity could describe an entire nation. However, national identity is still a belief Australians have found hard to give up. Over the years, scholars have debunked particular versions of *the* Australian national character or identity. For example, feminists demonstrated how women were excluded from the masculine bush legend and Anzac ideal. Indigenous peoples showed how ideas of national identity excluded them. The interesting point to note is that the sense of a national identity is hard to displace: it is persistent. If one national story of identity is discounted, another more expansive one is rapidly developed to fill the gap. The possibility of a national identity is not often rejected. So what cultural and political work does the perpetu-ation of the story of a national identity do?

Despite the perpetuation of singular nationalist stories, the unity of a nation is never complete or total. The notion that Australians are *all* proudly bonded together by a series of shared ideas and shared history is obviously not true. Citizens of Australia have a multitude of different attitudes about all sorts of things. However, nationalism and the idea of *a* singular national identity encourage citizens to conform to particular ways of doing or seeing things. This is why, if one citizen disagrees with another citizen's actions, an easy way to discredit their opinion is to call them 'un-Australian'. The insult suggests that the argument put forward by one person is outside the parameters of shared ideas about Australian-ness, insinuating the person does not love their country and is not worthy of it. This ploy closes off debate. However, calling someone 'un-Australian' also introduces the poss-ibility of different ways of being Australian—even if they are viewed by some citizens as negative. In this sense, dominant national stories are set up against un-national stories. Different—or other—stories are presumed to exist.

National identities and national stories are not truths that reflect the total experience of the citizenry. Rather, they reflect the experi-ences and desires of particular—often powerful—groups. This partial and invested aspect of nationalism is often not acknow-ledged. It is uncommon to hear a business person saying: 'I need Australians to love their country because I want to make millions of dollars selling subscriptions to them to watch their national sports team play on pay television.' A politician never says: 'I need Australians to identify with a specific story of Australian-ness because it makes it easier for my government to justify a particular policy.' Instead, stories of Australian-ness are told as if all Australians are equally invested and everyone reaps equal rewards. In truth, these stories suit dominant groups—groups with the most power to produce and sustain their own stories and to overwhelm (though not necessarily end) other stories. Importantly this dominant (or dominating) story encourages a sense of consensus and insists that the shared national story is the most pertinent one for all Australians. Given that consensus necessarily depends on omission, this has meant that women, Indigenous people, gay men and lesbians and non-white migrants have frequently been marginalised or omitted in Australian national stories. These omissions are sometimes acknowledged; however, more frequently these 'divisions or conflicts within society are minimised in deference to [what are suggested to be] the overriding, accepted priorities of the nation which unite the people' (Turner 1993: 108). A national story is not an innocent reflection of a state and its peoples; rather, it is a way in which complexity and differences can be silenced by reference to a 'bigger' unifying story.

Exclusion

The exclusion of particular ideas or people from national stories is not an unfortunate or innocent by-product resulting from the natural limitations of dealing with such a large concept as the nation. On the contrary, exclusion is intrinsically built into the idea of the nation. Philosopher Linnell Secomb (2003: 9) argues that stories of communities necessarily require some exclusion. She contends that the way humans exist is communal—what she calls 'being-together-in-community'. This 'being together' suggests more than just humans living in proximity; Secomb argues that people who live 'together-in-community' also share things in common. They form an 'in-common community'. However, Secomb goes on to explain that 'the formation and perpetuation of in-common community requires the estrangement of those who threaten its commonality'.

Community is something that humanness is defined by, yet often the way in which community is enacted by humans has built into it the need to 'marginalise', 'vilify', even 'brutalise' others in order to secure that community (2003: 9). Using Secomb's ideas of the 'in-community' of a nation, it is possible to see how stories of commonality are so frequently premised on exclusion. The 'in-common' stories of the national 'in-community' set up an us and them dualism. This can seem (and probably is) harmless in many cases. For example, a headline screaming 'Poms Thrashed by Aussies' creates for many Australians a sense of 'being in-common' with other Australians through a sporting victory. Although it marginalises the English; such a headline would probably be met with nothing more than a roll of the eyes or a sigh by any English people reading it. However, other 'in-common' marginalisations have more disturbing effects—for example the marginalisation of a female Muslim student at school because she wears the *hijab*; the vilification of people of a particular ethnicity or the violent bashing of a gay man have profound effects in terms of creating an 'in-common' story of the nation.

Though nations are a powerful way in which the world and its people are organised at the moment, and though it has so many pleasures for many citizens, given the limits of this idea it is necessary to draw on other imaginings about how communities could be organised.

Never-ending stories

Though the argument that nations are 'imagined communities' (Anderson 1983) and the ideology of nationalism suggest a lack of reality, this is not in fact the case. The concept of Australia as an 'imagined community' does not suggest that the Australian nation exists only as an imagined concept. There are obviously real laws that structure real relationships between real citizens who live in a real place. As Etienne Balibar (1991: 49) notes, a nation may have no ethnic basis 'but [still] they do have to institute in real (and therefore historical) time their imaginary unity against other possible unities'. This production of an 'imaginary unity' is a continual process. It takes place in official (legal, formal governmental, educational) as well as popular (journalism, film, television, advertising) sites. This process is what is termed 'narrating the nation' (Bhabha 1990). The nation needs to be continually 'told' in order to give it substance, to disavow the differences and to reinforce what it is not. Indeed, as Michael Shapiro (1999: 47) suggests, given the amazing diversity in a nation like Australia today, it is only the people's commitment to the national stories that can 'give themselves a historical trajectory that testifies to their collective coherence'. According to this view, if Australians stop narrating the story of being Australian, then being Australian will no longer exist as a concept.

Think about this question: if the national identity of Australia (or any nation, for that matter) is so secure, why do nationalist events, policies and laws need to be continually enacted? If it is in the Australian character to love one's country, then why do parliamentarians need to discuss banning the burning of the Australian flag? If Australians are so proud about their history, why has it been decided that national holidays need to be taken on the day on which they fall rather than allowing them to be moved to the nearest Monday to create a long weekend? For many, the answer is simple: within the nation there are those who do not love their country enough and therefore need to be educated (or eradicated). The potential flag-burners or long-weekenders might say they simply have another understanding of being Australian that does not concur with the dominant story. It is because the nation has no chance of ever being totally unified—because there are so many other stories—that nationalism has to be so strident and disciplining. For every dominant story, there are counter-narratives that challenge this story. The challenge may be weak or strong, it may be sporadic or continual, but it is always there.

Other stories

The story of national unity is not easy to maintain, and the contradictory stories that circulate challenge the 'coherence project of the state' (Shapiro 1999: 47–48). One strategy employed by dominant groups in order to maintain the myth of a unified nation in the face of contesting stories is what philosopher Michel Foucault calls 'commentary'. Within nations, dominant groups help to create or reinforce the sense of unity by invoking important books, key historical events or the words of exemplary authors. This 'commentary' reinforces a sense of national collectivity and belonging. Foucault suggests that what is happening in this process of commentary is not the reinforcement of a collectivity that has a long history and a point of origin (as set out in the books and key texts that are used). The commentary is actually only the repetition of 'perhaps nothing' (1976). It is the powerful retelling of an empty originary story. The power is in the continual telling, not in the 'facts' of the story itself.

As suggested in the Introduction, another useful issue when exploring the idea of the modern nation is the repressed or unacknowledged—that which is not spoken. As Elspeth Tilley (2002: 2), drawing on the work of cultural theorist Homi Bhabha, argues: 'every nation is based on a phantasm; that is every "imagined community" has some illusory entity or idea at its centre.' Different nations have different phantasms. For some, it is the mythical belief that the origin of the nation can be traced to an ethnically 'pure' or Indigenous people. In others, it is the mythical story of a war-like purging of an enemy from the nation. What is the 'phantasm' at the centre of Australian national feeling? What is the illusory entity? It is the story of *terra nullius*—the belief that the Australian nation is built on land belonging to no one. This story suggests that the Australian nation, originating with British colonisation, did no psychic or physical harm to the Indigenous peoples on whose land the non-Indigenous nation was superimposed. The phantasm of *terra nullius* masks other understandings of Australia as Indigenous land. Yet the story of originary Indigenous sovereignty remains—even though it is largely unacknowledged—in national stories. As Homi Bhabha (1990) argues, this makes nationalism ambivalent by nature. An important goal here is to explore what happens when these ambivalences and subversive other stories emerge to challenge the dominant story—to draw attention to the gaps, the phantasm.

The Sydney Olympics ⟵————

Various Australian governments spent millions of dollars hosting the 2000 Olympic Games. One of the benefits for the host nation of an Olympics is that there is the chance to use the amazing global television audience for the Games to tell a national story, especially during the Opening Ceremony. From the time Sydney was declared the winner right up to the night of the opening ceremony, the Olympics was used as a framing device for thinking about the contemporary Australian nation. The staging of the Sydney 2000 Olympics can be used here to illustrate some key aspects of Australian national stories. Early in the planning, there was a general demand that the story the world heard be one showing Australia in a 'good light'. After the Atlanta Closing Ceremony in 1996, where inflatable kangaroos were part of the showcase of Australiana on display, there was a general plea that the Olympic national story not make Australians cringe. As 2000 approached, there was an increasing insistence on a unified story. Alternative stories—anything from accounts that posited the Olympics as a gigantic waste of money to stories of social injustice—were moved to the periphery, sometimes literally. The New South Wales government enacted legislation making it difficult to protest anywhere near the Olympic sites. The public areas set up for large groups of people to congregate during the Olympics were designed to hold fans who were not able to attend sold-out events rather than protesters.

The staging of the Olympic Games revealed important issues about national identity and ideas about 'being Australian'. Specifically, the story—or narrative—told through the Opening Ceremony of the Sydney Olympic Games provides a wonderful opportunity to explore national stories, nationalism and national identity. The ceremony is a good example of the recurrence of motifs that have long dominated popular stories of the nation—'commentaries' and 'representational codes'—and their role in reproducing a particular set of relations between men and women, Indigenous and non-Indigenous Australians, British and non-British migrants, heterosexual and non-heterosexual people, workers and bosses. It is also an ideal place to see shifts and changes in the stories about the relations between these different groups.

On the evening of 15 September 2000 in the Homebush Bay stadium, when the crowd's countdown for the beginning of the Opening Ceremony finished, a lone horseman carrying a stock whip entered the stadium, the stockman's horse reared on its hind-legs in the centre of the stage, and so began the ceremony. More horses and their riders entered the arena, first carrying Olympic then Australian flags (see Figure 1.1). Then a young girl, Nikki Webster— representing the 'future' or 'young' Australia—appeared. She lay on a beach towel and fell asleep to dream a history of Australia. In this history, first came sea creatures, then Indigenous peoples, the fire of the bush, and the regeneration of nature—flowers and bush plants. Captain Cook arrived, bringing rabbits and rollicking good fun. In a riot of colour and sound, pioneers sheared sheep, played two-up, bushranged and eventually settled in suburbs with their lawn-mowers. Then migrants arrived from 'four corners of the globe' and the post-1945 economic boom—represented by the steel industry— made the nation strong. The labour of men and women frenetically, joyously, built to a climax—the word 'Eternity' appeared written in lights across a miniature Sydney Harbour Bridge. This is a narrative of the Australian nation. It is obviously a dominant and popular one—after all, various Australian governments paid millions of dollars to help stage it.

The slapstick and exuberant nature of much of the ceremony invited viewers to see parts of it in the lighthearted and slightly ironic way in which it was offered. And most likely the majority of the 200 million people who saw the ceremony viewed it in this way. However, another way of understanding the ceremony is as part of the ongoing (re)production of the Australian nation as an 'imagined community'. For Australian viewers the opening ceremony told an 'in-common' story. It was one that many of these viewers consented to understand, or enjoyed thinking of, as 'their' national history. If it was not their personal experience, it was still a story that was pleasurable for many people to believe in and see themselves as part of. The Opening Ceremony helped to reinforce or produce a particular narrative of the nation. Yet it was not a narrative that everyone in Australia shared. For example, Stephen Page, one of the choreographers of the Indigenous section of the ceremony, remembers the reaction when he was discussing ways of presenting Indigenous stories in the ceremony:

I'd be radical and say: 'Let's have Archie Roach sitting in the middle of the ground singing . . . "They Took the Children Away".' He'd be

Figure 1.1 The Sydney Olympic Opening Ceremony began its story of Australia with
dozens of stockmen and women riding across the arena, which had been
transformed by a ground cloth to represent a vast uncluttered desert space.
(© *Newspix/News Ltd/3rd Party Managed Reproduction & Supply Rights; Photographer Craig Borrow*)

surrounded by members of the stolen generation wearing t-shirts with
'Sorry' on them. But that was too much for some of those people
(Lawson 2003).

Page's political story did not fit with the dominant story being told.
His story of Indigenous peoples' suffering had to be excluded to
create the 'in-community' narrative.

To encourage the idea of a shared 'imagined community', the
Opening Ceremony drew on the bush man in the outback as its
'commentary' or 'representational code' about being Australian.
The popularity of this image can be traced back to the 1890s in the
poetry of Henry Lawson and A.B. 'Banjo' Paterson, and aspects of it
remain visible in beer advertisements in the 2000s and television
idols such as the Crocodile Hunter (the late Steve Irwin). Traditionally,
the story of the bush bloke is often matched by an image of a larrikin
city slicker. This image shares much in common with the outback
stereotype, but the characteristics of larrikin humour and drinking
are moved from the bush to the city or suburbs. The larrikin city

fellow has morphed into the stereotype of the suburban yobbo or ocker—with his beer belly, barbecuing skills and formal wear of thongs and stubbies. The Opening Ceremony drew on this story as well—at times ironically, at others seriously. The cavalcade of horse riders, cantering around the arena to the music from the film *The Man from Snowy River*, strongly evoked a bush history. The later scenes of pioneers moving into the bush, the rise of the sheep industry, the larrikin bushrangers refusing to bow down to injustice, and the carousing dancing and two-up games extended this stereotype. The tap-dancing workers and the lawn-mowing blokes brought out the urban dimension of this image.

As argued earlier, the power of this national type—the bush bloke—comes not from the fact that all Australians or even a majority of Australians live this life, but from an acceptance of it as a pleasurable and meaningful story that describes who Australians are. The image supposedly reflects a national character—that is, if you are Australian, some of these characteristics make up your identity. Many people would argue that this image is outdated and inaccurate. In fact, Russel Ward (1958) argues that the image should be understood as typical, not common. The slapstick manner in which many of these stereotypes were presented during the Opening Ceremony suggests that many Australians are aware of the way in which aspects of these stories are outdated and laughable.

However, the power of the story is unquestionable. The opening moment with the spot-lit stockman and his horse was designed to illicit pride, not self-deprecating humour. It was an image presented to Australians (and non-Australians) as a quintessential idea of who they are, not as a joke about how outdated this sense of self may be. The story draws on already existing knowledge (many Australians have read the poem 'The Man from Snowy River', or seen the film, or undertaken history classes about the pastoral expansion, or watched television advertisements that evoke this scene to sell a product). The story is reinforced through its reproduction at the beginning of such an important event.

The story of the bush bloke was central, but is was not the complete story told in the opening ceremony. There were many other stories produced around this central tale—land and nature, Indigenous peoples, work, multiculturalism and harmony. These stories appeared as other aspects of national identity or the national story of 'being Australian'. Given the diversity of the Australian people, it would be impossible to present a singular story. It is, however, easy to centralise particular stories. It is also, as Stephen

Page's comments suggest, regarded by some organisers as necessary to exclude other stories.

National phantasm

It was suggested earlier that *terra nullius* is the phantasm at the centre of dominant national stories. Did the *terra nullius* phantasm structure the Opening Ceremony? There were Indigenous people represented in the Opening Ceremony; for example, the two guides who took the audience through the experience were the non-Indigenous girl Nikki Webster but also Djakapurra Munyarryun, a member of the Indigenous Bangarra Dance Company. There was also an extensive and beautiful series of tableaux involving a thousand Indigenous people from all over Australia (see Figure 1.2). This part of the ceremony was designed and directed by Indigenous artists. Even so, overall there was a failure to recognise the prior and ongoing Indigenous occupation and ownership of the land and how this has shaped Australian national stories—the phantasm of *terra nullius* predominated.

Nothing negative was said about being Australian—what some Australians call 'black armband history'—in the entire Opening Ceremony. There was not even an allusion to the history of injustice

Figure 1.2 A segment of the Indigenous tableaux from the 2000 Sydney Olympics Opening Ceremony that brought together Indigenous dancers, musicians and participants from all over the country. The well-known Tiwi Islander image was lit up in Aboriginal colours of red, yellow and black. (© *Newspix/News Ltd/3rd Party Managed Reproduction & Supply Rights*)

that still structures Australian society today. For many non-Indigenous Australians, this history is shameful and had no part in the good story that was told to the world that night. So it was not included. What *was* included was a celebration of the beauty and power of Indigenous cultures as represented by Indigenous peoples themselves. This seems fair enough in a feel-good ceremony, but it came at a cost. Some Indigenous people would have liked the difficult part of the story to be told. When it was not, these Indigenous voices were marginalised.

Further, it needs to be noted that Indigenous peoples disappeared from the Opening Ceremony as the story of the nation unfolded, only appearing again in the massed display at the ceremony's end. In the ceremony, the representation of Indigenous peoples took place in one neatly bounded tableaux. From the end of the Indigenous section of the ceremony, Indigenous peoples—except for Djakapurra Munyarryun—were not visible in the arena. For example, in the scenes about the pioneers, Indigenous peoples were not repre-sented—either positively or negatively—as the group dispossessed by the expansion of Europeans in Australia, nor as the workers they were in the outback and bush. Though Indigenous peoples were integral to the pastoral industry, it was non-Indigenous larrikin bush blokes who dominated in this tableau. Indigenous peoples appeared only on the margins of the nation. The phantasm or illusion at the centre of this Australian national story is that non-Indigenous possession of the land did not entail the wholesale dispossession of Indigenous peoples. Yet Australian nationalism is ambivalent. There is a desire for Indigenous stories to be part of being Australian. However, this is matched by a fear that recognising these stories will have a cost.

Sociologist Jennifer Rutherford (2000) suggests that, even when we are trying to be good, the end result can be that racism is reinforced. Consider the way the welcome was staged at the Olympic Opening Ceremony. Remember it started with a lone male stockman entering the stadium, then more stockmen and stockwomen, before the Ken Done 'G'Day' welcome banner unfurled. After this, the series of tableaux started. The stereotyped, or iconic, images of welcome made up by 'G'day' and the horseman were easily recognis-able as Australian. They were what many people would expect in a true Aussie welcome.

Only those who attended the ceremony and the local Koori community in Sydney know that there was another welcome ceremony conducted just before the televised Opening Ceremony. In this welcome, elders from the local Aboriginal land councils of the

Sydney area welcomed spectators, participants and organisers of the Olympics to their 'country'. Why was this welcome not included in the televised ceremony or the commemorative DVD? The exclusion (or maginalising) of the Koori welcome to country from the televised ceremony reinforced the belief that the land of Homebush Bay, of Sydney, of Australia, was not really Indigenous people's land. The dominant narrative of Australia as told to Australians and the world in the Opening Ceremony reinforced the idea of *terra nullius*—that Indigenous people are not and were not the sovereign owners of this land. Again, the phantasm at the centre of stories of non-Indigenous belonging appears. Yet the original sovereignty of Indigenous peoples will not disappear.

The Opening Ceremony, while going some way to acknowledging other stories, still reinforced the dominant narrative of Australia. However, it also contained within it subversive elements. Again the views of Stephen Page are helpful. Page noted in an interview after the Olympics that he and Rhoda Roberts, another Indigenous director of the Opening Ceremony, considered organising an Indigenous 'theatrical boycott' of Olympic cultural events but 'instead, we brought a thousand people together on this Eora land and it made a much more powerful statement' (Lawson 2003). This, in combination with the welcome to country—witnessed by 100 000 people in the Olympic stadium—asserted another story: that of Indigenous presence and power as ongoing, and situated right in the heart of the city.

Women

Another group of Australians whose stories were marginalised in the Opening Ceremony's national story were women. This is not to say women were missing. There was obviously a considerable effort to make sure men and women, boys and girls, were part of the ceremony. The areas where one might traditionally have expected only men to appear included men and women. When the stock riders came into the arena, there were men and women. 'Young Australia' was represented by a young girl (Nikki Webster). When the workers tapped their way into the stadium, the flannelette-shirted, work-booted performers were men and women. And so it continued. Yet in the tableaux about the growth and expansion of Australia—that whirl of activity that saw sheep and lawn-mowers, bushrangers and builders improve the land—there was no image of pregnant women, new mothers or child-minders doing the work they did to build a nation.

There were men mowing lawns, but not women pegging nappies on the clothes-line. Even in contemporary Australia, when the value of such work is beginning to get recognition, it was not part of this national story of 'being Australian'. This type of 'women's' work is still mundane, natural and unremarkable. It does not build a nation. What does it mean if the work that women have traditionally undertaken for decades does not appear in the 'story' of the nation? What does it mean to a woman for her history to be invisible? What would it take to get these hidden histories into the dominant narrative? It would take more than good will and the adding of these narratives to the national storybook. It would require the disruption of the existing narratives and the realisation that these stories are premised on the exclusion of particular histories.

The challenge mounted by women—including feminists—that it is sufficient to represent Australia only in terms of what men have done has been going on for decades. Similarly, the myth of peaceful settlement—the idea of no war having ever been fought on Australian soil—has been countered by other understandings of violence and guerilla warfare. Simple pride in a form of Australian social egalitarianism has also been challenged. Writers such as Andrew Markus (1994), Marilyn Lake (1999), Aileen Moreton Robinson (2000), and Graham Willett (2000) have put forward a more complex picture that highlights the gender, sexual, ethnic and race inequality in Australia. It can be argued that the Opening Ceremony was just a bit of fun. However, stories of being Australian are produced in fun places as well as serious places (such as parliament or the courts). Even in fun events, the inclusions, marginalisations and exclusions that occur have an impact on people's sense of belonging. For this reason, it is necessary to think carefully and critically about the stories told about Australia and being Australian.

Though national identities—shared ideas of who Australians are—are powerful, they are never complete. There are always counter-stories and challenges to the dominant narrative. This is how change takes place. Michael Shapiro (1999) writes of this incompleteness. He suggests that people promote a sense of national coherence through 'identity stories' or 'unity-promoting articulations' (Aussie, Aussie, Aussie, Oi, oi, oi!). Citing Homi Bhabha (1990), Shapiro argues that these identity stories are 'conceived in a language that registers interpretive contentions between the legitimations of mainstream national culture and what Homi Bhabha refers to as "those easily obscured, but highly significant recesses of the national

culture from which alternative contingencies of peoples and oppositional analytic capacities may emerge'" (Shapiro 1999: 47). So, within
'assembl[ages] . . . identified as nations', there are 'complex sets of
forces' that can work to pull people together; however, in doing this
'assembling' work, there will be strains and fissures as the ambigui-
ties, contradictions and problems glossed over by the identity stories
are repressed.

FURTHER READING

Anderson, Benedict 1983, *Imagined Communities: Reflections on the Origin and Spread of Nationalism*, Verso, London.

Moran, Anthony 2005, *Australia: Nation, Belonging and Globalization*, Routledge, London.

Smith, Rodney 2001, *Australian Political Culture*, Pearson Education, Sydney.

Smith, Sidonie and Schaffer, Kay 2000, *The Olympics at the Millennium: Power, Politics, and the Games*, Rutgers University Press, New Brunswick.

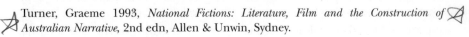Turner, Graeme 1993, *National Fictions: Literature, Film and the Construction of Australian Narrative*, 2nd edn, Allen & Unwin, Sydney.

White, Richard 1981, *Inventing Australia: Images and Identity 1688–1980*, Allen & Unwin, Sydney.

2

THE WORKING MAN IS EVERYWHERE

Class and national identity

THIS CHAPTER EXPLORES how the idea of class contributes to the construction of Australian-ness. It analyses the function of class in national stories of being Australian. The argument is that the concept of class has operated as the historical 'foundation stone' in stories of Australian-ness. Many early national stories about Australian-ness locate the essence of being Australian in a concept of a working man—an idea emerging from a class-focused approach to society. In these narratives, the figure of the working man is imagined both as a physical type and as someone bound up with a range of qualities and values emerging from working men's lives. Over time, the figure of the working man—especially one undertaking manual labour—has been modernised and complicated. He has come to represent not just a class specific figure but the archetype of Australian-ness. He has appeared as the bush bloke, selector, returned digger, plumber and even media mogul. The stories of this quintessential working bloke have been thoroughly critiqued in scholarship and popular writing for decades, yet they still circulate. Given the legendary status of the story and its easy use for multiple purposes, it is not the truth (or otherwise) of class-derived stories that make them important to study but their continuing power.

The centrality of the working man in the early stories of Australian identity makes it important to explore the historical circumstances drawn upon to create this archetype, or early model, of the quintessential Australian. It is also important to examine the relationship of the working man to the concept of class. The way class operates in this story of Australian-ness is not simply about a division between rich and poor, and the possibility or impossibility of moving across these class divisions. In Australia, egalitarianism has been a key trope, that is a key symbol or theme, in class stories. In Australian stories, egalitarianism makes class a neutral descriptor that adds colour to the story without inflecting it with the stridency of social and economic division. So, paradoxically, in national stories class is what unites Australians—not what divides them.

Here we also explore class in the context of contemporary politics and economic change. When thinking about issues of class in the twenty-first century, it is necessary to analyse the effects of rapid globalisation on the Australian economy and society. Globalisation has opened Australia to economic pressures that have challenged traditional ideas of class. Both the British experiences of economic change under former prime minister Margaret Thatcher and American neo-conservative approaches to the role of government have affected the traditional Australian understanding of class. Finally, the chapter considers other stories about class—stories that do focus on social and economic difference—and explores how they work to shape Australian-ness in terms of equality.

Before going any further, it is necessary to clarify what is meant by 'class'. Although class is a common term for thinking about how nations are organised, it is also a term for which there are many different definitions or understandings. Political philosopher Karl Marx (1962), writing about the relations of different groups in European communities in the nineteenth century, emphasised that a person's class was determined by their relation to the 'means of production'. By this he meant that, if a person owned the means of production (the factory, the field, the machinery, the money), then their class position was different from that of someone who did not own the means of production (a worker or labourer). This idea still influences many thinkers today, and the labour union rhetoric of 'workers' and 'bosses' draws on such a division. Other thinkers have offered different ideas on what class is. More recently, sociologists have suggested that class is best understood by reference to a person's occupation (CEO, piano tuner, factory worker). Some have suggested that property ownership is a good indicator of class, while others have said that a person's wealth is a measure of a person's class position. In the complex community of Australia, it is probably sensible to take into consideration most of these measures or indicators as well as an individual's own perception of where they fit into the community.

The working man

Given that economic inequality does exist in Australia, and given that the spectrum of this inequality extends from severe poverty to extreme wealth, the idea of class operating as a unifying factor in stories of being Australian is not a given. So how does it work? There are two important elements: first, the valorisation of the working man in the history of white Australia; and second, the place of the concept of egalitarianism in that history.

As suggested above, the valorisation of the manual labouring working man as the quintessential Australian has a long history and has played a large part in shaping stories of what it means to be Australian. In fact, it still does. As discussed in chapter 1, it was the stockman who turned up to open the Olympics in 2000 rather than a funky metrosexual stockbroker. Indeed, in the spate of popular television programs about suburban living, representations of the working man or manual labourer have re-emerged. Television shows such as *Backyard Blitz, Renovation Rescue* and *Better Homes and Gardens* have teams of these Australian working men (and women) renovating and improving people's homes and gardens in order to make them more pleasant and the property more valuable. The actual job of the wealthy television personalities who appear on these shows is to act, yet what is centralised is the manual labour of the stars (and the tradesmen who assist them) in the transformation of the house or garden. Australian politicians still position themselves as working men. Craig McGregor (2001) gives examples of contemporary politicians from both sides of the political spectrum deploying the story of their working-class roots to garner credibility with voters.

The 'commentary' or 'representational code' of a working man rather than, say, a professional man as the real Australian emerged from a variety of sources. An especially important one was the influence of a group of writers known as the *Bulletin* School. Working in the 1880s and 1890s, these writers—in particular, Henry Lawson and A.B. 'Banjo' Paterson—supported the idea of a new Australian nation and championed the cause of Federation. Their writing covered disparate themes, and the different authors often took up contradictory positions; however, the centrality of a working man as the heart of the nation was a common theme. Further, history as it began to be written for non-Indigenous Australians also privileged the working man. The emergence of a national history with a chronology of events highlighting the convict era, pastoral expansion, the gold rushes, more pastoral expansion, and then Federation followed by Gallipoli reinforced the centrality of the working man in the making of Australia.

Obviously there were men whose lives fitted with these stories being produced in literature and history. George Elder, a young migrant farm worker living in western New South Wales in 1925, wrote a letter home to Scotland telling a friend about his life in Australia:

> I live with the boundary rider in a tin hut and I had to make my own furniture. This consists of a wash-stand made from sunlight soap box [and] a table made from a kerosene box . . . a lot of time is spent in the saddle and I reckon my legs are like hoop iron. If they do not come up to that mark in strength they do in shape.

His description of life as a farm hand matches the *Bulletin* School's description of the working man—with his resourceful ways and dry humour. The lives of real working men were sometimes inspirational for the writers. For example, the story of Jack Riley, the horse-breaker who inspired Banjo Paterson's poem 'The Man from Snowy River', still appears on the side of a brand of organic milk produced in the area where Riley worked. However, not all Australian citizens had or have a life shaped by manual work and the ability to cleverly insert larrikin good humour into personal interactions. As has been emphasised already, it is not the access to this life by the majority of citizens that centres it in stories of being Australian. Rather, it is the desire to see it as a central part of what being Australian is all about that makes the story so powerful. It was not the fact that everyone was living the life of the working man that made it influential; rather, it was the reading of the *Bulletin* and classic Australian history books, the reproduction of family letters in memoirs, and staring at the stories on the sides of milk cartons over breakfast that helped reinforce the idea of this working man as representing real Australian-ness.

All Australians are not working men in the sense of being manual workers. In fact, the vast majority are not. Yet for decades the power of this story never waned. The trope of the working man centralised what were regarded as unique and positive characteristics of being Australian. It thus produced a national story Australians could use to define themselves against those who they considered not Australian. As suggested above, though the figure was a classed one—a 'working' man—this type came to stand for a real Australian-ness that could be attributed to people from a range of backgrounds.

When media magnate and multi-millionaire Kerry Packer died in early 2006 many of the stories written about him demonstrated this common deployment of the idea of Australian egalitarianism. Packer's Australian-ness was said to be represented in his deep under-standing of the lives and likes of the working man. Sydney radio personality, Alan Jones, the MC at his funeral, called Packer 'an everyman—the voice of Australians with no voice' (Salter 2006: 41). Prime Minister John Howard summarised Packer's life by saying: 'The key to the enormous impact [he made] on Australian the community was his understanding of what made the ordinary bloke tick' (*Huxley* 2006). His Australian-ness was said to be demonstrated through traits associated with the working man type rather than the bourgeois mores associated with the very wealthy. It was noted the meal served for guests after the funeral included pies (Huxley 2006: 27). In writing stories about the death of Australia's wealthiest man, the tension that might emerge from class differences—for example, Kerry Packer's extreme wealth and 'legendary unwillingness to pay any more tax than he had to' (McClymont 2006: 10)—is tempered by a powerful story of inverted egalitarianism—Packer's love of working-class culture.

Given the obvious stratification of Australian society, the egalitar-ian narrative suggests that what is distinctive about class in Australia is that citizens from any stratum of society are comfortable with and believe they are equal to people from other strata. Historically this story was told in relation to leisure. In a 1971 Reader's Digest coffee table book, *Australia—This Land, These People*, there is an article by Australian social commentator Donald Horne, no great believer in the legend of Australian perfection. On one of the pages of Horne's article, three images are used to illustrate the story. All refer to the absence of class prejudice. One image—the front bar of a pub—shows a range of men (and a woman) drinking—some in ties, some in open-necked shirts, one smoking a pipe, all drinking beer (see Figure 2.1). The caption informs the reader:

> Nowhere is egalitarianism demonstrated more clearly than in local pubs at the end of the working day. Company executives may prefer to drink in the saloon rather than the public bar, but no one objects if the storeman chooses to drink there also. On Saturday night in a high-priced city tavern, it may be difficult to tell which man is the employer and which the employee (1971: 34).

Another image showing the front of a New South Wales club tells the reader: 'New South Wales clubs, financed largely by poker machine

Figure 2.1 'Nowhere is egalitarianism demonstrated more clearly than in local pubs at the end of the working day.' (*Photographer: David Beal*)

profits, offer their members opulent buildings like this and absence of class barriers' (1971: 35). Finally, there is an image of dozens of private school boys in boater hats: 'The boys wearing these boaters, reminiscent of English public schools, are all Australian, but their features may be Anglo-Saxon, Celtic, Latin, Slav, Asian ... [sic]' (1971: 35). These images helped produce the story of egalitarianism. The story is that class exists in Australia, but it is trumped by an egalitarianism that sees the working man invite himself into the 'opulent' spaces usually kept for the rich in other societies. The suggestion to the reader is that high-priced places can be accessed by all Australians, not just the rich. Indeed, as represented in this pictorial story, the egalitarian narrative suggests that class is not even about wealth. In the 'high-priced city tavern', one cannot tell the difference between the boss and the worker. The presence of both of them in the pub suggests both are wealthy enough to enter the hotel and afford the drinks.

This commentary of a good egalitarian Australia still works today. In an Australia Day paean in the *Sydney Morning Herald* in 2005, a journalist wrote: 'A millionaire can look like a plumber or indeed be a plumber such is our relaxed approach to sartorial hierarchy' (Low 2005). Obviously the writer is making a slightly tongue-in-cheek reference to Australian (men's in particular) approaches to dress. The iconic references it draws on to do this are egalitarianism and class. The article suggests the millionaire may look like a plumber—that is, a wealthy man may look like a working man. More than this, a working man may be a millionaire—in other words, class position is not about your relationship to the means of production or about wealth (or lack of it). Here, being a working man signifies nothing more than the manner in which a person's money was made—by manual labour or a trade rather than professional or white-collar work. This author uses the archetypal values of the working man—primarily unpretentious-ness—combined with the notion of egalitarianism to create a story of a good Australia where all are equal.

Positing egalitarianism as a central characteristic of Australian-ness obscures class inequality, while paradoxically making class central to stories of being Australian. In dominant stories of being Australian, egalitarianism has been deployed to produce a narrative reinforcing the idea of class (some Australians are plumbers, some are media moguls) whilst obscuring the real social and economic outcomes that result from class differences (such as different health outcomes and educational opportunities). For example, in February 2005 Kim Beazley, the then leader of the federal opposition, said of class politics:

> In Australia, while there is always an element of class politics, the reality is that we're a very egalitarian society in spirit. We may not be in outcomes or experience, but in spirit we all see ourselves as much the same (Hartcher 2005: 9).

The argument put forward is not that Australia is classless; indeed, it is not even an argument suggesting that Australia has equal opportunity for all. It is simply an argument that, in 'spirit', Australia is egalitarian. Class, as it is deployed in these stories of being Australian, obscures social and economic inequalities and encourages citizens to see themselves 'as much the same'. To be Australian is to value the working bloke as much—indeed, more than—the up-town 'toff'. The hypothetical nationalist question being posed in these stories is: how could a nation be anything other than good when it values the ordinary, hard-working working bloke so much? Myths and stories of egalitarianism—that is, stories which reinforce the idea that there are no real ramifications resulting from class difference—encourage the primacy of the notion that being Australian is about being part of a nation all pulling together for the same end.

The working man is everywhere

What is interesting to analyse in these stories is who actually is repre-sented as the 'working man'—or, more recently, the gender-neutral 'battler'—in stories of class and egalitarianism. It needs to be said that these stories about class and the working man were originally couched in terms of masculinity without much consideration for how women were placed in the story of Australian-ness (this issue will be discussed in more detail in chapter 3). As suggested so far, the working man is represented as a manual worker (with those rough and ready practical skills) rather than as a professional. The working man is someone who gets his hands dirty. However, it is important to note that working men (or battlers) are not marked in terms of their relationship to the means of production (a wage worker or a boss), but rather their placement in a more nebulous story of their attitudes to the idea of hard work.

The working man in these stories crosses classes. In the 1971 Reader's Digest chapter mentioned earlier, the working man was a storeman, an employee and a club member. In 2005 in the *Sydney Morning Herald*, he was a plumber and a millionaire. In more gender-inclusive stories from the 1990s and 2000s, the working man has morphed into 'mum and dad' in the middle Australian family doing it tough. This fluidity of what it means to be a working man or battler highlights the openness of the category and locates issues of class conflict or social inequality outside this story. The farmer out working on the fences on the 10 000-hectare property he inherited from his father is as much the working man as the self-employed small business owner, who is as much a working man as the brickie's labourer. The working man is marked by a class, but he does not necessarily emerge from a particular class—the working class. He is simply Australian. Wealth differences are not understood as attached to particular classes. In turn, class differences are represented as unrelated to superiority and inferiority. This saw the development and valorisation of the larrikin or ocker as the type representing this refusal to recognise class distinction. Again businessman Kerry Packer is a good example of this type who occupies the working man category yet reinforces the fluidity of movement across society by this type.

Russel Ward (1958) argues that Australian culture emerged from the 'bottom' not the 'top'; from the worker not the boss; from the popular not the elite. This story of the democratisation of culture produces the impression all Australians are equal in the nation, because the engine of the nation is fuelled by working men's sensibilities. In the 1970s and 1980s, the comedian Paul Hogan (of *Crocodile Dundee* fame), who dressed for his television show in football shorts and socks with a shirt that had the sleeves cut out, exemplified these sensibilities. This 'ocker' bloke would interview the world's stars on his television show in the guise of the Australian everyman. More recently, until his death in 2006, Crocodile Hunter Steve Irwin, in his khaki shorts and shirt, filled a similar role—the everyman who mingled with the stars.

Though, in the twenty-first century, the images of the typical Australian have become more nuanced and diverse, they often still operate around a figure of the working man. And the story of the working man still reinforces a shared Australian-ness rather than a specific working-class sensibility. Take the example of Gallipoli veteran Alec Campbell. In the first few years of the twenty-first century, more than three-quarters of a century after the end of World War I, the last Australian veterans of this war have died. In honour of their contribution to the nation, many of these men were given state funerals. Alec Campbell who died in 2002 was the last remaining Australian who had been at Gallipoli. In the media coverage of his life and death, the focus was on his participation in World War I though, as his daughter noted, this was a very small part of his life (ABC 2002). Family and friends commented on Campbell's involvement in Anzac Day services, but couched this in terms of his pacifist leanings. They also recounted what they saw as other important aspects of his life, particularly his commitment to the trade union movement and his decades of work improving working men's access to education through the Workers' Educational Association (WEA).

What is interesting about the honouring of this ordinary and yet exceptional Australian, this Australian whose state funeral suggested that he was someone other Australians could look up to, was that Campbell was represented as the quintessential Australian because of his links to Gallipoli and the 'Anzac tradition'. The linking of Australian-ness and Anzac means that the genealogy of this exceptional Australian is traced back to that 'any-class' bush bloke whose ghostly presence still haunts the making of national stories. What is not taken up in the stories of this Australian man, whose long and productive life inspired so many, were his links to working-class politics. Campbell's positioning of himself within the stories of Australia as a fighter for the rights of those who were disadvantaged in the nation is not given pride of place. Alec Campbell approached his life in terms of working to challenge the social inequality that he saw as being shaped by class, for example, unequal access to education. Yet in the final official story—his state funeral—he was represented as the quintessential Australian bloke who sits at the heart of the nation by virtue of his classless Anzac status. He was a working man who worked for his country—the battler—but he was not represented as the working man, the working-class Australian who challenged the status quo. Here class, via the egalitarian myth, was used to posit a story about a united nation, not one where a man spent a lifetime trying to undo the effects of inequality.

Inventing egalitarianism

So far, it has been argued that the idea of class is placed at the centre of stories of Australian-ness through the valorisation of the image of a national type—a working man. Though the image of the working man derives from a class-inflected system, the figure itself is not necessarily attached to specific class but often to a type of work—manual labour—and a set of values emerging from the lifestyle of this type of worker. This emphasis on Australian national identity as emerging from an historically 'lowly' type of work, especially in the bush, functions to reinforce or produce a story of Australia as an egalitarian society. What this story of Australian-ness and egalitarianism does is to emphasise the idea of being Australian in terms of a shared (national) quality rather than highlight the differences (for example, class) that run through the community. This story of egalitarianism has a long history. This section explores the historical origins of the story in order to explain how ideas of egalitarianism and a culture shaped by working class values came to be seen as a central part of the dominant narratives of the nation. Three narratives will be considered: the story made in relation to Britain as the mother country from whom Australia had to break away; the story made in relation to Asia as a despotic region whose inhabitants sought to take over Australia; and the story made in relation to Australian workers who needed to be lifted up to the standard held by the working man.

Breaking away from the 'mother country'

It has often been argued that the fluidity of class in Australia and the innate feeling of equality in this nation emerged in opposition to the strict class system of Britain. In the nineteenth and early twentieth centuries, one of the stories the newly federated colonies told themselves and the world was that Australia would make itself in a manner different to the old country. As the chairman of an eight-hour day meeting held in Melbourne in the 1850s claimed: 'the old idea that prevailed at home that one class was born to labour and another to direct that labour ought not to find a place here' (Hughes 1961: 399). Many of the stories of national identity in Australia are structured in terms of this relationship to Britain, which is often seen as both the place of the origin of the nation (hence the mother country or home), and as the place against which Australia has to mark itself as different and better. It was argued this was achieved through the evolution of a non-Indigenous but local Australian culture from the bottom of Australian society rather than the top. Unlike Britain, where the aristocracy set the tone of the nation and its culture, in Australia it was argued that this came from the workers.

Kurt Iveson (1997) writes about the emergence of this working-class Australian identity in terms of bush ballads:

> The lyrical project of many bush ballads was to help construct a new Australian national identity, one in which the traditions and culture developed by the Australian working class were celebrated and embraced rather than repressed and denied. This was important as a time when the Australian ruling class and Australia's identity were still bound closely to mother England (1997: 39).

Though there was much to draw from the mother country Australia was going to be fresh. It was not going to be bound by the values of England—imported via a ruling class. In this context, Australia was often represented as a 'social laboratory' where new and better ways of organising society would evolve. This would include the eradication of British ideas of caste and class.

There was a certain pleasure at this time in the telling of stories about the role of ability and attitude to work as the key to success rather than a person's class status or their genealogy. C.E.W. Bean, the well-known documenter of the Gallipoli campaign, tells these types of stories in his book *On the Wool Track* (1910). He is clear in his belief that Australia's British heritage is central to its success: 'The boss knew from the first that if he was to make anything at all of his life he had to depend on his common sense, his courage and sheer ability to lead which generally exists somewhere deep down in people of British birth' (1910: 40). However, Bean also reinforces that for a British person in Australia 'his future depends, as nearly as is humanly possible, upon his brains and courage and energy' (1910: 139). Aspects of the British character are important, but they are being reworked in ways that ignore class and caste. These stories of egalitarianism mask the difference between the long-term prospects of most of the pastoral workers and the owner of the property. They also underplay the class differences that do exist. Again Bean gives an example when he recounts a story of a worker on a sheep property who called the bosses son by his first name—Jack: '"See here. Thompson," says the young boss, picking up for once the man's surname, a mode of address hardly ever used in the bush, "as long as I'm here I'm Mr M'Donald—and don't you forget it"'(1910: 41).

Richard White (1981) argues that the view of Australia as a 'working man's paradise' emerged in Australia in the mid-nineteenth century as part of the propaganda used to encourage new migrants to come to Australia. Immigration has been one of the main engines of growth for the Australian colonies and the federation. The nineteenth and twentieth centuries were periods of unparalleled global population movement. Of the millions who migrated from Britain, Ireland and Europe, the majority were not interested in coming to Australia. It was considered wild, distant and unknown compared with destinations in North America. The Australian colonial governments and their agents in Britain had to spend much time and effort encouraging men of modest financial means to give it a go in Australia. In the early days, there were some impressive success stories. Yet for every success story there was a matching story of difficulty. Over time, it is the story of a land of milk and honey that has survived as the dominant story of Australia. The experience of migrants in Australia is mixed, but the egalitarian story works to produce an homogenous story of success rather than—as Henry Parkes and others remember—an unequal community sometimes based on 'slavish' conditions (Cannon 1971: 148).

This story of egalitarianism posed in terms of a tension with the British class system also emerges in national stories of war. One of the proud claims about Australians' participation in wars, before the 1950s, was that the soldiers who fought in them were all volunteers. Unlike the United States or Britain, where unwilling or at least un-interested men had to be dragooned into the military and into battle in major wars through conscription, most fighting men in the Australian military were there because they wanted to be. This history helped in the production of the story of the egalitarian nature of the Australian nation. The story was that, in the military, the relations predominating in the workforce or on the pastoral property were replicated. An officer was not someone who was superior to you, but simply someone who, through luck or circumstance (or perhaps ability), held a position of authority over you. It made this man no better than you and perhaps no worse. A soldier's decision to obey an order from an officer was made because he agreed with the decision of the officer, not because he deferred to the officer as a person from a superior social position.

Concomitantly in this story, an ideal or good officer is often represented as one of the men. The final scenes of the well-known

Australian film *Gallipoli* (1981) help reproduce this legend. As the men prepare to go over the top of their trenches to a certain death at the hands of the waiting Turkish army, the officer loads his gun and announces that he would not make his men do anything that he was not willing to do. Contrasted with this exemplary act of egalitarianism are the English military officers who give the order for the men to die from the safety of their headquarters, while they sip tea. The film deploys a narrative contrasting the class-bound English and their ill-treatment or disregard for those who they see as their inferiors with the egalitarian Australian society where men may be from different social and economic positions in life, but this does not translate into ill-treatment of those who are less well off. Further, the scene reinforces the regional affiliation of the men, and by implication their status as rural workers—a group known for their mateship. As the officer in the film says: 'I want you all to remember who you are. You're the Tenth Light Horse, men from Western Australia.' Their shared regional and national affiliation trumps any class divisions. In this film, the message is that the over-arching feelings of egalitarianism, of being in this together, negate any possibility of class division.

This story of egalitarianism as opposed to British class-consciousness is also (re)produced less seriously elsewhere—for example, in comedy. The characters created in some Australian films of the late 1960s and early 1970s often surfaced in scenes set in London where brash Australian-ness rubbed up against snooty-English manners. In the film *Stork* (1971), one character at a party takes an hors d'oeuvre consisting of an oyster on a cracker and places the oyster up his nose and then turns to face some of the guests. He asks one for a handkerchief, then blows his nose and eats the contents. It is a scene that reinforces a story of Australians understanding the ludicrousness of a class system and the snooty manners associated with it. Australians therefore draw on the working man's larrikin humour to demonstrate this knowledge and implicitly celebrate the values of the working man, here represented as the ocker.

The pleasure in representing Australian-ness as thoroughly egalitarian in opposition to a stuffy Englishness has not disappeared. It was brought to the fore during the prime ministership of Paul Keating (1991–96) who, during a meeting with Queen Elizabeth II, put a hand on her back and gently steered her towards the correct room. Apparently no one touches the person of the monarch. The gesture caused an uproar in the tabloid press in England and a fiery response from incensed Australians who claimed they were not party to the class-ist paranoia of their forbears. Even this trivial piece of nationalist jingoism from both sides of the world works as part of a bigger story that sees a united Australia capable of thinking beyond an elitist system and knowing that this small hand gesture marks a superiority shared by all.

Class in the region

The story of Australian-ness created by juxtaposing the British class system against the egalitarianism of Australia is one mostly staged in terms of a friendly (familial) rivalry. National stories of Australian egalitarianism were also formed in relation to the excluded 'other'— Asia. In this case, the story is not framed in terms of familial tension, but a terminal inequality that could not be bridged. In the New South Wales parliament in 1881, a member argued: 'the Chinese are bred under the despotic government and inured to the oppression of mandarins and cannot enter in to British feeling' (NSW Parliament, 1881: 113). Here the British and colonial Australians are linked in terms of having a feeling for democracy while the Chinese are represented as being well behind in terms of developing ideas of democracy and equality. The idea of the Chinese (who operated as the 'type' representing all Asia in white Australian discourse) being part of the nation was seen as ludicrous. Difference, represented in terms of wildly different political systems signifying centuries of change, is characterised as a sign of the need to reinforce the integrity of the Australian nation against unequal outsiders. The Chinese worker is represented as unable to understand egalitarianism, and on these grounds as needing to be excluded. Again, this reinforced a story of sameness (a national shared story) for Australians. Those in Australia, with their 'British feeling', understood equality. Those outside needed to be kept out because they would undermine the egalitarian space of the Australian nation. The egalitarian story, with its emphasis on Australian-ness as refracted through the person of the working man and his catchcry of a 'fair go', operated to join Australians in a nationalistic story that seemingly united the citizens who understood fairness against outsiders who did not.

This story can still be recycled in the 2000s. In the discussions about the federal government's 2005 industrial relations reforms, one letter writer to a newspaper stated:

> Don't they [unions] realise that the world is changing and there is a huge and growing workforce in countries surrounding Australia only too anxious to take over all aspects of our industry unless we can keep our competitiveness? Instead of poncing around the streets sprouting

futile clichés, the unions should be getting together with the employers to see how labour costs can be reduced—not by wage cutting or lay-offs, but by efficiency, enthusiasm, multi-skilling and other means (Read 2005: 12).

Australian workers are represented as a group who should ally themselves with their employers, against both a 'poncing' union leadership and greedy outsiders poised to 'take over' Australian industry. In this story, the worker and boss come together to create an outcome that is fair. Placed outside this story are those who threaten the story, the un-manly unions who use the 'futile' idea of class and the threatening nations that 'surround' Australia.

In the late nineteenth century, the hysteria that accompanied the formation of stories about Australia in terms of the exclusion of the Chinese drew on various prejudices—not all of them about a failure to understand workplace and political democracy. The different players—workers, bosses, parliamentarians, professionals— were not as united as first might be suggested by the story. Further, the story of Asian inferiority was never total. There were stories where individuals in Australia argued for the recognition of Asian peoples' equality with all others. However, it was not until the twentieth century, especially amongst radical trade unions, that an egalitarian story was deployed to secure equal wages for all Australians regardless of their heritage.

Egalitarianism and exclusion

A Federal Arbitration Court was set up in 1904. In its early years the court made a series of important rulings about decent and just pay for workers, called the living wage. In 1907 Justice Higgins made a famous decision—known as the *Harvester Judgement*—that stipulated workers should to be paid wages that allowed them to live decently. This decision institutionalised many of the values about the fair—what Higgins called 'civilised'—and egalitarian nature of the new nation (Lake 1999: 55). However, reflecting dominant social values of the time Higgins' decision drew a distinction between the value of the living wage for men and women (Ryan and Conlon 1989: 86–111). Reproducing the general work and family patterns of middle-class Australians Higgins presumed that male workers had dependants (wives and children) and that female workers were single women who would quit paid labour and return to the private sphere after marriage. Accordingly the male living wage was set at a higher level—deemed a family wage—than the female living wage. Male workers were to be paid a wage 'sufficient to enable them to marry and keep a family in frugal comfort' (Bulbeck 1998: 51). Implied in the payment of this family wage was the idea that the male worker was 'under obligation—even a legal obligation—to maintain' his wife and children (Ryan and Conlon 1989: 92). However, it was often the case that male workers did not have dependants to maintain. Chilla Bulbeck (1998) points out that, in 1907, 45 per cent of male workers were single but many women in the same period were single parents responsible for children or the sole worker in a family supporting aged parents (1998: 51). So though the *Harvester Judgement* was envisioned by its designer as a means to produce a more 'civilised' society—and it did achieve this—it also institutionalised the ideal of the heterosexual couple with a private woman (working for lower wages) and a public man (earning the family wage); a vision of work which was not fully confronted until 1972. This meant that the inequity of the pay women were receiving was made invisible in the national story.

The institutionalisation of workplace inequality for Indigenous peoples was not so neatly tied up in one arbitration court decision. Their place in the story of working Australia was part of a colonial narrative where Indigenous peoples were controlled by a colonising power. Indigenous peoples were excluded from the national story of egalitarianism. Using scientific and religious ideas, they were positioned as inferior workers. As such, Indigenous peoples did not even earn the 50 per cent of a working man's wage non-Indigenous women were promised. Many earned nothing; some were given payment in kind—their work clothes and food. For those who earned wages, state governments often had them paid straight into trusts rather than to the individuals. Much of this money was never transferred to the Indigenous people who had earned it. Further, many Indigenous peoples were not free to move and find work if and when they desired to do so. They were under the direction of 'protectors' who controlled their daily lives, including work.

The story of Australian egalitarianism could be used to challenge inequality within the nation. For example, women and Indigenous people deployed the story to shame or encourage citizens and governments into making changes to their labour conditions. Sometimes an international narrative about equality, deriving from groups such as the United Nations, was also used to secure work and social justice where it was missing in Australia. If a group claimed to be treated unjustly, the egalitarian story suggested that once Australians were alerted to this inequity the problem would be fixed. The logic was that, because Australia is an egalitarian place when inequities are brought to their notice, the natural tendency of Australians is to right them. However, the international stories of human rights and the national egalitarian story were not always enough.

Other stories about Australian-ness—as white or masculine—were powerful. Take the example, used earlier, of the egalitarian pub. That 1971 story of executives and storemen drinking together in the saloon bar can be told and many readers (still) fail to notice that, at the time, if a non-Indigenous woman was working behind the bar she would be earning half the wages of a man. Further, if an Indigenous man was added to the scene, he would most likely be sitting outside the pub because only four years earlier it would have been illegal for him to access the facility. Racial prejudice would mean he would be unlikely to be given a job in a pub. Though it might be easy to say this story is over 30 years old, and these issues have been sorted out, today the egalitarian story still masks considerable inequality.

Politics and class

Though there is a strong story of egalitarianism in Australia, there are also stories reinforcing social and economic difference. At the level of formal politics, class has been an important marker of difference. In the post-1945 era, Australian politics was organised around three political parties—the Australian Labor Party (formed in 1891), the Liberal Party (formed in 1944) and the National Party (named in 1982, morphing from the Australian Country Party which emerged in Western Australia in 1914). Since 1949, the National Party and the Liberal Party have worked together, forming coalition governments when they could. Until the late 1980s, these three political parties dominated the political scene and were organised—not solely, but strongly—in terms of loyalty towards particular class or sectional groups.

In Australia, political parties representing the views of wage workers, or the working class, emerged in the different colonies during the 1890s. The Queensland shearers' strikes and the east coast maritime workers' strikes of the 1890s mobilised thousands of workers. Though these strikes were ultimately unsuccessful, they laid the foundations for widespread trade union membership in 'blue-collar' industries. In the west of Australia, labour parties emerged somewhat later. However, in the first federal election in 1901, 24 parliamentarians representing 'labour' were elected and they came together and formed a national Labor Party.

In the early period of Federation, there was no one party representing the interests of business and wealth. There were coalitions representing different sections of capital—both free trade and tariff protection parliamentarians. The United Australia Party, a non-labour party, was formed in 1931. In 1944, United Australia Party members met and formed a new party—the Liberal Party. This new political venture would be, in the words of its leader Robert Menzies, a 'progressive party, willing to make experiments, in no sense reactionary but believing in the individual, his rights and his enterprise' (Menzies 1967).

From the post-1945 period until the 1990s, these parties were commonly understood in terms of a 'left' and 'right' political dichotomy. Left politics was associated with the Australian Labor Party, the trade unions and the working class or poorer groups in the community. The Liberal Party, County Party and National Party were associated with the 'right' of politics and the rural and wealthy sections of the community. The parties were also understood in terms of a conservative/progressive dichotomy. The Australian Labor Party was associated with socially progressive reform such as equal pay for women. The Liberal Party and the National Party were associated with more conservative stands—for example, attempts to ban the Communist Party in Australia.

Neo-liberalism and globalisation

As Anthony Moran (2005: 38) writes: 'most accounts of Australian political culture begin by stressing the strong support of Australians for an interventionist state.' From the mid-1980s, a new brand of economic thought—neo-liberalism—came to dominate many avenues of political, economic and social life in Australia. Neo-liberalism, which entered Australia via Britain and the United States, is a radical form of free market orthodoxy, that is, it emphasises small government, centralising the place of the individual in society and placing choice at the centre of its philosophy. Given the historical emphasis on state intervention, the impact of neo-liberalism was perhaps slower than in other similarly placed nations, but there were many Australians who welcomed it. Further, as Moran (2005) points out, bipartisan political party support for this economic paradigm meant it was always going to enter Australia. It was simply a question of time and degree.

The Australian Labor Party governments in the period after 1983 were the first federal governments to implement neo-liberal policies.

They privatised public utilities and deregulated parts of the labour market. Since the coming to power of Liberal Party and National Party at a federal level in 1996, the takeup up of neo-liberal ideas has accelerated. The sale of the national telephone company, Telstra, is one example. Another is the introduction of massive workplace changes, including individual work contracts to replace labour agreements negotiated collectively through a union.

The prominence of neo-liberal ideology in Australia in the last two decades has shifted the place of class in political life. The notions of choice and 'user pays' have come to dominate at the popular level in many sectors of the population. Social surveys have found that younger Australians are much more likely to agree with statements about the need for citizens to 'look after their own interests first' than older Australians are. The idea of the Australian ethos of a 'fair go' has been extended to include the proviso 'but not a free ride'. The ideas of collectivity and social welfare, long associated with the politics of the left and the Labor Party, have begun to seem old-fashioned and irrelevant to many Australians. Instead, there is an increasing emphasis on the individual and individual effort rather than the notion of structural inequality. This has led to fewer Australians identifying with a collectivity such as the 'working class' or a trade union.

The egalitarian story has also helped to create a sense that if a person is located in one class, they should be aspiring to join the next one up. In the late 1990s, the term 'aspirational voter' came to prominence—referring to a voter who once had been a traditional Labor voter but was now looking to the Liberals for the outcomes they wanted, such as good education for their children, a bigger home and an investment portfolio. For many of these 'aspirationals', the Liberal Party held a further appeal. This party had what Judith Brett (2003) calls a local rather than cosmopolitan focus. Even though it was the neo-liberal policies of the Liberal (and Labor) governments that continued to open Australia up to some of the uncertainties associated with a globalising world, many Australians looked to the Liberals as the party which would protect Australian sovereignty and 'culture'.

Many Australians picture their 'way of life' as being undermined by new policies introduced by progressive parties. Policies such as increased immigration from Asia, native title rights for Indigenous peoples, the prominence of multiculturalism and increasing recognition for gay men, lesbians, transsexuals and same-sex couples have been seen as 'worries' for many Australians. For these citizens, who were often traditional Labor voters, being Australian was changing to a story they no longer recognised or from which they felt excluded. They envisaged the nationalist and conservative aspects of the Liberal and National parties as stopping these changes, of standing for a more 'traditional' Australia. So now added to the Liberal and National Party's adherents is not only the aspirational voter, but also the 'battler'—the Australian who feels excluded from the Australia of their memory.

In this new configuration, the divisions of 'left wing' and 'right wing' or 'worker' and 'boss' no longer described the political framework of Australia. Other divisions such as progressive or conservative, elite or mainstream and Australian or un-Australian made more sense. It was in this context that the One Nation Party emerged in Australia in 1997. The leader of this party, Pauline Hanson, began her political life as a Liberal Party candidate for a federal seat in Queensland. Her conservative rhetoric about the exclusion of 'mainstream Australians' in favour of minority group interests, especially Indigenous peoples and Asians, struck a chord with many citizens although it also led to her expulsion from the Liberal Party. Yet many of her other opinions about 'big business' and the globalisation process leading to the decline in living standards were closer to a traditional (pre-1980s) Labor Party view of the world.

Traditional class divisions were fading; instead, divisions such as 'mainstream' and 'elite' were favoured. These categories often crossed class lines, with divisions being made between inner-city 'bleeding hearts' and suburban and rural 'battlers'. As Christopher Scanlon (2004) explains:

> Terms such as battler and aspirational are solid enough to tap into basic human emotions and experiences, yet sufficiently inchoate that people can flesh them out with their own expectations. The people tagged with such labels may be worlds apart socially, economically and culturally, but they conjure into being the idea that we all share a common world-view and set of expectations, while leaving blank the details of what makes up that world-view and those expectations.

The fuzziness of terms such as 'mainstream', 'battler' and 'mums and dads' gives a sense of equality and inclusion; however, such terms often mask structural inequities that mean some 'aspirationals' will never have access to the wealth that others do as a result of education, job and family privilege.

Class as 'divisive'

In contemporary Australia, invoking class as a way of seeing the world and as a factor to be considered when designing policy has come to be regarded as 'divisive'. When federal treasurer Peter Costello was asked about the tax cuts his government had made in favour of middle- and upper-income Australians in 2005, he responded:

> Anyone who works is a member of the working class, right, anyone who works . . . This idea that you only work if you are engaged in manual labour—most Australians aren't engaged in manual labour, but they work, they are workers and they deserve tax cuts (Garnaut 2005).

Costello argues that all workers belong to the working class. Differences such as salary and relative wealth, and structural distinctions such as educational attainment are erased. Using the neutralised idea of the working man and woman discussed earlier, Costello invoked an all-inclusive notion of class that eradicated both social justice and equity as criteria for delivering tax cuts. A year or so earlier, in the campaign for the 2004 federal election, the then-leader of the Australian Labor Party, Mark Latham, argued that school funding by governments should be assessed on need. In this story, all schools and their students were not the same: some needed the public dollar more than others. Latham drew on a story of class and inequality in designing this policy; however, it was very easy for his political opponents to use this against him. He was accused of creating an 'us and them' mentality that divided the community. His approach was described as 'wedge politics'—the deliberate nurturing of differences between groups. This is perhaps one of the last mentions of class and equity in contemporary debate within political parties.

Class and social justice

Some stories of being Australian do take up the idea of class as a marker of social and economic inequality. These have never been the dominant stories in the production of Australian-ness, and are less so in the twenty-first century, but they have at times been a powerful way in which some citizens have imagined their place in Australia. These stories of class are an important way in which citizens organise their national identity through their identification as working class. They also challenge the egalitarian story, arguing instead that systemic inequality means that economic and social reform is needed in Australia. One of the reasons why the egalitarian story works so effectively as a nationalistic story of a united nation is that what constitutes egalitarianism is ill-defined. Nebulous phrases, such as 'a fair go', are used to explain how Australia is organised. If these notions of egalitarianism are put up against a clearly expressed description of what equality entails (for example, equal access to clean water, health care or the legal system), then the idea of Australia as an egalitarian nation is harder to sustain. In the light of specific criteria for equality, class differences within Australia immediately become obvious.

Though Australian governments have a history of approaching economic and social relations in an innovative manner emphasising equal access, this did not emerge from some innate national belief about what constituted a just society. Aspects of Australian culture that emphasise egalitarianism in the form of equality did not simply emerge from the proximity of citizens to sheep and the land. Rather, they are linked to long fights by workers (as a working class), trade unions and also a political party—the Australian Labor Party—that was set up to represent the needs of that working class. Though the egalitarian story may divert attention from this fact, it is the long history of workers' struggle and protest, their lobbying for change and justice, that has in so many instances led to social innovations in Australia. The social ideas that informed radical working-class Australian thinkers have always been part of a global discourse of equality and work. In this sense, these stories of egalitarianism are not framed in terms of nationalism, but internationalism—making it easier to see the limits of many of the nationalistic ideas of equality.

From the beginning of British colonisation, new migrants brought with them ideas about how communities should be organised. For example, the new European narrative of *liberté, egalité* and *fraternité* came in the minds of some migrants in the early nineteenth century. Other migrants brought with them Chartist principles of labour unions and equal parliamentary representation. Later migrants came with other utopian ideals deriving from the Russian Revolution and experiments with new social organisations.

In the context of international stories of reforming (or revolutionising) societies, workers' tactics did not simply involve using the national egalitarian story to make change around the edges of the dominant ideas of Australian-ness and work. Workers often discarded this story in favour of global and locally responsive narratives of justice and workers' rights. As a result, labour unions and workers were often at the forefront of campaigns to undo injustices faced by wage-workers. For example, in Australia—as in other areas of the

Western world—the end of the nineteenth century saw the increasing mechanisation of the factory process and the introduction of assembly line work. In this atmosphere, more workers were regarded as unskilled and easily replaced. This, in concert with the devastating economic depression of the 1890s, led to a new precariousness in daily existence for more and more Australian workers. Recognising this trend, and linking it to ideas of the development of capitalism, unions of these unskilled workers were dedicated to stopping the continual cutting of their wages. In this atmosphere, the tone of a strike was of large groups inspired by radical international ideologies. The struggle was seen as one between international capital and labour. There were acknowledged differences between Australian citizens: some were 'bosses', some were 'workers'.

These international ideas have also been taken up within the regional and national arena in Australia and used to fight for justice for workers who were discriminated against on the basis of gender or race. For example, the Indigenous stock workers' strikes in the Pilbara and Kimberley region in the 1940s and 1960s were supported both locally and from a distance by labour councils and workers around Australia who were influenced by the ideas of the Communist Party. In 1939, Tom Wright, working for the Labor Council of New South Wales, wrote a tract arguing that gaining a 'new deal for Aborigines . . . must be one of the tasks of the Labour Movement' (Hess 1994: 69). Wright's solution, drawing on a Marxist tradition of communism, was organised around a system of land rights and self-management (still a radical proposal today) for Indigenous peoples. For any sort of egalitarianism to be achieved by Indigenous peoples, the inequalities in the system had to be addressed—not masked by a national story of Australia being a nation that gave a 'fair go' to all. Similar campaigns run by radical women struggled to have the injustices faced by women in the workplace recognised by the state.

Nationalism is a part of some stories of being Australian. In the new economy that has developed in Australia as a result of the impact of globalisation and neo-liberal economic ideas, new types of poverty and hardship have emerged. The decline in tariff protection and opening up of Australian industries to free trade has led to the decline or closure of many key manufacturing industries with substantial blue-collar workforces. Industries such as metals, textiles, footwear and automotive manufacturing have shed thousands and thousands of jobs over the past two decades. Given that the declining industries are located in specific geographical areas, and given that many of those who have lost their jobs were in semi-skilled or unskilled occupations, this has led to regional concentrations of unemployment and poverty. Though the decline in manufacturing has been matched with a growth in other industries, such as the services sector and information technology, this has provided jobs for a different group of Australians—usually young and highly skilled. Trade unions have worked to defend workers when their jobs were threatened. In this case, rather than using an international story, unions often draw on nationalist stories of hard-working Australians who did not deserve to be thrown on the 'scrap-heap'. They use the nationalist language of it being 'un-Australian' to put workers out of a job—especially if the job is going to a non-Australian based overseas.

S11

More recently, changes brought about as a result of global neo-liberal idelologies have been challenged by groups that are thinking in terms of the global. In September 2000, a meeting of the World Economic Forum took place in Melbourne. Tens of thousands of Australians and international visitors protested outside the strongly fortified casino where the meeting took place. The protesters were a mixed group with differing agendas. There were trade unions, environmental groups, socialist political parties, anarchists, and many clusters and individuals not linked to any particular political party. This protest was of an international or global nature. Though quite a few groups were aligned with specific national campaigns, they framed their protests in terms of a 'global corporatism' which they saw as attacking wages, conditions and the sustainability of societies all over the world. The global trend of a neo-liberal 'freeing up' of the economy was seen as having adverse affects on the poorer groups in communities around the world. The needs of the Australian working class were linked to others around the globe.

In dominant stories about the issue of wealth and poverty in Australia, it is often suggested that representing the story in terms of class is divisive and destructive to the national story of working together. Yet this 'us' versus 'them' formulation of the economic structure of Australia made and still makes a lot of sense to many workers, especially those who are exploited. A citizen labouring in a sweatshop in Australia may not think Australia is ordered in terms of a natural ethos of 'a fair go'. The notion of an unfair system privileging those with more power may make more sense. It might be very heartwarming to suggest that under-paid workers are able to drink in the same pub as the person who pays these people $2.00 an hour to sew *haute couture* clothing. However, this egalitarian story does not change the experience of poverty. It might be pleasurable to imagine Australian egalitarianism in terms of the 'right' of the working man to sit next to 'old money' at a country agricultural show, or the fun of being in the working man's company when he is yarning, or the droll satisfaction of the working man making it to the top, but this is not enough. National stories of egalitarianism need to be interrogated more thoroughly to see what work they do in covering up difference.

FURTHER READING

Attwood, Bain and Markus, Andrew 1999, *The Struggle for Aboriginal Rights: A Documentary History*, Allen & Unwin, Sydney.

Brett, Judith 2003, *Australian Liberals and the Moral Middle Class: From Alfred Deakin to John Howard*, Cambridge University Press, Melbourne.

Fox, Charles and Lake, Marilyn 1990, *Australians at Work*, McPhee Gribble, Melbourne.

Frankel, Boris 2004, *Zombies, Lilliputians and Sadists: The Power of the Living Dead and the Future of Australia*, Fremantle Arts Centre Press, Fremantle.

Grimshaw, Pat, Lake, Marilyn, McGrath, Ann and Quartly, Marian 1994, *Creating a Nation*, McPhee Gribble, Melbourne.

Hollier, Nathan (ed.) 2004, *Ruling Australia: The Power, Privilege and Politics of the New Ruling Class*, Australian Scholarly Publishers, Melbourne.

McGregor, Craig 2001, *Class in Australia*, Penguin, Melbourne.

McKnight, David 2005, *Beyond Right and Left: New Politics and the Culture Wars*, Allen & Unwin, Sydney.

Peel, Mark 2003, *The Lowest Rung: Voices of Australian Poverty*, Cambridge University Press, Melbourne.

Wilson, Shaun, Meagher, Gabrielle, Gibson, Rachel, Denmark, David and Western, Mark 2005, *Australian Social Attitudes: The First Report*, University of New South Wales Press, Sydney.

3
THE INVISIBLE WOMAN
Gender and nation

FOR MOST OF the twentieth century, dominant stories of the
nation were understood as deriving from a particular class within
Australia. This classed individual also had a particular gender. Many
scholars have noted that national stories about being Australian tend
to depict a man or draw on men's experiences. Take, for example,
the globally popular figure of the 'Crocodile Hunter', the ubiquitous
Anzac legend or the lifesaver. These iconic images of the quintessential or typical Australian are not of bush folk, but bush *men*; they are
not of participants in war, but male diggers; they are not of volunteers
at the local nursing home, but of male volunteer lifesavers who patrol
the beach. So, though Australians live in a nation that has over ten
million women, when they are asked about a typical Australian, many
people still imagine a man.

Kaye Schaffer (1988: 3), in her book *Women and the Bush*, asks why
the Australian tradition is 'so resolutely blind to women'. Yet women
are not entirely absent from the story of Australia. They are represented as the people the digger fights for in times of war. The
Crocodile Hunter story of Steve Irwin is framed in terms of his wife
and children. And women as well as men volunteer to be lifesavers on
beaches around Australia. This chapter explores how the concept of
gender contributes to the idea of being Australian. The approach is
not simply to note where women are missing from stories of the
nation and then to add them in (though this has been an important
project). Rather, the chapter analyses the ways in which concepts of
masculinity or femininity shape stories of the nation. That is, how
gender frames stories of the nation.

Imagining Australian men and women

An important aspect of the dominant knowledge system in non-Indigenous Australia is that it draws on a logic depending on binaries: for example, right/wrong, good/bad, white/black and, importantly, male/female. In binary logic, the two parts of the pair are intimately related to each other and each term can only be understood in relation to the other. That is, masculinity makes sense in relation to femininity—being a man is to not be a woman. Further, this system of pairing works on the presumption that the pairing captures all that can be said or known about a particular topic or area of knowledge—the binary male/female represents all that there is to be said about a gendered identity; it purports to explain all experience in that realm. Another important part of the logic of the binary is it posits a hierarchical relationship between the two terms: man is not only not-woman, the term 'man' is privileged over the term 'woman'.

Traditionally, national stories frame the relationship of men to women in terms of a normative binary. For example, consider the postcard rack in a beachside newsagency in a tourist town that typically provides a gendered story of being Australian organised around a male/female and active/passive binary. The range of beach postcards available in Australia is quite standard. There are the generic shots of the long coastline with 'Greetings from Such and Such Beach' stamped in gold in one corner. Then there are the shots of the surfer out on a wave and the slightly risqué shots of topless women on the beach with some slightly lewd caption. The dynamics of the postcards as a world-view of the beach—an aspect of Australian life—usually shows an active male and a reclining (sexualised and passive) female. This is obviously not a representation of real beach life, but it is a powerful story of gender in Australia that is stamped, postmarked and sent around the nation and across the globe. In this story, the man is the doer and the woman is the done-to. The dominant logic is that the person who is a doer occupies the valorised position; the person who is passive is secondary. This gendered binary is not unique to Australia. If a tourist went seeking postcards to send home from a trip to a Californian or French beach there would probably be a similar selection.

The classic representation of war and the nation further illustrates this gender binary. In representations of war, it is men who are represented as active in going to war, and women as passive in staying at home to support or be protected by the men. Men occupy a position of action and courage. They operate in relationship to women (their wives, their mothers, their sisters) whom they protect. The logic of masculine action only makes sense in relation to a feminine need of protection. This logic pertains not just to real men who go off to war to protect real women, but to a symbolic national story where the masculine military protects a nation represented as feminine—'we will protect her'.

The nation is also organised in terms of homosociality. Miriam Dixson (1999: 17) suggests in her book *The Real Matilda* that: 'men like women less in Australia than in any other community I know'. She also writes: 'men often say that Australian women can be paralytically boring to be with—though I must admit I often find our men that way too' (1999: 16). Dixson, somewhat provocatively, argues that there is a mutual dislike between men and women in Australia. This type of mutual gender segregation is called homosociality. Dixson is not alone in arguing Australia was a nation structured around homosociality. Others have noted the early colonial gender imbalance (more men than women) in tandem with sex-differentiated workplaces, and the power of masculine world-views reinforced or helped to produce this outcome (Summers 1975, Schaffer 1988, Lake 1992). This argument of non-Indigenous Australia as profoundly homosocial sits, somewhat uneasily, next to the dominant understanding of heterosexuality as the normative form of gender relations. Even though there is a strong story about the separation of the sexes, and the dominance of men, the man/woman dyad is still important in stories of Australian-ness.

Hegemonic and subversive stories of gender

This man/woman binary is an important way of understanding gender relations in Australia, however, it does not explain all relations between women and men. Think of a real beach scene rather than the one represented on a postcard. There are women out surfing and men lying in the sun getting a tan. One can be a woman and occupy a masculine subject position and vice versa. Or consider the make-up of the Australian military—there are many women in the ranks of the army, navy and airforce. Further, within the homosocial space of just men or just women, there are hierarchies. This is particularly so in an all-male world. For example, in Australia the valorised form of masculinity—what Robert Connell (1995) calls 'hegemonic masculinity'—is the Anglo–Australian, heterosexual, physically fit or outdoor-living bloke—the working man from the previous chapter. Though there are other groups of powerful men in Australia (especially businessmen), it is the image of the physically active and heterosexual man that dominates national stories.

The power of the dominant form of masculinity can be demonstrated in terms of his relationship to a man who does not act this way. So, going back to the postcard rack, in the story of the nation circulating here, the surfer dude—active, outdoor, blond—represents the dominant and hegemonic form of masculinity. This operates in relation not only to the passive feminine (the cards of women topless on the beach), but perhaps also to a man who cannot surf sitting with the women sunbaking or an older male who is 'past his prime' and wandering along the beach preceded by his beer belly.

Rose Lucas (1995) gives a good example of this hierarchy of masculinity in her readings of Australian film. She draws attention to the relationship between the two protagonists in the film *Gallipoli*—Archie and Frank. She argues that Frank, as the knockabout bloke, is represented in relation to his more gentle, thoughtful mate Archie. She notes that, after the section of the film where Archie and Frank bond on the pyramids in Egypt, the homosociality of the film threatens to spill into homosexuality. It is the more feminised Archie—representing a rather dubious form of Australian masculinity—who is gunned down at the film's end, putting a stop to such subversive or worrying types of masculinity.

This same hierarchy can be seen, though with very different meanings, in terms of women and femininity. Women's femininity is regulated in Australia, and there are privileged forms of femininity. Some aspects of femininity are less carefully monitored than masculinity; for example, women's intimate friendships with other women—but others are more carefully scrutinised—their intimate relationships with men. The valorised form of femininity in Australia is monogamous, heterosexual, maternal femininity, and it has been imperative that women fit this type as closely as possible. Jill Matthews (1984) in her ground-breaking work *Good and Mad Women*, made this point:

> The process of becoming a woman is the process of the pursuit of femininity, the attempt to live up to various standards of her society, the struggle to behave like and be a good woman according to her own and her society's standards (1984: 8).

The parameters of being a 'good woman' in Australia have shifted over time and place, but they tend to include not being too sexual, looking good, being pleasant, not showing up men and not 'misbehaving'.

The validation of this type of femininity works by setting it up against other less acceptable types of femininity. Again, to use a film example, there is an episode in the film *The Adventures of Priscilla, Queen of the Desert* (1994) where the gay and transsexual male characters spend the night in a pub in Broken Hill. In these scenes, a highly masculinised woman (muscular, with short hair and a wearing a Bonds singlet) insults the gay men and then sits down to out-drink Bernadette, the transsexual of the group (played by actor Terence Stamp). This local 'dyke' is trounced in both the slanging match and the drinking competition. In this homosocial dyad, the masculine-looking woman is represented as outside her proper feminine place compared with the long-haired, elegant and well-mannered Bernadette. It is feminine Bernadette who puts the 'dyke' in her place without ever giving up any feminine niceties—a flick of the hair here, a softly murmured phrase there. She signifies an acceptable femininity compared with the unacceptable 'butch' behaviour of the other woman.

The parameters of being a 'good' woman in Australia are also inflected in terms of race. This can be seen in the framing of Indigenous femininities in relation to non-Indigenous femininities. Indigenous women have frequently been represented as possessing an inferior type of femininity in relation to non-Indigenous women. For example, in cartoons from the early to mid-twentieth century, non-Indigenous women are mostly represented as understanding the role of clothes, sex appeal, appearance and demeanour, whereas Indigenous women are often represented in men's clothes, barefoot, smoking pipes, suggesting they have no such understanding. These types of representations reinforce a race-based superiority through a gendered hierarchy.

Thinking about the importance of gender in tandem with homosociality and the issue of the imbalance in power between men and women, it is possible to explore how stories of Australian-ness came to be ordered in terms of a dominant masculine and a subordinate feminine.

Gender and colonial exploration

Jennifer Rutherford (2000) has argued that the exploration and mapping of the Australian continent by the British colonisers entailed the 'creation of the cultural symbolic' for the white nation.

The land the colonisers framed as being empty and belonging to no one (*terra nullius*) was mapped or created in the image of the new colonisers. This British mapping of the land had a gendered dimension. The process of 'exploration' (the marking of the land as British) was undertaken by men. There are no records of British women explorers in Australia in the nineteenth century. There were women who accompanied men, mostly as wives on expeditions, but they did not travel by themselves into unexplored land (though women such as Lady Jane Franklin were travelling early in the process of colonisation). So, not surprisingly, the narrative of 'discovery' and mapping of the landscape posits a masculine figure that crossed and conquered the new spaces.

Even though this exploration was principally a male undertaking, it was still framed in terms of a gender binary. Though no non-Indigenous women were physically present on treks, there was still a feminine presence against which the male explorer made sense of his experience. For example, a feminine presence was sometimes invoked by the male explorer through the naming of the newly conquered territory in honour of a woman (for example, the Queen, a patron or his wife). It was also experienced in terms of a hetero-sexual dynamic where the explorer understood himself as part of a pair (husband/wife) and the logic of the exploration experience depended on the woman waiting and supporting him in his quest. So the explorer undertook his duties for the empire/nation with his wife's blessing and returned to her when the expedition ended. The letters written to their wives by early British explorers such as Matthew Flinders and James Cook demonstrate this gendered dynamic. Though Indigenous women would have been in many of the areas crossed by non-Indigenous explorers, the idea of *terra nullius* would have rendered them invisible in non-Indigenous imaginings of discovery.

Matthew Flinders had been married only a short time when he left England in 1801 to explore the coast of Australia. This expedition separated Flinders from his wife, Ann, for ten years and he died not many years after his return to England. The national story of Flinders is framed as a heterosexual love story. For example, Ernestine Hill's (1941) famous book on Flinders, *My Love Must Wait*, presents the story in terms of the personal sacrifice he made—leaving a young wife with whom he was deeply in love to undertake explo-ration for the Empire. The story is ordered in terms of the gender binary of a passive feminine and an active masculine; Flinders travels while Ann waits. Yet the exploration story also works in terms of a homosocial dynamic. Most of Flinders' companions on the ship as he sailed from England and around the Australian continent were men. The bonds Flinders felt for these men, such as Joseph Banks, were deep. In one letter home to Ann Flinders, just after hearing of his father's death, Flinders writes of the sorrow he feels about the death of so many of his sailing mates:

> alas, I have lately had too much experience of death's power, for my eyes can scarcely be turned where some victim does not die. Douglas, the boatswain is gone—the sergeant, two quarter-masters and another followed before we got into this port . . . (Grant 2003)

Though the process of exploration is a masculine one, undertaken by men, it is shaped by relationships that reflect a heterosexual binary— masculine/feminine—as well as a deeply pleasurable and meaningful homosocial space. (These issues will be discussed more fully in the next chapter.) Gender in the national imaginary functions to centralise masculine activities, while still framing these activities in relation to the feminine.

The feminine other which worked in relation to the masculine explorer was not always obvious—as in the case of Ann Flinders waiting at home in England for her husband. For example the explorer Thomas Mitchell says of one of his trips: 'Of this Eden it seemed that I was the only Adam; and it was indeed a sort of paradise to me.' Here he sees himself—as the 'only Adam' that is as alone. Yet, the scholar and filmmaker Ross Gibson in a retort to Mitchell's nineteenth-century poetics wrote: 'the explorer is Adam. Eve is missing? No, she is the landscape' (Williams, 1996: 30). Though women themselves are not represented in the process of explo- ration—they do not cross the land, name it or conquer it—the land itself is often represented as feminine. Another example of the land's representation as feminine is a line from the Australian film *The Sons of Matthew* (1949). One of the male characters in this film notes that an area of Queensland is 'like a beautiful woman, lovely to look at, but tough to handle' (Williams 1996: 31). The images of nation-building are gendered—bodies, spaces and places are marked as masculine or feminine—but feminine images are subordinate to masculine ones. More recent representations of crossing the land still draw on this dualism. Advertisements for four-wheel-drive cars often show them in the bush or the desert. The cars are mostly driven by men and seem to suggest the powerful car tames the unruly land. There are dozens of films—*Mad Max* (1979) or *Wake in Fright* (1971), for example— where men in cars rev their engines and belt across the bush, often in search of prey—spotlighting kangaroos and dominating a passive feminised space.

Gender and the bush

Though non-Indigenous women were not present in those initial exploration parties, they have been part of the presence in the land. The mapping and traversing of land is no longer the provenance of men. Women now cross the space of Australia—often without men. In fact, women aviators and rally car drivers have been doing this since the 1930s (Clarsen 1999). Road movies set in Australia today are just as likely to have a group of women as a group of men singing badly to out-of-date music blasting from the car stereo as they cross the Nullarbor Plain. However, it is interesting to reflect on how women are represented in this process and what happens to them when they take up this masculine position. Stephanie Green (2002), in her article 'Wildflowers and Other Landscapes', notes the threat women can feel when out alone by themselves in the bush:

> alone in a tent in the Victorian highlands . . . [l]ate one night two cars drove hard and fast toward me in the dark, flashed their headlights onto full beam, braked suddenly and revved their engines. Nothing more than that. After a few moments the noise of the engines stopped and the cars went away (2002: 5).

There are filmic representations of this same masculine intimidation of women in the land without masculine protection. In the film *Shame* (1988), a woman on a solo motorcycle trek stops in a town to help another woman and is set upon by the town's men. Of course, women also occupy the masculine position of domination and control in terms of the land. The 'freedom' story associated with more recent narratives of women crossing the land needs to be seen (as do earlier narratives of men's crossing) in terms of trespassing on or traversing Indigenous land.

In the previous chapter, it was argued that a long-standing national archetype was the working man. This figure was popularly imagined to occupy the space of the bush. Women have stood alongside men on properties as workers in the bush, yet in the binary of rural/urban it is men who are associated with the rural space of land and women with the city. Many writers have suggested that women prefer the glamour of the city rather than the outback, leaving men to cope by themselves. Ernestine Hill, in her book *The Great Australian Loneliness* (1937), suggests the reason so many non-Indigenous men had relationships with Indigenous women in the outback was because selfish, single non-Indigenous women refused to leave the city. A farmer writing to the ABC in the 1950s asked whether the fictional radio serial *Blue Hills* could have a scene in it encouraging women to come to the bush and marry men to help stop their loneliness. And in the summer of 2004–05, the choice picks for television viewing included a series called *Desperately Seeking Sheila*, about British and Australian women being enticed to come and live with bush blokes in Australia who were unable to find partners because of their isolated existence. Another series—*Outback Jack*—was based on the premise of a dozen city models (from the United States) being parachuted into the outback to try to win the heart of a 'dinkum' Australian bloke. The squealing shown in the promos was enough to suggest that a few of the women would SMS an SOS home very soon. More importantly, the show—like the other representations discussed—reinforce the stereotype of women as being uncomfortable with life on the land.

Yet non-Indigenous women obviously do live in the bush, and are at times celebrated for their endurance in this space. Aeneas Gunn's autobiographical account—*We of the Never Never* (1908)—of her time in the early twentieth century living on a Northern Territory cattle station is a popular story of a non-Indigenous woman working with her husband in the outback. In 2002, Sara Henderson—a woman who ran a huge cattle property in the north of Australia—wrote a best-selling book on the struggles and joys of her life in the outback (Henderson 2002). Historically there have been fewer women than men in the bush, and the effect of their minority status in the bush reinforces the dominance of a masculine nation. If the traditional tendency has been to represent women as not at home in the bush, then where do they belong in the nation? Apparently they belong in the home. Gender is deployed in national stories as a means of ordering the lives of men and women in terms of a public/private dichotomy. In this conceptual framework, women have historically been associated with the private space and men with the public realm.

If women are often seen as not being at home in the bush, then in stories about Australia it is men who are most frequently represented as uniquely at home in this most Australian of places. As has been argued already, for many years the bush was seen as the archetypal Australian place and the bushman as the archetypal Australian. In more recent decades, this story has been contested and even parodied. Yet it has never truly gone away. There is still a soft spot in Australian national stories for the bush bloke, even though the rapid changes in Australian society over the past 20 years have sorely tested the resolve of this mythic type.

The opening up of the long-protected rural industries to aspects of free trade and economic rationalisation has changed the lives of bush blokes and their families, as have the long-term shifts in Australia from an economy dominated by agricultural industries to one dependent on tertiary industries. The decline in the importance of agricultural industries has challenged the emotional understanding of many Australians about the place of the rural sector and the men who dominate it in the national story. The bush and bush blokes are no longer the engine of growth in Australia. Long understood as a type who savoured their independence, bush men have also had their economic independence challenged in recent years as large industry conglomerates replace smaller economic units such as the family farm. For example, in 2001 the dairy industry was deregulated in Australia. As a result, very large dairy companies are taking over and replacing smaller dairy farms. Interestingly, many farmers have resisted the changes—especially the new technologies, such as automatic milking—in favour of maintaining the pleasures and independence of economically less rewarding traditions.

The changes wrought as a result of native title legislation have also displaced many rural men's understanding of their place in the centre of Australian national stories. Native title legislation is part of a group of changes that have slowly led to the recognition of Indigenous people's legal and spiritual connections to the Australian land. Given the traditional centrality in non-Indigenous national stories of non-Indigenous bush men as the economic and emotional 'custodians' of the land, this has challenged many rural men's (and women's) understandings of their place in Australia. The congruence of declining economic profitability and accusations of environmental degradation of their land, along with the challenge of Indigenous claims to the land, have decentred non-Indigenous rural men in national stories.

Gender and violence

In 1996, lone gunman Martin Bryant killed 35 people at the well-known colonial convict tourist site at Port Arthur in Tasmania. Following this, the federal government—in line with significant community support—moved to tighten Australian gun laws. The move to limit the availability of semi-automatic weapons had a disproportionate effect on men living in rural parts of Australia, who often kept the type of guns that were now being banned. As Melinda Mawson (1999: 159) argues, the aftermath of the Port Arthur massacre created a feeling that particular types of masculinity—especially those organised around violence and guns—were unacceptable. For many Australian men, for whom gun ownership was a rite of passage into manhood and a taken-for-granted part of their lives, to be recast as dangerous and their everyday activities (such as pest control with guns) to be understood as illegal was alienating. Again, this type of masculinity—once at the heart of Australian national identity—was marginalised and in some ways vilified.

Throughout the twentieth century, the masculinity of so many Australian men was shaped by stories centralising independence and self-reliance, but also violence. As the twentieth century drew to a close, many of these stories had been challenged by alternatives—especially feminist stories. In the first half of the twentieth century, young men learned the key place of violence in their lives as citizens through narratives of war and ideas about the importance of being willing to fight for their country. In the later part of the century, Simon French (1999: 143) notes that sport replaced war as the place where Australian boys could learn 'legitimate form[s] of violent behaviour'. They also learn that these behaviours are connected with 'prestige'. David Brown and Russell Hogg (1997) have similarly argued that media representations of sport—for example, in highlights packages—frame violence in ways that normalise violence and almost equate it with being a man. This culture of masculine aggression and violence does not shape all Australian men's lives, many men actively resist such identities, but for a large proportion of the male population the association of aggression with masculine prestige does shape who they are.

Though both Australian men and women can be violent, men are over-represented as both the perpetrators and victims of violence (see Table 3.1). Young men are more likely than young women to end their lives in a violent manner. The quaint Australian saying, 'be a man you woman', yelled out by football coaches and overwrought parents from the sidelines of sports fields, captures the way in which young Australian men are drawn into this form of aggressive masculinity. Yet, as Katherine Biber (1999) notes, those Australian men who do not perform the dominant form of hegemonic Australian masculinity are not simply feminised. What is happening is 'not so much the coding of men as women, but the uncoding of men as men' (1999: 29). For so many Australian men, there is always the potential that they will not perform masculinity in the way it needs to be performed to fulfill the mythic national story of being a man, so their lives are fundamentally anxious. According to Biber, they spend their lives masking this anxiety with 'multiple layers of unambiguous masculinity to deflect attention from the underlying and ever-present threat' (Biber 1999: 29). Ex-Rugby League player Ian Roberts said in 2005 that one of the reasons he was such an aggressive football player before he came out was to cover the fact that he was gay. Roberts eventually did come out, deciding to give away aspects of the myth of being a 'real' Australian man. Yet many more men organise their lives around the masochistic imperatives of the myth of the 'real' Aussie bloke, even though living up to the myth is a near-impossible task.

Table 3.1: Gender Profile of Victim and Person of Interest (POI) for Assault Incidents on Licensed Premises in Inner Sydney, 1998–2000

Gender of victim	Number of assault incidents	Percentage of assault incidents	Mean age	Median age
Male	930	80.9	30	28
Female	174	15.1	28	26
Both male and female	45	3.9	26	25
Gender of POI				
Male	512	87.5	29	28
Female	67	11.5	28	28
Both male and female	6	1.0	27	26

Source: Suzanne Briscoe and Neil Donnelly, 'Assaults on Licensed Premises in Inner Urban Areas', *Alcohol Studies Bulletin*, No. 2, 2001.

Yet Australian masculinity clearly offers significant pleasures for men. A number of ex-football players were recently interviewed about their lives post-football and, although all of them were physically battered as a result of the cumulative injuries they had sustained over their careers, they mostly said that if they had their lives over they would do the same again (Guilliatt 2005: 26–32). These players—who live with chronic pain, gnarly fingers that cannot grip, dicky knees and hips that will need replacing 40 years before they should wear out—suggest with the benefit of hindsight that they might have been more careful and not played when they were injured, but they all remember the exhilaration and feeling of invincibility they experienced as young elite athletes. Similarly, as the 2005 Australian Football

League (AFL) grand final drew to a close and the Sydney Swans and West Coast Eagles fought it out for victory, the commentators caught up in the moment exclaimed that the players who had come back on to the field despite their injuries and who tackled hard and who were tackled hard would be 'heroes'. The mythic model of Australian masculinity suggests men's bodies are meant to be battered, that violence is the norm. This is what makes them Australian men.

The home

Australia was one of the first countries in the world to grant women the right to vote. Most Australian women were granted this right in the first years after Federation—but not all. Indigenous and Pacific Islander women were excluded from this right (as were Indigenous and Pacific Islander men). So, while white women were placed with white men as equal partners in the public shaping of the future of the nation, non-white people were comprehensively excluded. However, even between non-Indigenous men and women there was not really equality. For example, Australian women could stand for federal parliament from 1902, but the right to stand for state parliaments was not granted until later.

Though Australia was one of the first countries to grant women the vote, it was one of the slower ones to elect women to public office. Women put themselves forward as candidates for the various parliaments, but more often than not failed to be selected. The first women to be elected to the national parliament were Enid Lyons and Dorothy Tangey, and this did not take place until 1943. And, whereas many other countries around the world have had or currently have women national leaders—presidents or prime ministers—Australian national political parties still seem to have a shortage of women leaders. In the more prosaic world of non-parliamentary work, the 2003 Australian social attitudes survey showed that the majority of men believed that if the work lives of a heterosexual couple became too busy and one of them had to take on more home duties, it should be the woman (Wilson et al. 2005: 59). The dominant stories of gender shaping national narratives perpetuate a public/private division that associates women with the home.

It would be simplistic to suggest that there is a watertight division between the masculine public and the feminine private. Many men and most of the women activists working in the early twentieth century took the approach Australia would benefit from women in public life. One argument was that women could bring special qualities to the public sphere. Patricia Grimshaw and her colleagues (1994) refer to this idea as the 'motherhood principle'. The logic of this belief is that it is in the home—women's sphere—where desirable characteristics such as 'altruism . . . peacemaking; judicious good judgment' (1994: 182) evolved and are supported. Allowing women into public life would mean they could bring these traits with them, guaranteeing the spread of these qualities into the broader world, thus creating a better Australia. Few people today would publicly support the suggestion that what women bring to public office is thrift developed from years of housekeeping or a firm hand coming from their experience raising children; however, the notion of women bringing different attributes to public office, and the public sphere generally, still resonates. For example, a *Sydney Morning Herald* article in 2004 reported the positive difference in management styles emerging as more women reached the upper echelons of the workforce (Horin 2004: 3).

If Australian women have so often been represented as belonging in the home, then Australian men have been represented in terms of a more ambivalent relationship to the home. The home has often been represented as the place to which men willingly return after a hard day's work. It has also been represented as a place from which they seek to escape. In the last few years, cultural and artistic analysis of Australian men and their backyard sheds has highlighted these as places where men can be by themselves and be themselves. Here, away from the pressures of life—sometimes retrenchment from long-term employment or divorce—men work at hobbies they love and regain the self-esteem they often feel they have lost.

For other Australian men, home is their 'castle'. In 1975, the *Family Law Act* substantially altered the landscape of the home in Australia. The introduction of no-fault divorce made it possible for unhappy spouses to end their marriages without public shame. Around the same time, there was increased surveillance of the home space by the state. For example, domestic violence was no longer considered a private issue. These changes altered home from a place almost totally controlled by a husband/father to a more equitable unit.

Thirty years after these transformations, there have been ongoing accusations that the Family Court, which oversees divorce and child custody proceedings, is anti-men or anti-father. Drawing on narratives that are in a large part imported from the United States, in particular Warren Farrell's book *The Myth of Male Power* (1994), a series of men's rights or father's support groups have accused the court of siding with women too often (Maddison 1999). The more radical men's groups have claimed systemic problems of unhappy wives concocting false allegations of child abuse against innocent male partners. Interestingly, many of the men's groups blame feminism—another narrative that is often seen to have been imported from the United States—as the underlying reason for many of these problems (Ellard 1999: 163). For many Australian men long used to the home being a world where they were in control, to have someone else end their marriage and to no longer be able to control the situation was enormously frustrating. For some men:

> fatherhood, within the context of marriage, offers them the opportunity to express love and affection, exercise authority and provide economically for their family, largely on their own terms. Post divorce, custody/access, maintenance and property arrangements place boundaries on their roles and behaviour in the family (Ellard 1999: 165).

Many Australian men are finding new ways of being fathers and husbands, but others are unable to come to terms with the loss of privilege that has accompanied economic and social change associated with the home in recent decades.

The paid workforce

The public/private binary also works in terms of how men and women are imagined as workers in the nation. Chapter 2 explored the ideas of work and workers, class and power in Australia. It argued that a central part of the story of Australian egalitarianism is the myth of a fair day's work for a fair day's pay. Yet, for most of the twentieth century, pay inequity based solely on gender was institutionalised. Despite the idealised vision of women at home, women were vital to the paid workforce in Australia—they just worked for lower pay, with poorer conditions and fewer perks (such as holiday leave and sick pay).

During World War II, lack of manpower in Australia meant governments needed women to take up men's jobs if the economy was going to survive. New stories had to be constructed about women and work. These new stories provided many women—particularly middle-class, non-Indigenous women—with new ways of understanding themselves as workers, and as workers for the nation. Women have a long history of undertaking paid and unpaid work in Australia. What was novel during World War II was that the request for women to enter paid work came from governments. More importantly, they were asked to undertake work designated as men's work. Women were formally made central to the work story of Australia—though, in a broader gendered story, it was suggested men were doing even more important work for the nation in the arena of battle. Bringing women into the world of men's work—the part of the public sphere from which they were traditionally excluded—meant women could use a different set of ideas in assessing their place in the nation.

In the extreme circumstances of World War II, a significant minority of non-Indigenous women began doing men's work and earning men's wages. The work they undertook varied from jobs on public transport and in radio stations to factory work in heavy industries. This was amazingly exciting for many women. However, it was also disturbing for many men and women. Even though this shift in women's roles was officially sanctioned, it contradicted the usual stories of the nation. First, it upset the system that had institutionalised lower wages for women. Second, it had the potential to disturb the gendered binaries of active/passive and public/private. The dominant way in which non-Indigenous women were imagined in the nation—even how many of them imagined themselves at this time—was as someone who was attached to, or related to, others. Women were less likely to see themselves or be seen as individuals. They were daughters, wives, mothers and lovers. During World War II, non-Indigenous women were also fully paid workers in the public sphere. With their husbands, fathers and lovers away at war, there was more space for women to see themselves and be seen as individuals—making decisions and choices for themselves. Feminists of the time emphasised these traits of independence and individuality in their struggle for women's equality.

However, it was not in the interests of a community organised around a system of men as economic earners and women as chiefly domestic workers, child carers and back-up paid employees to have a group of women who wanted to continue their independence and individuality. So women were encouraged to think they were undertaking war work for the nation or for their man, not for themselves. E.C. McGrath, a trade union leader, expressed this idea in 1943:

> A woman employed on the trams shows a nice appreciation of things when saying: 'My husband who was a tram guard, is now in the Middle East. I want equal pay so that he can get his job back when he comes home' (Fox and Lake 1990: 177).

The woman tram guard is represented as having her husband's job, not her own job. When he returns, it is not so much that he will get his job back and she will lose hers and return to the home, but that she will give him his job back. This woman worker is not represented as enjoying the independence of work, but as actually waiting for the moment when the world will be put to rights and she will once again be her husband's helper at home.

However, some of the changes set in place during World War II could not be reversed. As a result, the way gender figured in stories of what it meant to be Australian had to be reworked. Although most women were removed from 'men's jobs' after the war, they did not stop paid work (but they stopped working in such good conditions), and the campaign for equal pay never went away. It was not until 1972, under the Whitlam Labor government, that women finally achieved full and formal equal pay. Barrister Mary Gaudron presented the government's argument in terms of 'equal pay for work of equal value'. She argued—and it was accepted—that women should have their pay rates assessed on the same basis as men's pay rates. In December 1972, women 'were awarded a male pay rate of pay no matter what work they were doing' (Ryan and Conlon 1989: 162).

Yet significant pay disparities still exist (see Table 3.2). Due to the subjective valuing of the worth of different types of work, jobs associated with women or work seen as feminine tend to have a lower value than work associated with men. As a result, women's status in the workforce is still not commensurate with that of men. Numerous studies have demonstrated that jobs dominated by women are less well paid than those dominated by men. And, although women now have equal access to education and are increasingly well qualified for a growing range of jobs, they remain clustered in 'women's' jobs and at the lower end of the pay and status scale.

Table 3.2: Mean Weekly Earnings ($) of Australian Men and Women in their Main Job, 2002

Age group	Full time		Part time		All	
	Male	Female	Male	Female	Male	Female
15–24	550	513	196	171	410	327
25–34	839	732	402	336	794	596
35–44	967	751	438	347	933	547
45–54	895	730	432	358	924	568
55–59	802	654	364	317	823	492
All ages	864	688	303	298	697	508

Source: Diana Olsberg, 'Women and Superannuation: Still MS…ing Out, *Australian Journal of Political Economy,* June 2004.

Conditions for women in the workforce may have improved greatly, many still face the problem of juggling work and family. More workplaces are instituting supportive maternity (or paternity) leave options, but there is still no national government-funded maternity leave scheme. In late 2002, a thirteen-point plan for such a scheme was presented by Pru Goward, the federal sex discrimination commissioner; however, her suggestions have not been taken up. Instead, the Coalition government instituted tax benefits encouraging stay-at-home mothers. The Family Tax Benefit Part B provides a benefit for single-income families regardless of the value of the salary of the single-income earner. The idea of the nation underpinning the government's vision is one that imagines a woman in the home raising children and a man as the breadwinner earning the 'family wage'. In this way, gender still functions to underpin a conservative story of Australian-ness based on a traditional binary.

Motherhood

An important story of the nation to which femininity and women are central is the national population story. Dominating social policy for most of the twentieth century—though especially in the first half of the century—was the idea that Australian–Britons needed to populate the continent. At times this was an extreme belief—fuelled by understandings positing the superiority of the Australian–Briton over the Indigenous peoples of the continent and the region. At other times, it was more subtle—couched in terms of economic expansion rather than fear of an 'invading horde'. This anxiety about the nation and invasion was organised in terms of gender.

The worry about population resulted in an emphasis on the ideal of motherhood, and a higher level of surveillance of women and their sexual activities. The population story was also inflected with ideas of class and ethnicity. In fact, class and ethnicity come to the fore in the population story. Some groups of women were more likely to be subject to or represented as central to the population narratives than others. It was respectable Anglo–Australian women who were subject to, and actively involved in, a range of policies and techniques encouraging them to have more children and to raise these children carefully. In raising families, these women were seen as (and many understood themselves to be) part of a process of national self-definition. That is, government policies often suggested that having and raising children was not a personal issue, but rather a national one. A cartoon from 1920 demonstrates this point (see Figure 3.1).

We want something more than a sign to keep them out

Figure 3.1 Nineteenth-century cartoon mocking the declining Anglo–Australian birth rate and linking it with a future that will see an invasion of Australia from Asian countries. (*Smith's Weekly, 1920*)

A single 'white' baby is surrounded by children from China, India and Japan, eagerly climbing over a fence into the 'empty' space of Australia. The suggestion is that more 'white' babies are needed. In imagining invasion and the filling of the perceived empty space of the north Anglo–Australian women were called on to be the mothers of the nation and to stop the possibility of invasion by filling that empty space with their children. In this story, women did not just have children to fulfil their own desires, but to fulfil the dream of a 'white Australia'.

Anglo–Australian women were sometimes represented as recalcitrant in this national project of 'populate or perish', as it became known. At times, it was suggested that Anglo–Australian women were not doing the right thing and producing enough children to 'fill' the nation. The earlier case of women being chastised for not living in the 'empty' bush with lonely men is one example. Another is the 1904 New South Wales Royal Commission into the Decline in the Birth Rate—specifically the problem of the falling Anglo–Australian birth rate. The commissioners (all men) came up with findings that suggested many Anglo-Australian women were selfishly following their own desires and not having enough children. It was suggested that married women were using contraception and regulating the number of children they had (Pringle 1973)—and indeed, many women were doing precisely this. At a time when Australia governments were paranoid about other countries in the region being overpopulated, this choice by women was seen as selfish and anti-Australian.

So, far from being a private decision made between a couple or by an individual woman, family size was represented as a national issue. In response to the declining birth rate, the regulation of the availability of contraceptives, an emphasis on the noble nature of motherhood, and social incentives to encourage the 'cult of motherhood', all played their role in constructing the notion of the heterosexual family, with a large brood of children as the national ideal.

No amount of regulation or propaganda has been able to slow or reverse the decrease in the birth rate. In the 1800s, the average number of children a woman had was seven; today it is fewer than two (Hicks 1978; Goward 2002). Large-scale immigration programs replaced the emphasis on childbirth as the solution to slow population growth; however, the idea of a low birth rate and women's decisions to limit the number of children they have still informs national stories of population and the state. For example, in 2004 the federal treasurer suggested: 'If you can have children, you should have one for your husband, one for the wife and one for the country' (Haywood 2004). Prime Minister John Howard chimed in by saying: 'Come on, come on, your nation needs you' (Farouque 2004). Again, the issue is not posited as personal choice—the treasurer does not say 'if you *want* children', but 'if you *can have* children'. This government encouragement came in the midst of an extended political discussion on the birth rate, women's role in the community (workers or mothers or both), what policies are required to support them in these decisions, and who should be having babies. But it also came at a time when the issue of 'invasions' has once again surfaced as a catch-cry in Australian politics.

Un-Australian mothers

The discussion about motherhood and the nation has not only been a story about the fear of an external 'other' invading Australia. As suggested earlier, it is also a story about *which* women *within* the nation should have children. In national policies about motherhood, the mother was represented as a non-Indigenous woman. For many Indigenous women, their right to mother their children was denied. Instead they were subject to policies that led to the removal of their children, who were brought up by non-Indigenous women (in foster families) or in institutions. The Indigenous children removed from their families were not imagined in national stories as making new families when they grew up. They were imagined as domestic workers and labourers—cheap labour for the nation. Many Indigenous women spent their lives working in or for another family. As Jackie Huggins (1998) poignantly argues in her work on Indigenous domestic servants, when the feminists of the 1970s were demanding the right to get out of their kitchen and into the workforce or education system, many Indigenous women faced quite different issues. They wanted to get out of the non-Indigenous woman's kitchen, where they looked after someone else's home and children, and back to their own kitchens and children.

The policy of Indigenous child removal has had devastating effects in terms of generational mothering. Young Indigenous women removed from their families and brought up in institutions had little or no experience of love and mothering, so when they had their own children they often struggled to cope. This outcome simply reproduced the cycle of removal as state governments could argue they were poor mothers and take their children away. The refusal to pay any proper compensation to the stolen generations means the money required by Indigenous peoples to develop support services that will help them cope with issues such as inadequate parenting skills are not available. Even though the national family is no longer imagined as white, the chances for Indigenous peoples to be part of happy, well-functioning families is sometimes impeded by a failure to recognise the trauma of the recent past.

Indigenous women had their children removed regardless of their marital status. For most of the twentieth century, young non-Indigenous women who became pregnant when they were single were marginalised in the community. Many of these young women experienced extreme guilt about the shame their pregnancy caused their families. Most of these women were forced to give their children up for adoption. Even if women were not bullied into adoption, the combination of the social and economic circumstances they would face as a single mother meant many chose to give up their child. Even in the twenty-first century, young single women who have children are often vilified and lack support. So, although the Family Tax Benefit Part B encourages women to stay at home with their children—based on an idea of the benefit this has for the children and the family—other welfare changes have been mooted that see single women with children moved into work or on to lower benefits as soon as their youngest child reaches school age. In this case, the young woman's status as mother is not privileged; rather, her status as welfare recipient and non-worker marks her as needing to contribute more to the community than simply bringing up her children. The circumstances of young non-Indigenous women's loss of their children through adoption—or more recently their vilification for decisions to have children when they are young and unmarried—is very different from that of Indigenous women; however, they are both women whose motherhood is not understood to be part of the national project.

Fatherhood

Fatherhood has, over a long period, been represented as being 'in crisis' in non-Indigenous Australia. This is not surprising, given that the privileged national narrative centralises a larrikin, knock-about single man. There have, of course, always been alternative ways of being a man in Australia, and this has included being a great dad. However, traditionally men have been understood as being invisible or absent as fathers. The long-standing division of men as breadwinners and women as nurturers has privileged a system where being a father was not about the day-to-day work of raising a child, but about being out of home all day, returning for night-time baths and weekend play. If Australian men had a (re)productive role, it was to nurture and bring into being the nation—not children. As Marilyn Lake (1992) argues in an influential article, the dominant national story of the birth of Australia is that it was men who gave birth to the nation through their sacrifices at Gallipoli. Understanding this sacrifice as productive rather than a waste of lives makes it possible to rethink this war experience as being integral to the nation.

The changes that came about as a result of the women's movement and feminist thinking in the second half of the twentieth century had profound effects on the ways in which women understood their role in the nation. They had better and more equal access to the public sphere, and their traditional duties of child-raising and domestic duties slowly gained more prestige. For many Australian men, these changes in women's lives were welcome, but for others they represented a threat. Men had more to lose than women in this reworking of national life. For example, for women the shift from the under-valued private sphere to the more highly valued public sphere was exciting, whereas men—used to having this space to themselves—now had to share their power with women.

It has tended to be women, not men, who have been 'forcing the pace of change in the family', because it is women whose options have expanded so rapidly in the past few decades (Edgar and Glezer 1992: 37). For example, feminist stories of empowerment and inde-pendence mean the majority of divorces are now initiated by women (Crawford and MacDonald 2002: 1). These changes have left many men feeling confused and lost. Australia is not alone in this 'crisis of masculinity'. It is a global Western phenomenon. Although the rearrangement of family life has opened up the possibility of men having more access to the private sphere—domestic duties and child-raising—this is frequently a difficult and fraught option for many men. In everyday life, men have long been represented as the providers in relation to stay-at-home mothers. They used to be the head of family, just as men were traditionally the heads of the nation. Now many feel this traditional role as breadwinner means they do not have sufficent time with their families, but they are still required to work long hours to pay for their children's needs.

As a result, a powerful contemporary story of the Australian family has emerged. In this story, men have lost their national dominance. The story is not expressed in terms of loss of power, but in terms of loss of opportunity. It has its most strident manifestation in the story of men's loss of access to their children and their right to father after divorce. In the post-divorce situation, it is the case that most resident parents are mothers. Men do have less contact with their children after divorce—only about 27 per cent of separated fathers have weekly contact with their children. Yet studies have shown that, even before divorce, women are far more likely to spend more time with their children (Craig 2002). Further, when women are with their children, they are more likely to be in primary carer roles, undertaking necessary tasks. By comparison, the time men spend with their children is more likely to be playtime, with the other parent present. Generally, fathers sacrifice less of their leisure time for childcare than mothers do. So, as Lyn Craig (2002) notes, there is a gap between the 'popular support' for shared parenting and actual practices.

In the late 1990s and early 2000s, the issue of men's lack of access to their children led to a great deal of discussion about the need for change. In 2003, the prime minister noted that young boys raised in households with their mothers and no male siblings could be fifteen or sixteen years old before they had a male role model. The federal government solution was to institute what is known as 'rebuttable presumption of equal-time shared parenting' through the Family Law Amendment (Shared Parental Responsibility) Bill 2005. This means that when parents divorce, the default position is shared parenting where children spend equal time with each parent—unless there is a reason why this is not in the best interests of the child. It is important, when thinking about stories of fatherhood in Australia, to analyse which stories are about new ways of being a father and which are about regaining the power lost in the changes brought about by the women's movement. Sometimes this story focuses on reasserting the father as the boss rather than encouraging men to participate in daily child care as a way of achieving gender equity (Everingham and Bowers 2005).

Many of the reasons men spend less time with their children have to do with work demands. The dominant story of the nation at present is that Australia should be productive and globally competitive. Higher productivity usually comes about through longer working hours. Historically, men have been the key full-time workers in the national economy. So, although men and women may have personally shifted their ideas on how to raise their children, many of the institutions they come into contact with are not similarly disposed. Australians are working longer hours and while many large companies have parenting policies and provide some basic parenting facilities, such as breast-feeding rooms or child-care centres, most workplaces do not even have these. Further, in 2006 new industrial relations legislation was passed that radically changed the way workers negotiate their workplace conditions. In this new era the emphasis is on individual negotiation and a set of pared back allowable matters in awards. Historically it was union bargaining power, through test cases such as the family test case, that led in time to the inclusion of family leave in many awards. However, in the new environment where the emphasis is on individual negotiation and economic productivity it is harder for men to negotiate around paternity leave. First, even if a male worker is employed in a company that does have family leave policies there is often subtle pressure not to make full use of these entitlements. Second, in many workplaces there is far more sympathy for women having to take time off to care for sick children than men needing to do the same thing (Edgar and Glazer 1992: 4). Third, in individual negotiations, where most workers have diminished bargaining potential, men are more likely to focus on key issues—such as salary and annual leave—rather than issues such as paternity leave which can be seen as marginal. Not surprisingly, the vast majority of Individual Workplace Agreements to date do not have paid maternity or paternity leave provisions included in them.

Indigenous fathering

Indigenous men experience aspects of fatherhood differently to non-Indigenous fathers. Today, Indigenous fathers undertake their fathering role in the context of colonisation. This can mean that many Indigenous men father in the context of a ' "vicious cycle" of limited education and employment opportunities [which] significantly influences living conditions (including the capacity to form and maintain a family unit)' (Parliament of South Australia 2005: 27). Contemporary Indigenous fathering takes place in the context of the long-term policy of Indigenous child removal. This has meant that a significant proportion of Indigenous men have had no positive experiences of being parented. They therefore become fathers without much idea of how to nurture. Because of the extended family structures of most Indigenous communities, other significant adults (aunties and uncles) can step in to fill this gap; however, many Indigenous men still miss the opportunity of being an influential parent.

It is not only limited resources that shape Indigenous men's capacity to parent. Culture differences in parenting can mean that Indigenous men's (and women's) practices are understood from a western viewpoint as inherently lacking. Given the high level of surveillance of Indigenous families, this can mean that Indigenous fathering takes place within an ongoing anxiety about government workers classifying them as 'unfit' parents. One problem faced by a higher proportion of Indigenous than non-Indigenous men is the issue of fathering while in prison. High incarceration rates increase the marginalisation of Indigenous men in families, put more stress on families and make male role models scarce.

In traditional non-Indigenous families, many men have been grappling with the loss of power that has come about as a result of social changes. Non-Indigenous men's anger often targets non-Indigenous women as the reason for the loss of their fathering role.

For Indigenous men, this loss of access to their families is not seen as the fault of Indigenous women. Rather, the non-Indigenous colonial state and its institutions are the source of this loss.

Gender, sexuality and families

The dominant national stories of parenting represent it as taking place within a family created by a heterosexual couple. The 2003 Australian Social Attitudes survey showed that 99 per cent of participants viewed a heterosexual couple with children as a family. Only 54 per cent agreed that a single-parent household was a family, and 42 per cent felt that a same-sex couple with children constituted a family (Wilson et al. 2005: 13–19). Men had more conservative views than women about whether single parents and same-sex couples constituted a family.

Another invisible group of fathers in Australia comprises gay fathers. Being a gay man and father is a complex role. Up to 10 per cent of gay Australian men are parents (Gay and Lesbian Rights Lobby 2003: 5). Some men are parenting their biological children after coming out; others have donated sperm, most frequently to lesbian couples. These men have a range of roles from active parent to a person who will appear if the child asks. Legal institutions in Australia are heteronormative, that is they draw upon and reinforce the belief that heterosexuality is the only natural expression of sexual desire. Other sexual identities are legally invisible. This means that gay men who donate sperm (in fact, any men who donate sperm) are not the legal parents of children. Unlike heterosexual men, gay men have more limited options when it comes to parenting so this invisibility has serious implications for their lives as fathers. In terms of gay men who donate sperm privately to a known lesbian couple, this legally cuts them out as fathers regardless of their level of interest in their child's life.

One part of the recent discussions on mothering and the birth rate has been a fierce debate about the right of women who are not in heterosexual relationships (both single women and lesbian couples) to access IVF (in-vitro fertilisation) technologies to have children. There are groups against the idea of non-heterosexually active women having access to this service. These include many Christian churches and Prime Minister John Howard. At one time, the prime minister went so far as to say that marriage was about 'having children, raising them, providing for the survival of the species' (ABC 2003). The angry response from older heterosexual couples and infertile couples who did not plan to have children perhaps explains why Prime Minister Howard has not repeated this line. This debate has again demonstrated that the government is thinking about specific women when it encourages 'Australian' couples to have three children. Though homosexuality is not illegal in Australia, the idea of fertility and children is still dominated by visions of heterosexual women—more specifically, heterosexual women with male partners.

There are many lesbian and single women who are having babies and creating families. The very existence of these alternative families works to subvert the commentary of the heterosexual family. Yet these challenges to the dominant national story of gender and motherhood do not go uncontested. This was apparent in 2004 when the ABC children's show *Play School* had a story about a young girl and her two mums visiting a fun park. There was both outrage and support for this scene. Deputy Prime Minister John Anderson said: 'I think before the views, interests and perspectives of adult parents are put forward, the first consideration should be for the children who can't speak for themselves.' Minister for Children and Youth Affairs Larry Anthony warned the ABC against becoming 'too politically correct':

> I think I'm representing the majority of Australian parents . . . My kids watch *Play School*. I think it is an excellent production, but I think it's important for those program producers to ensure that they are not just responding to minorities . . . I don't think it's appropriate (Marriner 2004).

Labor Family and Community Services Spokesman Wayne Swan said: 'I haven't seen the program but I'd be concerned if a children's program explored issues of sexuality, because that's a matter for parents' (Marriner 2004).

Of course, the children of Australia are constantly being informed about sexuality. Many of the books selected and read to them in *Play School* are about sexuality. It is just that they are mostly about the unremarkable story of Australian sexuality consisting of two heterosexual parents and a child. So when heterosexuality is being explored it is invisible to most Australians. In the explorations taking place in children's television about sexuality, heterosexuality is understood as the national ideal. Reading stories about mummy and daddy is not seen as 'politically correct'; it is only when other types of families are represented that sexuality becomes visible to many people, and suddenly discussions about it (via innocuous stories of visiting a fun park) are said to be unacceptable. For the critics of *Play School*, reading a story about daddy and daddy or mummy and mummy is understood as creating a type of Australian-ness that is unacceptable.

The debates about fatherhood and motherhood demonstrate that not all men and women are equal in the national story of parenting, and not all means of increasing the national population are validated. In the arguments about the declining birth rate that went back and forth between different groups in the early 2000s, there was occasionally a mention of the population and the need to 'fill the nation'. Prime Minister Howard, in particular, was taunted by his detractors with the question about why he refused entry for potential refugees, often with young families, when he was seen to be supporting a general program that entitled Australian women to stay at home and lift the birth rate and the population. A particular masculine experience of being Australian is still generally privileged in these conservative stories of the nation. Yet, because of the hetero-sexual imperative of the national stories (babies and a growing population), women are required. In these stories of all the women who make up the Australian population, only a section is represented as truly Australian. Yet other stories about being an Australian women or man exist to challenge this traditional narrative—stories that imagine work and family and public and private in different ways.

FURTHER READING:

Dixson, Miriam 1999, *The Real Matilda: Woman and Identity in Australia 1788 to the Present*, 4th edn, University of New South Wales Press, Sydney.

Evans, Raymond and Saunders, Kaye 1994, *Gender Relations in Australia: Domination and Negotiation*, Harcourt Brace, Sydney.

Grimshaw, Pat, Lake, Marilyn, McGrath, Ann and Quartly, Marian 1994, *Creating a Nation*, McPhee Gribble, Melbourne.

Lake, Marilyn 1999, *Getting Equal: The History of Australian Feminism*, Allen & Unwin, Sydney.

Pocock, Barbara 2006, *The Labour Market Ate My Babies: Work, Children and a Sustainable Future*, Federation Press, Sydney.

Ryan, Edna and Conlon, Ann 1989, *Gentle Invaders: Australian Women at Work*, Penguin, Melbourne.

Summers, Anne 2003, *The End of Equality: Work, Babies and Women's Choices in Twenty-first Century Australia*, Random House, Sydney.

Wilson, Shaun, Meagher, Gabrielle, Gibson, Rachel, Denmark, David and Western, Mark 2005, *Australian Social Attitudes: The First Report*, University of New South Wales Press, Sydney.

4

POPULATE OR PERISH

Sexuality and nation

As WITH GENDERED bodies, sexed bodies are central to the framing of dominant stories of the nation. Gender and sexuality fit quite closely together as concepts, so many of the ideas discussed or alluded to in the previous chapter will appear in this chapter as well. Chapter 3 argued that gender ideals inform many of the iconic representations of being Australian, which are generally organised in terms of heterosexuality—the man/woman dyad. Yet heterosexuality is not the limit of these gendered stories. Other stories—especially those that intrude into the worlds of homosociality and suggest homosexual, bisexual and transgender identities—also exist. Here the focus is on heterosexuality and homosexuality, rather than masculinity and femininity. The spotlight will be on how sexuality functions in national stories to produce feelings of being Australian.

In the modern world, of which Australia is a part, sex is identified as something beyond a physical act or bodily designation. It is understood, via Freudian psychology, as something 'central and formative to the social . . . as the arena in which the subject is made' (Bhattacharyya 2002: 5). That is, one's identity as sexed and sexual shapes one's way of being in the world. Sexualities are not essences—something that is hardwired into your brain. A person's (or subject's) understanding of their sexuality does not simply evolve from the recognition of particular secondary sex characteristics. Rather, sexuality can be understood as the cultural, biological, gendered, personal and psychic aspects of identity formed in terms of desire.

It is also linked to what you do: sexuality is performed. Sexualities can be formed in opposition as well as attraction to an object of desire.

Though radical shifts have taken place in the last 30 or so years about sex and sexuality, it is still a topic understood to be private, intimate and personal. Yet because sex is often confined to private spaces, and sexual identity is generally understood as a private issue, it would be inaccurate to suggest that these aspects of life are not regulated. They are highly controlled aspects of identity. For example, in the popular Australian film *The Sum of Us* (1994), the gay characters' sex lives are quite highly monitored. The film is about the relationship between a father and son. The father (played by quintessential Australian bloke Jack Thompson) is a heterosexual working-class ferry driver and his son is a plumber. The father is very accepting of his gay son, and this is part of the charm of the film. The film has a series of slapstick scenes where the over-caring father bursts in on his son and potential lover as they are about to kiss to check that they are alright—'Would you like a beer?' he asks. Kym McCauley (2000) points out in a reading of the film that these scenes operate as part of a narrative of intrusion into and regulation of the gay couple's lives. Indeed, in one promotional photograph for the film, the happy trio is seen drinking in a pub—with Jack Thompson, the father, placed in the middle of the couple. This intrusion and regulation of sexuality carries over into real life. Part of the gay law reform campaigns in Tasmania in the 1990s focused on changing laws which allowed police to arrest gay men who were having private consensual sex in their own homes. It is not just gay sexuality that is under surveillance, however; heterosexuality is also produced under a watchful eye, though in different ways.

The monitoring and shaping of sexuality is undertaken through many mechanisms: some organised around pleasure, others around punishment. Sexuality is controlled through the law. For example, some forms of sex are illegal, and the law protects young people by stipulating the age at which a person can have sex. Religion is also a place from which sexual behaviour is regulated. Many religions argue that celibacy before marriage and monogamy within marriage are morally right. Though Australia is a secular state, religions—especially Christianity—have some power in shaping national narratives. One example is the availability of abortion and the 'morning-after' pill. Governments are sensitive to the feelings of many churches on these issues, and therefore proceed carefully. Sexuality is also shaped through custom and popular culture. Debutante balls are still organised by schools or local community organisations, and at these coming-out ceremonies young women and men perform in a ritual organised around a heterosexual couple. Schoolyard slang posits being a 'poofter' as negative and to suggest someone or something is 'gay' is not a compliment.

In Australia, the two main sites of the regulation of sexuality are the heterosexual family and the homosexual individual. Of these two, heterosexuality is the normative sexual identity, though in Australia today there is more room for other sexual identities. This shift can be seen in adaptations in the media, governments, medical professions and some mainstream religions. Many have changed their representations, laws, procedures and beliefs to be more accepting and understanding of homosexuality (Willett 2000). Homosexuality is no longer illegal in Australia: gay male and lesbian de facto couples are recognised by legislation in all states. Some schools allow same-sex couples to come to dances and formals, and even provide support for gay and lesbian students. Yet this shift is not total. In August 2004, the federal government, with the support of the Australian Labor Party, passed legislation reinforcing the legal presumption that marriage was something that could only take place between a man and a woman. This move was not legally necessary, as other existing laws and customs already meant gay men and lesbians could not marry in Australia. Yet the federal government and major opposition party decided to introduce a piece of legislation reiterating the heterosexual nature of marriage. In exploring the place of sexuality in the production of Australian-ness, the normative status of heterosexuality in relation to the marginal status of homosexuality needs to be kept in mind.

Regulating sexuality

The regulation of sex and sexuality is not specific to the Australian nation. Nations have long associated themselves with particular types of bodies doing certain things (Shapiro 1999: 112). The propaganda images of the 1930s in both the former Soviet Union and Germany, displaying healthy, strong, muscular, male bodies to denote the idea of the health, strength and muscularity of the nation, are an example. Similar images existed in Australia in the same period. This representation of the ideal national body signified what was seen as respectable in the nation (Mosse 1985). In most western nations, national respectability is associated with physical health, heterosexual marriage, physical work and bourgeois manners. National bodies need to be understood as behaving in 'respectable' ways. This led, from about the mid nineteenth century, to 'high levels of surveillance of sexual and other practices that moralists associated with the maintenance of "decency"' (Mosse 1985: 112). Given the emphasis on population and bourgeois sensibilities, this meant the state had preferences about the type of citizens having sex, and the times and places where that sex should take place.

In Australia, this management and surveillance of sexual practices is organised around the heterosexual couple and family. These are seen as the basic units of the state (Pearce 2000: 245). Take as an example the place of the concept of the family in the 2004 federal election campaign. Both the Liberal and Labor parties had slogans giving primacy to the family. The Family First party, which emerged in the 2004 election, explicitly named the type of family it supported as a heterosexual family. More generally, welfare payments and taxation are organised in terms of an understanding that men and women will form couples (and later have children). The heterosexual couple has long received legal recognition through marriage, whereas gay marriages are not recognised. Recently, legislation has been passed in all states that recognises same-sex de facto couples. However, they do not share the same status as heterosexual couples. For example, the receipt of spousal benefits is often based on the stated understanding that a spouse will be an opposite-sex husband or wife. Accessing the superannuation benefits of a deceased partner is easier for a heterosexual partner than for a same-sex partner.

Heterosexuality

As suggested earlier, the heterosexual family and the homosexual individual are the two main sites of regulation of sexuality. Given the historical use of a punishment model by the state towards homosexual behaviour, it is easy to see how this area of sexuality is regulated. However, 'the family rather than homosexual desire is arguably the site where law and state most actively regulate and act upon the sexual and intimate dimensions of their subjects' lives' (Chedgzoy et al. 2002: 11). The reason for this active regulation of the family is clear: if the population of a state is of national significance, then the way both men's and women's sexual energies and desires are directed becomes a national issue. As discussed in chapter 3, the Australian state has had a high level of interest in regulating women and the birth rate. The national story of Australia has been framed in terms of a small, young nation needing to grow up quickly so it could emerge from the maternal shadow of Britain and the threatening shadow of a menacing Asia. Further, the story contains the repressed memory of illegitimate non-Indigenous possession of the land. Given this narrative, increasing the non-Indigenous Anglo–Australian population has been crucial. Therefore, how men and women act in their sexual lives is central.

In the increasingly affluent Australian society emerging from the mid twentieth century, political rhetoric positioned the heterosexual family space as the centre of national life. Politicians arguing about how best to support the family may have differed in their approaches, but the idea of the centrality of the family to the nation was everywhere. Labor Prime Minister John Curtin said in 1941: 'There has never been any doubt of the value of the services, infinite in variety and extent, which the family renders up to the nation' (Murphy 1995: 559). At about the same time, Liberal Senator Annabelle Rankin located the family as the space where mothers in particular 'build the foundation of good health among children and through them a better and stronger nation' (Murphy 1995: 560). Given that the family space was represented by governments as central to the health of the nation, there was little sense of it as a free-for-all for the indulgence of heterosexual pleasure without responsibility. For example, after the Liberal government of 1950 expanded its child endowment policy, a group of Catholic chemists wrote to Enid Lyons suggesting that now heterosexual couples had this new financial payment, there should be 'no financial difficulty in having a normal family and in 20 years' time our population should increase to that [sic] extent that we could expect to defend our country against aggression' (Murphy 1995: 561).

However, just because government social policy reinforces a particular way of understanding Australian-ness, it does not mean this is the only way of understanding one's place in the nation. As Hera Cook (2000) has pointed out, for most of the twentieth century, heterosexual Anglo–Australian women in Australia were quite active in using contraceptives as a means of controlling their fertility. More importantly, women used contraceptives they (rather than their partners) bought and controlled. Whether Australian women adopted these types of contraceptives because it allowed them to not have to worry about pregnancy and enjoy themselves during sex, or because they felt their partners could not be trusted, is hard to know. Perhaps it was both. However, the active use of contraceptives by women and the high level of sexual activity this suggests encourages the view women and men understood themselves as more than just parents in the family unit.

From the 1930s, there was a rise in the availability and purchase of 'sexology' literature, with its emphasis on the importance of pleasure for both men and women in sexual encounters. This again suggests a change in attitudes to sex. English sex manuals (such as Marie Stopes' *Married Love* [1918]), in tandem with local magazine and radio commentators giving advice on sex, gave many Australians unprecedented access to information on sex, not just in terms of procreation and hygiene but in terms of pleasure. It needs to be added that this mainstream sex literature emphasised the place of heterosexual sex, and most of it located this sex as belonging to the monogamous and committed couple. So, just as the family space was the place where the national population was boosted, it was paralleled with a proviso that this was the only place in which citizens of Australia should indulge in sexual activities.

Homosociality

Historically, Australia has been represented as a male-dominated, homosocial culture. Men worked, played and socialised together and so did women. National images often formed around particular stories of masculinity and men together. Images of Australian soldiers together in wars around the globe, the representations of squads of male lifesavers going through their drill, cinema images of men in shearing sheds, television advertisements of men in bars drinking beer, newspaper pictures of victorious football teams falling all over each other with joy—these all (re)produce pleasurable feelings of Australian male homosociality and camaraderie. This idea of men together has been and continues to be a common representation of the nature of being Australian—or at least being an Australian man. Yet this pleasure of men being in each other's company has always had an edge of anxiety to it. For many men, the desire for closeness has been undercut with a fear that the pleasure in each other may go too far. Given the negative understanding of homosexuality, and the venerated position of many homosocial activities (such as sports locker-room highjinks, military carousing and shearing bunkhouses), it has always been necessary to police the boundaries between homosocial and homosexual cultures and behaviour in the nation.

Given the emphasis on heterosexuality in social policy, it is interesting to note in many of the longest-standing national stories that the heterosexual dynamic is not central. As outlined in the previous chapter, though women may have been literally giving birth to future citizens, it is men's endeavours as mates at Gallipoli that are often represented as having given birth to the nation. In a nation that so often privileges heterosexuality and still punishes homosexuality, such an all-male story of birth may seem at odds with a heterosexual model. Yet this privileging of the desire between men in national stories is quite common. The chief places where the stories of the Australian nation are located—the bush, the beach, the battlefield— are all places dominated by men. There is even a small part of the national story representing the heterosexual family as drudgery. In the late nineteenth century, the *Bulletin* school writers and artists imagined the new nation they hoped to see in terms of the homosocial world of work and freedom in the bush. Marriage and domesticity were understood in this story to be antithetical to such a lifestyle (Lake 1992).

As was noted in chapter 3, these homosocial scenarios are not empty of feminine imagery. In fact, the presence of some sort of feminine representation is key to how they work. To use and slightly rework the ideas of Joan Landes (2001), the proliferation of images of women in spaces dominated by men emphasises the erotic or sexualised side of being Australian through representations of heterosexual romantic desire without the space needing to be filled with *actual* Australian women. This works in two ways. First, it allows a space dominated by men (say, a parliament) to still be imagined as gender-neutral—just Australian—even though it is filled only or mostly with men. Second, it works to allow the participants in these male-dominated or male-only spaces the pleasure of homosociality without the spectre of homosexuality.

One example of this is the story of war and Australian-ness. In the previous chapter, it was argued that the national stories about war emphasised men as the active participants in war and women as passively waiting at home. The military is highly charged in terms of desire: this is a place where men are taught to be and are willing to die for their country and their mates. Yet, because the state privileges a particular form of heterosexuality—one that might be challenged by the intense homosociality of the battlefield and barracks—the emphasis on the place of women in the project of a nation at war has to be maintained. So, in representations of war and what men are doing in war, the stress is on the romantic heterosexual stories of dying for a feminised nation. There is also the important story of the soldier as undertaking his job for an individual woman at home. Take the trope of the love letter the digger carries close to his heart throughout the war. This piece of paper works to emphasise the heterosexual dynamic of war. Though the Australian digger loves his mates and dies for them, his erotic desire is directed towards a woman. Sometimes the letter is from a sister or mother. Yet again, this places the story of love back into the heterosexual family.

This is not an argument suggesting that all men who experience the intense atmosphere of an all-male arena, such as war, wish to or do take up homosexual lives. It is an argument pointing out that, in the powerful Australian story of a nation—predicated as it is on heterosexuality and the marginalisation of homosexuality—for men to sexually desire each other is a problem. As a result, the state works quite vigorously to minimise this possibility. It does so by emphasising other stories, punishing homosexual behaviour, and separating out any intense male-to-male desire and naming it as 'mateship' rather than an erotic love for other men.

Mateship is the dominant national story of men loving men. As suggested above mateship is most powerfully represented in stories of war. It is also a strong component of narratives of work and sport. When the two miners Todd Russell and Brant Webb were trapped underground in a gold mine in Beaconsfield, Tasmania, in April 2006, the dedication of their fellow workers in labouring for two weeks to find and free them was understood in terms of mateship. The teamwork in sport is also represented as the outcome of mates working together; trusting each other, depending on each other. The bonds of mateship are obviously powerful, and they signify some of the deep connections between men. At one level the story of mateship that is drawn from war, work and sport demonstrates the positive ways men love each other. At another level it works to centralise a particular form of homosocial desire; one that is cordoned off from a marginalised and historically despised story about homosexual desire between men.

A less intense space that also demonstrates the story of homosociality and heterosexuality in a place dominated by men is the pub. Though the pub has recently become a more welcoming space—with spaces for families, and for men and women as both customers and workers—there still exist the iconic pubs that are male bastions. For example, there is the lunchtime pub with topless or lingerie-clad barmaids serving an all-male clientele, or the old country pub where the front bar is still a place for blokes only. Though pubs are no longer the male bastion they once were, they are still good places to demonstrate the contradiction between the practice of homosociality and the desire to reify heterosexuality in Australian-ness. For most of the twentieth century, the local pub was the preserve of men. It was a home away from home, a pleasant stop on the way home, a way of life for some men (Fiske et al. 1987). Though there were no laws barring women from pubs, the social conventions keeping them out of the public bar and in the women's lounge were especially strong. Descriptions of the public bar in the mid twentieth century paint an image of a space marked by male customs and desires. There is a scene in the 1966 film *They're a Weird Mob* where a new migrant is introduced to the 'six o'clock swill' in a pub. As pubs closed at six in the evening, men hurried to drink as many beers as they could between finishing work and closing time. In this scene, dozens of men shoulder each other to get to the bar and order drinks; they then hurriedly skol their drinks—one even vomiting—before moving on to the next drink.

This intense atmosphere of all-male drunken bravado and sentimentality was, of course, a perfect space for masculine excess, including declarations of undying love—'Mate have I told you how much you and Macca mean to me?' slurred out after the fifteenth schooner. But pubs were maintained as heterosexual spaces by the presence of a select group of women: barmaids, women who owned pubs and sex-workers. The barmaid is understood in this context as the sexy woman who is available (at least for a chat about how hard life is at home or a half-hearted sexual offer) and so secures the heterosexual nature of the pub while allowing the frisson of homosocial desire between men. The story of the pub privileges the respectable heterosexual man (and, by association, woman) as the real Australian. This works in tandem with a positing of homosexuality as deviant, while still allowing a delicious homosocial desire to operate in the form of drunken intimate time with mates.

Heterosexuality and 'white Australia'

Though the heterosexual family unit has been widely understood as the building block of the Australian nation, it has still been an anxious place. In national stories of the family, the privileged family has been the white family. The placement of the Anglo–Australian heterosexual couple as the core of the Australian family/nation has meant that, in the same way Indigenous peoples and Asian peoples have been excluded from the nation, they have also been excluded from the family. Yet this exclusion—or desire to exclude—was never complete: there was also a desire for these other peoples. The anxiety about the white family centres on threats to it posed by (white people's) inter-racial desire and what this means for future of the white family.

Non-Indigenous representations of relationships between non-Indigenous men and Indigenous women have a long history in Australia. Poetry, novels, memoirs, diaries and films have been written about inter-racial sexual relations. These non-Indigenous stories often draw on more widespread Western representations of black women as highly sexualised. Though there was a pleasurable erotic aspect to these stories for non-Indigenous peoples, there was another side to them. Eroticism and desire operated in tandem with stories about the inferiority of Indigenous peoples compared with non-Indigenous peoples. In recent years, Indigenous artists have engaged with this non-Indigenous presumption. For example, Brook Andrew's *Sexy and Dangerous* (see Figure 4.1) and Destiny Deacon's *Blak Like Me* (Figure 4.2) artworks respond to non-Indigenous stories of black and Indigenous exoticism, danger and difference.

The desire for inter-racial relationships was represented as improper by non-Indigenous peoples, even though it was a popular

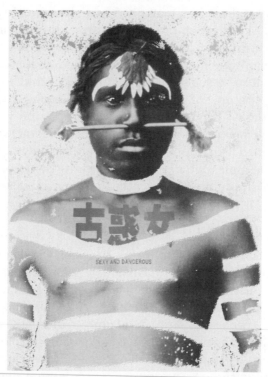

Figure 4.1 Brook Andrew's artwork, *Sexy and Dangerous* (1996), represents under-standings of Indigenous men in the context of colonialism—'this guy is seen as sexy, but he's also really dangerous for lots of different reasons' (Andrew 2004). (© *Brook Andrew, 1996, Licensed by VISCOPY, Australia, 2007*)

Figure 4.2 Destiny Deacon's *Blak Like Me* (1991/2003) explores the way the black female body is objectifed and represented as exotic in the colonial context. (*Image courtesy of the artist and Roslyn Oxley9 Gallery*)

fictional pastime. So, although there are plenty of popular fictional stories of inter-racial relationships, men who really had such relationships were often described by other non-Indigenous men by the pejorative term of 'going native' (Herbert 1938, Mann 1963). The implication was that, if there were non-Indigenous women in the area then the non-Indigenous men would have no need of sexual relationships with Indigenous women. That there were and are relationships between Indigenous and non-Indigenous people in Australia is now taken for granted. Both Indigenous and non-Indigenous writers have recorded the complex history of non-Indigenous men's sexual relations with Indigenous women—a history that was often based on unequal power (McGrath 1987; Evans et al. 1993; Huggins and Blake 1992; Haskins and Maynard 2005). There has also been a history of systemic abuse and use of Indigenous women by non-Indigenous men. (It needs to be added here that memoirs of many Indigenous women note that non-Indigenous women were implicated in the abuse of Indigenous women, in particular playing a role in the removal of Indigenous children [Huggins and Blake 1992].)

The circumstances of colonisation meant there was an intimacy between Indigenous peoples and non-Indigenous peoples in bush or outback spaces. Indigenous men and women often provided the labour for outback stations, and relationships—both voluntary and coercive—between non-Indigenous station owners or managers and Indigenous women workers were common. Well-known country singer, and now the Northern Territory's chief administrator, Ted Egan, gives an example of an intimate sexual and working partnership in his song 'The Drover's Boy'. The song tells the story of a drover mourning the death of his 'boy'. The 'boy' was actually an Indigenous woman who had been his sexual companion and co-worker on the track. Since it was mostly illegal for non-Indigenous men to enter into relationships with Indigenous women, drovers would dress Indigenous women in men's clothing and pass them off as boys.

Another example of disavowed inter-racial intimacy can be found in country towns. There was often significant interaction between Indigenous people and non-Indigenous people in regional areas. In particular, non-Indigenous men would have relationships or casual sex with Indigenous women. The clandestine nature of some of these relationships was not always about the law, but due to feelings of shame. In another literary example, the plot of Leah Purcell's and Scott Rankin's play *Box the Pony* (1999) is organised around an Indigenous woman whose father lives in town with his non-Indigenous family. Steph lives out of town with her Murri mother. Given the primacy of the non-Indigenous family, the illegality of many inter-racial relationships and prejudice, Indigenous women were often not accorded the status of partner, and the children born of these relationships were often not recognised by their non-Indigenous fathers. As the twentieth century progressed, more and more children born as a result of inter-racial relationships were removed from their Indigenous mothers and brought up in institutions where they were isolated from their Indigenous families yet not really welcomed into non-Indigenous society. This reinforced the primacy of the non-Indigenous heterosexual family in the nation.

Non-Indigenous narratives of inter-racial relationships often follow a pattern where the anxious yet pleasurable desire between an Indigenous person and a non-Indigenous person is eventually replaced by a more acceptable desire for a person of the same race. In other stories, the violent death of one member of the couple marks the forbidden nature of the desire but also solves the problem of what to do about inter-racial desire. The film *Walkabout* (1971), based on a children's novel by James Vance Marshall, tells the story of an adolescent girl and her younger brother who survive an accident and are stranded in the desert. They are rescued by a young Indigenous man who is alone in the desert as part of his initiation into his community. The young man and the boy find a way to communicate through a happy-go-lucky sign language. The adolescent girl and the young man, both on the cusp of a sexualised adulthood, have a more fractured relationship—represented through a repressed desire for each other. In the end, the young Indigenous man commits suicide to make right his inappropriate desire for the non-Indigenous woman. More recently, in the film *Dead Heart* (1996), an Indigenous man and non-Indigenous woman have a sexual relationship. The fraught nature of the relationship is represented in the initial sex scene that takes place (very inappropriately) at an Indigenous sacred site. The inter-racial couple is represented as transgressing important boundaries.

The anxiety in non-Indigenous communities about the prevalence of inter-racial relationships probably far outweighs the actual incidence of relationships. What motivates the anxiety is not simply racism, but something more complex—something linking back to the issue of dispossession and the need to represent Indigenous peoples as excluded. In a nation where a colonial population has dispossessed an Indigenous population and appropriated their land, the mixing of populations in any way muddies the question of who owns the land. If an Indigenous person has a non-Indigenous father (or mother), then their claim to the land as their country exists at the level of Australian law; however, it also still exists at the repressed or disavowed level of someone Indigenous to the land—the land is their country. This double claim upsets a national story where the owners of the land are understood to be the colonisers (and their children), not Indigenous peoples. So, even though the possibility of large numbers of Indigenous people repossessing their land through non-Indigenous Australian laws of inheritance has never been a real threat, the nightmare of Indigenous people's sovereign claim to the land has been. One way in which this repressed fear was expressed was through a disapproval of inter-racial relationships.

Homosexuality

Along with the monitoring of heterosexual families, the other carefully monitored behaviours in terms of narratives of national identity are those of homosexual men. As has already been suggested, in Australia (and most other nations), individuals come to understand their desires and feelings in an environment that valorises heterosexual desire and denigrates homosexual desire. Ideas about sexual identity are always framed in the context of a 'homophobic national imaginary' (Shapiro 1999: 161). So what is understood as real Australian-ness is not just masculine, but heterosexual.

Acceptable national configurations of sexuality and sexual desire were shaped through the criminalising and pathologising of homosexuality. When the British colonised Australia, there were only two crimes deemed worthy of the death penalty: murder and sodomy (Johnston and Johnston 1988). Regulation of what actually constitutes the criminal element in male-to-male sexual activities has changed over time. These changes chart the shift in self-identification and public classification of homosexuality. So in 1788, when English law decreed that the crime of sodomy was punishable by death, this was not about a sexual preference (desiring men) being understood as deviant, but about a particular act (anal intercourse) being seen as deviant. This fits with philosopher Michel Foucault's (1976) ideas that before the nineteenth century there was only a category of 'forbidden acts' rather than a particular 'deviant' sexual identity that was targeted by law. Similarly, in the nineteenth and early twentieth centuries, the laws targeting homosexual men in the different colonies tended to punish public sex rather than homosexual sex (Carr 2000: 34).

In the early part of the twentieth century, laws forbidding homosexual activities began to be passed in Australia. Male homosexuality was at some stage criminalised in all states in Australia. Female homosexuality has never been illegal in Australia: dominant ideas about feminine sexuality being passive led to an attitude that lesbian sexuality was oxymoronic. More importantly, the understanding of women as subject to men in national stories meant that independent female sexuality was not understood as part of the dominant story. Homosexual men and women have often been presumed to be less than perfect Australian citizens. For example, within the armed services, homosexual men and women have often been assumed to be security risks. In the 1970s teachers in the public school system who were homosexual could not let this information be generally known or they could lose their jobs. The laws and customs regulating the Australian state for most of the nineteenth and twentieth century not only presumed that a heterosexual subject or citizen was preferable, but that any alternative was unacceptable and needed to be punished.

What activates and centralises the fear of homosexuality within the national imaginary is not an understanding that there are pockets of gay men and lesbians in a community positing itself as straight. Rather, it is that homosexuality is contagious. As Fiona Nicoll (2001) argues, the threat to the nation was not the existence of homosexuals as a group in the community, it was the fear that straight men and women might be seduced into a homosexual lifestyle (2001: 196). The gay man was at once represented as pathetic and powerful—as not masculine enough, but also as having the power to lure men from their deeply held heterosexual convictions. Similarly, the lesbian was at once asexual, but also had the power to entice women out of satisfying heterosexual relationships. Extending on this is the consideration that the latent or unacknowledged desire men may have for each other has often been rechannelled as violence towards any man who challenges the divide between the desire understood as mateship and a physical same-sex sexual desire.

The frequent violent punishment of gay men (and women) says as much about the anxiety felt by the bashers as the bashed. It is because of the very uncertainty of Australian heterosexual identity that it needs to be violently asserted again and again. This is reinforced in the national legal story. Until recently, it was a defence in law that if you assaulted someone (usually another man) because they offered you the opportunity of homosexual sex, it was a lesser crime than other forms of assault. These attitudes towards homosexuality would also have powerfully regulated the lives of men who did not think of themselves as gay but who had more complex feelings towards other men than thinking a punch on the arm said it all. Such a strong anti-gay culture may have kept ambivalent men straight, and demonstrative or sensitive men restrained.

Yet, in so many public forums—both historical and contemporary—men flirt with other sexual identities. For example, men on television football panel shows quite regularly appear dressed in fishnets, silky frocks, sock-filled bras and high heels. The international icon of Australian-ness overseas is Dame Edna Everidge (the cross-dressed Barry Humphries). And drag queens—whether in films about large buses crossing the desert or in the annual Sydney Mardi Gras celebration—are a crowd favourite. Yet this celebration of polymorphous perversity is not quite the free-for-all it seems. As Heather Brook (1997) points out about the footy blokes, they are never perfect representations of women. They are hairy men dressed *as* women, making sure no one can mistake them for real women or 'poofs':

> Footballers use comical drag to construct their own masculinity through a kind of elaborate performance of denial—to show what they are not, what they 'cannot' be. Not women . . . not 'poofters' (1997: 8).

The reinforcement of the impossibility that these quintessential Australian men could be either gay or feminine centralises a particular gender and sexual identity in the story of being Australian. Of course, when football players began to out themselves as gay in the 1990s they looked nothing like the parodic spoofs doled out by television Rugby League personality 'Fattie' Vautin and his mates, but just like dozens of other fit and buff football players.

Homosexual communities

Even in the face of legal and social discouragement, homosexual individuals and groups remained, and homosexual sub-cultures continued to emerge. Throughout the first two-thirds of the twentieth century, gay and lesbian communities were 'a scene of the night and . . . very largely invisible to the rest of society' (Willett 2000: 9). The emphasis in these communities was not so much on politics and fighting for civil rights as on providing social, sexual and friendship circles—places to meet safely and regularly. The plan was to keep out of the eye of the law, religion, the medical profession and the rest of society—that is, to remain outside the national story. The emphasis on low-visibility communities reflects the codifying and punishment of homosexuality.

From the 1950s onwards, there was a distinct shift in government policing of homosexuality from a passive to a proactive approach. In the story of the nation, heterosexuality worked as a marker of the norm and homosexuality as deviant. In this period, deviance was not acceptable even if it kept itself to itself. Its supposed danger to the nation had been recognised. Even if it could not be seen, it had to be eradicated. The proactive state sought to flush out the invisible homosexual. This type of surveillance meant policies of entrapment and eradication began to be actively pursued (Willett 2000: 10–11). Aggressive policing meant that more gay men were found, arrested and charged, and came to court. These court cases were often given prominent placement in tabloid news. As both Willett and Wotherspoon (1991) note, the heightened interest in homosexuality from the mid twentieth century at so many different levels—medical, judicial, media—led to homosexuality having a higher profile overall in the community. Information on what homosexuality entailed—however negative—was now easier to access. As Foucault (1976) might suggest, the desire to police and eradicate homosexuality actually helped to (re)produce it as a visible identity. The endless discussion of this forbidden and what was considered abnormal behaviour placed it everywhere. Something previously unnamed—or at least not on the front page of the tabloids—was now identified. Even if it was represented as deviant, homosexuality was from this point a part of the national story. However, in the dominant story, it appeared as something needing to be eradicated from the nation.

It was in the face of this increased policing, and the associated publicity that led to the outing of so many individuals, that a political edge started to develop in gay and lesbian communities. Slowly but steadily groups formed to respond to these injustices: gay and lesbian social groups expanded their charters or just increased their visibility, operating as support organisations as well as social groups. By the late 1960s and early 1970s, a range of political groups had emerged: CAMP—Campaign Against Moral Persecution—formed in 1970; and Sydney Gay Liberation in 1972 (Reynolds 2002). Other groups focused on legal redress for workplace injustice, such as the Australian Capital Territory Law Reform Society. A body of materials—not just the tabloid press with its lurid stories of 'perversion' but scholarly work from North America and Britain— emerged from which gay and lesbian activists could draw on when thinking about and running their campaigns for change. As with the discussions about class that took place in Australia in the 1930s, issues of gay and lesbian identity were framed in a global or international framework. Links were made across national boundaries, not just within them.

For lesbians in Australia, one of the transnational frames for their stories was feminism. The impact of feminism in Australia in the 1970s was considerable. However, its meaning was not the same for all women. For some Australian women, the political message they took from feminism—the overthrow of patriarchy—meant they sought a separatist life without men. For these women, being or becoming a lesbian was a political stance (O'Sullivan 1997: 115). Drawing on mostly American separatist feminist writings and practices, they set up women-only communities in urban and rural spaces (Ion 1997). Political events and rallies such as Reclaim the Night were styled on overseas models and highlighted men as the problem. Robert Reynolds (2002: 5) notes that the remaking of gay and lesbian identities in the 1970s was often undertaken at the expense of 'other homosexual styles'. This was the case for many lesbians. For them lesbianism was something predating the women's movement of the 1970s. The new gender separatist tactics of the newly converted political lesbians contrasted with long-standing coalitions other lesbians had developed with gay men. These new models and their contradictions when it came to other ways of being homosexual caused anger, unrest and factions. As a young queer activist quipped to a gay man whose approach to change they considered outmoded: 'One day, as you old buggers lie comatose in yet another committee meeting we will sneak in and unplug your life-support system' (Reynolds 2002: 159). By the start of the 1980s, it was not possible—if it ever had been—to speak of one homosexual community in Australia. There were now many disparate communities.

HIV/AIDS and the nation

In the early 1980s another significant transformation took place in the way gay men (and to some degree lesbians) lived their lives as Australians. The emergence of HIV/AIDS changed the landscape of gay men's lives irrevocably. As Gary Dowsett (1997: 82) writes: '. . . at times the obituary page of the *Sydney Star Observer*, the lead weekly gay community newspaper, is so full as to wrench the heart unimaginably'. HIV/AIDS was a serious and mostly fatal illness when it first emerged, and the one group of people who were vastly over-represented as victims of the illness were gay men. The illness became known pejoratively as the gay plague. The severity of the disease and the significant levels of homophobia in the community meant gay men were often represented, first, as responsible for their illness; second, as dangerous and uncaring carriers; and lastly, as people who needed to be avoided, isolated and punished for their HIV status. As in earlier decades, lurid headlines meant there was a high level of negative discussion about homosexuality.

However, an outcome of the emergence of HIV/AIDS was that various state and federal governments began to develop health and education campaigns to increase awareness about how the virus was transmitted and how to live with HIV/AIDS. The early government campaigns were directed at a national population. For example, a 1987 television campaign to raise HIV/AIDS awareness was a fear campaign involving a ghoulish anthropomorphised HIV virus represented as the 'grim reaper', indiscriminately taking the lives of innocent Australians. The campaign drew on a dichotomy of a good Australia plagued by a bad disease, implicitly and popularly associated with gay men. Homosexuality was represented as not-Australian.

Yet, at the same time, Australian governments began to fund medical research to develop better drug regimes to fight the disease. They also developed public health information directed specifically at sexually active gay men. Interestingly, this was more informative and clear than the general HIV/AIDS material. These targeted campaigns focused on giving the group most vulnerable to HIV explicit information about how to remain sexually active and yet safe. Further, as Dowsett notes, gay groups were given responsibility for the design and delivery of HIV/AIDS programs—'an enormous responsibility that represents significant trust on the part of the government' (1997: 81).

There was a noteworthy tension in the development of HIV/AIDS health programs for gay men. In their potential vulnerability to a very serious illness, gay men were understood as part of a national population. These men needed to be protected if the nation was to remain healthy. Government-funded research programs worked to achieve this end. However, the sex practices and techniques (of safe sex) outlined were understood as taboo subjects, considered perverted by many and still illegal in some states. The government health programs helped undermine the story of homosexuality as un-Australian. Yet the gay citizen was still in a liminal and precarious position in terms of being understood as Australian.

The increasing need for health and educational resources for gay men led to a growing number of advocacy groups and government-funded groups that were run by gay men. Though some limits were put on the types of campaigns designed, and though homophobia did not miraculously disappear, this meant that the *lives* of gay men were now a part of the public health agenda of the nation. However, the level of homophobia, medical ignorance and the marginal place of gay men in the narrative of the Australian nation meant there was still a large measure of neglect or lack of interest in the issues gay men were dealing with in the 1980s and 1990s. For a nation that prided itself on egalitarianism and had such a pride in its compassionate response to the senseless loss of young lives (for example in war), the response to the loss of life and the grief experienced by so many gay men in this period (and on to the present) was limited. As Fiona Nicoll points out, the sacred understanding of the deaths commemorated on Anzac Day makes it almost impossible to criticise; by comparison the Mardi Gras, which also has a commemorative aspect, 'regularly attracts criticism from conservative sectors of the Australian community' (Nicoll, 2001: 194).

Many gay and lesbian activists in the 1980s and early 1990s found the level of action taken by the government to deal with HIV/AIDS inadequate. They also disagreed with the 'integrationist logic' underpinning many of the changes taking place for gay men and lesbians. Historian Jeffrey Weeks argues there are two main approaches to thinking about homosexuality and the nation: citizenship and transgression (Reynolds 2002: 5). So while some gay activists worked within the bureaucracy, others worked outside the state. Citizenship approaches focus on asserting claims 'to rights within existing practices and institutions' (Reynolds 2002: 5). For example, campaigns for the right for gay men and lesbians to marry, or the campaign for the age of consent to be the same for same-sex and heterosexual couples, are citizenship demands to be included in the dominant national narrative. By contrast, transgressive claims 'overturn convention and def[y] existing social relations' (Reynolds 2002: 5–6). The demand by some gay men to be able to safely use beats (secluded areas for anonymous public sex) works outside the existing dominant narrative that sex should properly take place in private with the expectation of an ongoing relationship.

In the arena of HIV/AIDS, ACTUP (AIDS Coalition to Unleash Power) was a transgressive queer global activist group. Their actions and protests were based on the premise that the state, with its hetero-sexual and homophobic paradigm, would never provide a world that had a place for gay men and lesbians as well as bisexual and trans-sexuals. ACTUP actions were often witty and in-your-face, rather than working around the edges and negotiating by ameliorative measures. ACTUP's post-national vision of the world went beyond the assimila-tion of gay men and women into the nation. Instead it demanded a world that did not work around a division of homosexual/hetero-sexual. Gay and lesbian activism today still has these different dimensions—people working within or with the legislature to change law and those who work outside the national story seeking to rethink the world.

Global sexual cultures

For individual gay men and lesbians, a long-term alienation from national stories often makes it easier to imagine themselves as 'global citizens' rather than national ones. However, global can sometimes be a synonym for 'white middle-class respectable gay and lesbian cultures' (Berry 1994). Further, this global identity is often formed around capitalist consumption. There is a demographic of gay men in Australia who are high-earning, high-spending consumers. Not surprisingly, they have become a target of transnational companies selling desirable lifestyles. Even within Australia, there are gay and lesbian identities that do not fit this type. And, as Chris Berry (1994) warns, other identities should not be measured against this dominant global one as if it was the 'original, the true' gay or lesbian identity.

Sexuality is a key place where ideas of what it means to be Australian are being negotiated. Because sex and sexuality are seen as private issues these negotiations, and in some cases legal fights, are not as obvious as those negotiations around issues such as ethnicity. However, they shape the stories of Australian-ness. Discussions around issues such as maternity leave, the falling birth rate and who should have access to taxpayer-funded fertility services are questions about belonging and being Australian. They are also discussions about discrimination and equality. Historically the Australian state privileged and supported particular types of citizens as potential mothers and fathers and particular children as the 'future of the country'. Today these exclusions made around ethnicity and indigeneity are understood as discriminatory and moves have been made to undo such inequality. Yet discrimination still exists—in particular around gay and lesbian citizens.

In the early twenty-first century, most state legislatures have moved in some way to recognise gay and lesbian rights, with a key change being the legal recognition of gay and lesbian couples. There has also been some recognition of gay and lesbian forms of family. For example, Western Australian legislation recognises gay and lesbian couples' rights to adoption. The Australian Capital Territory legislature has passed a bill allowing gay and lesbian couples' to form civil unions however marriage celebrants are not allowed to perform the ceremonies as federal legislation forbids same-sex marriage. For some gay and lesbian activists and thinkers, this general shift to acceptance has many everyday advantages and reinforces the rights of gay men and lesbians to live as equal citizens within the nation. For other activists, though they recognise the advantage of these liberal moves, they understand the outcome as assimilatory rather than radical—gay men and lesbians are being assimilated into or accepted into a world where they fit a heterosexual model. Other ways of experiencing one's sexual identity or organising one's life are repressed or eradicated, or considered deviant in a nation that still valorises stable, heterosexual reproductive two-person units. And even the formal recognition of equality masks ongoing discrimination. The Australian Capital Territory legislation allowing civil unions was overturned by Federal legislation on the grounds that it was unconstitutional. In May 2006 a Marrickville day care centre hit the New South Wales media when it was discovered they had children's books about kids with same-sex parents in their libraries. The state opposition labelled this policy social engineering, not equality.

FURTHER READING

Altman, Dennis 2001, *Global Sex*, Allen & Unwin, Sydney.

Grimshaw, Patricia, Lake, Marilyn, McGrath, Ann and Quartly, Marian 1994, *Creating a Nation*, McPhee Gribble, Melbourne.

Lake, Marilyn 1992, 'Mission Impossible: How Men Gave Birth to the Australian Nation—Nationalism, Gender and Other Seminal Acts', *Gender and History*, vol. 4, pp. 305–22.

Matthews, Jill 1997, *Sex in Public: Australian Sexual Cultures*, Allen & Unwin, Sydney.

Phillips, David L. and Willett, Graham (eds) 2000, *Australia's Homosexual Histories: Gay and Lesbian Perspectives V*, Australian Centre for Lesbian and Gay Research and the Australian Lesbian and Gay Archives, Melbourne.

Reynolds, Robert 2002, *From Camp to Queer: Re-making the Australian Homosexual*, Melbourne University Press, Melbourne.

Willett, Graham 2000, *Living Out Loud: A History of Gay and Lesbian Activism in Australia*, Allen & Unwin, Sydney.

5

WHITE AUSTRALIA MEETS MULTICULTURALISM

Ethnicity and nation

As the two previous chapters implied, dominant narratives of Australian-ness presume a real Australian to be someone with British heritage. This chapter explicitly analyses the ways in which ethnicity—a person's cultural heritage—contributes to stories of being Australian. Two quite different stories of ethnicity have been central to ideas of Australian-ness. One is a very powerful story of Australia as white. This white Australia story covers a range of narratives focusing on Australia as an Anglo–Australian nation, a Judeo–Christian nation and a democratic nation. The white Australia story posits being Australian in terms of sameness. The second story is of Australia as a nation of immigrants. The notion of Australians all being immigrants implies that all citizens have come from somewhere else but are united in their commitment to their adopted country. This is the story of multicultural Australia; it posits Australian-ness in terms of difference and diversity.

Though these two stories seem to exist as opposites, they have some aspects in common. This chapter focuses on the relationship between the white Australia story and the 'we are all immigrants' or multicultural story. Many people would argue that the relationship between the two stories is chronological—white Australia is the historically earlier story, replaced by the more liberal and forward-thinking story of multiculturalism. The argument put forward in this chapter is that the relationship is more complex. Rather than understanding the two stories in terms of one replacing the other, they can be identified as having always existed and continuing to exist, side by side. Even at times of extreme racism in Australia, there were always citizens who supported diversity. Similarly, though in recent times the multicultural story has displaced the dominance of the white Australia story in everyday and governmental discourse, the white Australia story still lingers in the shadows.

In the previous chapters, the terms used to refer to the heritage of Australian people were mostly 'Indigenous' and 'non-Indigenous'. In this chapter, the limits of this pair of terms become obvious. Non-Indigenous peoples are not an homogenous group, but a diverse group (as, of course, are Indigenous peoples). Not surprisingly, in dominant stories of being Australian, differences in ethnicity are represented in terms of binaries such as white/ethnic, Anglo/non-Anglo, or perhaps even Australian/NESB (non-english speaking background) or Australian/CALD (culturally and linguistically diverse). In slang, the binary is sometimes skip/wog. The inadequacy of these terms—especially those describing non-British Australians—is obvious. Most strikingly, many of the terms describing this group are negatives: non-English speaking, non-Anglo. As Nicola Joseph (1996) notes, there is something unsettling about having one's identity within the nation expressed as that which it is *not*.

Ghassan Hage, in his work *White Nation* (1998), explores the dynamics ordering the dominant conceptions of Australian-ness in terms of ethnicity. Hage argues that dominant stories of being Australian privilege being white. The field of whiteness is not homogenous: there are different kinds of whiteness. Hage suggests that Anglo-ness is the most valued type of whiteness and argues that whiteness can be 'accumulated' by non-Anglo–Australians, but not Anglo-ness itself (1998: 191). Added to this, the groups who are represented as not-white are those understood as being 'third world looking'. It is this group (the members of which change over time) that is marked as outside whiteness and so occupies the most precarious positions within the stories of being Australian.

One of the key issues this chapter explores is racism in Australia. It needs to be stated that the capacity to be racist is not restricted to Anglo–Australians. Racist attitudes can be—and are—held by members of many different cultural groups. There is ample evidence of individuals from minority ethnic groups in Australia holding prejudiced views about Anglo–Australians. Ien Ang (cited in Hage) notes that some Asians, when asked to describe Anglo–Australians, will answer with the same prejudices Anglo–Australians put forward when asked the reverse question. Some members of both groups suggest members of the other exhibit poor hygiene and are uncivilised (Hage 2003: 117). However, what is important to note when analysing racism is power. In the historical context of Australia, one group has been able to deploy its prejudices in ways that reinforce them and reproduce inequities. So although, as Ghassan Hage suggests, a Lebanese–Australian person might be able to create a 'micro-space' where they can air their ethnic prejudices and wield power so that their small world is ordered around their vision, in general this Lebanese–Australian person would exist in a space where the dominant prejudices ordering the nation were those held by Anglo–Australians. (Hage 2003: 118).

The issue of racism is not about the moral superiority of one group over another, but rather the political power of one group over the other. The example of 'ethnic' gang rapes is apposite here. The Lebanese–Australian men who raped women in Sydney in 2001, choosing them on the grounds of their ethnicity and subjecting them to violent and humiliating assaults, were exhibiting extremely misogynist and racist behaviour. Their actions—both the rapes and the racism—were odious and were severely punished by the courts. These men had a certain amount of power—power mostly accruing to them as men—and they used it to abuse Anglo–Australian women. What the men did not have was much political or institutional power. This is reflected in the representations of them in the media. By comparison, in the lead up to the day in December 2005 when hundreds of young Anglo–Australians rioted in Maroubra and Cronulla, seeking out Australians they deemed un-Australian to vilify, they stood in a different relation to powerful media institutions. For example, Steve Price, a talkback radio personality in Sydney, encouraged a 'community show of force' in response to the incident where Cronulla lifesavers were beaten up by non-Anglo–Australians (Marr 2005a, 2005b). Alan Jones, another very popular talkback radio star, ran the story of the original violence against the Cronulla lifesavers for days and on some occasions, when listeners phoned in and suggested a violent response, he did not disagree (Salter 2006). Some days before the riot, he also read out on air one of the text messages inciting violence and suggested he 'understood' the feeling rather then condemning the call for lawless actions. The racism of the Anglo–Australians took place in a context where aspects of their hatred were supported by some powerful institutions. So, when analyses of racism in Australia end up focusing on Anglo–Australian power and institutions, it is not because this group is the only one that exhibits racist behaviour, but because it is the group with the most political and institutional power. Keeping these ideas in mind, the logic of the white Australia story is now explored.

The 'white Australia' story

This story hinges on the importance of Australia's British heritage. However, it also depends on the idea of Australia as separate and independent from Britain. As is well known, Australia—as a non-Indigenous space—began life as a convict dumping ground. Many of the first British immigrants who came to Australia arrived not by free choice but by decree of the court. Even amongst these convicts and their masters there were ethnic and cultural differences. In particular, Irish convicts—and later Irish colonists—were treated by the government as a lower order of person. Irish political prisoners, fighting English occupation of their country, often ended up in Australia as transported convicts. For decades, prejudice towards Irish–Australians, and especially Irish–Catholic–Australians, was commonplace.

From the early nineteenth century, feelings that Australia was more than an extended prison started to develop. Australia was recognised as a place to which a person could have loyalty. As a result, there was a concerted effort to populate Australia with free immigrants rather than convicts, who were considered to carry a 'stain' or pass on their hereditary propensity for wrongdoing. Sturdy English and Scottish men and women of some financial means and hard-working labourers were sought as the colonisers for this new land. By far the largest group of immigrants coming to Australia between the early nineteenth century and 1945 were those from England, Ireland, Wales and Scotland. Immigrants came as assisted migrants (that is, the government paid part of their fare in return for work) or unassisted migrants (the immigrants paid their own way).

The white Australia story is about loving Australia *and* about British-ness. Even though Anglo–Australians frequently represented themselves as part of the 'civilisation' of the British Empire, they also argued that they were native to Australia:

> Culture in Australia if it ever develops indigenously, begins not from the Aboriginal, who has been suppressed and exterminated, but from British culture . . . We inherit all that Britain has inherited, and from that point we go on—to what? (Stephenson 1935)

Cultural critic Percy Stephenson's 1930s picture of Australia is of a nation shaped by British immigrants who bring culture to Australia.

He does not imagine 'indigenous' Australian culture as linked to Indigenous peoples, but as a distinct and new version of British-ness. Indeed, Stephenson excludes Indigenous peoples from his vision of the nation—deploying the vision of Indigenous cultures and peoples as 'suppressed and exterminated'. This allows him to ignore Indigenous people's ongoing presence in Australia and locate the dynamic space of culture as emanating from non-Indigenous British natives.

Over time, this emphasis on British-ness was matched by virulent stories vilifying all that was not Anglo–Australian. This sentiment, reaching its most intense expression in the late nineteenth century, was given one of its most crass and now infamous airings in the *Bulletin* magazine in 1887:

> . . . all men who leave the tyrant-ridden lands of Europe for freedom of speech and right of personal liberty are Australians before they set foot on the ship which brings them hither . . . No nigger, no Chinaman, no lascar, no kanaka, no purveyor of cheap coloured labour is an Australian (White 1981: 81).

This distaste for difference began in the gold rushes of the 1850s. Of all the non-British groups who arrived in Australia seeking gold, it was the Chinese miners who were most scrutinised by the colonial governments. The Chinese were physically the most distinctive group on the gold fields. Their clothing and hairstyles, drugs of choice, food and language were very different from those of the British and European miners. These cultural differences had little or no meaning by themselves; however, beliefs held by most Anglo–Australians that Asian peoples were not civilised compared with Western Europeans were used to suggest that Chinese miners were a threat and did not belong in Australia. In the 1850s, and again in the 1880s, many of the colonies introduced anti-Chinese legislation.

By the late 1880s, the Chinese in Australia were frequently described as being responsible for the unemployment of Anglo–Australian men. The first national conference of trade unions, held in 1879, unanimously passed a motion opposing *all* Chinese immigration (Jupp 1991: 73). The Chinese men who came to Australia were regarded as a danger to the democratic systems of the colonies and later the commonwealth of states. The Chinese were also understood as bringing disease into a nation frequently figured as a pure and clean island nation (Bashford 2002). The aspect of Chinese people's arrival in Australia perceived to be most threatening was the fact that Chinese men came to Australia alone, without wives and families.

Gender and 'white Australia'

Gender was significant in the way the Chinese men who came to Australia were represented; they were seen in terms of a hetero-sexual threat. They were viewed as a danger to Anglo–Australian women—for example, they were frequently portrayed as luring Anglo–Australian women into their 'depraved' opium dens. Yet these representations of Anglo–Australian women and danger were double-edged. In one sense, the women were *in* danger from Chinese men and therefore needed to be protected by Anglo–Australian men; the dominant gender order was reinforced. However, Anglo–Australian women were also presented as vulnerable to the Chinese men's 'immoral' world—that is, they were willing to be lured into the dens. In this sense, Anglo–Australian women were seen *as* the danger. They were the site of vulnerability in white Australia. This was a key anxiety in the story of white Australia—that whiteness itself was under threat. By this logic, Anglo–Australian women could never be *the* exemplary Australian. Their vulnerability meant they needed to be protected or controlled. Exemplary Australian-ness was something that was the exclusive domain of the white working-class man (Walker 1997: 134).

The gendered representation of danger, Chinese masculinity and Anglo–Australian femininity was not only about real white Australian women being in or being the danger. It sometimes also worked as a metaphor for Australia's situation—a feminised colony or nation threatened by a Chinese masculine presence and needing to be protected by Anglo–Australian men. In the late nineteenth and early twentieth century this metaphor of danger was frequently represented in cartoons. In these Australia was portrayed as a vulnerable feminine figure open to a sexualised threat from a menacing Chinese man (see Figure 5.1). This feminine nation was imagined as protected by a masculine figure. In reality this protection took the form of the military, the legal system, and labour regulations. This complex set of protective measures came to be known colloquially as the white Australia policy. Its central control mechanism was the piece of legislation known as the *Immigration Restriction Act*. This act passed in 1901 sought to control immigration to Australia by granting government authorities the right to refuse entry to unfit entrants. In particular it

WAKE, AUSTRALIA! WAKE!

Figure 5.1 The cartoon 'Wake Australia Wake' appeared in *The Boomerang* in 1888 and it demonstrates the gendered representation of Chinese immigration as a danger to the vulnerable feminine nation. (*Image courtesy of the State Library of Victoria*)

sought to exclude non-white people from the nation through a dictation test.

Desire and 'white Australia'

There is another side to the white Australia story: it is not only premised on a notion of anxiety but also one of desire. Asian countries have long been places of fascination for Australians. Like people in many other western nations, Australians desired cultures they saw as different from their own. Edward Said (1978) named this western desire for the Middle East and Asia as, 'Orientalism'. He describes Orientalism as a 'subtle' Euro-centred prejudice about the

'Orient' that could be deployed to justify colonial expansion into these areas. This desire had many manifestations: some were sustained through a fetishisation of Chinoiserie and later Japon-eserie—Chinese and Japanese arts and fashion—other desires were sustained through literature and the popular genre of romance fiction set in the East; travel and study were yet further ways in which these desires manifested themselves.

Other examples of this desire were more straightforward. For many capitalists or pastoralists, the attraction of Asia was the avail-ability of cheap, hard-working labour. Many of the earliest arrivals from China and India were indentured labourers hired to work in areas seen as unsuitable for Anglo–Australian men. These labourers undertook work seen as back-breaking or located in the tropics. Many Anglo–Australian employers had a secret, or even open, admiration for what they saw as the stamina of the workers who came from Asian countries. This admiration changed over time. In the post-1945 period, when Japan, and then Korea and Taiwan, became economic powerhouses, the result was often attributed to the commitment and dedication of the workforce. The Anglo–Australian admiration morphed into a dedicated study of Japanese business practices in the hope that they could be adopted in the Australian workplace.

The invasion complex

Though the stories about Asia were never singular or coherent, there was a dominant story pervading the white Australia era. The conglomeration of negative ideas about Asia was brought together in the form of an invasion narrative. The 'invasion complex' is an important part of the white Australia story. Though culturally Australia allied itself to Britain, geographically it was a long way from the country considered as home. This distance meant the white Australia story took on a paranoid edge—the belief was that the people refused entry to white Australia coveted the continent. The Chinese in particular were imagined as just waiting to pour down from the north and take over the country (see Figure 5.2). The hysterical responses accompanying the arrival in Australian territorial waters of a few boatloads of potential refugees in the 2000s is a contemporary manifestation of this long-standing 'invasion complex' (Papastergiadis 2004). Although the specific stories of invasion have changed from one period to another, and although they have focused on different groups of people, the logic has been constant.

LANDING CHINESE AT COOKTOWN, QUEENSLAND.

Figure 5.2 Image from an Australian magazine in the 1890s encouraging the idea that the borders of Australia were permeable and 'hordes' of unwanted visitors were entering the nation. (*Image courtesy of the State Library of Victoria*)

Taking the complexity of feelings of both desire and repulsion into account allows for an understanding of the ambivalence underpinning the white Australia story. The mixture of both desire and repulsion for the rejected group meant the policy of exclusion was never complete, but similarly any welcome was never wholehearted. Further, as Asha Varadharajan (1995) writes, just because you desire something or someone does not mean you value them or do not ending up harming them. An example of this ambivalence is found in the story of Vietnamese immigration to Australia. Between 1971 and 1975, the Australian government pulled its troops out of the war in Vietnam where it had been involved for nearly ten years. As a result of the war's end there were many refugees from the non-communist south of Vietnam, which had supported the United States and Australia in the war, living desperate lives in refugee camps outside their own country. In this same period, the last vestiges of the racially discriminatory white Australia policy had been dismantled. In these circumstances, it was possible to offer refuge to many of these Vietnamese people in Australia.

In the mid 1970s Vietnamese refugees started arriving in Australia as part of an extensive and well-organised refugee program designed by the federal government to support these displaced people. Not all refugees arrived in an orderly fashion. A small number came without official clearance, sailing in rickety boats from South-East Asia to Australia and landing as unauthorised entrants in the north of Australia. The invitation from the Australian government for the refugees to come and make their homes in Australia in part reflected a desire to remake Australia as a multicultural nation. It reflected some citizens' desire to create a new way of being Australian—Rutherford's (2000) 'desired state'. The Vietnamese refugee program took place within a set of broader changes. The previously minority view—that all people who wished to come and make Australia their home should be treated equally—shifted to centre stage. The story of Australian-ness was being rewritten in terms of ethnicity.

Yet the new wave of migration to Australia in the 1970s reignited many of the old fears and prejudices Anglo–Australians had exhibited in the late nineteenth century. The arrival of the refugees was referred to by many Australians as an 'Asian invasion'. There was extensive anti-Asian sentiment and far right-wing groups lobbied for an end to immigration from Asian countries. As with earlier migration from Asia, the Vietnamese refugees were represented as too different to fit into the nation. Many of the same prejudices were aired—their very different languages, different food, and different understandings of how the world worked—to argue that Vietnamese refugees should not be allowed to enter Australia. The representations of these immigrants often drew on themes used in earlier narratives. Images tended to show the few unauthorised migrants arriving by boat on the north coast of Australia, rather than the orderly arrival of the majority at Mascot or Tullamarine airports. Popular responses in the form of graffiti exhorted 'Asians go home'. An editorial in the *Australian* in 1977 recommended 'we . . . fumigate every shirt and slipper they arrive with' to prevent disease entering the country (Carton 1994: 64).

In the twenty-first century, the 'invasion complex' has still not completely disappeared. Though it has been critiqued, and is now most commonly represented as marking a less acceptable racist moment that was discarded with the white Australia policy, it still informs some of the ways in which international affairs and immigration are understood. In her 1996 maiden speech in federal parliament, One Nation Party leader Pauline Hanson suggested that the large population of the Asian nations compared to the small population of Australia was a threat. The mentality underpinning the original nineteenth century fear of invasion can also be found in contemporary media images. For example, in 1999 the *Sunday Telegraph* ran a huge banner headline (see Figure 5.3) that said simply 'Invaded' when a rusty old ship with approximately 80 Chinese unauthorised entrants ran aground at Scotts Head Beach on the north coast of New South Wales (Gora 1999). The threat of invasion was less than negligible—perhaps the headline was meant to be ironic. Whatever its intention, it still drew on the stereotype of 'Asian invasion'.

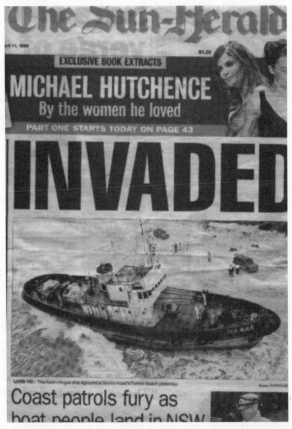

Figure 5.3 A headline of the *Sun-Herald* when an unauthorised rusty old ship carrying unauthorised arrivals reached the beach of Northern NSW in 1999. (*Image courtesy of News Ltd, 11 April 1999; Text: Bronwen Goray, Image: Stefan Moore*)

The motif of invasion can even come into play when it is actually Australia extending its reach or entering another country. In 1999, when the Australian government authorised the support of the East Timorese people in their bid for independence from Indonesia, there was a flurry of worry about the 'empty north' of Australia. This fear seemed to be inspired by an anxiety that, having supported the East Timorese rather than the much larger state of Indonesia, there would be some form of retribution and Australia would be invaded. The odd thing was that, though there was a spate of letters to the editor and political pronouncements about the need to populate the Northern Territory, the troops who were outside their national borders were the Australian troops in East Timor.

The most famous recent reinvigoration of the invasion story took place in 2001. Australia was on the front page of newspapers around the world when the federal government refused to allow the potential refugees who had been saved from an un-seaworthy boat by a passing Norwegian tanker—the MV *Tampa*—to land on Australian soil. Many commentators have argued the federal election of that year was won by the conservative government because of its hard-line stance on asylum seekers. 'When John Howard put his foot down and said "keep out!", the people of Australia roared their collective approval' (Mares 2001: 133). In the wake of the *Tampa* crisis, a series of legis- lative changes were initiated by the federal government to further curtail the ability of asylum seekers to reach Australia. Legislation such as the *Migration Amendment (Excision from Migration Zone) Act 2001* and the *Border Protection Act 2001* were introduced to help control, in Prime Minister Howard's words, Australians' 'absolute right to decide who comes to this country'.

Sara Wills (2002) argues that this desire to decide who comes to Australia is nothing new. She notes that from Federation in 1901 national governments have worked to exclude people they consider undesirable from the nation. Wills argues that many Australians have so focused on the story of Australia's immigration generosity after World War II that systematic policies of exclusion throughout the twentieth century have been forgotten. More than this, the ongoing discrimination within the exclusion policies often goes unremarked. Since 1989, federal governments in Australia have used their power to more consistently detain unauthorised arrivals. Unauthorised arrivals are people who arrive in Australia without visas or their passports in order. As many refugee advocates have made clear, there are unautho- rised arrivals who have been in Australian detention camps for years. Children were born and lived in detention for years. Yet, another group of non-citizens who are in Australia without the proper permission—the 50 000 or more people who have overstayed their visas—are hardly ever detained. As Don McMaster (2001: 68) notes, this is because about 20 per cent of them are British or American tourists who have decided not to go home. These 'illegals' are not understood in terms of the 'invading Asian horde', and so are not seen as a problem. By comparison, the 'third world looking' arrivals are kept in geographically isolated detention centres, their misery operating as a deterrence to 'others' who might want to come to Australia.

It also needs to be noted that the increase in the number of potential asylum seekers who arrived on Australia's shores in the late 1990s was due largely to a huge humanitarian crisis of global population displacement. Sara Wills (2001) points out that at this time conservative estimates suggest 22 million people around the world were refugees. Most western or wealthy northern nations are dealing with huge numbers of applications from potential asylum seekers. Australia deals with a small number by comparison. And though Australia does have a generous quota for refugee resettlements, the overall policy, legislative and popular attitude towards this global issue is punitive and focused on the danger to Australia (and the so-called Australian way of life) rather than the needs of millions of displaced people.

It is important to note that the invasion story is not associated with the British colonisation of the continent, but only with other outsiders who turn up uninvited. Within the non-Indigenous story, the first invasion of Australia takes place with the arrival of Chinese gold-seekers and workers in the colonies rather then the British arrival in 1788. In 2001, when a wave of the 'invasion complex' was circulating in Australia, a group called Boat People (www.boat-people.org) released an image showing a nineteenth century sailing ship with the caption below reading 'boat people' (see Figure 5.3). The image was designed to get Anglo–Australians to think about how their arrival in Australia might be posited as an invasion. It also showed how hard this dominant group works (both consciously and subconsciously) to make sure they are not positioned as invaders in stories of the nation.

The 'we are all immigrants' or the multicultural story

In a 2005 news story about Australia Day, the authors note:

> Some may regard January 26 as invasion day, but for most it is a day for all Australians: for those whose connection with the country dates back millennia, for those whose citizenship is only hours old, and for all those in between (Huxley and Ireland 2005).

Figure 5.4 Poster used in the 'We are all boat people' 2001 campaign to counter racism about the supposed increase in unauthoried arrivals in Australia. (*Image courtesy of boat-people.org*)

The ready dismissal of the view of January 26 as 'invasion day' and the move towards a story of easy coexistence is a version of the we are all immigrants story. This national story flattens out the different meanings attached to arriving in Australia over the last few hundred years. This story proposes Indigenous peoples are simply the first of a range of migrant groups who have come to Australia. They were followed by the British, Italians and Greeks, the Vietnamese and Lebanese and most recently Afghani refugees. One outcome of this story is that it displaces Indigenous understandings of themselves as being of this land. It conflates Indigenous belonging and non-Indigenous belonging. (This will be discussed in more detail in chapter 6.) Further, it fails to recognise that from the earliest times, there emerged hierarchies and differences between British immigrants—who morphed into the 'natives' of the land—and migrants who came from a range of non-British countries—Hage's (1998) white but not Anglo–Australians.

A more nuanced version of the we are all immigrants story is the story of multiculturalism. This story is explicitly set up in opposition to the story of white Australia. It is represented as a more progressive story, replacing an earlier and narrower narrative about being Australian. This new story takes into account the fact that all citizens do not come from Britain and not all of them are Christians, with a cultural history that links them to the English Westminster system of government and the Magna Carta. The multicultural story acknowledges the cost of the white Australia story for many immigrants, and works to undo the inequalities set in place by that story.

The origin of the multiculturalism story is often located in the post-World War II period. This period saw a substantial change in the size and focus of the Australian government's immigration policy. The government plan for postwar reconstruction in Australia was based on heavy industry (compared with agriculture and small-scale manufacturing before the war). This emphasis on significant economic expansion was tied up with an increased fear of invasion fuelled by the early Japanese successes in World War II. However, in the post-1945 period there was near-full employment in Australia so a new source of labour was needed to fuel economic expansion. The government believed that Australia required a supply of cheaper labour to undertake this expansion (Buckley and Wheelwright 1998: 188). The original emphasis was on British migrants, but not enough British people wanted to come to Australia. More nationalities had to be included in the immigration program. This combination of large-scale immigration and the diverse national origins of immigrants who came forever changed the demographic profile of Australia. Australia moved from being a nation whose population was predominantly British-derived in 1945 to one where citizens came from over 220 countries in 1990 (see Table 5.1).

Assimilation

In the early stages of post-1945 immigration, Australian governments considered it a compromise to allow non-British migrants to settle in Australia. The first minister for immigration, Arthur Calwell, declared in 1946 that for every foreign migrant there will be ten people from the United Kingdom (Zubrzycki 1995). The tradeoff for extending

Table 5.1 Top 10 Countries of Origin of Migrants to Australia, 1901 and 2001

1901 Census		% of total population	2001 Census		% of total population
	Birthplace			**Birthplace**	
1	United Kingdom	13.1	1	United Kingdom	5.5
2	Ireland	4.9	2	New Zealand	1.9
3	Germany	1.0	3	Italy	1.2
4	China	0.8	4	Vietnam	0.8
5	New Zealand	0.7	5	China	0.8
6	Sweden and Norway	0.3	6	Greece	0.6
7	India	0.2	7	Germany	0.6
8	United States	0.2	8	Philippines	0.6
9	Denmark	0.2	9	India	0.5
10	Italy	0.2	10	Netherlands	0.4
% of total population made up of top 10 countries		21.5	% of total population made up of top 10 countries		12.9

Source: Department of Foreign Affairs and Trade, *A Diverse People: Australia in Brief*, May 2005

hospitality to non-British migrants was that they would assimilate and become like Anglo–Australians. The logic was that white Australia would be created culturally if it could not be created ethnically. A particular focus was on language. Migrants were encouraged to speak English, and they were not encouraged to teach their children their first language. Overall, there was little support for cultures other than those of British origin. By the mid 1960s, it was becoming apparent that assimilation was not working. Though immigrants were supposed to become like Anglo–Australians, they were poorer, did not have equal access to education, were not as healthy and were more likely to be in a poorly paid job.

Underpinning assimilation is a notion of sameness, including a belief that all Australians should be treated the same. For many Anglo–Australians schooled in beliefs in their own superiority, to treat non-Anglo people as equals was a significant change and improvement in attitude. For others, the long-standing egalitarian ethos meant that such an approach based on equality was taken for granted. But, however well-intentioned, the idea of sameness and equal treatment is flawed. Newly arrived migrants were invited to come and settle in Australia and make it their home. They were asked to live by the laws of the country and in return receive the benefits of life in Australia. Migrants had to assimilate—be the same—and the type they had to assimilate to, or become the same as, was Anglo–Australian. This was the standard that all citizens or potential citizens had to meet. One problem with this logic is there is no reason why, just because of earlier and longer occupation, the substance of Australian cultures should always be British-derived. Second, this belief immediately disadvantages all those who were not of British heritage. For example, in the 1960s, government literature for citizens was in English. If a new citizen, whose first language was Italian and they spoke only some English, required information on the law, child immunisation or how to vote, they only received information in English. If they did not read English, they were not able to access information about their citizenship rights. In what sense was this person sharing equally in the rights and benefits of being Australian?

Multiculturalism

Government attitudes to new immigrants shifted away from assimilation to multiculturalism in the mid to late 1970s. The emphasis of a multicultural policy was not that everyone should be the same; rather, it was an approach that stressed 'unity in diversity'. The idea was that all citizens should be loyal to Australia, but this did not mean everyone needed to speak the same language, practise the same religion, eat the same food or have the same family structures. As Fiona Nicoll clearly explains: 'Policies of multiculturalism are designed to ensure that, rather than furthering the interests of a particular culture, the state functions as the neutral arbiter of the interests of an array of different, but equal, cultures' (1999: 77). Most importantly, multicultural policy also recognised that particular migrant groups were disadvantaged and required government assistance to achieve the equity promised to them as Australian citizens. So, for example, in the multicultural story the government needs to spend money to translate government information so all citizens can access and understand it.

In thinking about multiculturalism in Australia, it is necessary to distinguish between government policies and popular imaginings. Multiculturalism as government policy emphasised equity; multiculturalism in popular imaginings emphasised cultural diversity. Diversity rather than equity is the most prominent understanding of multiculturalism in Australia. For example, the success of multiculturalism is often said to be evident in the wide variety of national cuisines available in restaurant strips in big cities in Australia. Diversity as the signifier of multicultural success is also found in the media and popular culture, where the use of images showing a range of cultures as making up Australia is common. Advertisements will use a range of different ethnic faces to sell a product rather than the traditional 'typical' Aussie face. Of course, the vast array of Thai and Vietnamese restaurants is testimony to one type of successful multi-culturalism. However, for all this visual and nutritional diversity, there are so many ways in which the success of multiculturalism as an equity program and a shift in understanding about what makes up the cultural life of Australia has been remarkably limited.

The limits of multiculturalism

The most obvious limits of multiculturalism are the social and economic indicators that demonstrate more recently arrived migrants are placed at the bottom of the Australian social-scape. These limits are also indicated in the ways in which citizens with non-Anglo heritage are figured in government and popular ideas of the nation.

Since 1988, federal governments have radically reshaped migrant programs. One change has been to the mix of migrants allowed into the country each year. In recent years, there has been a growing emphasis on business migrants. This has been accompanied by a reduction in the number of migrants admitted as part of family reunion schemes. Given that for a long time Australia controlled the ethnicity of migrants, changing the terms of family reunion schemes has an uneven impact on different migrant communities. Migrants who have arrived more recently (for example, Vietnamese and Afghani migrants) have a more difficult time bringing other members of their families to Australia than migrants from earlier periods (Mellor 2004: 635). This limits multiculturalism.

In mid-2005, a Muslim cleric in Australia made a comment about non-Muslim women, suggesting that if women adopted immodest forms of dress and were sexually assaulted, they had no one to blame but themselves:

> A victim of rape every minute somewhere in the world. Why? No one to blame but herself. She displayed her beauty to the entire world . . . Strapless, backless, sleeveless, nothing but satanic skirts, slit skirts, translucent blouses, miniskirts, tight jeans: all this to tease man and appeal to his carnal nature (Devine 2005).

There was quite a response to this comment, which argued that if women dress in certain ways they are responsible for men's illegal actions against them. The cleric's comments were interpreted by some people as evidence of the 'un-Australian' beliefs of some Muslims in Australia. The belief was seen as evidence that some Muslims did not understand the Australian way of life.

Sadly, Australians from many different religions believe this myth of women being responsible for sexual assault against them. Rape trials run by non-Muslim judges and non-Muslim lawyers sometimes use a similar line as a defence for sexual assault. In 2004 a school-aged girl who was raped while on a school trip overseas was questioned in court about the short skirts she wore (Wallace 2004). Again in 2004, when a woman accused a group of footballers of rape there was extended debate in the Australian community about the behaviour of women who seek out highly paid sports stars for sex and whether these women weren't 'asking for it' (Bone 2004). Advice to women on rape crisis centre information constantly reminds women to remember 'It wasn't your fault. No one asks to be sexually assaulted' (New South Wales Rape Crisis Centre 2006). The Queensland Police Service's web advice on rape reiterates that 'safety' advice to women advising them not to dress 'provocatively' 'often perpetuate[s] the many myths of rape' (2005). If in twenty-first century Australia it is still necessary to tell women rape is not their fault, then it is possible to conclude such beliefs are not 'un-Australian', but part of a story circulating in many different cultural groups in the nation. The cleric's sexist comment was taken up by some Anglo–Australians anxious about their nation. The comment became a tool for these people to argue against multiculturalism. It exposed their hopes that the nation should be 'white' rather than their desire to bring about gender equality.

On World Refugee Day in 2005, a group of West Australians gathered in Fremantle to celebrate. A story about this event appeared in the *West Australian*. It was accompanied by a photograph of a woman carrying a placard reading: 'Refugees are welcome. Racists are not.' The next day the paper's letters page included letters about the woman in the photograph (*West Australian* 2005). One reader called the image 'heart warming', noting that the woman—who was identified by the letter writer as having Asian heritage—was probably someone who had benefited from the refugee intake after the Vietnam War in the 1970s. The writer argued that she was the latest in a 'vast mob of convicts and refugees' who had escaped persecution by coming to Australia. This letter was matched by another suggesting that, as a person who either directly or indirectly had been on the receiving end of Australian generosity towards refugees, the woman in the photograph should be more grateful for this kindness and not make trouble by protesting:

> I take it that the Asian woman pictured . . . holding a poster appreci-
> ates that she and her family have been allowed to settle in Australia
> and should not abuse the privilege. Her poster accuses hard working
> Australians of being wrong in rejecting illegal entry and 'racist'. If
> rejecting her protest and illegal immigrants makes me a racist then
> amen to that (*West Australian* 2005).

There was no evidence provided by the paper about the identity of the woman. Yet the presumption by both letter writers was that her Australian-ness was more precarious than that of other non-Asian Australians. She was not simply an Australian taking up her rights as a citizen to engage in public protest. Rather, she was a marginal person whose welcome needed to be reinforced or who needed to learn better manners. It was her Asian face in tandem with protest action that marked her as potentially un-Australian. Again, the limits of multiculturalism were reached.

In August 2005, government backbencher Bronwyn Bishop revived an ongoing sore point for many non-Muslim Australians— the issue of the *hijab*. Bishop and another Liberal backbencher, Sophie Panopoulos, argued that the Muslim headscarf should be banned in public schools. She said: 'In an ideal society you don't ban anything . . . but this has really been forced on us because what we're really seeing in our country is a clash of cultures and indeed, the headscarf is being used as a sort of iconic item of defiance' (AAP 2005). A similar response was made after a Muslim woman, Maha Shiyab, appeared on Andrew Denton's ABC TV program *Enough Rope*. Shiyab explained why she wore the *hijab*. In the web discussion after the show, a number of participants wondered why Muslim women had to 'force' their difference on others. As with the earlier examples, there is a sense that these Australians—including the members of parliament—have reached the end of their tolerance for difference. The presumption is that the norm is Anglo–Australia and differences unacceptable to this group are outside the bounds of what it means to be Australian. Again, it is only specific groups' actions that are perceived as different in a negative way. The headwear of Catholic nuns is not 'defiant': it is simply religious. The vows of chastity taken by young Christians are not 'defiant', but reflect someone being true to their values.

What is also disavowed in comments about the so-called forceful and defiant actions of Muslim–Australian women wearing the *hijab* is that it is actually these women who are vulnerable not the Anglo–Australians 'forced' to view the headscarves. Since the attacks on the World Trade Centre on September 11 2001 Muslim–Australians have been subjected to increased assaults and vilification. The Human Rights and Equal Opportunity Commission's report *Isma-Listen: National Consultations on Eliminating Prejudice Against Arab and Muslim Australians* (2004: 3) states Arab and Muslim Australians have reported an increase in 'various forms of prejudice because of their race or religion' after September 11 but also after the Bali bombings. Young Arab and Muslim–Australians feel especially vulnerable and young Muslim–Australian women 'were especially afraid of being abused or attacked. Many have restricted their movements and reported becoming more isolated since September 11' (2004: 3). One woman stated: 'Many people think and feel that a woman wearing a *hijab* is a moving bomb' (2004: 45). Another woman reported being called 'wog' and told to 'Go back to your country! . . . We don't want to see you here with your veil' (Poynting 2004: 10).

Some Arab and Muslim Australians reported support in the post September 11 period. For example one woman told this story: 'I put the scarf on after 9/11 as a form of being an Aussie courageous young woman. And nothing happened. People would smile at me and I'd smile back' (Human Rights and Equal Opportunity Commission 2004: 46). This woman tells a story of acceptance; however it is also a story about a young woman, living in her own country, for whom getting dressed in the morning and leaving the house requires an act of courage. This 'Aussie' had to wait for the non-Muslim Anglo–Australians to recognise her, to accept her, before she could relax and smile back. This is a very limited form of acceptance. In Suvendrini Perera's (2005: 31) 'hierarchy of belonging and entitle-ment' this young woman is placed below the non-Muslim Australians. It is the Anglo–Australian 'host' group who have power to accept her as Australian or not. And many Arab and Muslim Australians were not accepted. They were vilified: spat at, yelled at, attacked, insulted and followed and threatened with rape (Human Rights and Equal Opportunity Commission 2004: 47–69).

The common fantasy of Australia for so many Anglo–Australians is that Australia embodies a 'realised and privileged good' (Rutherford, 2000: 15). In this story, Australians are exemplary hosts to all cultures. If this were the case, then Muslim– and Vietnamese–Australian citizens would simply be different voices in an equitable Australian (multicul-tural) space. However, as Rutherford points out, the ubiquity of the egalitarian fantasy of the 'good' Australia only serves to underline existing inequality. How powerful must a group be to make a fantasy story of equality seem accurate in the face of a very different reality? There is no similarly powerful place from which those who disagree can air their views.

'Ethnic enclaves'

Many migrants who have arrived in Australia in the last 50 or so years have done so in difficult circumstances. They often arrive with little money and few resources. Many migrants, when they arrive, seek out other migrants who are related to them, who are from the same area or who speak the same language. For example, many Vietnamese migrants on arrival have headed for southwest Sydney. In this area, there are other Vietnamese speakers, as well as restaurants and grocery shops selling familiar products. Yet this tendency is often translated as a problem; as creating ethnic enclaves. Sometimes the problem of enclaves is framed in terms of lack of opportunity. The areas to which new migrants move are not the wealthiest areas of Australia. They often have many social and economic problems, such as high levels of unemployment, drug trafficking and use. In the opportunity story, living in an enclave is read as limiting new migrants' chances of prospering in Australia. The ethnic enclave is also represented in terms of a refusal to assimilate. One comment-ator on this issue asked whether Vietnamese–Australians who remained in Fairfield in Sydney were 'trapped, unable or unwilling to integrate into the wider society' (Carroll 2003). In an investigation of what Australians see as 'un-Australian', two sociologists found that a common understanding for many Anglo–Australians, especially those from rural or regional areas, was that migrants living in 'their own communities' or 'ghettos' was un-Australian. As one respondent put it: 'They don't need to learn our language because they have whole communities that speak their own' (Smith and Phillips 2001: 330).

There are enclaves of migrants from all sorts of ethnicities in Australia. For example, in northern and southern Adelaide there are clusters of migrants who arrived from Britain. Similarly, many small country towns are made up of Anglo–Australian or European families who have lived in the same area for generations. Only some enclaves attract media and popular attention as problems. For many Anglo–Australians, visiting a suburb where many of the signs are in languages they do not understand is exciting. For others it is confronting—it creates a sense of loss of control. For non-Anglo–Australians, being able to walk through an area with signs in their first language is probably comforting: it reinforces aspects of their cultural heritage that are important. Some Australians find enclaves anxiety provoking because they still imagine an Australia that is white and where English is the dominant language spoken in the streets. For other Australians, these enclaves are havens, local neighbourhoods and home. They are the reality of multicultural Australia.

The 'typical' Australian

The limits of multiculturalism are most evident in the failure of one type of Australian-ness—Anglo–Australian-ness—to be decentred. As discussed already, the story of Australian-ness is often expressed through the idea of particular qualities that are seen as making up a quintessential Australian 'type'. This has been a long-standing, if ironic, way of expressing stories of Australian-ness. The parameters and challenges to this type have been discussed in the chapters on class, gender and sexuality. However, the spectre of this 'typical Australian' appears yet again when the issue of ethnicity and nation is discussed. In early stories of being Australian, an Australian was imagined—mostly, if not exclusively—to be of Anglo heritage. That bush bloke who appeared in the Olympic Opening Ceremony was most certainly an Anglo–Australian. Later popular cultural icons such as actors Jack Thompson and Paul Hogan, and cricketers Steve Waugh and Mark Taylor, also fit the mould. More recently, in multicultural Australia, other faces have become Australian icons: actors Anthony La Paglia and Gia Carides, sportsmen Mark Viduka, Hazem Al-Masri and Mark Philippoussis, for example. Yet are these Australian faces really accorded the status of being typical? In Hage's (1998) schema, these faces could be accorded whiteness, but not Anglo-ness. Could a 'third world looking' face be typically Australian?

The Chinese–Australian artist Hou Leong, in a series of photographs called 'An Australian', emphasised the ongoing uniformity and singularity of identity in Australia. Leong—an Australian citizen—imposed his Chinese face in place of a 'typical' Australian face in 'typical' Australian situations. This substitution of a blond, blue-eyed, white face with a dark-eyed, dark-haired Asian face playfully makes the point that 'real' Australians are still imagined by most people as white Australians. When Leong substitutes his face for that of Paul Hogan in a still from the enormously successful 1980s film *Crocodile Dundee* (see Figure 5.5), most viewers of the image giggle at the juxtaposition. The same reaction occurs when Leong superimposes his face on a country town pub scene and a photograph of an Anzac Day march. Though

Figure 5.5 Hou Leong's 1995 'An Australian' image challenged ideas of the egalitarianism of the Australian multicultural nation. Some Australians are still considered more typical than others despite rhetoric. (*Image courtesy of the artist*)

the story of multiculturalism suggests there is no longer a 'real' or 'typical' Australian—or, more precisely, that any citizen can be a 'real' Australian—the reaction these photographs elicit suggests otherwise. There are still some citizens who seem *more* Australian than others—or, to put it the other way around, there are Australians who are represented as *less* Australian than others.

This understanding—conscious or not—can have serious implications. The result of this blindness to the Anglo-heritage standing as the exemplary form of Australian-ness means this type of Australian-ness comes to stand as the norm by which others are judged. For example, in mid 2003 there was an incident on a Qantas domestic flight from Melbourne when a passenger took two wooden stakes and tried to break into the cockpit. The flight attendants and passengers stopped the man and the plane returned to Melbourne. Given that the incident took place in a time of heightened awareness of terrorism, there was much media interest, particularly in who the man was and what his motives were. In a story in the *Sydney Morning Herald*, one passenger was quoted as describing the man as 'just a normal looking Australian' (Cornford et al. 2003: 1). Part of that normality seems to be the man was wearing a suit and was by appearance white. The implication here is that an 'abnormal' Australian would not be white and not in a suit. White or Anglo–Australians still occupy what is considered the normal ethnicity of the nation. The point here is not that the passenger who described the attacker to the *Sydney Morning Herald* was outrageously racist, but more that the representational codes shaping dominant national stories in terms of ethnicity are long-standing, often subtle, and almost invisible to white Australians.

A-'typical' Australians

Non-white and non-Anglo–Australians are much more aware of the representational codes shaping Australian-ness because they are more frequently excluded or insulted by them. Their experiences of being Australian are different from those of the exemplary Australian. Speaking for themselves, non-Anglo–Australians have told different stories about Australia to those told by Anglo–Australians. For example, non-Anglo–Australians have subverted the story of the quintessential Aussie bloke. Rather than suggest the universal experience of this bloke is his knockabout charm, other interpretations have been offered. Poet Ania Walwicz expresses another attitude to the laconic Aussie bloke in her poem 'Australia':

> You don't go anywhere. You stay at home. You like one another. You go crazy on Saturday night. You get drunk. You don't like me and you don't like women. You put your arm around men in bars. You're rough. I can't speak to you. You burly burly. You're just silly to me. You big man (Walwicz 1986).

Performance artist and photographer William Yang, who grew up in country Queensland in a large Chinese–Australian extended family that had come to Australia decades before Yang was born, wrote of his experience of racism: 'One day when I was six years old one of the kids at school called me "Ching Chong Chinaman, born in a jar, christened in a teapot"' (Graham 2002: 156). Yang has spoken of the disconnection he felt from his Chinese heritage during his youth, and the negative feelings that accompanied this. In growing up as a Chinese–Australian, there was a general racism Yang and many others internalised, ignoring their non-Anglo cultures as much as they possibly could in a society that still marked them as 'Chinamen'. Playwright Tony Ayres notes this about his experience of being Chinese-Australian:

> I had already developed a native understanding that East was inferior to the West, the legacy of growing up in Australia in the 60s and 70s. But my way of dealing with the personal implications of ethnicity was to write myself out of the picture. In my head I recreated myself as something other than Chinese. The fact that I looked Chinese was a physical aberration (1998: 112).

Other non-Anglo–Australians experience being Australian as 'an amalgam of everything put together' (Butcher and Thomas 2001: 23) '. . . you grow up thinking you're Australian, but you don't grow up with *Home and Away* or something and you don't have roast dinners, instead you have rice dinners. But then you still speak with an Australian accent . . . so it's bicultural, tricultural whatever' (Butcher and Thomas 2001: 24). For this young Australian the multicultural nature of her daily life—where she is both similar and different from a 'norm'—is sometimes experienced positively as 'whatever'.

Other non-Anglo–Australians experience being Australian as being 'lost'. They explain that they especially feel distinct or as if they do not belong in Australia when they experience discrimination:

> People having been rude or mean just because of you being Asian, that is what I incorporate into my idea that I'm not part of Australian culture . . . I've been a good ambassador for my country when I've been overseas. And I find it funny because you feel like it's your home . . . but it won't recognise you . . . I feel like I have done a lot for Australia but it doesn't recognise me (Butcher and Thomas 2001: 24).

Non-Anglo–Australians identify strongly with Australia and see the country as their home. However they also understand that the cultural influences that make them who they are are broader than vegemite and kangaroos. Katy, a Fijian–Indian–Australian expresses this feeling: 'I've accepted that idea of you can be of different cultures, but . . . you can still be Australian' (Ghosh 2003: 81). The family home is often an important space where this experience of being 'of different cultures' and 'Australian' is generated. Through meals, watching videos from their family's other home, or relatives visiting, young Australians develop a sense of their Australianness being produced through many influences.

Anglo–Australian uses of multiculturalism

It is important to note that the multicultural story is often deployed by Anglo–Australians to find out more about themselves rather than to encourage intercultural exchange. Though multiculturalism is a popular topic, the focus is not always on issues of being a migrant, being a minority or even about the relations between different cultures. *Death in Brunswick* (1991) and *Strictly Ballroom* (1992) are good film examples. Critics argue that these films involve an Anglo–character who works out important aspects of their identity through their interaction with another culture. The exotic 'other' is a mirror through which one can learn more about oneself. As Ghassan Hage (1998: 201) argues, the use of multicultural elements, such as the ethnic girlfriend or boyfriend and their ethnic fathers and grand-mothers, demonstrates the 'capacity to appreciate and productively exploit difference' without actually challenging the 'white protago-nist's place in the story of Australia'. Access to other cultures sometimes clarifies Anglo–Australians' sense of who they are without them ever really needing to engage with the culture they mine for self-knowledge.

Other cultures can be used as ways to signal an exotic and desirable other without any impact being made on the dominant national story. Authors Selvaraj Velayutham and Amanda Wise (2001) make this point in their discussion of the 1999 Gay and Lesbian Sleaze Ball in Sydney. This ball used the theme 'Homosutra' in all its adver-tising and design. The theme was a spoof on the Hindu religion. The authors point out that the ball's theme had been workshopped with Indian gay and lesbian locals, but not with any Hindus whose religion was parodied. They suggest that the use of an Orientalist theme simply reinforced ideas of the exotic 'other' as something or someone of 'sexual promise, untiring sensuality, unlimited desire' (2001: 152). Velayutham and Wise argue that this simply meant the mostly white Australian gay and lesbian audience was using the 'outsider' or the 'other' to their own ends. They were not interested in finding anything out about Hinduism or seeing what it might mean in terms of homosexuality. It was simply a way of having fun, and the overall product 'remains an "Anglo-looking" phenomenon' (Hage 1998: 191), with inter-cultural dialogue limited.

Though Anglo–Australians may not put non-Anglo–Australians in the centre of narratives of being Australian, non-Anglo–Australians do. As earlier examples demonstrated, these narratives often reflect negative experiences of being in Australia and an Australian. Other stories tell of the mix of amusing, confusing and hostile experiences of racism. Many of these narratives are framed in terms of humour. A generation of comedians have used stand-up club comedy, television and film to reproduce and rework their stories of being different in Anglo–Australia. Effie, Mary Coustas's comedic figure of 'wog femininity', is a classic example. The characters of the SBS television comedy series *Pizza*—Pauly, Rocky and Habib—are more recent examples. The humour of these comedians often uses stereotypes and the everyday for its power. For example, the film *Wogboy* (2000) begins with a scene of a young Greek–Australian boy in the schoolyard. He is dressed in a traditional Greek outfit and is eating a lunch that is comic in its difference from the accepted Anglo–Australian norm of a sandwich. This story of having to eat strong-smelling cheese on brown breads while being teased by children eating white bread vegemite sandwiches has been told by hundreds of kids whose parents were born in Malta, Greece, Italy or Lebanon. Through this comic process, feelings of isolation or difference are translated into a good dinner table story or a scene for a movie to be told to modern multicultural Australia. But the use of self-parody can be two-edged. It allows people whose experience is different from the Anglo–Australian norm to express their stories without having to frame them as entirely negative. It allows the comedian to both represent their experiences lovingly (kooky relatives and national customs) and yet express the discomfort they felt as outsiders. Yet the parodic mode also opens up the possibility for some types of racism to be authorised. In the audience, along with the fans, are those who believe in the stereotype or joke as a reality.

Racism and imagining Australian-ness

The multicultural story of Australia has never completely replaced white Australia. As suggested from the outset, there are ways in which the racism of the white Australia story still circulates. Jennifer Rutherford, in her book *The Gauche Intruder* (2000), argues that one of the reasons why the white Australia story is represented as gone, replaced by the multicultural story, has to do with an anxiety about past racism. Her argument is that some Anglo–Australians are so ashamed or conscious of a strong racist past that they are creating new stories and new ways of being, such as multiculturalism. She suggests that this anxiety with the past leads to a mixing up of the story of the *desired* Australia and the Australia which Anglo–Australians are *actually* producing. Rutherford argues there is a gap between the two. Many Anglo–Australians desperately want to be free of racism, but this is not necessarily what they are producing in their attempts to remake Australia. In some cases, racism is being reproduced, but this is not clear to Anglo–Australians because they are so focused on the desired story—the desired good Australia. For example, in late April 2003 the New South Wales Anti-Discrimination Board launched a report on racism in media debate titled *Race for the Headlines*. The report suggested that some elements of the media are helping racism to circulate. The then premier of New South Wales, Bob Carr, announced to the parliament that the report was 'ill-informed, inflammatory and tendentious': 'This report cloaks this slander in a veneer of spurious scholarship, of moral superiority reflected in its pompous language.' The premier went on to say:

> I treat with contempt any report that brands Australians as racist, contradicting the whole happy experience of this country in the postwar period when we established a reputation second to none for receiving people from diverse backgrounds and making them welcome (O'Malley 2003: 7).

Rutherford's concept of the desired Australia is useful here. She argues that notions of goodness are fantasies, and these 'fantasies of [Australians as] good provide a camouflage for aggression at both a national and local level: an aggression directed both to an external and an internal Other' (2000: 10). Rutherford contends that 'the good, as camouflage, as point of identification, as authorisation, provides a fantasmatic frame for the enactment and consolidation of white Australian culture at the singular and collective level' (2000: 10). Rutherford is not denying that Australia is a multicultural place where people with different heritages, religious beliefs, sexual preferences and politics all live. This is obviously the case. Further, she agrees that it is possible to find old, new and emerging alternatives to the white Australia story in Australia today. What she is suggesting is there is often 'a critical confusion between the desired state—Australia, the multicultural . . . and the social and political reality':

Different laws, different voices, different fantasies do not have equal regulatory power in Australia, and the fantasy that they do only serves to perpetuate this fact. It does so in a way that is endemic to white Australia, via a fantasy of Australia as the site of a privileged and realized good (2000: 15).

Bob Carr's distaste for the Anti-Discrimination Board's report on racism and media demonstrates this 'confusion' of the fantasy of a non-racist (good) Australia with the reality of a place where racism is a common occurrence in all sorts of circumstances, including media and community debate. But, more than this, Carr's eager savaging of a report suggesting Australia is less than perfect, and is not the sum of the fantastic understanding of the nation, is oddly aggressive. Anglo–Australian fantasies of Australia as 'good'—that is as 'not racist'—can often hide this aggression, an aggression directed at the other.

This failure to acknowledge the history of Australian-ness as in part emerging from a belief in the inequality of the races reflects the historical Western understanding of nations as monocultural (as discussed in chapter 1). Nationalism is heavily dependent on a fantasy of sameness. The power of national stories often comes from their ability to draw out feelings of shared history, culture, language and spiritual belief. The immigrant—as an outsider, and as someone who has a different language, history and culture—can challenge this story. Immigrants 'constitute a disturbance to the mythic stories [that] states are alleged to contain single nations' (Shapiro 1999: 40). Further, because nations are by definition limited, all nations have outsiders. The role of the outsider is to reinforce some citizens' sense of national identity. So ideas of racism are built into some stories of being Australian, but if this is revealed the response is anger.

Ghassan Hage (1998) suggests that the shift to multiculturalism has not meant the creation of a national space where all Australians treat each other with respect and equality, but a situation where one group of Australians—the dominant Anglo–Australian or white Australian group—agrees to tolerate other groups as long as they 'behave': 'When those who are intolerant are asked to be tolerant, their power to be intolerant is not taken away from them. It is in fact reasserted by the very request to exercise it' (Hage 1998: 85). This tolerance can be withdrawn at any time—as happened in the last decade in response to the Iraq wars and the War on Terror. Muslim- or Arab–Australians (or anyone who looked 'different') were seen as a threat to Australia, and often became an 'acceptable' target of violence and vilification. Muslims were spat on; women reported they had had their *hijabs* pulled off or were insulted, told to 'go home' or 'act Australian'. In these crisis moments, for some Anglo–Australians the tolerance extended to 'third-world looking' Australians ends. Instead, they are seen as outside the nation, represented as lacking 'real' Australian-ness. The desire to be the good and welcoming multicultural nation is challenged by a fear of difference. The fantasy of the good is challenged by the fear of losing one's grip on power.

Australia is without doubt an ethnically diverse nation. It is also a nation where successive governments have experimented very successfully with policies of multiculturalism in the hope of making the state a more equitable place for all citizens. Yet Australia is not a nation free of systemic racism. In 2000 and 2005, the Australian state was criticised by the United Nations' Committee on the Elimination of all Forms of Racial Discrimination. In fact, in 1998 Australia became the first western democratic nation to receive an 'urgent action' notice in response to concerns about systemic racism. The power of the egalitarian story and the multicultural story does much to hide this racism, as do Bob Carr's and the federal government's responses to accusations of racism, but the racism is still there. Coming to terms with ongoing racism is more useful than the defense of the fantasy of the good nation. Another story about the imperfect nation needs to be cultivated.

FURTHER READING

Burke, Anthony 2001, *In Fear of Security: Australia's Invasion Anxiety*, Pluto Press, Sydney.

Collins, Jock, Noble, Greg, Poynting, Scott and Tabar, Paul 2000, *Kebabs, Kids, Cops and Crime: Youth Ethnicity and Crime*, Pluto Press, Sydney.

Hage, Ghassan 1998, *White Nation: Fantasies of White Supremacy in a Multicultural Society*, Pluto Press, Sydney.

——2003, *Against Paranoid Nationalism: Searching for Hope in a Shrinking Society*, Pluto Press, Sydney.

Jordens, Ann Mari 1995, *Redefining Australians: Immigration, Citizenship, and National Identity*, Hale and Iremonger, Sydney.

Jupp, James 1991, *Immigration*, Sydney University Press, Sydney.

Kalantzis, Mary and Cope, Bill (eds) 2001, *Reconciliation, Multiculturalism, Identities: Difficult Dialogues, Sensible Solutions*, Common Ground, Australia.

McMaster, Don 2001, *Asylum Seekers: Australia's Response to Refugees*, Melbourne University Press, Melbourne.

Mares, Peter 2001, *Borderline*, University of New South Wales Press, Sydney.

Perera, Surendrini (ed.) 2006, *Our Patch: Australian Sovereignty post-2006*, API Network, Perth.

Poynting, Scott, Noble, Greg, Tabar, Paul and Collins, Jock 2005, *Bin Laden in the Suburbs: Criminalising the Arab Other*, Institute of Criminology, Sydney.

Walker, David 1999, *Anxious Nation: Australia and the Rise of Asia 1850–1939*, University of Queensland Press, Brisbane.

6

THE MYTH OF *TERRA NULLIUS*
Indigeneity and nation

THE PREVIOUS CHAPTER explored the relationship between two different ethnicity-related narratives of what it means to be Australian: the white Australia story and the multicultural story. The white Australia story plays a role in producing Australian-ness in relation to Indigenous peoples, and the emphasis is on sameness and exclusion. But the white Australia story cannot exclude Indigenous peoples by keeping them outside the boundaries of the state, as Indigenous peoples are by definition in this space. Exclusion has a different meaning here because the stranger to be excluded is *inside* the nation. Further, Indigenous peoples are excluded from the national story for different reasons than non-white migrants. In the story of Indigeneity and national identity, the central issue is land. Non-Indigenous peoples' claim to the land comes through the erasure or marginalisation of Indigenous peoples' claims to the land. An Indigenous presence (through prior and ongoing occupancy) in the land is a continual challenge to this.

Exclusion is not the whole story. There is also a simultaneous desire by non-Indigenous for Indigenous peoples to be in the national stories. Indigenous peoples are sometimes desired because there is a recognition that Australia is Indigenous peoples' land and there is a wish to reverse the wrong committed in the exclusion story. However, more commonly Indigenous peoples are desired because of the legitimacy they can bring to non-Indigenous peoples' occupancy of this land. If, as an outsider or newcomer, one can indigenise oneself—that is, make oneself native—then one can claim equal status with *other* Indigenous peoples. In this sense, Indigenous peoples are desired to certify white occupation. Indigenous peoples are often understood as the real connection non-Indigenous peoples have with Australian-ness. As a result, aspects of Indigenous cultures are appropriated or used by non-Indigenous peoples to help create a feeling of belonging. This chapter will explore both the exclusion and the desire and appropriation aspects of the Australian national stories.

A third important narrative running alongside the exclusion and desire stories is that of self-determination. This is the story of Indigenous people's resistance and sovereignty. Though most non-Indigenous narratives of Australia draw on limited understandings of Indigeneity—those that suit non-Indigenous peoples and exclude Indigenous peoples when necessary—Indigenous peoples have their own narratives. Some of these narratives have always existed and others were developed in the face of colonisation. These stories also produce Australian-ness. The chapter will not be an exploration of Indigenous cultures, *per se*, but an analysis of the relationship between Indigenous peoples and non-Indigenous peoples in the two centuries since British colonisation in the context of exclusion, appropriation and self-determination stories.

An important point that needs to be kept in mind when thinking about the exclusion (or inclusion) of Indigenous peoples and the nation–state is that, historically, Indigenous peoples had different rights and were subject to different treatment depending on when and where they lived. Laws controlling Indigenous people's lives were mostly made by the state (or colonial) governments, not a federal government. Prior to 1967 only Indigenous peoples living in Australian territories (in particular, the Northern Territory) were subject to federal law. This meant a Torres Strait Islander person on the small island of Mer would be living under a different set of laws from a Noongar person living in Perth. One state (or colony) might have granted Indigenous peoples a right denied to Indigenous peoples in another state. In extreme cases, this meant a person might be considered an Indigenous person in one state but not in another.

It is also necessary to clarify the differences, but also the links, between the 'real' process of exclusion and the telling of stories about the process. As argued in the Introduction to this book, the focus is on analysing representations of Australian-ness—that is, the production of national stories. It needs to be remembered that these stories are related to real events. In fact, the two aspects—the real events and the stories surrounding them—can work to mutually reinforce one another. For example, the stories of Indigenous peoples as a 'dying race' that non-Indigenous peoples consumed in literature, poetry, art and cinema throughout the nineteenth and twentieth centuries are largely why the actual absence of Indigenous peoples from the space of the nation (the parliament, the law, the streets) becomes understandable or expected for non-Indigenous peoples. The focus here will be on the stories produced in the courts and in the parliament, as well as in the cinema or in novels; however, these stories need to be understood in relation to the real experiences of Indigenous peoples.

Finally, it is worth reiterating that issues of racism and national identity are not about the moral worth of one group of people as measured against the lack of moral worth of another. As suggested in the previous chapter, arguments about the racism structuring the relationship between Indigenous and non-Indigenous peoples are not arguments about the inherent immorality of one group and the perfection of another. Indigenous communities and cultures—just like non-Indigenous communities and cultures—can be organised around prejudices about the outsider. Similarly, Indigenous communities have members who are bad, behave poorly and commit crimes, just as non-Indigenous communities do. As Ghassan Hage (1998) argues, non-Indigenous, anti-racist commentators often attribute a perfection or moral superiority to Indigenous peoples as a way of assuaging their discomfort about the effects of non-Indigenous racism on Indigenous communities and individuals. It seems churlish to note a capacity for bad behaviour in a group so comprehensively harmed by colonialism. Yet to refuse to see Indigenous peoples as imperfect—including a capacity for racism (just like all people)—is to refuse, at some level, Indigenous peoples' humanness. Such a refusal also works to 'fix' Indigenous peoples' identity, and therefore to limit their capacity to be who they wish. Yet again, the coloniser is defining the Indigenous person. Even if the definition is positive this time, it is still someone else's understanding of Indigenous identity.

Terra nullius

One of the chief ways Indigenous peoples are represented as excluded from the nation is through the narrative of *terra nullius*. In 1788, when the British arrived in Australia, Captain Arthur Phillip was authorised to act as the administrator of a piece of land (from latitude 10°37' to 43°49' south and to longitude 135° east) in the name of the British Crown. In declaring the land the sovereign territory of the English monarch, the British colonisers did not fail to see that Indigenous peoples occupied this land—they obviously did. The issue was more that they did not recognise that Indigenous people occupied the continent in any way that the British believed demonstrated they cared for or improved the land. Since the late 1980s, this refusal to acknowledge prior Indigenous claims to the land has been popularly understood in terms of the concept of *terra nullius*—which means that the British colonisers saw the land as belonging to no one and so claimed it for themselves (Reynolds 1987b). The exclusion of Indigenous people from their land via legal processes was quick—it simply required the raising of a flag. Actually moving Indigenous people physically off their land was a longer and more violent process, extending over more than a century. This process took place and was imagined in terms of the three stories of eradication, protection and assimilation.

The eradication story

When the British first arrived in Australia, the relationship of most non-Indigenous peoples to the land was one of fear and a desire to escape or return to Britain. In this atmosphere, the issue of land ownership or occupation was not particularly contentious. However, whether they liked or loathed the place, from the beginning of colonisation non-Indigenous people started to write new stories of the space of Australia. The colonisers saw this place as empty and sought to fill it. Yet in 1788 the land of Australia was already totally inscribed with stories. The land provided a comprehensive narrative 'arranged in kinship patterns across her skin' that different Indigenous peoples could read, or translate for others (Mudrooroo 1995: 54). As soon as the British arrived and cleared land, felled trees and quarried rock, they were erasing one narrative and writing another. However, the *terra nullius* story meant non-Indigenous peoples could imagine they were telling a story where no other story existed. The non-Indigenous story of bringing a wilderness to life demonstrates how blind colonisers were (and often still are) to Indigenous narratives and how powerful the story of *terra nullius* is.

Though the displacing of Indigenous narratives began almost immediately, it was the change in non-Indigenous people's understanding of this continent—from the initial perception of it as an oversized gaol to one viewing it as a desirable land—that shifted the relationship between Indigenous and non-Indigenous peoples permanently. It was at this point that the physical exclusion of

Indigenous peoples from the land became an issue, and violence was a central part of the story. The fact that British sovereignty had been established with the decree of the monarch meant the British colonisers had a powerful way of understanding their 'right' to own the land and their sense of belonging to this place (in this period, the story would not have been framed as being Australian). Yet the contradiction between this legal story of non-Indigenous belonging and the obvious way in which Indigenous people were literally at home was stark. It was not lost on non-Indigenous peoples that Indigenous peoples could get around this land whereas the British were continually getting lost and feeling overwhelmed by the place. Non-Indigenous peoples understood that Indigenous peoples' knowledge signified a deep belonging they could not match. But the desire for the land—especially as an economic resource—meant this story of Indigenous belonging had to be challenged. And it was.

The eradication stories were imagined in both benign and violent ways. For example, narratives of Indigenous peoples as 'noble savages' and the 'dying race' suggested that, though Indigenous peoples certainly did belong and were a people who had a long association with the land, they could not survive the inevitable onslaught of the modern world with its new technologies, its fast and furious pace of life and its complex economic and social systems (McGregor 1997). This type of eradication story is clearly represented in an advertising poster from the 1930s for the Indian–Pacific train route (see Figure 6.1). In this image, an Indigenous man stands in the foreground with a large train approaching him. The construction of the image suggests the Indigenous man—clothed in what would be considered by some non-Indigenous people as traditional loincloth and holding a spear—will be overwhelmed by the new forces of modernity—that is, British occupation—here represented by the oncoming train. Framing a lone man in the landscape suggests pathos in this outcome. The poster creates a feeling of loss and perhaps nostalgia about this change, but the size and speed of the train also suggest the inevitability of the event and that it is out of the control of non-Indigenous peoples.

This travel poster was designed decades ago, so it could be understood as representing quite outdated ideas. However, the ongoing presence of this sentimental 'dying race' image today implies it still has resonance. This image has been widely reproduced as part of a contemporary postcard series available all around Australia in newsagents, airports and card shops. The postcards from this series, reproducing nostalgic images of Australia's past, usually

Figure 6.1 A 1930s advertisement for Trans-Australian Railway. (*Image courtesy of Percy Trompf Estate*)

sit in a display rack which, when twirled around by the viewer, tell a sentimental story of white Australia. It is a story reproducing the eradication of Indigenous people in pastel hues and as part of the greater story of the arrival of non-Indigenous peoples. For example, another postcard from the same series shows a young blonde girl, again in the pre-World War II period, in a field of Western Australian wildflowers (see Figure 6.2). The young girl, unlike the small figure of the Indigenous man in the train travel postcard, fills the scene. With her arm shading her eyes and looking outward, she is represented as the sole occupier of a land evacuated by Indigenous peoples.

Another postcard, using the same design of an oversized non-Indigenous figure filling the space, advertises travel to north Queensland (see Figure 6.3). In the spirit of an old army recruitment

Figure 6.2 Advertisement by the Australian National Travel Association from the 1930s encouraging travel to Western Australia. (*Image courtesy of Percy Trompf Estate*)

poster, the caption informs the viewer: 'North Queensland calls you'. This image suggests the man—the epitome of the colonial conqueror—is occupying a space again evacuated by overwhelmed Indigenous peoples, and he is calling others to come fill the space. The story of eradication told here is one pithily expressed by Australian war correspondent C.E.W. Bean when he was comparing American and Australian frontier expansion. Bean wrote that, in Australia, 'there happened—nothing' (Morris 1998: 243). The implication of Bean's comment is that, in the face of non-Indigenous people's arrival, Indigenous peoples evaporated. More recently, tourism and travel campaigns have put Indigenous peoples into the story—but often in the past tense. A Murri woman travelling through her own country remembers coming across a plaque acknowledging

North Queensland calls you
to a winter holiday in the tropics

Figure 6.3 Travel advertisement from the early twentieth century with a pith-helmeted 'white man' calling others to join him in North Queensland. (*Image courtesy of Percy Trompf Estate*)

that the land she was walking over was the country of her community. However, the plaque—written in the past tense—expressed the idea that her people had crossed this land at some distant time not connected to the present, even though she and her family were undertaking the same crossing very much in the present. Here, even the benign acknowledgement of Indigenous peoples still eradicates Indigenous peoples' presence.

There are alternatives to the C.E.W. Bean nothing happened story. Interestingly, though, when there is an acknowledgement in non-Indigenous stories that something did happen on the Australian frontier, what happened is mostly understood to have happened to non-Indigenous men: 'Stories of deadly encounters in Australia are stories where the land *is* the danger and the white man is *in* danger'

(Morris 1998). The narratives non-Indigenous peoples tell themselves are organised around 'scenarios in which white people are *victims*': 'the bush and the desert act as inhuman agents of *de*-population' that lead to 'lone white men dying of nothing in an "uninhabited" land' (Morris 1998: 247). This serves to 'condense and censor a history of Aboriginal deaths and black resistance to white settlement', and it shifts 'responsibility for colonial violence' to a homicidal land (Morris 1998: 247). The image of a 'white man' in hunting gear suggests a person who needs to be ready for attack, a person in a wild place—a savage land. Yet this image also hints at a ghostly and shameful story of Australian-ness where the hunted are Indigenous peoples.

Violence and eradication stories

Indigenous peoples were hunted. Represented as savage and cruel within some non-Indigenous narratives, it was argued that Indigenous people could 'legitimately' be killed, poisoned or moved on because they were vermin infesting the land non-Indigenous colonisers sought to make productive. Stories of massacres and the question of their veracity have been hotly debated in Australia in the early 2000s. There is no doubt Indigenous peoples in many different regions were killed, massacred and tortured by non-Indigenous peoples who often deployed a vermin story as inspiration or justification. As Henry Reynolds (1987a) points out, there were always colonisers who resisted the vermin story and repeatedly spoke about the inhumanity of the treatment of Indigenous peoples on the frontiers. Yet the killing continued. Massacres were recorded well into the early twentieth century. And in the late twentieth century, Indigenous peoples were still recording the inhuman ways in which they were treated by non-Indigenous peoples who considered harming Indigenous peoples a sport. It needs to be stated that Indigenous peoples responded to this violence in myriad ways—sometimes with reciprocal violence, sometimes through guerilla warfare, at other times through petition to the colonial, state or even British governments demanding protection.

The violent exclusion of Indigenous peoples is still a motif of contemporary non-Indigenous representation of Indigenous peoples. For example, consider Australian film. When Indigenous peoples, especially men, appear in Australian films they are quite often seen as troubling the story and frequently violently killed. As Alan McKee (1997: 192) writes: 'Representations of Aboriginality in Australia have been consistently fatal . . . in a literal sense'. In *The Chant of Jimmie*

Blacksmith (1978), a fictional film based on a true story of an Indigenous man in early twentieth century Australia trying to find a place in the white world, and when rejected, murdering non-Indigenous people, the angry protagonist is dead by the film's end. In a more recent film—*Blackfellas* (1993)—the more troubling and troubled Indigenous man in this story dies at the film's end, saving his mate who has more of a chance to go 'straight'. Katherine Biber (2000) argues that Indigenous men are troubling because the type of Australian masculinity they represent does not have its origins in the bush bloke (and later the digger). As such, they are 'impossible men' (2000: 28) who do not fulfil the requirements of masculinity as it is set out in the bush legend. More than this, they are impossible because they contest the bush bloke for the land. In cinema, this contestation is avoided by placing 'Aboriginality on a narrative trajectory ending in death . . . Australian narratives erase any promise of possibility for these men . . . young black men cease to be imagined in our national stories' (Biber 2000: 30–31). To metaphorically eradicate Indigenous men in such a violent manner both reinforces and reproduces the dominance of the narrative of a non-Indigenous masculinity as central to being Australian and belonging to or owning the land.

Having been both sentimentally and violently excluded from the narrative of the nation, Indigenous people reappear on the margins. As Mandawuy Yunupingu writes, what happens is that Indigenous peoples appear as a smudge on the edge of the page, marginal, easy to get rid of (Yunupingu et al. 1993). For example, as Biber (2000) notes, in Australia cinema older Indigenous men retain a place in national narratives, but as she points out they remain as signifiers of a passing race—the remnants of a once-proud culture. They exist for non-Indigenous people, along with those sentimental postcard representations, as comforting stories to consume even as Indigenous land continues to be appropriated.

Interestingly, in more recent Australian films Indigenous men have been represented in a new way—the tracker. As a number of writers have noted, in this guise the Indigenous character brings to the fore the limits of non-Indigenous knowledge about the land. In Rachel Perkins's film *One Night the Moon* (2001) the refusal of a father to allow an Indigenous tracker on his land to help locate his lost daughter is represented as sealing the fate of the girl (Langton 2006: 63). David Gulpilil who plays 'The Tracker' in the eponymously named film (2002) is the one 'who is "at home" . . . Indeed The Tracker's hospitality extends to a willingness to share cultural knowledge, opening the eyes of The Follower and the spectator to his cultural understanding of the land as "country"' (Collins and Davis 2004: 16). These representations perhaps emerge from the shifts and changes of the 1990s brought about by the reconciliation movement. The tracker is the cinematic audience's guide in moving towards reconciliation in a place where non-Indigenous viewers often cannot read or see the signs to follow (Probyn 2005).

Protection stories

The logic of white Australia operates not just through the story of eradication of Indigenous peoples, but also through stories of protection and assimilation. In these narratives, the Indigenous person in danger of being overwhelmed by the culture of the new colonisers is offered protection by the British Crown and later the Australian state. The official aspect of this story is found in the protection legislation that emerged in the late nineteenth century. Protection began as a response to the eradication intentions of many of the newcomers to Indigenous land. The state and churches provided havens where Indigenous peoples could escape the fury of the new occupiers who were set on removing their competition for the land. In time, this paternalist protective principle developed into a comprehensive system of control. Protection legislation controlled where Indigenous people could live and where they could work. It regulated when Indigenous people could travel and who they could visit. It gave government officials the power to regulate Indigenous people's lives (Haebich 2000: ch. 4). For example, in some states, Indigenous people needed to get permission to marry or to move house. The overall effect of this legislation was that Indigenous adults were denied the rights non-Indigenous adults took for granted.

If the original impetus for protection is imagined as providing a physical space of safety for Indigenous peoples, then over time this space came to be understood as operating outside the nation. Indigenous peoples were protected by the government, but not understood as equal members of the national community. Over time, many Indigenous people were given exemptions to the *Protection Acts*. That is, they were allowed to move into the white Australian nation. They were given rights as British subjects or later as Australian citizens. These exemptions came at a price. An Indigenous person given an exemption was not allowed to fraternise with any Indigenous people who were living 'under the Act', other than their immediate family. That is, if an Indigenous person was given the rights of a non-Indigenous citizen, then he or she could only socialise, live and work with the non-Indigenous community. This frequently cut Indigenous people off from their communities. It forced them to make impossible decisions—to gain a basic right (for example, to work where they pleased), they had to give up a vital part of their lives (their extended family). Many Indigenous people refused to take up exemption certificates because they were not willing to make this sacrifice. This often meant that they lived in more difficult economic circumstances.

Paternalistic or protection narratives still operate today. One example is the experiment of ATSIC (the Aboriginal and Torres Strait Islander Commission)—the self-determining Indigenous governance body—which has recently been decommissioned and replaced with a federal government-appointed advisory committee. It was only in the mid-1970s that Indigenous peoples started to hold positions of power within government bureaucracy and to be consulted in decisions about their health, education, cultural and economic needs. Even so, most financial decisions were made by non-Indigenous bureaucrats who, however well intentioned they might have been, were still controlling Indigenous peoples' lives. When ATSIC was established in 1989, a national Indigenous-elected government body controlling its own finances finally existed. ATSIC was closed down in 2004 amidst a range of problems involving both the personal lives of some of the ATSIC representatives and accusations of financial impropriety. Many Indigenous peoples, as well as non-Indigenous people, were disappointed with the problems in ATSIC and considered it required large-scale reform. What is more important for this analysis are not the reasons for the dissolution of ATSIC, but the shift from a democratically elected, self-determining commission for Indigenous peoples to one controlled by non-Indigenous peoples. The new National Indigenous Council is made up of a group of impressive Indigenous people, however, they can only advise the government—they have no legal or governmental power to make and implement decisions. The shift is away from the logic of self-determination and back to protection. Many bureaucracies in Australia suffer small-scale to widespread corruption. For example, a number of state police forces have endured Royal Commissions to deal with systemic problems of this type. Yet the response has not been to close them down or to presume that these institutions are incapable of reform. ATSIC was not seen as being capable of managing a similar process of reform. Instead, the state took over the decision-making.

Assimilation stories

Indigenous people who were given exemption from the *Protection Acts* were imagined as entering the white Australian nation through the process of assimilation. Assimilation is a complex and anxious narrative in the story of non-Indigenous Australian identity. Assimilation stories are the most intimate of exclusion stories. In these stories, paradoxically, Indigeneity or blackness is excluded from the nation by Indigenous peoples being made white. Assimilation was at times a comforting story for non-Indigenous peoples—Indigenous peoples would be assimilated and so disappear into the white community (and thereby offer no contest for the land). It was also an anxious story—did non-Indigenous peoples really want Indigenous peoples in their community and would Indigeneity really disappear (or reappear generations hence—as a 'throwback'—to haunt white people)? Assimilation narratives operate in two ways. Sometimes they are stories of cultural assimilation—that is, exempted Indigenous people will be made white through adopting non-Indigenous cultures. At other times they are stories of biological assimilation— that is, Indigenous peoples will have sexual relationships with (working-class) non-Indigenous peoples, creating generations of lighter and lighter skinned children until Indigeneity is eradicated.

State (and colonial) governments, in tandem with anthropologists and scientists, had complex formulae for calculating grades and possibilities of assimilation. In the mid-period of the twentieth century, this hinged on a presumption that Indigeneity disappeared after three generations of intermarriage between Indigenous and non-Indigenous people. Kim Scott (1999), in his novel *Benang*, responds to this non-Indigenous fixation on biological assimilation. The central character in Scott's novel is a man, who is fair-skinned and Indigenous, growing up in Western Australia. In one scene he reads a section of a government document:

> Breeding Up. In the third or fourth generations no sign of native origin is apparent. The repetition of the boarding school process and careful breeding . . . after two or three generations the advance should be so great that families should be living like the rest of the community (1999: 28).

A central part of the assimilation story depended on the removal of children from their Indigenous families. Scott's reference to 'boarding school' refers to the widespread removal process that operated across all the states and territories. The basic intent of this almost century-long project was to assimilate fair-skinned Indigenous children into white Australia. This story worked in tandem with the 'dying race' and protection narratives. In these stories, those Indigenous people who were old and could not adjust to the new Australia would be protected (kept on reserves) and eventually disappear or die out. Those who were judged as too young to be marked by Indigeneity and capable of what was called uplift were to be assimilated into the white Australian nation. Removing young Indigenous children from their families was part of this process. Children were taken from communities where their life chances were considered minimal and placed in children's homes to be educated and eventually made part of the nation.

In reality, what happened was that children were often removed from loving homes, against their parents' wishes, and moved to institutions where they were maltreated. The education they received was one that equipped them to be domestic servants or farm labourers for white families. A National Inquiry into the Separation of Aboriginal and Torres Strait Islander Children from Their Families was established in May 1995 in response to efforts made by key Indigenous agencies and communities to bring this maltreatment to light. Indigenous peoples were concerned that the general public's ignorance of the history of forcible removal was hindering the recognition of the needs of its victims and their families and the provision of services.

When the National Inquiry report, *Bringing Them Home*, was released (it was tabled in the federal parliament on 26 May 1997), it had a huge impact on the non-Indigenous community. Indigenous communities had been dealing with the fall-out and impact of the practice of child removal and the Inquiry for many years before 1997, because they were part of the process. However, for many non-Indigenous people this was their first exposure to the policies of Indigenous child removal. The sense of shame and guilt was overwhelming for many non-Indigenous Australians. Copies of the 700-page report sold out again and again as non-Indigenous people bought the report to read and so inform themselves about this aspect of their history. It is out of this process that many of the most productive cooperative efforts between Indigenous and non-Indigenous peoples have emerged in the last decade. Some of these will be discussed later in the chapter.

Desire and appropriation

Julie Marcus (1997: 29) defines cultural appropriation as the 'processes by which meanings are transformed within a political hierarchy'. In Australia the colonisers needed to feel connected to the land they claimed as their own—to build a sense of themselves as the ones who not only owned this land but belonged in it. Through the cultural appropriation of a vast range of Indigenous ideas, spaces and arts, it was hoped that this belonging would be achieved (Figure 6.4).

The traditional understanding of belonging and national identity emerging through a long-term association with a space is only available in a limited way for non-Indigenous peoples in Australia. They cannot tell stories about their connections with this space being so ancient they are lost in the mists of time. The date of arrival is known—and it is not that long ago. One way in which this lack of longevity is dealt with is for non-Indigenous peoples to link themselves with this land by connecting their belonging with concepts of Indigeneity. An example of this is the 1940s and 1950s literary group the Jindyworobaks. The Jindyworobak manifesto argued that an authentic Australian voice could be produced through the harnessing of non-Indigenous cultures to Indigenous stories and approaches to life (Gifford 1944). The theory was that non-Indigenous peoples could 'aboriginalise' themselves in order to express their sense of belonging to a place. Heidi Ellemor (2003) provides another example. She cites a case where the non-Indigenous peoples' claims to connection to land in a native title

Figure 6.4 Advertisement for the main resort at Uluru—the company used the idea of 'our' sacred sites to sell the idea of coming to the resort. (*Image courtesy of Voyages*)

hearing mimic quite closely the ways in which Indigenous people express their belonging. Indeed, non-Indigenous peoples even liken their feelings of belonging to those of Indigenous people: 'I suppose you could be like the Aboriginals and say [my attachment to the forest] is spiritual' (Ellemor 2003: 244). The appropriation of Indigenous ideas fills a gap in non-Indigenous ways of understanding feelings of belonging. Further, national companies often use Indigenous motifs to mark themselves as Australian. The flagship jets of the international fleet of Qantas airline are painted with the artworks of Indigenous artists such as Pitjantjatjara woman Rene Kulitja and Balarinji Design Studio. The passion for ochre dots and boomerang shapes also appears in company uniforms, t-shirts and cultural logos. In creating stories of being Australian, Indigenous signs are often used.

The recognition of Indigenous cultures in narratives of the nation does not necessarily mean the full recognition of Indigenous peoples, however. To begin with, often the representations of Indigeneity deployed by non-Indigenous peoples do not come from Indigenous peoples themselves. As Marcia Langton (1993: 34–35) argues: 'Safe, distant, distortions' of Indigenous peoples are 'recycled, retold and represented in conversations between white people. Indigenous peoples appear only as stereotype and icon.' Langton notes that non-Indigenous peoples' understandings of Indigenous peoples are self-referential: 'they do not know and relate to Aboriginal people. They relate to stories told by former colonists' (1933: 33). Langton's argument is that Indigenous peoples are represented by non-Indigenous peoples in non-Indigenous terms and for non-Indigenous ends. She argues that this is best illustrated by:

> the appropriation of all things Aboriginal, sacred and profane as a form of cultural wallpaper decorating the back stage. Sacred dreaming designs have become the Olympic Games logo . . . and the sacred didjeridu sound is on in-flight entertainments (Sculthorpe 2001: 73).

The aspects of Indigenous cultures that suit non-Indigenous people are often taken without full consultation or care for the impact on Indigenous peoples.

Authenticity

As Langton suggests, non-Indigenous peoples' desire for Indigeneity is shaped by their own needs. This means Indigeneity is often structured in terms of a binary: 'authentic' and 'inauthentic' Indigenous peoples. In this binary, authentic Indigenous peoples are those living in remote areas—living lives, as Langton suggests above, equating with non-Indigenous stereotypes of Indigeneity. These include eating bush tucker, having dark skin, speaking an Indigenous language and maintaining an intimate and extensive knowledge of the Dreaming that is enacted through ceremony. These perceived authentic Indigenous persons are contrasted with Indigenous peoples who are understood as not authentic—or, as it is sometimes put colloquially, not real. These Indigenous peoples are not regarded by non-Indigenous peoples as real because they have fair skin, are wealthy, live urban lives or simply seem to be like most non-Indigenous people. For example, an Indigenous person who has moved to Perth from their country, gone to university and works as a commercial lawyer might be represented as a not-real Indigenous person in non-Indigenous stories of Australian-ness. They are seen as distanced from so-called real Indigenous culture because of their perceived failure to fulfil non-Indigenous people's fantasies about what Indigeneity is.

This dichotomy of real and not real is deployed to control which aspects of Indigenous cultures are allowed into the national story. For example, well-known Tasmanian Aboriginal activist Michael Mansell is often delegitimised as both a representative of Aboriginal Tasmanians and as an Indigenous person by reference to his blue eyes and fair skin. He is represented as not a real Indigenous person, but as an urban troublemaker, and contrasted with a supposedly real or authentic Indigenous person. When Mansell makes demands about how Indigenous peoples should be treated (for example, that they should be able to have their own government), he is contrasted with a non-Indigenous fantasy of authentic Indigeneity: a person who would never inconvenience non-Indigenous Australians with claims of sovereignty and rights. Of course, the beauty of this system is that any Indigenous person who is seen as rocking the boat can be marked as not authentic and their position undermined. There are, of course, significant variations between Indigenous peoples, and Indigenous peoples have discussions between themselves about the implications of these differences. Indigenous peoples must deal with these models of themselves as 'real' or not, and not surprisingly it has affected some Indigenous people's identity. For example, a lighter skinned Indigenous person may at some time wish for darker skin or wonder about who they are as an Indigenous person.

Inner-city areas dominated by Indigenous peoples, such as Redfern in Sydney, are key spaces where this binary works to reinforce a particular story of being Australian. The Block in Redfern is an area of Indigenous-owned housing and the Indigenous majority population has lived in the area for decades. Yet, as Ceridwen Spark notes, the 'inhabitants are frequently seen to represent absolute displacement' (2003: 33). By using the logic that authentic Indigenous peoples live in remote areas and non-authentic ones in urban areas, the Indigenous residents of The Block, who are living in their self-owned properties, can be represented as being in the wrong place. This logic is not meant to imply that the residents of The Block and similar neighbourhoods and communities in Australia are understood as non-Indigenous or as white. It simply suggests that Indigenous peoples have no deep or real connection to the urban spaces they occupy; it suggests they are 'improper inhabitants of domestic and city space' (Spark 1999: 58).

This displacement and dualist strategy—whether it is conscious or not—limits the ways in which Indigenous peoples' complex and dynamic beliefs and community organisations are recognised in, or by, the contemporary state. It restricts how they are included in stories of the nation. For example, in enacting the *Native Title Act*, the parliament made it a condition that Indigenous peoples who claimed land through native title must show an unbroken connection to that land. Not surprisingly, given the impact of colonisation, not many Indigenous communities in eastern Australia can do this. This limits Indigenous communities' legal rights. It also limits the ways in which their connection to country is understood. So real connection only comes from an unbroken physical occupation of one's country—this is not how most Indigenous people understand their relation to their country today. Indigenous peoples may live and work away from their country, but they are still connected to it, and often make sense of who they are via that relationship.

Indigenous cultures as unchanging

Earlier in this chapter, the image of the thundering train and the overwhelmed Indigenous man was used to illustrate one way Indigenous peoples are imagined in Australia. In this story, change and progress are understood as associated with non-Indigenous cultures, whereas Indigenous cultures are represented as fixed. Non-Indigenous cultures are understood to embrace new technologies and use them to build railways connecting the east coast with the west. By contrast, Indigenous cultures are presumed to be fixed in what is often seen as a primitive mode. This notion of fixity often makes Indigenous cultures attractive to non-Indigenous peoples. What non-Indigenous peoples desire in this story of fixed Indigeneity is a sense that they can, through their communion with Indigenous peoples, access a primal and primitive truth lost to them as a result of their modern lives. Many new-age discourses are premised on this idea of returning to a simpler or more authentic life via Indigenous cultures. What is often unacknowledged is the level of fantasy and projection on the part of non-Indigenous peoples in this story and the costs of such stories for Indigenous peoples.

Fixed and caught outside time is not how Indigenous peoples see themselves, their cultures or their communities. For example, Mary Magulagi Yarmirr (1997), from West Arnhem, expresses her understanding of Indigenous peoples' relationships to land:

> we had our legislation long before it was put upon us by the coming of the white man's interpretations of our land (foreign law) . . . this was reflected in our names, our kinship ties, our languages, ceremonies, stories, dance (1997: 80).

Yarmirr sees foreign laws as being 'put upon' Indigenous peoples, and frames the relationship her people have to the land as ongoing. However, she recognises the need for Indigenous peoples to take 'their traditional lifestyle a step further [and fight] for recognition and [fight] for their country to make the wider community aware that there is and always has been a law that controls the land and its people as one' (1997: 83). This is not a community or culture which is ossified and unable to change.

For many Indigenous people, their relationship to their country and community is framed slightly differently from that expressed by Yarmirr. Change is at the centre of their experiences of everyday life—child removal, *Protection Acts*, seeking work. For many of these Indigenous people, a central part of their life is the process of coming to know a community and place from which they have been distanced. Jeanie Bell (1997) describes this feeling in her book about her aunt, *Talking About Celia*: 'I feel very strongly about this country, Yuggera country, and in recent years I have renewed my traditional connections to this land' (1997: 100). Bell has both Indigenous and non-Indigenous heritage, and lived in Brisbane as part of a large and active Murri family and community. Throughout her life, she had strong social and political connections with Indigenous civil rights activists and struggles. Bell understands herself as a politically active, urban-dwelling Murri. Her Indigeneity did not only come through an everyday proximity to her country. However, she still wanted to renew a particular type of connection to country through her Aboriginal grandfather.

For many Indigenous peoples, this reconnection is difficult. Koori poet Anita Heiss (1998: 12) expresses this in her poem 'Deprived of Culture':

> She's uptown, lives like a gub
> Yeah, talks like a whitefella too.
> Grew up in the city.
> Father's white, yeah
> Mother's deadly, she's black.
> But her, she's a textbook blackfella.
>
> Get off her case, it's not her fault,
> She's been deprived of her culture!

Heiss' piece expresses the difficulties experienced by Indigenous people who have been distanced from their culture. One of the voices in the poem chides to the other one when she refers to a women as a 'textbook blackfella'—someone who gains their knowledge of Indigeneity through reading, not being. The final voice firmly asserts the deprivation this distancing causes and asks what caused this deprivation. There are conversations going on within Indigenous communities about the various ways Indigenous people experience colonialism and how this affects the way they live as Indigenous people. As Juanita Sherwood (1999: 6) puts it:

> We are a diverse nation. Until two hundred and ten years ago we managed diversity and community need in an extremely effective manner. Our subsequent experiences of invasion, dispossession and colonisation are equally diverse. Solutions to the problems arising from colonisation will also be diverse and need to be acknowledged as such.

Sherwood makes clear the complexity of being Indigenous in Australia today, and stresses the need for both non-Indigenous and Indigenous people to grasp this.

As Mary Yarmirr's comments above suggest, the British colonisation of Australia in 1788 introduced a powerful new group of people to this land. The British implemented a wide-ranging system of law, economic, labour and social relations. In the face of this imposed colonial system, Indigenous people have struggled to have their own systems of law and social relations recognised. The struggle for land rights is an example of this fight for the recognition of Indigenous understandings of land ownership within non-Indigenous legal and economic systems. Indigenous peoples have also struggled for justice and equality within the British-based or non-Indigenous system of law, economics and society.

Art

Indigenous art practices are diverse. They obviously vary from artist to artist, but also between different communities. Historically, Indigenous art was a part of the Dreaming. It was often corporeal—painted on the body—and explained the relationship between Indigenous peoples and their ancestors as well to their country (Perkins and Fink 2000: 79). This is still an important part of Indigenous art practices; however, the arrival of non-Indigenous colonisers in 1788 meant that other dimensions have been added to the production of art. As Galarrwuy Yunupingu (1998: 65) explains: 'painting became central to the expression of the conflict between Indigenous and other Australians . . . Our painting has paralleled our political struggles to maintain our culture and our rights to our land.' Art has also been an important part of Indigenous communities maintenance of history and memory in the face of the dislocation brought about by colonialism: 'Many [Indigenous artists] are involved in resurrecting memories and reconstructing experience driven by the need to unearth the truth from the past in order to make sense of the present' (O'Brien 1999: 59).

One of the main roles of art in Indigenous communities is the communication of stories of connection and custodianship over land. Historically this communication process took place through the production of artworks on bodies or impermanent paintings on the earth—ground paintings—undertaken as part of rituals and then obliterated after the ceremony (Brooks 2003/4: 200). As the process of assimilation took hold and more Indigenous peoples were moved from their country to reserves the production of art took on another dimension. Eric Michaels (1987: 139) explains this process for the artists of the Indigenous community Yuendumu in the Western Desert. He argues these artists were, by the very act of painting, 'describing their responsibility to "care for"' places they could no longer easily access. However, this painting of country and custodianship from a distance does not mean there is an estrangement from country. Ngarralja Tommy May, an artist from the Kimberley region, explains: 'our painting, our country, our *ngurrara* [country]. They are all the same thing' (Anker 2005: 92). Paintings do not simply represent a part of the Dreaming, they are the Dreaming: 'the painting is not a picture of land or evidence for land but the country itself' (Jorgensen 2004: 113).

Indigenous artworks are sometimes also claims to land. When Arrente artist Albert Namatjira undertook his world-famous water-colour paintings in the 1930s he was seen by most non-Indigenous people as working in a medium alien to Indigenous peoples, yet he was claiming his country. His paintings were of his country. In painting their country Indigenous artists are expressing their connection with this land. This claim to connection has taken on new meaning in the era of native title. Ngarralja Tommy May, one of a group of artists from the Walmajarri, Wangkajunga, Mangala and Juwaliny communities in the Kimberley, when asked to provide a map of the territory they were claiming in a native title claim, painted his country. Each artist painted the section 'represent[ing] their own areas of responsibility on the land and in lore [then] each witness stood on their respective portion of the canvas and recounted their stories associated with it' (Anker 2005: 91–92).

In the early to late twentieth century much Indigenous art production has taken place in circumstances shaped by colonisation. The Carrolup artists of Western Australia were a group of young Indigenous people living in a reserve in the 1940s. Under the tutelage of their non-Indigenous teacher they took up painting. Many of their works were undertaken as a way of 'maintaining continuity with the old' (O'Brien 1999: 57). As with other artistic works from this period the artists were often representing something that had not been expe-rienced first-hand—Revel Cooper's *Imagined Corroborree* (1948) for example. As Philippa O'Brien (1999: 57) puts it:

> Many of the artists . . . have adopted some specific strategy to deal with the dislocated world in which they find themselves . . . Just as many Aboriginal people comb through government records to recon-struct their family histories and locate lost relatives [some artists use] visual records to reconstitute experience.

The experience of the Western Desert artists of Papunya Tula can also be understood in terms of a response to dislocation. The community of Papunya Tula was made up of a number of different Indigenous communities and language groups who were 'rounded up' and brought in from their desert camps by the Northern Territory Welfare officers as part of the assimilation drive of the post-World War II period (Perkins and Fink 2000: 76). In the 1970s the local school teacher Geoffrey Bardon described the community as 'a quiet desperate place of emotional loss and waste with an air of casual and dreadful cruelty' (cited in Perkins and Fink 2000: 76). Bardon attempted to encourage school children to paint the Indigenous images he had seen drawn in the sand. The children showed little interest, but the older men took the opportunity to paint and the art of the Papunya Tula artists is now world-renowned. Indigenous art from the Kimberley region has similar origins—the community around Fitzroy Crossing is made up of various communities and language groups who moved to the area after the equal pay decisions of the 1960s saw Indigenous stock workers sacked and asked to leave properties. The art communities gained a similar international reputation in the late 1980s: Rover Thomas perhaps the most well-known of the group. For many Indigenous artists in northern and central Australia painting was a 'way to make *wangarr,* or shadow images, of what was now gone, and thus restore *mangi'*, the spiritual and physical trace of a person (Brooks 2003/4: 203).

If Indigenous artists' interest in painting was about the assertion of connection and a continuation of belonging, then what explains non-Indigenous people's interest in this art. Marcia Langton (2000: 12 &16) suggests:

> The fascination with Aboriginal visual representations of landscape in the last twenty years surely reflects a desire for a homeland and a sense of loss and shame at the fate of so many Aboriginal societies . . . For the settler Australian audience, caught ambiguously between old and new land, their appreciation of this embodies at least a striving for the kind of citizenship that republicans wanted: to belong to this place rather than another.

Yet this desire to belong and the idea that this can be achieved through Indigenous art sometimes slips into appropriation. Indigenous art has often been used as a way of attaching non-Indigenous people to the land. Artist Margaret Preston's use of Indigenous iconography in the 1920s and 1930s was explicitly about a desire to belong (McLean 1998: 289). However, as Jennifer Isaacs (1999) points out what often marked these 'genuine' attempts to incorporate Indigenous themes into national art was:

> the view that Aboriginal designs were like a set of ingredients to be remixed by the hand of a master chef. This remixing constituted the *art* as such with the indigenous originators providing inspiration through a 'primitive' vitality of themes, colour and style suitable for a national image (Isaacs 1999: 68).

This appropriation of Indigenous art sometimes led to the use of sacred motifs in public art (Isaacs 1999: 71). It usually also involved a failure to recognise Indigenous artists' claims to ownership of the images and their rights to these as intellectual property.

Not all Indigenous art has marketability as 'genuine' Indigenous art. What is generally recognised as Indigenous art is usually confined to the art of so called traditional or remote communities—the very famous dot paintings. It is this artwork that circulates in the global art world and gallery scene as 'Aboriginal Art'. However, as Murri artist Richard Bell says:

> I don't do Aboriginal art! When I make art I'm talking about the politics of this country; and I'm talking about it from an Aboriginal perspective. I want to be recognised as an Aboriginal artist, but I don't want to be forced into doing 'Aboriginal art'—whatever people feel that is (Hoffie 2003: 48).

Bell is responding to suggestions that as an Aboriginal artist he should create a particular type of art—'Aboriginal art'—but also to the claim that other types of art undertaken by Indigenous people are not really—authentic—Indigenous art. Bell suggests that many galleries and curators still work on the assumption that 'the "real blackfellas" don't live in the city' (Hoffie 2003: 46).

Urban Indigenous artists are often members of the Indigenous communities that have 'been through the hardest part of the British colonisation' process (Mundine 2005: 22). Influenced by non-Indigenous art styles their work often engages with the history of Indigenous/non-Indigenous relations in Australia. One of the catalysts for a flourishing in urban Indigenous arts was the bicentenary in 1988. Many Indigenous people used art—especially photography—to challenge the celebration of 200 years of colonisation (Gellatly 1999: 8). Key Exhibitions such as *Inside Black Australia* and *After 200 Years* exposed the ongoing poverty and racism that many Indigenous people still dealt with. However, as Kelly Gellatly (1999: 9) points out the relentless 'creation and perpetuation of negative images of Aboriginal people' was a problem for Indigenous artists. There was a desire to engage with history but also to present the diversity of Indigenous life. In the 1980s a group of Indigenous urban artists got together to form an arts co-operative—Boomali. The artists associated with this co-operative—the most well-known is perhaps Tracey Moffatt—used a variety of styles and produced stunning but very different types of art. What drew them together was their belief that:

the social inequities and unsympathetic Representation of Aboriginal and Torres Strait Islander culture by non Aboriginal and Torres Strait Islander artists and curators throughout Australian history is one of the driving forces for the desire of Aboriginal and Torres Strait Islander artists representing themselves and their own artistic perspective (Boomalli).

These artists, and dozens more in the decades that followed, produced works that engaged with the history of colonisation in myriad ways. Artist Gordon Bennett's early work explored the ways in which Indigenous peoples were 'caught' in Western systems of representation (Bennett 1996: 36). His works also explored issues of identity—how he came to understand who he was through his 'own day-to-day experience of living in Australia' (Coslovich 2004). Bennett's painting *Self Portrait (But I Always Wanted to be One of the Good Guys)* explored growing up in a community tinged with racism where being good was often associated with being white (see Figure 6.5). Indigenous peoples' art also engages with issues within Indigenous communities. For example Maningrida artist Les Midikuria's 1998 work *Petrol Sniffers* deals with the devastating impact of petrol sniffing in remote Indigenous communities (Andrew 2001: 22). Destiny Deacon's 1997 art show 'No Fixed Dress' engages with representations

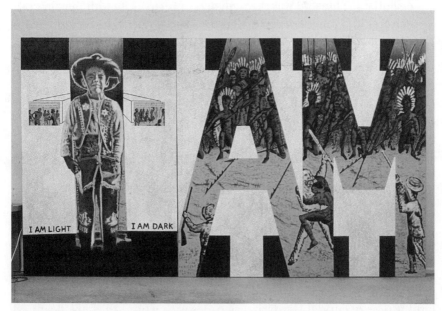

Figure 6.5 Gordon Bennett's *Self Portrait (But I Always Wanted to be one of the Good Guys.* (*Image courtesy of the artist*)

and stereotypes of Indigenous women both within and outside
Indigenous communities (Langton 1998: 102). Koori artist Lin Onus's
work references discussion and interaction between different
Indigenous communities. In the mid 1980s Onus spent time with the
Gamerdi community in Maningrida in Arnhem Land and his later
works use the crosshatching *rrark* technique in his photo-realist
paintings of the land. As Jennifer Isaacs (1992: 25) puts it, this use of
rrark is 'an immediate allusion to the presence of Aboriginal spirituality in every natural place'.

Self-determination

As the art and literature of Indigenous peoples suggests there has
been a strand of Indigenous story-making countering non-Indigenous
narratives. These are stories of self-determination. What underpins
these stories is the Dreaming. The Dreaming is the dynamic and
comprehensive story of Indigeneity chronicling the peopling of this
continent. More than this, the Dreaming orders Indigenous peoples'
worlds:

> The Dreaming explains our creation and the deep and connected
> relationships between the land and all the living creatures of this
> country. Our Mother is the earth who provides us with the nutrients
> essential for life and it is through acts of reciprocity with her that our
> cultures and the lores that govern our social norms and relationships
> develop (Sherwood (1999: 5).

Different Indigenous peoples access the Dreaming in different ways.
For some, the stories are still passed from elders to other community
members as part of everyday life and ritual. For other Indigenous
peoples, finding out about their Dreaming entails reading texts
where stories they have not heard first-hand are recorded.

The Dreaming not only provides a framework for Indigenous
peoples' lives, but the very logic of their claim for sovereignty. As well-
known Yolngu activist Galarrwuy Yunupingu (1997: 3) puts it:

> We believe the land is all life. So it comes to us that we are part of the
> land and the land is part of us. It cannot be one or the other. We
> cannot be separated by anything or anybody.

Indigenous peoples have never shifted from an understanding of
their status as first peoples. They do, however, recognise that their
land is now occupied by myriad peoples with whom they are destined
to share the space. The framing of Indigenous self-determination

stories also involves seeking justice using the logic of non-Indigenous stories of law, rights and equality. More than this, Indigenous peoples are creating narratives in relation to other groups in Australia who have also been the subject of racism. Not all stories comprise a dialogue between the dominant non-Indigenous group—Anglo–Australians—and Indigenous peoples. Conversations also take place with other peoples who have been excluded from the dominant story of being Australian (Stephenson 2003).

Indigenous peoples' fight for justice in the non-Indigenous system included campaigns for citizenship, the right to vote and equal access to the law. They have also campaigned for an end to racism—for example, a demand for equal access to public spaces in Australia. They have demanded all the freedoms non-Indigenous people have—the freedom to travel, to enter semi-public spaces (hotels, clubs), to live where they choose, to marry whom they wish, to work when and where they want. Many of these demands seem like such basic rights it may seem unimaginable that Indigenous peoples did not have them. But Indigenous peoples have had to fight for every single one of them.

From the mid nineteenth century, Indigenous people wrote letters and petitions to the various governments, to newspapers—even to the British government and the Kings and Queens of England—protesting the injustice of their treatment. For example, the following letter was written in 1882 to the Melbourne newspaper the *Argus*, from a group of Koori people led by William Barak, from the Coranderrk reserve in Victoria. They are protesting at the increasing controls put on their lives:

> Sir— ... we have heard that there is going to be very strict rules on the station and more rules will be too much for us, it seems we are all going to be treated like slaves ... we wish to ask those Managor [*sic*] of the station Did we steal anything out of the colony or murdered anyone or are we prisoners or convict. We should think we are all free ... (Attwood and Markus 1999: 49)

Indigenous peoples continued to contest the unjust treatment they received on the state- or church-controlled reserves, missions and stations well into the mid twentieth century. They used the non-Indigenous narrative of equality to challenge their slave-like treatment. Another reform group set up in the 1930s—the Aborigines Progressive Association—protested about economic discrimination, poor conditions on the reserves and forced movements of Indigenous people using the same approach of equality (Goodall 1995: 87).

In 1965, a group of students from Sydney University, inspired by the freedom rides in the United States, went on a freedom ride through western New South Wales (Curthoys 2002). Their hope was to challenge the racism of the non-Indigenous communities. Charles Perkins, one of the Indigenous people on the ride, explained an objective of the ride:

> to integrate certain theatres, swimming pools etc. which discriminate against Aboriginal people. The tactics will follow the pattern set by the Rev. Martin Luther King. It is passive non-violent action . . . We do not intend to create confusion or disturbances that will lead to violent action. We merely wish to stimulate both Aboriginal and European towns-people into doing something practical themselves about the situation (Attwood and Markus 1999: 81).

Drawing on global stories of equal rights and decolonisation, Perkins and his fellow riders sought to challenge an informal system of apartheid that existed in Australia. Perkins made explicit links between his project and the Black civil rights movement in the United States. These transnational links have only strengthened over time. Indigenous peoples in Australia are now part of a global network of Indigenous peoples from all continents. As part of this global group, they work within and in cooperation with international bodies such as the United Nations to develop protocols and declarations to improve the status and treatment of Indigenous peoples worldwide.

Land rights

This chapter began with a reference to the fact that land was at the heart of Indigenous peoples' claims for justice, and at the heart of non-Indigenous peoples' need to ignore these calls. Land rights has been a central political issue since the mid 1960s when, in the face of new victories in civil rights, Indigenous peoples were better equipped to take on state and federal governments in their claims to have their rights to land recognised. The types of claims made by the various Indigenous communities differ. As with all large communities, Indigenous peoples do not all have the same wishes. However, since the 1970s, a pan-Indigenous movement has demanded a suite of basic rights in terms of land.

One of the first significant changes in terms of land rights was the *Northern Territory Land Rights Act* 1975. The result of this Act was that a range of Indigenous communities in the Northern Territory were granted title over their land. The federal Labor government then started to discuss with the state governments the possibility of national land rights legislation. (The federal government could only make law for the Northern Territory and the Australian Capital Territory.) However, as the land occupied by Indigenous peoples came to be seen as a more and more valuable asset—for example, no longer just outback space for cattle, but a mineral-rich plain—the states refused. Indigenous campaigns continued but by the time another Labor government came to power in the 1980s, it was unable to offer land rights and instead offered the lesser prize of a treaty. A treaty would in some ways have recognised Indigenous peoples' sovereignty—that is, their status as equal but different occupiers of the land in concert or opposition to the non-Indigenous government, state and nation. Again, this plan was stymied. By 1988, the bicentenary of British colonisation, a *Makarrata*—a Yolgnu word meaning 'the end of a dispute and the resumption of normal relations'—was being offered but has not yet been enacted.

These backdowns by the federal and state governments did not stop Indigenous peoples fighting for their land. The most influential case was perhaps that of Edward Koiki Mabo, who undertook a long battle with the Queensland government to prove his people—the Meriam people of the island of Mer in the Torres Strait—had title to their land and had never ceded this to the British. In 1992, the High Court found in favour of Eddie Mabo and the era of native title began. In the light of the High Court's *Mabo* ruling, the federal government quickly passed legislation both supporting and limiting the impact of the ruling. The court ruling found the original and continuing understanding of Australia as *terra nullius* could be challenged. This meant there were grounds for Indigenous peoples to claim their land had wrongly been taken from them and to argue they should have it back or be compensated. To limit this happening, the legislation included clauses reducing the chances of Indigenous peoples successfully claiming their land as Eddie Mabo had done.

In the weeks and months that followed the *Mabo* decision, there was hysteria amongst some non-Indigenous people about the likelihood of Indigenous people taking the backyards of innocent Australian suburbanites. (This is discussed in more detail in chapter 11.) In fact, the High Court ruling always had limited applicability, and the legislation further minimised its reach. More than this, there was no call from Indigenous peoples for backyards to be surrendered to them. Rather, there was a call for non-Indigenous peoples to consider the injustice of the land grab of the past, and to think about how this injustice could be rectified in ways that made it possible for the two groups to live together in a system that was equal, rather than in a relationship that was premised on one group's dispossession. Many non-Indigenous peoples argue that they did not personally take Indigenous peoples' land, so to visit the guilt of dispossession upon them is unfair. They argue that they are innocent and so should not be punished for the actions of earlier generations of non-Indigenous peoples. However, though no non-Indigenous people today personally took Indigenous peoples' land, they still benefit from this historic injustice and Indigenous peoples still suffer as a result.

How are non-Indigenous peoples to right past wrongs? How are Indigenous peoples to live if the life-source of their cultures (their country) is not open to them? At the moment, non-Indigenous peoples get the good feelings of being attached to what they value in Indigenous cultures—the spirituality of the Dreaming, the association with a vibrant and world-renowned art movement, the glory of Indigenous athletes performing overseas, the generosity of Indigenous peoples in reaching out to them in the reconciliation process—without having to give much themselves. What are non-Indigenous peoples going to give or give up in the renegotiation of relations between the two groups?

FURTHER READING

Behrendt, Larissa 2003, *Achieving Social Justice: Indigenous Rights and Australia's Future*, Federation Press, Sydney.

Cowlishaw, Gillian 2004, *Blackfellas, Whitefellas and the Hidden Injuries of Race*, Blackwell, Malden.

Curthoys, Ann 2002, *Freedom Ride*, Allen & Unwin, Sydney.

Haebich, Anna 2000, *Broken Circles: Fragmenting Indigenous Families 1800–2000*, Fremantle Arts Centre Press, Fremantle.

Heiss, Anita 1998, *Token Koori*, Curringa Communications, Sydney.

Moreton-Robinson, Aileen 2000, *Talkin' Up to the White Woman: Aboriginal Women and Feminism*, University of Queensland Press, Brisbane.

——(ed.) 2004, *Whitening Race: Essays in Social and Cultural Criticism*, Aboriginal Studies Press, Canberra.

Mudrooroo 1995, *Us Mob: History, Culture, Struggle—An Introduction to Indigenous Australia*, Angus & Robertson, Sydney.

Neill, Rosemary 2002, *White Out: How Politics is Killing Black Australia*, Allen & Unwin, Sydney.

Purcell, Leah 2004, *Black Chicks Talking*, Hodder, Sydney.

Tickner, Robert 2001, *Taking a Stand: Land Rights to Reconciliation*, Allen & Unwin, Sydney.

Part 2
WAYS OF BEING AUSTRALIAN

7

THE CULTURAL NATION

Art, cinema and music

MOST NATIONS USE the arts to tell national stories. All countries have national anthems—formal songs where national values and virtues are put to music. Sometimes a love of nation inspires artists, writers and musicians in their work—the expatriate Australian musician Peter Allen famously sang 'I Still Call Australia Home'. The meanings of being Australian have frequently been expressed in such songs, symphonies, poetry, novels, operas, musicals, films and paintings. In fact, these cultural texts often explicitly aim to introduce people to stories of the nation. They seek to instruct and encourage feelings of Australian-ness. The arts also reproduce and reinforce ideas of what Australia is. In so many Australian people's heads there are scraps of these stories—the phrase 'I love a sunburnt country' is mixed up with an image of a painting of a bloke shearing a ram, and this sits next to a memory of a teacher reciting a Banjo Paterson verse or a crowd at a sports match roaring 'Waltzing Matilda'.

This chapter focuses on how art, cinema and music come to be understood as being Australian or national. It is quite common to hear people talk about Australian films, Australian music, Australian literature or Australian art. What qualifies as an Australian artistic product? *The Matrix* trilogy (1999, 2003, 2003) was filmed in Australia—on local studio sets and along the streets of Sydney—but not many people think of it as Australian. Baz Lurhmann's film *Moulin Rouge* (2001) was also filmed in Australia. It had an Australian director, an Australian costume designer and an Australian star. It resonates a little more strongly as Australian than *The Matrix*. However, a film such as *Wolf Creek* (2005), which has Australian producers and technicians, and a well-known Australian actor, and draws on Australian horror myths and the archetypal Australian outback for its setting, is understood as totally Australian. What defines a cultural product as Australian? More importantly, what purpose do artistic endeavours marked as Australian serve in the national stories? This chapter explores these questions, but also explores what use these products are put to in making or remaking national stories. In thinking about these questions, the focus is on painting, film and music in three different eras. The section on painting focuses on the art of the Heidelberg School, a group of artists working in the decades before Federation. Film is explored in the 1970s—a period often referred to as the renaissance of Australian cinema. And for music the emphasis will be on a more contemporary moment.

Painting a nation: The Heidelberg School

From the moment the British First Fleet arrived in Australia in 1788, people began drawing and painting the new place. Though they may not have come to Australia because of their artistic talents, these artists, draughtsmen and painters were interested in capturing their novel environment. This ongoing interest in art meant that, by the 1830s, the colony was broad and sophisticated enough to support professional artists (Sayers 2001: 34). The stories told in these colonial paintings are diverse. However, a common way in which art historians classified the varied body of work produced in the first 100 years of colonisation was to divide it into two types: works harking back to Europe and its heritage and artworks that idealised the new land. The group of painters associated most strongly with the shift from the so-called European style towards a focus on the local Australian style is known as the Heidelberg School of painters.

The Heidelberg School, a group of men who were painting in the 1880s and 1890s, was made up of Tom Roberts, Arthur Streeton, Frederick McCubbin and Charles Conder. The group was so-named because the artists would leave their city/suburban life and camp out in the area of Eaglemont and Heidelberg in Victoria to paint. In time, the Heidelberg artists went their separate ways. Charles Conder left for Europe and lived in Paris, painting amongst the bohemian artists of the city. Tom Roberts and Arthur Streeton moved even further out from the city to paint the 'real' Australia— as Roberts said, he wanted to move away from 'the suburban bush and paint the national life of Australia' (Clark 1985: 128); Streeton wrote in 1892: 'I'm not a bit tired of Australia . . . I want to stay here, but not in Melbourne . . . I intend to go straight inland (away from polite society) . . . and try and translate some of the great hidden poetry that I know is here.' (Clark 1985: 128). The collective works of this group of artists have metaphorically been pulled together over the years and circulated as the quintessential Australian artworks.

Obviously the Heidelberg School style of art did not emerge out of nowhere. Much art from the earlier nineteenth century also celebrated or drew on aspects of Australian cultural life. Many Australian artists trained overseas, and travelled between Australia and Europe; many were born overseas. So, not surprisingly, the art of the Heidelberg School painters also has quite visible links to European art traditions and movements. Some of the obvious influences on the Heidelberg School are plein-air, impressionism, sentimentality (Victorian painting) and narrative painting. However, these transnational influences did not stop the creation of a powerful story about the Heidelberg School inventing a unique Australian art style.

The Heidelberg School is often represented as reflecting the coming of age of Australian art. Indeed, it is sometimes even suggested that the members were the first decent painters of Australia. Earlier painters were not said to be unskilled; rather, their failed efforts to paint the country as it really was are attributed to their lack of understanding of the land, the light and the space. With the Heidelberg School, Australian art is represented as finally being undertaken by people who loved the land. These 'native' painters are said to have painted from the heart, and their national-ism enabled them to really see and transmit the essence of Australian-ness.

The Heidelberg School painters worked in an atmosphere of increasing nationalism. In the 1880s, the movement for the federation of the individual British colonies into an independent state was underway (and soon achieved). As a result, an increasing number of people were searching for and creating stories to describe this new soon-to-be nation. The Heidelberg School brought this nationalist agenda to their painting, and their paintings were viewed in terms of it. As Allen (1997) explains:

For the first time the dry land, the harsh glare, the scrawny trees appear beautiful not because painters had finally solved the technical problem of representing them but because they had discovered the historical and political vision which made it possible to build a home among them (1997: 58).

The Heidelberg artists were not just painting a land that they were familiar with, but a land they imagined and represented as their nation. This group of painters had different styles and approaches, but as a rule their work tended to portray bush life rather than city life. They often focused on men at work in the bush. They painted scenes of pioneer life—building houses and fences—and bush industry—droving, shearing and farming. This was their story of the nation.

Similarly, those who viewed (and bought) the paintings did not simply take pleasure in the technical skills of the painters in rendering a gum tree accurately. Consumers were drawn to the images because they were (becoming) familiar to them as markers of Australian-ness. The painting and buying of the Heidelberg artists' canvases, with their images of the eucalypt bush peopled with heroic pioneers, hard workers, and scenes of commitment in the face of loss, were producing the nation. The images and people's interpretations of them helped to create a new story of the new nation, Australia. It is not that a group of artists finally had the sense to paint the real Australia that other artists had somehow missed. Rather, the circulation of these paintings—with their heroic scenes of the bush—helped produce and reinforce a particular story of Australia. The Heidelberg art reproduced a story of the real Australian-ness as located in the bush and dominated by bush men.

The scenes the Heidelberg painters committed to canvas were nostalgic images. They were already remembrances of the past, and the past they reflected related to the lives of a small minority of people. The use of historical and minority images is not unusual in the creation of national stories; however, it is interesting to explore the effect of this. When the Heidelberg School artists produced nostalgic scenes, and audiences consumed them as the real Australia, they knew there was a gap between these representations of Australian national life and their daily lives. Though the stories resonated with them, this did not mean they were their direct experiences. In viewing a Heidelberg School rendition of pioneer bush life, it was often the values represented in the painting that were recognised. The resonance came from the feeling in the viewer that these values fitted with their view of themselves and key ideas about what it meant to be Australian. For colonists, the art created a sense of *being* Australian. Heidelberg School art told new or emerging Australians that being Australian was about hard work and a love of the land. Many viewers recognised a fit between their values and the values represented in the painting—a connection they understood as recognising 'real' Australian-ness.

This nationalist art of the 1880s and 1890s created and reproduced a very specific idea of what it meant to be Australian— exemplified by the life of the bush bloke. Robert Hughes (1970: 59) notes that Tom Roberts and Frederick McCubbin drew on the same set of figures and ideas celebrated by many of the writers of the time: pioneers, bushrangers and shearers, with their 'virtues of mateship, courage adaptability, hard work and resourcefulness'. The Heidelberg painters 'endowed images of Australian life, especially pioneering history, with overtones of heroic grandeur and nobility' (Clark 1985: 128). They consciously created their painting on a grand scale. For example, Tom Roberts' extremely popular and large-scale painting, *Shearing the Rams* (1888–90), draws on many well-known European painting techniques and styles to create an image of heroic masculine labour (see Figure 7.1).

Figure 7.1 *Shearing the Rams* (1888–90) by Tom Roberts draws on many well-known European painting techniques and styles to create an image of heroic masculine labour. (*Tom Roberts born Great Britain in 1856, arrived Australia in 1869, died 1931. Shearing the Rams (1888–90). Oil on canvas on composition board. 122.4 × 183.3 cm. Felton Bequest, 1932, National Gallery of Victoria, Melbourne*)

Women and the family

Though it is generally non-Indigenous men who are represented as pivotal in nationalistic art, women are not totally absent from this genre of artistic representation of Australian-ness. However, the representations of women have different meanings to those of the bush men. Non-Indigenous women's place in national art is secondary to men, but still very important. Women's images secure the heterosexual and familial imperative of Australian colonialism. Men are everywhere in Australian art—by themselves and in all-male groups. Women are often represented either surrounded by family or accompanied by a man (most commonly a husband). Family is an important dimension of stories of nation-building. Often, when women appear in Australian nationalistic art, they signify the patriarchal heterosexual social order that is so important in imagining the new society of Australia. Though homosocial masculine endeavours present such a pleasurable story of Australia, the corollary story of the 'civilised' heterosexual family needs to accompany this narrative. Frederick McCubbin's 1904 triptych *The Pioneer* reproduces this story (see Figure 7.2). The central panel of the triptych presents a heterosexual

Figure 7.2 Frederick McCubbin's three-panelled work illustrates the gendered nature of the pioneering project. (*Frederick McCubbin Australia 1855–1917. The Pioneer 1904 oil on canvas (three panels) 225.0 × 295.7 cm. Felton Bequest, 1906. National Gallery of Victoria, Melbourne*).

couple—the woman holds a baby, suggesting her role as mother; the man sits resting on a log he has felled, his axe next to him, suggesting his key role as labourer in the clearing of the bush that is taking place behind him.

Art and exclusion

The stories of masculine endeavour that are so central to so much nationalist Australian art exclude some people from ideas of being Australian. Work is a central and important motif of the Heidelberg painters' work. The paintings suggest: 'It is through work that we learn to be at home in the new land. It is through work that Australians earn the right to be in the land' (Allen 1997: 81). This visual story of working the land as a quintessential aspect of being Australian subtly excludes those who do not have this type of relationship with the land from exemplary Australian-ness. As argued earlier, a person does not actually have to do the things represented in the artworks to identify with them; however, identification with the values produced in the art of the Heidelberg School was easier for some than others.

The representations of the heroic labour of making Australia in these works is raced and gendered. That is, the stories told by the Heidelberg School privilege non-Indigenous men's endeavours as truly Australian. Indigenous peoples are not understood to have undertaken this type of labour, and so are excluded from the status of true national belonging. Women and later non-white migrants will also never have the same status as Anglo–Australian men—again, because of their absence from the pivotal moment of nation-building that is mythologised in this art. Women in general, Indigenous men and non-British men are understood to be absent from the bush in the mid nineteenth century, the time when Anglo–Australian men are seen to have undertaken the physical labour that made Australia.

These exclusions were never total. As shown above, non-Indigenous women frequently appeared in the art of the Heidelberg School, though they were limited to a few set types: a bourgeois woman strolling on a beach, for example. Similarly, Indigenous peoples were not always excluded—the very early paintings of the land and landscape produced by the British colonisers often included Indigenous people—but these artists desired to capture and represent something they saw as new and exotic. Paintings were produced of Indigenous life—including corroborees and camps—as well as portraits of individual Indigenous people but they tended to draw on two different beliefs about Indigenous people: the discourse of a 'noble savage' and that of the 'wretched of the earth'. The 'noble savage' story imagined the Indigenous peoples of Australia as a culture untouched by the greed, corruption and depravity of the European world. Paintings drawing on this belief tended to represent Indigenous life as a Romantic bucolic existence where people were engaged in a pure and noble community life. The 'wretched of the earth' discourse drew on a negative understanding of Indigenous peoples. They were understood as primitive and unable to exhibit the emotions and feelings of 'civilised peoples'. Images produced by painters influenced by these ideas represent Indigenous peoples as rough and vicious. However, both these approaches to representing Indigenous peoples acknowledged their presence in the land. Whether positive or negative, Indigenous people were shown in the land doing what they do—fishing, hunting, trading, undertaking rituals and socialising.

Non-Indigenous Australians have always grappled with the problem of how to inhabit this continent. This difficulty was not simply about a lack of familiarity or a lack of experience with the place. It was also about the issue of dispossession and the ethical question about whose land this was. Non-Indigenous artists dealt with the same issue in their art (Allen 1997: 123). Whose land were they painting? It is important to note that, in the high moment of nationalistic painting associated with the Heidelberg School, representations of Indigenous peoples almost completely disappeared from canvases. In painting the story of the nation, Indigenous peoples were erased. Whereas the earlier artists had shown Indigenous people as economically productive, these nationalistic artists transferred this economic and cultural connection to the land from Indigenous peoples to non-Indigenous bush men.

Parochialism

In the early twentieth century, the nationalist focus of Australian art began to seem parochial to many artists. There was a desire to develop a more international perspective that acknowledged the many political and social issues of the wider world. The social unrest and economic pain of the depressions of the 1890s and the 1930s, and of World War I and then World War II were huge concerns in the new Australian nation. However, they were also transnational problems shared by other nations. The issues faced in Australia in the post-World War I period are often glossed over today in favour of a nationalist story of glory. However, in 1918 there was no escaping the problems of a nation of maimed men and social divisions that led to tension and unrest. In much of the art of this period, there was a shift away from an emphasis on the individuals in the context of the bush and a move to explore ideas of communities. In this context, a focus on cities made more sense and a global awareness was vital. Connections between the experience of Australians and other peoples were valorised rather than ignored.

Of course, shifts in art are not total. The repertoire of techniques and images of the artists of the 1890s are still available and were taken up by artists over the next century. They were never so dominant again, but they are still there. Max Dupain's photograph *The Sunbaker* (1937) is an example. This iconic image of a broad-shouldered man lying on the beach after a surf in the ocean was immediately popular. It shows a non-Indigenous man at home and at rest in the land. As he lies on the sand, his shoulders are exposed to the sun, which has made his skin dark—made him 'native'. Here the valorisation of the perfect Australian dominating the landscape and making it his home draws on the motifs of the nationalist painters of the late nineteenth century. And again, it is a male and non-Indigenous body filling the landscape.

National literature in the Heidelburg era

A nationalist literary tradition emerged at the same time as the Heidelberg School art movement. The slogan of the literary nationalism of the 1880s, 1890s and the first decade of the twentieth century: 'temper democratic, bias offensively Australian' (Gelder 1998: 10). Literary critic Vance Palmer elaborated on this sentiment in his 1954 analysis of the 1890s. He argued that for the nationalist writers of this period Australian-ness as:

> a way of life should be simple and frugal, centred in the idea of mateship; economically, a gradual increase of collective power; nationally, an exclusion of all elements likely to make trouble and even a keeping of the surrounding seas as free as possible from foreign neighbours. Isolated by geography and their own will, Australians were to construct a society that would be the pattern for free men everywhere (Palmer 1971: 2).

As Ken Gelder explains: 'an Australian literary tradition was constructed out of a confident assertion of difference' (1998: 11).

Australian-ness was about being different; and this meant being different from both Europe and Asia.

In the decades leading up to Federation a group of novelists, journalists, poets, short story writers and cartoonists—now known as the *Bulletin* School in recognition of the journal in which much of their work was published—sought to produce a national spirit. The *Bulletin*—established in 1881, whose famous contributors include Henry Lawson, Joseph Furphy and Banjo Paterson—was explicit in its desire 'to stimulate among Australians a love of their own country for its own sake' (Green 1930: 70–71). These authors wrote in the idiom of Australian bush dwellers: 'Mother, I won't never go drovin' blast me if I do', says Henry Lawson's Australian child at the end of 'The Drover's Wife' (Ackland 1993: 70). For them Australian accents were not a sign of inferiority—of being colonial—but of being at home. Though the work produced by the loose group of *Bulletin* writers was diverse and encompassed many different agenda and ideas, there are themes in common: 'The [*Bulletin*] writer accepts his reader on equal terms, takes for granted interest in and knowledge of Australian bush and city life' (Levis 1971: 55). These writers wrote for an audience who knew Australia and wanted to hear about it. They wrote for readers who self-consciously wanted to be Australian.

As with the Heidelberg School, the *Bulletin* School writers centralised the place of a particular group of Australians—the bushman, the larrikin, and the good mate. Richard Waterhouse (2000) makes the point that, similar to the Heidelberg School, this writing depended on a nostalgia for a disappearing type of Australian man. Further, Linzi Murrie makes the point that it was not particular men that were celebrated but particular forms of masculinity, that is, specific ways of being an Australian man. She also notes the nostalgia the *Bulletin* authors held for this type of bloke reflected the anxiety of these urban writers about their own distance from this type:

> The exemplary masculinity of the bushman . . . [operated] at a more profound level: it functioned as a response to the fears of late nineteenth century manhood, that society was inherently 'feminising', and that the opportunities for expressing masculinity were becoming increasingly limited (Murrie 1998: 71).

The problem for the *Bulletin* School authors was that writing was not a career that resonated with the privileged form of masculinity that they were exalting. They wrote of outdoor men while being trapped in the city. They privileged hard manual labour when they often sat at desks all day. And further, they extolled the virtues of independence and freedom when they were frequently tied to jobs and debt. Yet, the other part of the *Bulletin* equation is the readers. The magazine had a large circulation in the bush and the editors encouraged its readers to be contributors. Anxieties about being Australian men were different for this group of readers—they had other reasons for 'foster[ing] a group myth about the unique qualities of their society' (Walker 1988: 164): a growing sense of this place as familiar and of Australians as being at home in the landscape:

> By the 1880s and 1890s the bush had become a label for both the landscape and a social reality characterised by egalitarianism, collectivisms and 'mateship'. Central to this perception of the bush was the dignity of rural work, the elevation of the bush worker as hero, and the celebration of radical nationalist values which were presumably to be found in their purest form in the bush among bush workers (Walker 1988: 162).

Yet there is also a 'psychic disturbance'. Shirley Walker (1988: 159) argues the repetition of motifs of madness and being lost in the bush that appear in writings throughout the nineteenth century and into the twentieth suggest a 'fear of the vast and unknown bush'.

The *Bulletin* writers were only one of an array of local authors. Their story of being Australian was not the only one. An extremely popular form of literature in Australia throughout the nineteenth century was the romance novel. This type of literature was written at home—Rosa Praed and Rolf Boldrewood—as well as imported from overseas—Rider Haggard and Rudyard Kipling. Many of the *Bulletin* authors sought to challenge the romance novel. Women's romance with its focus on the wealthy classes and 'erotic satisfaction' (Lever 2000: 41) was at odds with the realist focus of the *Bulletin* School. Men's adventure romance was also sniffed at; seen as 'a form of British propaganda' (Lever 2000: 33). In opposition to this form of writing the *Bulletin* authors celebrated Australia as different from a feminine and problematic Britain. They wrote stories about the Australian bush—not European, or even Australian, cities. Egalitarianism and mateship are their politics; and generally their writing is devoid of erotic themes. Though many of their stories included sympathetic portraits of women's lives in the bush—Lawson's 'The Drovers Wife' (1892) and 'Water Them Geraniums' (1901) are good examples—they are not interested in the social issues of the domestic space.

Marilyn Lake (1992) argues that in the production of an Australian national literature in the 1880s and 1890s 'one of the greatest political struggles in Australian history' took place. She contends it was a struggle 'for the control of national culture'. What was being fought over was the form of masculinity that was to represent being Australian—the 'Lone Hand' or 'Domestic Man'. Many of the *Bulletin* writers valorised the Lone Hand as the quintessential way to be an Australian male—a life of freedom, independence and care-free existence as noted above. Lake (1992) argues this form of masculinity had serious consequences for women and families who were dependent on these care-free and independent men. Poverty was an outcome for many families where husbands made a virtue out of being rolling stones. Other writers drew on the model of Domestic Man in their fiction and journalism. Here Australian masculinity was represented in terms of romantic love, the nuclear family and a muscularity that came from taking care of dependants. In time the realist writings of the nationalist *Bulletin* School eclipsed romance fiction as the form of writing understood as Australian literature and the Lone Hand was much more popular as a masculine type in this nationalist literature.

Literature of this period—though not the *Bulletin* School—also concerned itself with a new type of Australian—the 'Australian Girl'. This character appeared most frequently in romance fiction although she also had a life in discussions in newspapers and magazines. The Australian Girl was most frequently understood in relation to English women. This new type was fresh, unpretentious and 'gay as a trout in a stream' (Dalziell 2004: 1). As Marilyn Lake (1992) suggests about the struggle over the control of 'national culture' that centred on forms of masculinity, a similar struggle took place around the Australian Girl. The Australian Girl was the centrepiece of a discussion about whether the new national type—the Australian—would lead to a deterioration or strengthening of the British–Australian race (Dalziell 2004: 5). Allied to the 'New Woman'—the early Western feminists who provided critiques of marriage and supported women's rights to sexual, economic and social equality—the Australian Girl was represented as a figure who both unsettled the white Australian family but was also represented as its salvation. The Australian Girl could, like Miles Franklins' protagonist in *My Brilliant Career* (1901), not marry and so figuratively she challenged the idea of being Australian that centralised heterosexual marriage and children. In romance fiction the sexual freedom of the Australian Girl could unsettle the certainty of white Australia in another way, as the romantic temptation in this fiction was often not the solid and dependable

Australian but a more mysterious and unknown figure (Teo 1999; Elder 2003; Dalziell 2004).

In the 1970s a new interest in Australian cultural production emerged in the publishing world and in university literature courses (and in film as will be discussed later). 'A group of writers who spoke directly to the nation's self-image' were identified as 'Australian Literature' (Gelder 1998: 10). The writers included Henry Lawson, Patrick White, Ray Lawler, Henry Handel Richardson and Miles Franklin. Whereas nineteenth century literature had emphasised the homogeneity of Australian national identity, the literature that was gathered together under the heading 'Aust Lit' in the late twentieth century was understood as Australian in terms of its heterogeneity: 'a pluralistic, multicultural image of this country's writing' (Gelder 1998: 11). What defined Australian literature was no longer its focus on the bush and the bushman but its 'pluralism and diversity' (Gelder 1998: 11). From the 1980s onwards several compendiums were published and these collections 'undo nationalism' by 'making a case for its redundancy in the face of multicultural realities' (Gelder 1998: 12). In this new category there were sub-genres such as women's writing, Indigenous writing, migrant writing, gay and lesbian writing. For example, whereas nationalist and feminist concerns had been seen as anathema in the early twentieth century, by the 1970s the shift from a narrow masculinist idea of Australian-ness saw the recuperation of many authors whose work had disappeared from the Australian canon. However, there are still many questions about what makes a particular novel, poem or short story 'Australian'. The near impossibility of answering the question suggests the constructed nature of the term.

Filming a nation: 1970s cinema

The Australian film industry is one of the oldest in the world. One of the world's first feature (length) films was made in Australia—a 1906 film on the life of a bushranger called *The Story of the Ned Kelly Gang* (Shirley and Adams 1983: 12–19). The medium of film as a form of representing the story of the nation has existed for as long as the Australian state has been in existence. The Australian film industry was quite successful in the 1910s and 1920s, but went into decline soon after. Marek Haltof (1996: 5) suggests that in the middle decades of the twentieth century Australia's only real role in the global film industry was as 'a cheap location for British, American and other foreign films wanting an exotic backdrop for exotic stories'. There were a few glorious exceptions to this rule—in particular Charles Chauvel's films *Jedda* (1955) and *40,000 Horsemen* (1941)—but over the next few decades Australian national stories were not told through cinema even though film has been an important genre for the production of stories of the nation in the last 30 or so years.

The popular motifs in the nationalist art of the 1890s re-emerged with a vengeance in the 1970s when the Australian film industry made a comeback after decades in the doldrums. Images of male achievement, the land and also the story of the masculine bond of mateship were everywhere. The origin of the 1970s film renaissance lay in the early 1960s when a senate committee, known as the Vincent Committee, drew up a series of recommendations for the future development of a national cinema. Though ignored at the time, the recommendations were revived in the late 1960s when both state and federal governments became interested in the project of a national cinema. Governments at this time began to see film as a cultural product (like painting or literature), deserving of the support of governments and their agencies. However, even though Australian governments were enthusiastic about Australian film, they did not have much money to allocate to this particular aspect of cultural production. Given the limited availability of government financial support, films needed to make a profit if the industry was going to survive.

Around the same time as governments began to think about the usefulness of a national cinema as a way of exporting Australian culture, there were changes in the film industry. One important change was the addition of a new 'R'—restricted—classification to the film classification code. Changing social circumstances, in particular the sexual revolution of the late 1960s, meant there was a growing market for films aimed at an adults-only audience. The new rating system was designed to recognise these changes and the R classification extended cinema from simply being an afternoon family activity to an acceptable adults-only event. A third factor that enabled the expansion of the Australian film industry was the opening of new independent cinema venues willing to show smaller local and alternative films (Moran and O'Regan 1989: 89).

The combination of government attention, a general growth in local cultural production and structural changes in the film industry led to a round of new films being made in the early 1970s. In fact, the number of films produced in Australia rose from seventeen in the 1960s to 153 in the 1970s (Haltof 1996: 7). These early 1970s films, called sexed cinema, are known for their 'vulgarity, philistinism and energy' (O'Regan 2004). These slightly wacky, small-budget, humourous sex films matched the new social and industry conditions perfectly. Some of the films—*Alvin Purple* (1973) and *Alvin Purple Rides Again* (1974) in particular—were quite successful and achieved the 'frankly commercial' bottom line seen as the hallmark of a good film by the Vincent Committee.

Although the Vincent Committee imagined a new national cinema as being commercially successful, it had not imagined national cinema focusing on sex and ribald humour. The government had envisaged a national cinema that would show the country to the world and show Australians an image of themselves of which they could be proud. This was not meant to be filled with boors and drunks. The state's idea of a national cinema was one comprised of 'quality' films which could be the cultural flagships of the nation (Turner 1989: 103). Not surprisingly, as the federal and state governments developed better and more generous funding schemes and bodies for film—including the establishment of an Australian Film Commission (AFC)—the films they sponsored in this period were not the ribald sex comedies of a maverick group of local comedians but rather the type of film that could be a:

> more worthy bearer of the nation's pride: the visually stylish, low key, highly aestheticised period dramas which offered the visually exotic of the Australian landscape. [In these films] Australia was caught in the amber of its history, its present credentials implied by the style and sensibility of its filmic representation of the past (Turner 1989: 203).

In these films, such as the breakthrough *Picnic at Hanging Rock* (1975) and *Sunday Too Far Away* (1975)—which played at Cannes—the new emphasis on national myths of mateship and the bush come to the fore. These films contrast strikingly with those made in the years just before the AFC, with their contemporary setting and stories about ockers, nudity, sexual innuendo and lavatory humour.

The Australian Film Commission

The AFC, set up in September 1974, was the body designated to encourage the production of quality national films. It was imagined as a 'manufacturer of cultural products for export' (Williams 1996: 44). As Ina Bertrand notes, the idea of a national cinema was not to recreate an accurate history or narrative about Australia, but to create a sense of Australian-ness:

> Truth is not an issue here. As a nation we can live without truth: perhaps we prefer not to know if the truth is unpleasant or, even worse, boring. But we cannot continue to exist without a sense of self, identity, in this case 'Australian-ness' (1984: 181).

This idea is reinforced by Phillip Adams, who around the same time wrote: 'We got into this industry for one reason: to give ourselves a national voice, to give ourselves a sense of national purpose and a national identity' (1984: 71). As with the art world discussed earlier, national cinema was seen as a place where ideas of what it meant to be Australian could be produced and consumed by Australians.

The films associated with this period, known as the Australian New Wave, include *Picnic at Hanging Rock* (1975), *Caddie* (1976), *The Getting of Wisdom* (1977), *My Brilliant Career* (1979), *Breaker Morant* (1980) and *Gallipoli* (1981). Dermody and Jacka (1988) refer to this group as films influenced by what they call the 'AFC genre'. The AFC genre involves:

> [cinematography] dedicated to the glory of Australian light, landform and vegetation, often with clear traces of a romantic, even charm-school, Australian post-impressionism. The approach of the camera is ... [to give] brief, rapturous play to cinematography's recognition of what is our own. This includes not only distinctly beautiful place, but space, history and cultural tradition (1988: 33–34).

Deane Williams suggests that the dominance of landscape images in films of the 1970s and early 1980s 'can be linked to a re-emergent nationalism at the time ... when landscape was seen as a delimited, manageable source of "Australian-ness"' (Williams 1996: 7). As Graeme Turner (1993) notes, this revival of nationalism drew explicitly on earlier nationalist forms of cultural production. He cites the cinematographer for *Picnic at Hanging Rock* as saying he drew on Tom Roberts for his inspiration for the lighting in this film. Similarly, producer Gillian Armstrong was influenced by Tom Roberts and Frederick McCubbin in designing her film *My Brilliant Career* (Turner 1993: 114). The AFC genre films were marked by their excellent quality, attention to period detail, high production values and exquisite photography. As with the nationalistic art and literature movements that went before them, they focused on local settings and Australian speech patterns.

These films were also predictable: the stories drew on quite narrow social and demographic groups. As with the paintings of the Heidelberg School, these were films marked by a nostalgia for an Anglophile and imperialist era. They often offered a simplistic view of Australia. As Graeme Turner (1989: 115) has noted, the films were mostly historical costume dramas re-enacting the same sort of stories first produced in the nationalistic paintings of the 1880s. For example, *Picnic at Hanging Rock*, an adaptation of a Joan Lindsay novel about the disappearance of four young women in the bush, is a beautifully filmed and lavish costume drama set in rural Australia in the early 1900s. The film draws on classic Australian stories about the mystery of the bush and the danger it holds for those who are not 'of' it—in this case, the young, single Anglo–Australian women and English men. The film *Sunday Too Far Away* also exemplifies many of the tropes of the AFC genre. Gone are the schoolgirls; they are replaced by a gaggle of male shearers working a shed on an isolated property in the outback. Here the men both compete for the glory of being 'gun' shearer—the fastest—as well as negotiating with the boss about the intricacies of daily work life. Like Roberts' heroic painting *Shearing the Rams*, the centrepiece of the text is the work life of the Anglo–Celtic bloke, working with and for his mates.

The enormously successful and now iconic film *Gallipoli* developed and further reinforced these narrow nationalist themes of what it meant to be Australian. It is the young men (from both the bush and the city) here who exemplify the spirit of Australian-ness as they demonstrate their willingness to die for each other and their country in a war thousands of miles from home. Again, it is the combination of an historical setting (far away from the complexity of contemporary Australian life), beautiful cinematography (capturing unflawed Anglo–Australian masculine beauty) and a lyrical sound-track that enable the production, or reproduction, of a narrative reinforcing particular myths of Australian-ness—myths that are organised around male homosociality and mateship. The slightly less well-known film *Breaker Morant* also uses a war setting—this time the Boer War—to (re)produce almost identical myths: the love of men for their mates and their country. And, like *Gallipoli*, the narrative suggests that these traits emerge from the specific life of the bush 'educated' bloke.

In the AFC cinema of the 1970s and early 1980s—one that is celebrated as helping to produce Australian national identity—there is an absence of Indigenous people, women and non-Anglo–Australian citizens. The AFC genre of film does not fill the whole spectrum of film-making in this period. There are AFC films made by women (an example is *The Getting of Wisdom*). There are also independent films made by women and about women. There are independent films made with and about Indigenous peoples. What is important to note, though, is that in general much of the film product that was most successful in the 1970s told a story which was not very different to the one told almost 100 years earlier on canvas. The Australia represented in these films 'was defined by its landscape and by its colonial history rather than the complex contemporary realities of an urban, middle-class, post-colonial, "multicultural" society' (Turner 1989: 115). This meant in this national story Anglo–Australian men were at the centre of an heroic history that produced Australia.

Other films

Just as there were films in this period by and about women, there were many films that were not period pieces set in the bush. Films such as Paul Cox's *Lonely Hearts* (1982), Michael Thornhill's *The FJ Holden* (1977) and Tim Burstall's *Petersen* (1974) were intricate and intimate portraits of contemporary life in inner city or suburban Australia. They told a different story to that of mateship, war and the bush. However, these films also never seemed to stand for the nation, nor were they seen to be about the essence of Australian-ness. Their focus on men and women—not represented in the 'ocker' tradition—who were dealing with love, loss, boredom and suburban life does not meet the heroic standards of the AFC genre.

Indigenous people are almost non-existent in the commercial films of the time, appearing only on the fringes of the stories as trackers, farm hands or exotic extras. Important exceptions are *The Chant of Jimmie Blacksmith* (1978) and *Backroads* (1977). Remember Mundawuy Yunipingu's suggestion that putting Indigenous peoples in the margins means it is easy to smudge them out, erase them from the scene? Given the emphasis on AFC genre films as being historical narratives that establish the story about where Australians came from, it seems astonishing that Indigenous people are virtually absent. Yet it also fits with the history of the day. Just as secondary education in this period focused on convicts, the gold rushes and federation, so did film. However, it is not just a question of emphasis. As was explicitly stated in the government policy documents that set out the plan to reinvigorate Australian cinema and make it national, the films were going to do work. They were going to create a story about Australia that Australians could be proud of and that could be exported to the world. This did not include stories of the violence that marked colonialism.

The 1970s was a period of change and unrest in relations between Indigenous and non-Indigenous peoples. In 1967, Indigenous peoples had been granted full civil rights, and an increasingly politicised generation of Indigenous peoples were campaigning for national land rights legislation through protest. In producing films about Australian-ness, the mainstream non-Indigenous film industry sought comforting nostalgic images of Australia in the past. They draw on a period already mythologised in a body of artistic work by the writers and artists of the 1880s. Australian film of this period tended not to deal with the long-standing issues about who owned the land. Rather, most government-sponsored cinema was implicated in the reproduction of nostalgic stories about the heroism of settlement and the bravery of particular groups of white men who were willing to—or in fact did—die for this land. In this genre of film, the Australian-ness being produced was not one dealing with the complexity of two peoples and one land, but one that erased one group of people and emphasised the glory of the other.

Of course, the films made in this period were not homogenous, and there were striking and effective films made about the complexity—including the violence—of colonialism. *The Chant of Jimmie Blacksmith,* made by Fred Schepisi, told the story of Jimmy Governor, an Indigenous man with non-Indigenous heritage. It sought to contextualise the explosive violence that saw Governor hanged in 1901 for multiple murders of non-Indigenous people. The film tells a nuanced story about racism, violence, and cross-cultural and inter-cultural relationships. Sean Maynard (1989: 223) argues *The Chant of Jimmie Blacksmith* has much in common with the AFC genre films of its era: for example, as with other films of the time, some of the films scenes imitate the look of the Heidelberg School; in this case the painter Tom Roberts. However, the film was a box office failure and, as Colin Johnson (Mudrooroo) argues, though the film was seen as a 'sensitive portrayal of racial issues in Australia ... the image lingering on is that of a beserk boong hacking to death white ladies' (Turner 1989: 112). Over time *The Chant of Jimmie Blacksmith* has been an influential film. However, its iconic status does not stem from its representation of an engaging and pleasurable story of being Australian. Rather the film is one that many non-Indigenous Australians could view in the 1990s in terms of the revisionist histories of race relations on the frontier. Over time this film worked to help non-Indigenous peoples rethink the stories of being Australian represented in many of the AFC genre films.

Australian film has in the last 30 years become more diverse and complex. Deane Williams (1996: 54) argues that a growing understanding of the complexity of Australian-ness from the early 1980s onwards saw the stories told in films move away from the outback and the bush into the city. From the late 1980s, urban films were no longer an oddity but more the norm. This 'new wave' of Australian cinema was represented by films that explored issues, cultures and identities outside those of the Anglo–Celtic bloke. Films such as *Strictly Ballroom* (1992), *Blackfellas* (1993), *Silver City* (1984) and *Head On* (1998) explore and rethink the type of Australian-ness that ignores difference. More recently, *Jindabyne* (2006), *Ten Canoes* (2006), *Lantana* (2001), *The Tracker* (2002), *Rabbit-Proof Fence* (2002), *Japanese Story* (2003) and *Little Fish* (2005) have extended this project.

Understandings about what makes a film Australian have also shifted in other ways. Cinema has always been a transnational industry. For English-speaking countries like Australia, the hub is Hollywood. In the 1970s, much Australian film was made in opposition to what was seen as the all-consuming Hollywood monster. Today, increasing global cultural and economic exchange means there is much more fluidity in the industry. More Australian actors, directors and technicians work overseas, but also make 'non'-Australian films in studios in Australia. As Elizabeth Avram (2004) argues, what Australians recognise as Australian is broader. Australian film goers may still look for indicators of the Australian-ness of a film, especially land, but they find them in a broader field than they did in the past. Further the global nature of the film industry means that viewers have different understandings of what makes a film Australian. Ask Australians if *Finding Nemo* (2003) is an Australian film—some people are adamant that the Sydney and Barrier Reef setting make it Australian; while others are equally convinced its American accented animated characters and Disney feel make it American. *Babe* (1995), a film directed by an Australian, still feels English to many viewers because the rolling hills of the Southern Highlands of New South Wales, where it was filmed, are not the archetypal landscape of Australian film. By comparison *The Proposition* (2005), directed by an Australian and with a cast of Australian and overseas actors, can still seem more Australian to viewers because the setting of outback Queensland still retains some cachet as the real or unique Australia.

Contemporary music and the nation

In the 1950s and 1960s, if an Australian wanted to be a famous musician (or actor) they went overseas—mostly to England or the United States. Matching the 1970s Australian film renaissance was a musical renaissance. This was not a government-sponsored revival; it was more a grassroots' phenomenon of young people starting up garage bands, with some of them eventually playing in pubs and clubs. As with art and cinema, the success of the bands was associated with nationalism. Kurt Iveson (1997: 41) comments that one of the great things about the bands emerging in the 1970s and 1980s was the way in which they challenged the dominance of American and British music. A steady stream of Australian musicians and bands have appeared on the pop music charts both in Australia and overseas over the last 30 years. Bands and musicians as diverse as Nick Cave, The Go-Betweens, Midnight Oil, INXS, Human Nature, Keith Urban, Kylie Minogue and Silverchair have been successful internationally. Yet there is also still plenty of overseas music in the Australian scene, often accompanied by cultural cringe. For example, in the 1990s a 'pre-packaged' British rave dance party scene was imported to Australia and its presence was often cited as evidence that Australia was on the hip global music map (St John 2001: 11). Yet it can also be interpreted in terms of an overseas product being preferred to a local one.

American cultural imperialism

Australian music is often represented as needing to battle an ever-present American cultural imperialism. This fear has fuelled Australian culture industries for well over half a century. The fear of local and nationally specific cultural products being swamped by an American accented one has been attached to both film and music production. One part of the nationalist agenda of the 1970s and 1980s film industry was designed to halt the Americanisation of Australia. This desire continues today. Last-minute changes were made to the United States/Australia Free Trade Agreement of 2004 to make it harder for large American companies to sell their film and music to Australia. Minimum quotas on local content for television and radio are also designed to hold back the wave of American mega-media product that is seen as always threatening Australia. Even into the twenty-first century, the logic of national identity being produced through citizens consuming local cultural products is still strong. And music is a forum where this production is seen to be taking place. Music is often understood as a place where Australians can hear their own accent and so reinforce their sense of Australian-ness.

The impetus behind the creation of Australian music is twofold: to support a local cultural scene for local people, but also to take a world-class local product and share it with a global audience. The local-product-for-local-people mantra is perhaps best exemplified in the suburban pub rock experience. Throughout the 1970s and 1980s, and into the 2000s, the ritual of going to see a band in the local pub was understood by many as the quintessential authentic Aussie music experience (Homan 2003: 2). This authentic pub/club experience was represented as different from the highly commercialised and commodified American music product also available in Australia. However, this pub scene was remarkably culturally homogenous. Although pub music was not generally about bush bands and bush ballads, the pub scene was still dominated by Anglo–Australians. Today, locally produced music is more diverse, but it still reflects the marginal social spaces occupied by non-Anglo peoples in the national stories of Australia.

Two interesting challenges to this Anglo–Australian music scene in Australia today are the music communities of Indigenous and other non-Anglo people. It is, of course, ridiculous to suggest that these large and diverse communities have some sort of homogenous music tastes. As with other sectors of the Australian nation, tastes vary from country music or Maria Callas to Acid or bouzouki ballads. However, keeping this proviso in mind, it is useful to explore some aspects of music in non-dominant communities and see how it works in the creation of stories of Australian-ness.

In 1986, the Australian band Midnight Oil had a hit song, 'Beds are Burning'. At one level the lyrics reprised the songwriter's painful memories of his own house on fire. At another level, it was a song about Indigenous rights:

> The 4-wheels scare the cockatoos from Kintore East to Yuendemu,
> The western desert lives and breathes in forty-five degrees.
> The time has come to say fair's fair, to pay the rent, to pay our share.
> The time has come, a fact's a fact, it belongs to them, let's give it back!

The song was quite influential, both as a local rock anthem and as a part of the increasing call within the arts for Indigenous rights. At the same time as this non-Indigenous band was passionately advocating land rights, a number of Indigenous bands were undertaking the same project. The Warumpi Band's song 'My Island Home' (written by Neil Murray) has had many incarnations as a hit song, but its central message about the links to land or country felt by Indigenous peoples has never changed:

> For I come from the salt water people, we always lived by the sea
> Now I'm out here west of Alice Springs, with a wife and a family
> And my island home, my island home, my island home is waiting for me

This non-Indigenous penned song about Indigenous land and home reflects some of the collaborations taking place in the music industry at this time between non-Indigenous and Indigenous musicians. The well-known Yolngu band, Yothu Yindi, is another example of these intercultural musical connections. The band is made up of Yolngu and Balanda (non-Indigenous) members. It's enormously successful song 'Treaty' was written in collaboration with non-Indigenous musicians Paul Kelly and Midnight Oil. It still stands as the quintessential land rights song:

> Well I heard it on the radio,
> and I saw it on the television.
> Back in 1988,
> all those talking politicians.
> Words are easy,
> words are cheap,
> much cheaper than our priceless land.
> But promises can disappear
> just like writing in the sand.
> Treaty yeh, treaty now, treaty yeh, treaty now.
> Nhima Djat'pangarri nhima walangwalang Nhe Djat'payatpa nhima gaya nhe
> Matjini
> Yakarray
> Nhe Djat'pa nhe walang
> Gumurrt Jararrk Gutju

This song was the first by an Indigenous band in Australia to reach the Top 40.

Peter Dunbar-Hall (Dunbar-Hall and Gibson 2000: 2) contends that Indigenous popular music has become increasingly important as a means of getting non-Indigenous peoples to think about 'Aboriginal viewpoints and agendas'. He argues that, even though music companies might sign up Indigenous musicians because of the money they can make based on the popularity of what might be viewed as exotic world music genres, music from Indigenous musicians still gets non-Indigenous Australians thinking about their relationship with Indigenous people. Melinda Hinkson (2004: 11) makes a similar point when she writes about bands from the Walpiri communities of central Australia. She argues that these Walpiri bands sometimes write songs with 'political themes' as a way of starting a 'dialogue' with 'wider Australia'. These songs let non-Indigenous Australia know the 'aspirations of the Walpiri community'. Similarly, Joel Beasant, the organiser of an arts festival in The Block in Redfern, stated that part of his interest in staging the festival was 'to overcome that barrier that people have to being involved with the Indigenous community' (Lobley 2006). Many non-Indigenous peoples listen to Indigenous bands as part of a global-lounge music experience but for Indigenous peoples it is often about a political musical conversation. Obviously not all music is overtly political; however, the engagement Indigenous peoples make with non-Indigenous Australians through their music is a central part of their assertion of alternative understandings about their relationship to the country. Indigenous music demonstrates other 'representational codes'—other ways of thinking about Australia and belonging.

Music, like other cultural products, is not only a way of asserting an identity or telling a story: it is also a way of *making* an identity or *constituting* a story. Many aspects of Indigenous music-making focus on communications *within* or *amongst* Indigenous communities. Contemporary music helps in the creation of identities for and by Indigenous peoples. For example, the role of local radio programs operating in Yuendemu (an Indigenous community in the Northern Territory) is as much about communication between Indigenous people as about the music (Hinkson 2004). The listening audience for the Yuendemu radio programs covers a vast area—about 480 000 square kilometres. During programmes, many of the listeners phone in and dedicate songs to their friends, family or workmates. Hinkson argues that these radio dedications create a new way of being a community for Walpiri peoples. Members of this community used to live close to each other. Today, more members are travelling to towns and cities to live. The radio dedications help create connections as the communities become more geographically disparate.

Hinkson also notes the centrality of music in Walpiri culture. Dozens of local bands write and perform their own songs:

These songs conjure up diverse aspects of contemporary Walpiri life: the problems posed by alcohol, the challenge to keep relatives and friends from being lured away from home to regional centres and drink, the premium on looking after family, love of home, love of desert country love of women (Hinkson 2004: 11).

Much of this songwriting and performance is a dialogue between Indigenous peoples. Songs written and sung by Indigenous bands are often written partly in English and partly in their own languages, so some stories in the music are only comprehensible to other Indigenous peoples from the same community. For example, the sections of 'Treaty' written in Yolngu language are accessible only to people who speak this language. These lyrics, as with other lyrics in Indigenous languages, constitute a story between Indigenous peoples.

Country music

Since the period between World War I and World War II country music has been an important aspect of Indigenous community life. From the early twentieth century, as part of the process of assimilation, many Indigenous people living on missions or in institutions were forbidden to speak their Indigenous languages or practice cultural rituals—including singing in their own language. This ban was designed to eradicate Indigenous cultures. It also left a gap in Indigenous peoples' cultural life that was filled by non-Indigenous music. On Christian missions the new music might be hymns; in schools it was often nationalist songs; and in homes and meeting places one of the most popular new music forms was country music (Ryan 2001: 43–45). There are many reasons put forward for the attraction of country music. Gay Breyley (2005: 14–20) suggests the themes of country music—loyalty, strength, breaking unjust laws, sustained courage, and a willingness to fight for lost causes—resonate with Indigenous peoples' lives. Clinton Walker (1996) argues that the fact that most Indigenous people live outside the major cities gave them exposure to a type of music that is generally more popular in regional Australia. Country singers were often the only musicians to tour remote parts of Australia (Brett and Smith 1998: 11). Well-known country singer Slim Dusty always included concerts in Indigenous communities in his tours of regional Australia.

Indigenous peoples performed as well as listened to country music. They took country music and made it their own, though they also recognised its origins. The nickname of singer Roger Knox as the 'Black Elvis' make this clear (Ryan 2001: 44). Indigenous country singers not only covered classic American country music but wrote and performed their own songs. Many of these songs made humourous or heartfelt reference to the problems of life. Others were political anthems: 'Brown Skin Baby' written in the early 1960s was a song about the policy of child removal and 'Gurindji Blues', from the early 1970s, was a land rights' song (Ryan 2001: 44). Early Indigenous country singers were not generally recognised in the non-Indigenous country music scene. Racism as well as the constraints on Indigenous peoples' lives contributed to this exclusion (Brett and Smith 1998: 11). The exception was Jimmy Little and today many Indigenous country singers, such as Troy Cassar-Daly, have high musical profiles.

Indigenous popular music, as Aaron Corn (2002) points out, often uses a mixture of genres. A song may combine reggae or country style with lyrics and structures deriving from more long-standing Indigenous forms of music. He gives the example of a band from Arnhem Land called the Letterstick Band. This band's music seems to fit the three-minute, electric guitar, drum-kit rock song format, yet is indebted to, and draws on, song forms and themes the band members have learned as part of their custodianship of country and kin affiliation (Corn 2002: 80–82).

Hip hop and rap

Telling and hearing your own stories is obviously part of the attraction of listening to or being in Indigenous bands in Indigenous communities. It perhaps also explains the popularity of genres such as rap and hip hop for Indigenous, Pacific Islander, Southern European, Middle Eastern and Asian youth. Young people from these communities often have experiences of growing up that are different from those of Anglo–Australian youth. This can range from the issue of not seeing oneself represented in popular culture to experiences of racism. Creating an identity that is both self-respecting and somehow Australian in this context can be fraught. At one level, these young people are seen as a central part of multicultural Australia; at another level, they are a 'wog', a 'gook' or an 'Abo'. Music is one way in which marginalised youth have rethought who they are in the face of this mixed message of belonging and rejection. The music that black youth in Australia are taking up is a kind of global music. It is the genre of music that emerged from poorer African–American-dominated cities of the United States—hip hop and rap—that resonates with many of these kids. Kurt Iveson (1997) argues that, via this music, this often-alienated group of Australian youth:

found a culture which has the means to fight back against their experience of racism by addressing the segregation and victimisation experienced by people of colour . . . The appeal of hip hop to ethnic and indigenous young people in Australia lies significantly in its valuing of that which isn't white in a white racist society (1997: 41).

In hip hop, black youth are not the outsider or the marginalised listeners, as they often are in mainstream Australian music. In fact, given the origin of hip hop, black youth in Australia are part of the audience to whom the music is directed and part of the gang who use the genre to express themselves.

Interestingly hip hop and rap music is often understood by other Australians as an example of the broad experience of American cultural imperialism in the Australian arts. Criticisms have been levelled at Australian hip hop practitioners that they are simply wanna-bes who mimic the American music scene. This criticism is often signified by mocking Australians who adopt African–American dress styles, in particular the backwards baseball cap. In this reading Australian youth who take up hip hop or rap are represented as adopting a foreign music form that rightly belongs in the United States. What these critics have failed to understand is how alienating so much of the home-grown national music scene was for non-Anglo–Australian youth in particular. What seems local and home grown to Anglo–Australians can seem white and exclusive to others. With hip hop non-Anglo–Australian musicians can use aspects of their Lebanese, Maori, Fijian, Indigenous, Indian or Maltese heritage in tandem with a powerful black music form to produce stories of who they are in the white-dominated space of Australia. As South West Syndicate puts it:

> 208 years ago, immigration started on this land,
> us blackfellas couldn't understand about the invasion of the land
> when they tried to eliminate my people
> but still I don't discriminate.
> People have been migrating from all over the world
> but it's intimidating to some that see it as a threat to their authority,
> they wanna snub their noses at minorities
> all the way from the east coast to the west coast
> Aboriginal people are the hosts (Tony Mitchell 2003: 198).

Written in 1996, by Munkimuk (Mark Ross) and performed with BIG Naz and Brotha Black, this song 'Definition of Danger' makes a powerful response to Anglo–Australian stories of belonging and dominance. Read in the wake of race riots in South Sydney in December 2005 it captures what is a key problem in Australian society today: the fear many Anglo–Australians feel in relation to the changes multiculturalism and Indigenous self-determination have made to their authority.

Hip hop is a musical subculture that sees authenticity as important. To be marked 'hardcore' as opposed to 'wack' (inauthentic) is central to the idea of belonging in this music world. In hip hop: 'Blackness has become [the] . . . measure of "realness"' (D'Souza and Iveson 1999: 59). In the hip hop world, it is the Anglo–Australian youth who have adopted hip hop style who lack authenticity. This outsider status is hard to dislodge whatever their skill level. By contrast, for non-Anglo–Australians, hip hop style gives them a certain subcultural standing (Tony Mitchell 2003: 8). Black youth are not marginal in this music world, but the real and authentic practitioners. It is therefore not surprising that hip hop has a hold in non-Anglo and Indigenous communities.

Hip hop is often understood as a way of life and the members of this lifestyle are seen as part of a global community (Tony Mitchell 2003: 7). Being black is what draws a group of disparate cultures together across national boundaries. These global links made between local black musicians with fans of overseas' black musicians have given them access to new sounds and connected them with social movements and change. The politics and ideology of the music have resonances with many Indigenous and Arab–Australian youth. As Nicola Joseph argues:

> Hip hop has the potential in Australia, to cross cultural boundaries like they have never been crossed before. I see this potential regularly at Radio Skid Row. A studio full of black kids of every race doing a show that is nothing short of a celebration of black culture (1996: 275).

Though the roots of the hip hop music scene are American, it is nurtured in the local community. Fred Pollard, for example, notes the place of the community centre as the training ground for hip hop practitioners (Tony Mitchell 2003: 9). Successful practitioners maintain their connections with local communities. For example, MC Trey, Maya Jupiter and Indigenous rapper MC Wire have all 'been involved in working with underprivileged youth in western Sydney' running workshops on rapping and breakdancing and 'generally rais[ing] the profile of hip hop as a positive expression of youth culture in the community' (Tony Mitchell 2003: 206). Performers take part in music festivals connected with their local communities as well as working in a broader music field. Hip hop and rap styles are also used as vehicles for expressing local stories. In a project designed by the National Museum of Australia, rappers Wire MC and Morganics travelled around Australia encouraging young school students to use rap to express themselves. And so, to a hip hop beat, the students rapped about their lives with no over-emphasis on American slang. For example, students from Swan Hill sang about the local issues of gun control, nightclubs and the Murray River:

I wish we had underage nightclubs
And hot boys
Crazy roller skating rinks for
Us to enjoy

No drugs, no fights, so we can
Live our life.
Strict gun laws, yeah, that's right
Protect our native animals day and night
And treat the Murray right

Australian World Music

These global links not only create ways in which black Australians can import and deploy music forms from the United States that help them express particular stories of national (be)longing. These links also mean that styles of Australian music travel overseas and form other global links. Not only has Anglo–Australian-dominated pop music been part of this global sharing, but aspects of Indigenous people's music has become part of a global traffic. Indeed, Indigenous Australian music is a component of what is known as world music. The didjeridu is the central motif of the sound of Australian Indigenous music in world music. The didjeridu has been appropriated within non-Indigenous Australia as an iconic tourist souvenir, signifying an authentic Aussie experience. The didjeridu also has a global meaning as part of an alternative traveller experience—it is part of a series of objects (along with other 'ethnic' art forms from travels in Thailand, Bali, India and North Africa) that are purchased to signify an authentic non-tourist trip overseas. Gibson and Connell describe these travellers as neo-tribes, a global group of ever-changing backpackers who tend to:

collectively appropriate sites and construct identities based on a range of styles and attitudes and consumption patterns, but also because those identities involve appropriations from diverse 'non-Western cultures' (2003: 182).

The didjeridu stands for the Australian leg of this worldwide musical journey. It is an instrument and sound that signifies the links to be made between Indigenous peoples around the world. It is also a way in which non-Indigenous Australian peoples can link themselves to cultures that are seen as authentically belonging to this place.

Music, along with other aspects of the arts, is a key site where stories of being Australian are produced. Art and literature were important cultural forms where painters and writers self-consciously sought to produce works that appealed to viewers or readers as Australians. There were always limits to this national product. Nineteenth-century artists drew on cultural traditions outside Australia—especially from Europe. In the twenty-first century the film industry is global and an Australian film is most likely to be made by an international group of financiers, technicians, producers and actors who move between Australia, Hollywood and film festivals around the world. The arts have also been important spaces where counter hegemonic stories of being part of this nation were narrated. These counter-stories have worked both to suggest the ways in which a broader group of people might be included in any story of Australian-ness, but also to critique the central pillars of these stories that have seen some citizens continually excluded from Australian-ness. For example, many films made in the early 2000s—such as *The Tracker* (2002), *Black and White* (2002), *Rabbit-Proof Fence* (2002) and *Aussie Rules* (2002)—sought to challenge this exclusion and tell stories that not only included Indigenous peoples in the stories but to explore how earlier ideas of Australian-ness had marginalised Indigenous peoples. These films brought issues of racism and inequality to the forefront and in doing this they created the possibility for other stories to be told.

FURTHER READING

Butcher, Melissa and Thomas, Mandy (eds) 2003, *Ingenious: Emerging Youth Cultures in Urban Australia*, Pluto Press, Melbourne.

Collins, Felicity and Davis, Therese 2004, *Australian Cinema After Mabo*, Cambridge University Press, Melbourne.

Creswell, Toby and Fabinyi, Martin 2000, *The Real Thing: Adventures in Australian Rock and Roll, 1957–Now*, Random House, Sydney.

Hughes, Robert 1970, *The Art of Australia*, Penguin, Melbourne.

Mitchell, Tony 2003, 'Australian Hip Hop as a Subculture', *Youth Studies Australia*, vol. 22, no. 2, pp. 40–48.

Murray, Scott (ed.) 1994, *Australian Cinema*, Allen & Unwin, Sydney.

Sayers, Andrew 2001, *Australian Art*, Oxford University Press, Oxford.

Turner, Graeme 1994, *Making it National: Nationalism and Australian Popular Culture*, Allen & Unwin, Sydney.

Walker, Clinton 1996b, *Stranded: The Secret History of Australian Independent Music, 1977–1991*, Pan Macmillan, Sydney.

Williams, Donald 2002, *In Our Own Image: The Story of Australian Art*, McGraw-Hill, Sydney.

Willis, Anne-Marie 1993, *Illusions of Identity: The Art of Nation*, Hale and Iremonger, Sydney.

8

THE HEART OF THE COUNTRY

Place, space and land

THE CENTRAL CONCERN of this chapter is land. It sets out the links made between land and national stories, investigating how and why connections are established between being Australian and the environment. Here I will focus on the changing meanings of the desert (from 'dead heart' to 'national icon'), the place of national parks in the Australian imagination and understandings of a distant part of Australia—the Australian Antarctic territory.

Travelling to the 'centre'

Anthony Hassall (1988: 405) suggests many non-Indigenous people imagine the interior of Australia to contain 'a reservoir of meaning about the essential Australian experience'. That is, the real Australia is found in what is often referred to as the 'red centre'. In this story it is in the centre where the people, places and feelings that make up the kernel of being Australian are found. Roslyn Haynes (1998: 6) extends this, arguing that the trip to the centre 'enacted a mythic journey into the self'. So the red centre is also where an Australian can find their essence, their real self. From the early to the mid twentieth century, before the development of relatively safe and cheap travel, most Australians only travelled to the centre in the metaphorical sense. Therefore, this journey to the real Australia or real self was delivered to most people through art, literature and film. As Hassall (1988: 405) suggests, mid twentieth-century literature—such as Patrick White's *Voss*—sought to make the magic of the centre available to suburban Australia.

By the latter parts of the twentieth century, the development of air travel, better roads and larger cars made travelling to the centre easier and cheaper. It has become a common and sought-after experience for many non-Indigenous Australians. The visitors to the centre are not only Australians; such a trip is also part of a global tourism experience. A visit to the centre—Uluru in particular—is marketed to international visitors as a way to experience the real Australia. Today, hundreds of different tourist packages—by 4WD, bus, plane, single or group, luxury or camping—are available to travellers wanting to visit or experience the centre.

The sense of Australian-ness produced for domestic visitors is probably different to that produced for overseas visitors, and it is probably different for the many different groups within Australia. However, there are some motifs of Australian-ness that dominate in red centre narratives. To travel to the red centre is often represented as going to the heart of Australia. Tourist information is often couched in these terms:

> 'The Alice' (as the town of 20,000 is affectionately known), is also the gateway to Australia's heart and soul. You can hear the 'heartbeats' as you visit Uluru (Ayers Rock) . . . Just take a moment and you'll feel the ancient beat (Australian Tourism Net 2005).

The centre is represented as the source of the lifeblood of the nation. Words such as 'heart', 'soul' and 'heartbeat' are commonly used to describe the geographic centre of Australia. And, as suggested, the tourist experience of what was considered to be the heart of Australia is represented as the real Australia:

> Our 7 day package links two of Australia's best loved destinations, the Red Centre and the Great Barrier Reef. The Desert Venturer will show you the 'real' Australia with places and sights that only the most adventurous travellers see (Vacation Australia 2005).

In the centre tourists can brush up against or experience real Australian-ness. As one blogging tourist explains the Aussie bush is the real Australia and at the centre of this real place is Uluru:

> And therein lies our reasoning for venturing beyond the cultured cities into the Aussie bush—to experience the *real* Australia. We crossed deserts, dried salt pans, underground towns, waterholes and cattle stations (some bigger than European countries) eventually arriving at one of Australia's most famous natural icons—Uluru (Kelly 2003).

The young overseas students demand to see the real Australia signified by the outback and centre has led to one university setting up a 'gap year' course where students can work on a cattle station south of Katherine in the Northern Territory (Carbone 2003).

And this real Australia is peopled with real Australians. As another tourist blog (Bury 2001) of a trip on the Oodnadatta Track states: 'All those images of outback Australia you see in the movies and on TV are here—this is real Australia with real Australians, warts an' all!' For some overseas tourists, the centre is where they find the living replicas of the Australian stereotypes represented in popular culture—crocodile men, for example. However, it is also the place where many Australians believe they can access real Australians not available in their city lives. The outback is often imagined as the place where the types found in Australian foundation stories are said to be located. The belief is that the people in the centre and the outback still fit Russel Ward's (1958) stereotype—men who are laconic, hard-working when they have to be, there for a mate, and most importantly still attached to the land—working it, owning it, taming it.

The outback space is also understood to reflect disappearing lifestyles around which a level of nostalgia is attached: 'the tourist experience . . . idealizes [a] way of life in which people are supposed to be freer, more innocent, more spontaneous, purer and truer to themselves than usual' (Wang 1999: 360). Tourism allows people to relive 'these ways of life . . . at least temporarily, emphatically and symbolically' (1999: 360). Travelling in the outback increases this feeling of nostalgia for a free life. Travellers believe they are in a space that is literally purer or truer than the rest of the nation. Many tourist experiences offer the opportunity to sleep in a swag, under the stars, surrounded by the sounds of nature. For many, this experience is understood as a real Australian moment. Further, life in the outback is represented as more closely reflecting early twentieth century Anglo–Australian life. In the outback, there are fewer non-British migrants. The family can still be imagined to be heterosexual and intact; women are more easily understood as strong but loyal helpmates of their husbands, husbands as hard-working individuals providing for a family. Younger members of the family are more easily seen as loyal to a family tradition, such as the farm, and willing to take it on in the next generation. There are some aspects of this imaginary that are accurate; however, outback towns have as many social problems and variations as the urban and suburban spaces of Australia. The emphasis on the traditional and real in these stories is often simply a fantasy about the outback being a little oasis of an older and more desirable Australia.

The centre as terror

Though the centre of Australia is often imagined as the heart of the nation, it also operates as a place of terror in many non-Indigenous stories. The outback, the desert and the centre have all signified a terrifying unknown at times for non-Indigenous peoples. Nineteenth century non-Indigenous explorers such as Burke and Wills and Leichhardt who perished or disappeared on their treks fuelled this fear. Even in the twenty-first century, stories of tourists or workers who set off to travel from one town to the next in the outback and die after their car breaks down circulate as cautionary tales of the terrible power of the desert. The archetypal twentieth-century story of the threat of the outback was perhaps the disappearance of Azaria Chamberlain in August 1980 from a campsite at Uluru. The child was seen by her mother, Lindy, being dragged from her tent by a dingo. The body of Azaria was never found and Lindy Chamberlain's story was not believed. Instead Chamberlain was convicted of murder. The confluence of the missing body, the trope of the bad mother, and the representation of the desert as a cruel feminine presence made it possible for many people to believe that something sinister and terrifying underpinned the disappearance of the child. As Julie Marcus (1989: 16) argues there is a longstanding story in non-Indigenous mythology of the child who gets lost in the bush. This child, who wanders from the safety of the domestic sphere, is claimed by the threatening bush. Marcus argues that what made it easy for the trial by media of Lindy Chamberlain was that she had taken 'her young and vulnerable child into the heart of the dangerous Australian bush'. She had 'entered the wild and exposed her child's purity to its danger' (Marcus 1989: 16). Lindy Chamberlain served three years of a life sentence before she was exonerated but the myth of a bad woman in a cruel land still circulates.

More recently in July 2001 two English backpackers travelling in the outback were attacked, and one was murdered by an Australian man. The body of Peter Falconio has not been found. His girlfriend, Joanne Lees, who managed to escape into the bush, was at times vilified in the press. Her innocence was questioned first through the narrative that her evidence to the police was inconsistent and then through the production in the media of tales of her sexual infidelity, and finally 'because she didn't fit the image of a tearful, distraught heroine' (Williams 2005: 1). Comparisons were made with Lindy Chamberlain. Again in the outback the feminine presence is not seen as entirely innocent. The woman is both uniquely vulnerable in this place and never completely above suspicion.

In 2005 the cult horror film *Wolf Creek* was released in Australia. This film brings together many of the classic elements of the outback horror story. The film is supposed to be loosely based on a series of backpacker murders that took place in the south-east of Australia throughout the 1990s. The murderer, who is played by an actor often represented in Australia as a typical Australian bloke, in a twisted and terrifying way reprises the Mick Dundee character of the *Crocodile Dundee* movies. The setting of the film is the Kimberley region not the Belangalo State Forest in New South Wales where the real murders took place. This shift places the victims in the iconic space of terror—the outback—rather than the more homely space of semi-domestic southern New South Wales. The film is both a generic Hollywood horror film that has appealed to global audiences of teens and a very local acting out of Australian mythologies of terror.

The outback became a site of terror for another group of people in Australia in the late twentieth century. Significant changes took place in migration law in the early 1990s, including the introduction by the federal Labor government of mandatory detention for un-authorised arrivals in Australia in 1992 (McMaster 2001). In 1991 and 1999 two detention centres were built in isolated parts of Australia— Port Hedland in northern Western Australia and Woomera in central South Australia. These barren and isolated prisons were surrounded by high perimeter fences, razor wire and desert, and housed hundreds of potential refugees, including children. The detention centres were partly designed to act as a deterrent to future unautho-rised arrivals to Australia. As Minister for Immigration Philip Ruddock in 2002 put it:

> Detention arrangements have been a very important mechanism for ensuring that people are available for processing and available for removal, and thereby a very important deterrent in preventing people from getting into boats (Ozdowski 2003).

For many of the people detained in these isolated centres, the years spent in these spaces were terrifying. They had extremely high incidences of mental health problems. Separated from the main population centres of Australia the inmates often had difficulty accessing legal and medical support; the long distances also meant the possibility of links between Australian citizens and the potential refugees were kept to a minimum. In this story, the outback may be the real Australia but this reality was for many future citizens of Australia terrifying, not heartwarming. (The Woomera detention centre was closed in 2003 after a series of inmate demonstrations and riots as well as support and demonstrations from concerned Australians—in particular ChilOut, a group dedicated to removing children from detention. Port Hedland was closed in 2004. Children were removed from detention in 2005.)

Indigeneity and the centre

For many people, this real Australia and the real Australians who inhabit it are reducible to a non-Indigenous, heterosexual white bloke doing a certain type of work—the crocodile man or a little Aussie battler. However, there is also a narrative that suggests the centre is the place to access another or related real Australia: an Indigenous one. For many visitors to the centre, it is the association of the red centre with Indigenous peoples and cultures that gives the place much of its power. This understanding can often draw on the appropriation of Indigenous cultures rather than sharing. There is a sense that the red centre is the place to go if you wish to interact with Indigenous people—or, more specifically, 'real' Indigenous people. Just as the centre is the source of real (white) Australians, it is also the place for real Indigenous Australians.

In contemporary Northern Territory tourism, Indigenous cultures are represented as central to the tourist experience. The mystical power of the centre is represented not just in terms of the beauty and grandeur of natural formations such as Uluru or Kata Tjuta but their association with Indigeneity. Whereas in advertisements for travel in the 1930s and 1940s the emphasis was on non-Indigenous occupation and understandings of the land, in the contemporary period it is the presence of Indigenous peoples that gives the journey its meaning. For example, in a poster advertising travel to Central Australia in the 1930s, the scene is dominated by a non-Indigenous couple in colonial hunting gear (including a zebra skin print tent!) and Indigenous people are posed in the scene as small figures who are attending to the needs of the non-Indigenous travellers (see Figure 8.1). In the 1990s, advertisements for travel to the same area show Indigenous people as central to the experience. In one advertising campaign, the emphasis is on the opportunity the travel package gives tourists to learn from the Anangu people about

Figure 8.1 Percy Trompf poster advertising travel to central Australia in the 1930s. (*Image courtesy of Percy Trompf Estate*)

their country (see Figure 8.2). The link with Indigeneity makes travel to this land special. However, it needs to be noted that not all land and not all Indigenous people are brought together in non-Indigenous stories of the land and tourism. Indigenous peoples in urban spaces are not usually accorded the same level of respect by non-Indigenous visitors or tourists.

What is it that makes the centre and the Indigenous peoples of the desert the 'real' Indigenous Australians and the 'real' Australia? For many visitors, access to the Indigenous peoples of the central parts of Australia is linked to stories of authenticity and spirituality. Indigenous peoples imagined by Westerners as untouched by the corrosion of Western modernity are frequently seen as having access to a purity that Westerners have lost but still desire. A tourist experience in central Australia with Indigenous peoples gives the tourist 'some discernible connection to the timeless, the ancient, the primal, the pure, the chthonic; [they want this] since their own world is often

Figure 8.2 A 1997 advertisement for travel to the Northern Territory. (*Image courtesy of OZAD and Anangu Waai*)

conceived as ephemeral, new, artificial, and corrupt' (Taylor 1997: 26). To be with, learn from or draw on the wisdom of Indigenous peoples and their cultures and beliefs is seen as a way in which non-Indigenous people can detoxify. This feeling of accessing a purer or more real people living closer to nature or living more authentic lives has many manifestations. For some tourists, it means living with Indigenous communities for extended periods. For others, it means including some activity in their itinerary where they will engage with, or at least see, Indigenous peoples via cultural shows—corroborees, dances, bush tucker walks. For others it is the purchase of artefacts—especially the didjeridu—that makes the connection.

Uluru

Visiting the red centre or the real heart of Australia is often distilled into the act of visiting Uluru, previously called Ayers Rock by

non-Indigenous peoples. The serendipity of Uluru, the iconic
monolith of the red centre sitting almost in the geographic centre of
Australia, reinforces the story of this desert space as the heart of
Australia. Given its location, it is easy to imagine The Rock as the organ
generating a life-giving force. The liner notes for a CD titled *Naked
Didge* (1997) read: 'The heart centre is manifest on earth as Uluru, the
sacred rock in the heart of Australia' (Gibson and Connell 2003: 181).
Uluru is one of Australia's top visitor spots, and responses from visitors
are overwhelmingly positive. The ever-changing monolith almost never
fails to awe those who see it. Interestingly, though, many visitors to
Uluru are disappointed that their visit to this national icon does not
include meetings with Indigenous people. In fact, they often note they
did not see *any* Indigenous people.

Part of the contemporary story of Uluru marks this place as
Indigenous. So in some ways, there is a need for an Indigenous
person to authorise and authenticate tourists' visits. The presence of
an Indigenous person facilitates the connection to the 'pure' and
'primal'. Yet the Anangu people, who are the custodians of Uluru
and co-managers of the national park in which it sits, do not often
interact with visitors. There are historical and structural reasons for
this. Anangu were forcibly moved from their land in an earlier period
when the presence of Indigenous peoples was thought to upset
tourists. Though Anangu have returned to their country, they do not
live near Uluru where the tourist facilities are, but in a community
some distance away. The gap between tourists and Anangu is also
reinforced by the fact that most of the big tourist buses do not stop at
the Anangu-run visitors' centre. It is more common for the itinerary
to include a champagne sunset viewing of Uluru than a tour of the
visitors' centre.

It also reflects the tension between the non-Indigenous uses
of Uluru to help create feelings of Australian-ness and the ideas of
Anangu people about how their country and knowledge should be
used in this process. Like the rest of Australia, colonisation meant the
land around Uluru became crown land. In an attempt to keep local
Indigenous people away from non-Indigenous communities and
industry the land around Uluru was made into a reserve in the early
twentieth century. The increasing non-Indigenous interest in Uluru
meant that in 1958 some of the reserve land, including The Rock, was
excised for a national park (Hill 1994: 275). In 1985, the area around
Uluru and Kata Tjuta was handed back to Anangu. The decision to
hand back the land was part of a deal that included an agreement
the Anangu would immediately re-lease the land to the federal

government, who would develop the national park. The park was to be co-managed by Anangu people and National Parks personnel. Though the co-management has had many positive effects for the Anangu, it is not seen as a perfect arrangement. Anangu understandings of Uluru are in conflict with those of many non-Indigenous visitors. One of the main issues of contention is the climbing of Uluru by tourists.

Anangu have explained to governments, park personnel and individual tourists their reasons for opposing the climbing of Uluru. As Barbara Tjikatu, an Anangu custodian of Uluru, explains in a pamphlet made available to tourists at Uluru:

> If you worry about Aboriginal Law, then leave it, don't climb it. The chain is still there if you want to climb it. You should think about Tjukurpa and stay on the ground. Please don't climb it (*Welcome to Uluru-Kata Tjuta National Park* brochure).

Tjukurpa is the social, economic and spiritual system underpinning Anangu culture. It is their Dreaming. For the Anangu custodians, Uluru is a sacred place. The route tourists take up the rock is an ascent taken by Anangu ancestors—Mala men. Added to this, the Anangu have explained that, as custodians of this country, Tjukurpa means that they are responsible for the wellbeing of visitors who come to Uluru. Every year tourists die in their attempt to climb the rock. As the deaths occur in their country the Anangu feel responsible and have to deal with these deaths.

Yet the Anangu or Indigenous meaning of Uluru has to exist in tension with non-Indigenous meanings. There are a number of aspects to these non-Indigenous meanings, including the feeling of Uluru as the heart and lifeblood of Australian-ness. Uluru as a national—rather than specifically Indigenous—place means many non-Indigenous Australians feel they have a right to have access to it. This is often expressed in terms of egalitarianism:

> It is now common to hear settlers explain that 'We are *all* Australians' and to continue by saying, 'We *all* have equal rights in these places, not just Aborigines. We want our children to be able to see and understand their heritage' (Marcus 1997: 33).

In this scenario, the Indigenous meaning of land is not completely ignored; it is appropriated. The deep meaning of Uluru, via Tjukurpa, is transformed into something 'all' Australians have a right to access. More than this, The Rock has a cachet because it belongs to an 'other' culture. It is saturated in Indigenous meaning, and this is one reason why non-Indigenous people want their children to know it. It is the sacred nature of Uluru in Indigenous terms that adds to the power of Uluru in this non-Indigenous story.

Although Indigenous connection to aspects of Australia gives those places significance, Indigenous spiritual and knowledge systems are not seen as the equivalent of contemporary non-Indigenous legal or political systems. The Indigenous request not to climb Uluru is understood as a custom rather than a law equal to non-Indigenous laws. Most tourists would feel obliged to heed the law of Australia and pay the entrance fee to the national park, but not feel the need to heed Tjurkurpa and refrain from climbing The Rock. Non-Indigenous tourists, including Australians, can climb Uluru and understand the experience as significant because of the supposed link to the heart of Australia. They can also feel it gives them a way of accessing Indigeneity, even though Anangu state it is against their law. Over the last decade, more and more visitors to Uluru are choosing not to climb. Instead, they are walking around the base of the rock on a trail designed with Anangu. This alternative gives them a chance to share aspects of Indigenous cultural knowledge and respect Tjukurpa.

Visiting Uluru is also part of global adventure tourism. For young international travellers, Uluru is something to be conquered. A pair of trainers, shorts, a stopwatch, an early start and a brief moment to reflect on the power of Uluru (by reading the plaques acknowledging those who have died on the climb) translate into the hope of a record-breaking race to the summit. The conquest can also be more leisurely. In this case, Uluru is just one of hundreds of signifiers of adventure found in countries around the world. When young (or even older) Australians visit and climb Uluru, they may not be producing Australian-ness but rather a sense of themselves as global travellers. They are part of a global group of people who travel the world in search of adventure. In this story, the conquest of Uluru exists alongside a bungee jump in New Zealand, an elephant ride in Laos or Thailand, or a mountain trek in Patagonia.

In May 2001, a senior elder associated with the development of the Uluru–Kata Tjuta National Park died. He was a person who had played a central role in the plan to hand back Uluru to Anangu people. When he died, the Anangu asked that the climb up Uluru be closed until his funeral (about a month later) in respect for the deceased person. Grief in most cultures is an intense and private time where those who are grieving tend to curtail their public lives. It was not easy for the Anangu community to metaphorically draw the curtains of their house and grieve in private because part of their 'house' is understood as public and open to all. The overlap of the Anangu meanings of Uluru with the more general non-Indigenous/national meanings of the Rock meant the members of the elder's family could not enact their mourning rituals by themselves. They needed support from the non-Indigenous community, in particular Parks Australia, the managers of the National Park in which Uluru is located. Parks Australia management did respect the wishes of the Anangu and decided to close the climb for 20 days.

There was some opposition to this decision, mostly from within the tourism industry and parts of the Northern Territory government. Spokespeople argued it would mean a loss of millions of dollars in tourism revenue. Senator Grant Tambling said the passing of an elder was normally respected on the day of death and on the day of the funeral or other ceremonies: 'But we don't close down the economic apparatus' (Metherell and Kennedy 2001: 11). However, generally there was support for this act of respect. As Minister for the Environment Robert Hill said: 'It's a demonstration of sensitivity towards an eminent man's death' (*Adelaide Advertiser* 2001). The ban was lifted after about twelve days. As soon as the ban was lifted, tourists returned to climbing Uluru. The other meanings of The Rock as a peak to be 'bagged' as well as secular national icon came into play again. Though another meaning of being Australian was asserted and respected for a short time, it was quickly replaced with the imagined egalitarian story where access to Uluru for all Australians meant the marginalising of the Anangu's story.

Antarctica

Nowhere near the numbers of Australians who travel to the centre even think about travelling to the Antarctic, but it is becoming a more popular tourist destination and also plays a role in the production of Australian-ness. Like the deserts of the red centre, Antarctica has a history of mystery and has mesmerised many explorers who hoped to map and conquer an unknown land. Unlike Australia and the central desert, Antarctica really was a *terra nullius*—inhabited only by birds and sea-based animals. In terms of Australian national stories the Antarctic presents a less problematic space than the desert in which to construct stories of conquest and idealisation. The story of the desert as the heart of Australia in national stories is quite fraught. The earlier non-Indigenous story of the emptiness of the desert has been significantly challenged by Indigenous peoples. Further, the desert reminds non-Indigenous Australians of the limits of their understandings of or connections to Australian land. For so long they saw it as worthless, as devoid of meaning, now it is key to ideas of Australia. This historical mis-reading can reinforce a contemporary sense of belonging. Australians ask themselves how can something we saw as worthless turn out to be so precious and so enchanting? What did we miss? The fact that non-Indigenous Australians can now see the value of the desert, a value Indigenous peoples of the desert always knew, reinforces non-Indigenous understandings that they are now at home in Australia. The Antarctic is understood as empty and pristine. It is therefore a space where non-Indigenous Australians can again try to establish their relationship with a new place. As Christy Collis (1999: 24) puts it: 'The nineteenth century desert has, in effect, moved to Antarctica.'

Australia is one of seven nations asserting some type of sovereignty over Antarctica (the other nations are Argentina, Chile, France, New Zealand, Britain and Norway). Australia's claim to this continent is significant—42 per cent as sovereign Australian land. A further group of nations assert the right to have a say in how the Antarctic is used and governed (for example, the former Soviet Union, the United States and Japan). The sovereignty declared over Antarctica by Australia (via Britain) is not a sovereignty similar to that declared over the continent of Australia. However, the ownership pattern of Antarctica does reflect the history of colonialism and wealth-seeking by European nations who claim portions of this continent. Alongside these colonial desires for Antarctica are sentiments acknowledging the need to manage this near-pristine and unique space so that it will not fall prey to the same fate as other 'new lands'. Given this range of issues, how does Antarctica appear in Australian national stories? And how is any sense of its Australian-ness asserted in this icy continent?

From the mid nineteenth century, many countries had whaling and sealing fleets in the oceans around the Antarctic. While in the pursuit of their prey, the crew—and occasionally a cartographer who was on board—saw new land, which they would add to the rudimentary and incomplete maps they had of the area. Sailors often named the new places they sighted, and sometimes claimed the land for their nation or sovereign. In the period when Antarctica was being added to maps and becoming accessible, the British colonial project was seeking new spaces where its young men could prove themselves as exemplary British subjects. The little-known southern oceans and lands were such places. The high point of Antarctic mapping and colonial endeavour was 1870 to1920, a period often called the era of 'new imperialism'. In Britain, new imperialism was associated with a particular type of subject and practice of British-ness. Young middle-class men were encouraged to complete higher education and then undertake service for their country by working in the bureaucracy, industry or military in one of the British colonies before returning to the motherland to reap the rewards of this service. Anglo–Australian men included themselves in this project of imperial endeavour and service.

In going to work in the colonies, young men were asserting a particular type of 'heroic imperial masculinity' involving both service—perhaps as a public servant or a botanist—and adventure—climbing mountains never scaled by Britons before (Collis 2004: 2). In this sense Antarctica was seen as a playground. As the famous Antarctic explorer Douglas Mawson himself put it: 'I am so contented and happy. It is great to realize an ambition and I have always wanted to get into the new lands' (cited in Hains 1997: 156). In Australia, this idea of heroic masculine service and adventure was the impetus for many of the men who travelled throughout the continent mapping new areas and naming them for their monarch. In time, the adventure extended to the Antarctic. In 1908, two Australians —the aforementioned Douglas Mawson and Edgeworth David—were part of Ernest Shackleton's British expedition to Antarctica. In 1911, Mawson would return to lead his own expedition—the Australasian Antarctic Expedition.

It is also important to remember that, by the early twentieth century, European empires were crumbling. Many colonies were asserting their wish for independence. In this changing world, the new untouched continent of the Antarctic was a place for old and waning colonial powers to reassert their dominance or reinforce for themselves a sense of superiority. In 1883, E.F. Du Faur, a prominent member of the Geographical Society of Australasia, chastised Australian men of science, suggesting that in their provenance were two vast uncharted continents—Australia and the Antarctic— 'awaiting the enterprise of hardy spirits', and so far they had 'done nothing' (Home et al. 1992: 391–2). These men were not showing the sort of commitment expected of those of British stock.

The dominant approach to knowledge at the time centred on humans being able to know and subjugate their world to their needs. There was also a sense that, even though the entire world was not yet known, it was in our grasp to map or track it all. These beliefs fuelled a drive to map and catalogue the complete world: every insect, every mountain, every language. For example, in the 1880s both the Royal Society of New South Wales and the Geographical Society of Australasia were established. These societies supported the collection, collation and sharing of new knowledge. Antarctica was a place where scientists from all fields went to seek new knowledge. Most of the expeditions to the Antarctic included scientists or those who were dedicated to science. Geologists, meteorologists, botanists and zoologists all wanted a place on expeditions to this new space with its unknown limits and surprises. In this context, Antarctica was also a place in which men could 'come to test their skill at tracking and inscribing and thereby containing the limits of the world' (Lucas 1997: 159). By bringing their scientific systems and knowledge to this challenging place, colonial men could assert a sense of control over their world and feel as if it was all known to them.

As with many adventures, the experience of going to Antarctica is fraught. It is ambivalent. Some of the representations of Antarctica in Australian national stories reprise those of the interior of Australia in an earlier period. Just as Australia was often seen as an ancient continent occupied by unique creatures out of time, so Antarctica was represented as a 'museum continent', inhabited by 'creatures, often crude and quaint, that have elsewhere passed away and given place to higher forms' (Hains 1997: 156). In these stories, as Australia is primitive so is Antarctica. Antarctica was also represented as worn out or drained of life: '"weird" and desolate: all this land is death. Here is both death and decay—it might have been the graveyard of centuries it looked so old' (Hains 1997: 156). This same story often dominated historical representations of the Australian deserts and the centre. In stories of Antarctica, as with the desert, there was both fear and a desire.

It was the alien wonder of the Antarctic that made it desirable. Consider this fragment of the poem 'The Last Land' by Robert A. Swan (1946):

They sailed ever southwards
Beyond Van Dieman's Land
Beyond the Land of the Holy Spirit:
Plunged deep into howling seas
Where winds raved from beyond the stars;
Peered at ringing ice-mountains
Toppling from iron skies, and roaring
At the affrighted, echoing moon.

It expresses all the thrill of conquest, excitement and an escape from the drudgery of everyday life. It is the very weirdness and desolation of the Antarctic that makes it attractive. The poem continues:

> They went back, back from the south,
> Back to the dull hours and old futilities,
> Back to the fungoid sprall of life
> With all its murky dreams and shapes;
> But ever they knew, sleeping and waking,
> A dreadful yearning, a strange cold calling
> Drifting from the jewelled iciness of empty spaces
> And the pale, clear glitter of immemorial snows.

These sentiments are common in the framing of stories of the masculine experience of non-Indigenous colonial Australian life. Compare the evergreen A.B. 'Banjo' Paterson poem 'Clancy of the Overflow':

> I am sitting in my dingy little office, where a stingy
> Ray of sunlight struggles feebly down between the houses tall,
> And the foetid air and gritty of the dusty, dirty city
> Through the open window floating, spreads its foulness over all.
> And in place of lowing cattle, I can hear the fiendish rattle
> Of the tramways and the buses making hurry down the street,
> And the language uninviting of the gutter children fighting,
> Comes fitfully and faintly through the ceaseless tramp of feet.
> ...
> And I somehow rather fancy that I'd like to change with Clancy,
> Like to take a turn at droving where the seasons come and go . . .

As with the story of Antarctica, here a tale of the beauty and freedom of the bush is juxtaposed with the harried and pallid life of the city. These unconquered places reinforce some version of the bush myth. Even though a much smaller number of Australians go to the Antarctic than to the bush or outback, these representations reproduce the idea of these places as reflecting values central to an Australian character.

Yet the other side of the image of Antarctica is as the ultimate masculine adventure: one outside civilised experience. In dominant stories, this immediately suggests the Antarctic is 'no place for a lady'. However, the ice continent has also been represented as a place that would send a man feral (Hains 2002: 157). Living in Antarctica is often described using the same terminology as living outside the western world. Adventurers who stayed too long were referred to as 'going native', and the space was described as 'no white man's land' (Hains 2002: 157). Like the desert and the outback, Antarctica is represented as unknown and unknowable, and as such is seen as a dangerous place where a person's identity is easily lost. Paradoxically, Antarctica as ambivalent space both reinforces Australian-ness (through its ability to enact a type of colonial masculinity) and strips it away (through its inhuman landscape).

As stated earlier, Australia claims just over 40 per cent of Antarctica as sovereign land—but what does this mean? Claims to sovereignty have historically rested on occupation and productive use of the land. This was the basis of the British claim to the continent of Australia—that the Indigenous occupiers were not using the land productively. People cannot live all year in the Antarctic without serious health risks, and at the moment humans cannot or choose not to make the space economically productive. Given these limits, how is a sense of Australian-ness projected on to this space? Christy Collis (2004: 2) argues that, since it is nearly impossible for Australia to claim Antarctica physically or spatially (though some other claimant nations have sent pregnant women to Antarctica to give birth to Antarctican citizens), it needs to be asserted textually. That is, the claim takes place through the reproduction and circulation of images and stories about the Australian occupation of the Antarctic. This is a common strategy in reinforcing a sense of spatial ownership. It is why so many images of James Cook or Arthur Phillip planting British flags on the Australian continent are in circulation. Because Antarctica cannot be peopled, this textual assertion is even more important. Collis (2004: 4–5) gives the example of the key role of a Frank Hurley movie in the textual stamping of Antarctica as British (and by association Australian).

Frank Hurley accompanied the Douglas Mawson-led British, Australian and New Zealand Antarctic Research Expedition (BANZARE) in 1931, photographing and filming the trip. His film from the trip, *Southward Ho! with Mawson* (1931), was travelling the country ten months after the men returned to Australia (Collis 2004: 3). This film about an exciting expedition captured the interest of many Australians. The circulation and viewing of the film contributed to a sense of the ownership of the Antarctic space by Anglo–Australians. As Collis explains, the film first shows the empty space of the continent—nothing but ice and howling winds. This is then replaced by the image of Mawson and his men, the British flag and the voice of Mawson proclaiming possession. In watching the film, the audience feels part of and contributes to a sense of creating the space as Australian.

This textual claim to occupation has also been asserted through the issuing of postage stamps featuring the Antarctic continent, and through the support of artists or writers in residence who produce literature and artworks that represent Australian occupation of Antarctica (see Figure 8.3). The repair of Mawson's Hut and its listing as a heritage building of national significance was another textual claim to occupation. Mawson and his men built the hut in 1911 as their base camp. In 1931, Mawson revisited the hut; interestingly, he reenacted the 1911 ritual of raising the flag over the hut. This was captured in Hurley's 1931 film. In 1978, a wave of sentimentality over the dereliction of the hut spurred a campaign to restore it and have it listed as part of Australia's heritage—this was achieved in 1984. As Christy Collis (1999) points out, this re-enacting of the spirit of conquest—both the re-raising of the flag and the rebuilding of the hut, and the poetry and artwork about Antarctica—reproduces and reinforces Australia's claim to this space, even though no Australians live in Antarctica permanently.

Figure 8.3 Jan Sensberg's painting *Borchgevinck's Foot* (1987–88) is from his time in Antartica. Carsten Borchgevinck claimed to be the first man to go ashore on the Antarctic mainland in 1985. He was Norwegian but living in Australia at the time he joined the expedition. (© *Jan Sensberg, 1987–88, Licensed by VISCOPY, Australia, 2007*)

Australia cannot simply claim Antarctica through the circulation of pictures of Australians being there in the summer of 1930–31 and because of the presence of an historical hut. There need to be other ways in which the Australian-ness of the places is asserted. These other ways include legal means and a real physical presence (Collis 2004: 4). To this end, Australia has funded—and continues to fund—expeditions that criss-cross the Australian Antarctic space, more fully documenting and mapping its intricacies. In particular, the federal government funds scientific expeditions to document the life of this ice land. This knowledge and the evidence of time spent on the continent is then drawn together by the government to help support a legal case about Australia's right to possession, based on the idea of original *terra nullius* and Australian exploration. The historical story of Australian presence (captured in the film and the hut) gives this legal story a past.

There are moves to classify Antarctica as something other than a space understood in national terms—a pie divided up between seven nations. There have been suggestions over the last few decades that Antarctica should be made '*terra communis*'—land belonging to all (Collis 1999: 26). Other national governments have suggested making it a global park—a space all the nations of the world agree to protect from development and harm. This will be difficult. The mineral potential under the Antarctic is stunning. What will happen as the world runs short of fossil fuels? The space is no longer pristine: there are scientists who come and go, and tourism is an increasing phenomenon. As Mawson sought happiness and the fruition of his ambitions through the conquest of Antarctica, so a new generation of Australians seek to do the same thing. They yearn to experience a place that is both home and yet unknown. Will Australians give that up in favour of a global pristine wilderness? That remains to be seen.

Parks and wilderness

As with the Antarctic, there is on the mainland Australian continent a tension between the love of a beautiful place and a desire to turn that place to economic benefit. These contradictory hopes have been an issue for Australian colonists and citizens for centuries. The intense battles taking place in Tasmania today between those in favour of using old growth forests for logging and those who wish to keep them as wilderness have precedents in earlier periods. It is obviously a place where different ideas about what Australia is clash with each other. The place of national parks in Australian stories is one of the areas where clashes occur.

The view that nations needed parks emerged in the late nineteenth century. As many countries became increasingly urbanised, movements emerged seeking to protect and reserve natural or non-urban areas. Kings Park in Perth is an example of a successful attempt to keep one part of a thriving metropolis untouched. Parkland was not just set aside in cities, but large areas of 'wild' land were also kept aside outside cities. In 1866 the colony of New South Wales declared the Jenolan Caves a reserve in order to protect them for the colonial tourists who had been visiting them for 40 years. In 1879, the same government declared an area just south of Sydney to be The National Park, the world's second national park. (The park was renamed the Royal National Park in 1955 after Queen Elizabeth II visited the area.)

The nineteenth-century belief about the function of national parks was very different from the dominant contemporary view. A national park was not simply viewed as an untouched space that provided refuge for native flora and fauna. Rather, the nineteenth-century national park provided a refuge where urban-dwelling folk could escape from the dirt and bustle of their city lives. Parks afforded visitors vistas and scenes considered peaceful. This often meant removing native vegetation and animals and replacing them with British or European trees, plants, waterways and views. Non-native animals for hunting were also introduced in early Australian national parks and reserves. The idea was to create a sense of being at home. 'Home' in Australian national parks was not Australia; it was often not even Europe—it was Britain. The 'national' in national park was a way of demarcating one nation from another. The type of Australian-ness being produced was not just about a connection with places outside the Australian continent; it was deeply inflected with the idea of Australia being attached to Britain. By the mid twentieth century, there were further shifts in understanding and perspectives about national parks. The growth in the idea of the intrinsic value of Australian flora and fauna and a growing nationalism meant that the practice of shaping natural spaces to look like places overseas was dwindling and being replaced with the desire to preserve and protect the native species of different areas. A different understanding of Australian-ness was being produced. The new idea of being Australian included a belief in the intrinsic value of the 'native'.

The name 'national park' infers that the space set aside is not for any individual, family or community, but for all citizens of the nation. Researchers at the Migration Heritage Centre (MHC) (2003) argue that calling a park national suggests the park is 'both the property of the nation and expressive of certain national virtues'. The peace offered by the natural space is not simply a refuge from the physical difficulty of the urban and modern life—pollution, over-stimulation, hyped-up work lives—but from the complexities of the life being set up in the new national space (MHC 2003). However, they also argue that the representation of national parks as untouched or natural places suggests they exist outside history. This creates an understanding of national parks as being outside all the complexities of colonial nation-making, in particular the dispossession of Indigenous people. The national park is seen as a place away from the conflict, violence, effort and corrupted processes integral to the coloniser making themselves at home in a new place. Paradoxically national parks are spaces that suggest a distance from the nation. Their representation as untouched wilderness means they can be seen as recuperative places not marked by an Indigenous presence or traces of colonial violence.

The increasing use of national parks by Australians has taken a toll on these spaces. By the 1970s, there was a growing awareness of the fragility of planet Earth and an increasing knowledge of the adverse impact of humans on it. This meant national parks came to be seen more often as places needing protection from humans, to stop Australians and non-Australians from loving these areas to death. A good case is the use of raised walking platforms in popular national parks, which stops the trampling of delicate ecosystems by enthusiastic visitors. By the mid 1970s it was not just plants and animals that were seen to be in need of protection. There was also a move to begin to preserve Indigenous peoples' cultures as they were represented in national parks. For example, in Tasmania the *Aboriginal Relics Act* 1975 was designed to protect Indigenous heritage in the state. It does need to be reiterated that moves to protect Indigenous peoples' cultural heritage was often only included in legislation designated to protect natural heritage. In this way, Indigenous peoples' cultures were seen as outside the urban space and only to be found within nature.

The 1970s also saw new (non-Indigenous) stories of imagining the relationship between humans and nature. These provided a philosophy suggesting there was a need to protect nature beyond the objective of keeping it beautiful for humans. These new philosophies challenged traditional rationalist philosophies which posited that anything not human (and rational) was inferior and only had a value insofar as it could be of use to humans. They suggested non-human things—sentient or non-sentient—could have an intrinsic value away from and outside of human need. Interestingly, in Australia, some of these newer understandings drew on Indigenous knowledge systems where the connections between nature and humans were intimate and often expressed in terms of kinship. This acknowledgement of the usefulness of Indigenous knowledge systems in helping to reshape non-Indigenous peoples' ecological relationships to land was not without its problems. This acknowledgement of the profound connection Indigenous peoples have to their country was often an appropriation, and it frequently failed to translate into an under-standing that Indigenous peoples might own this land, or that they should have a say in its management. In the past few decades the recognition of Indigenous peoples' claim and expertise in managing national parks that are in their country has increased. In 1979 Kakadu National Park became a co-managed space. The Uluru and Kata Tjuta National Park was handed back in 1985 and is also co-managed. More recently, in May 2006 the New South Wales government handed back Guluga and Biamanga national parks to the Yuin people of the south coast of the state.

By the early twenty-first century, Australia had well over 3200 national parks, conservation parks, reserves and refuges. Some are huge, others small; some are tramped through by thousands every month, others are almost without human presence. Many are co-managed by National Parks personnel and local Indigenous communities. The way in which different groups use and understand their relationship to the parks is diverse. Indigenous managers of parks understand the park as part of their country, and therefore their role is as ongoing custodians of the land. As seen in the earlier section on Uluru and Kata Tjuta National Park, for many Indigenous people this means sharing their knowledge of the place with others. However, it also means trying to encourage users of the parks to respect other ways of being in the place. Even understanding that exclusion is part of that use.

Multiculturalism and parks

The increasingly multicultural nature of the Australian nation has also had an impact on park use. For many new immigrants, visits to older national parks planted with exotic plants and trees provide a nostalgic return to their homeland. Walking through forests of non-native Australian trees creates a sensory replica of home. The smell and sound of non-native trees are a pleasure for many to experience.

For example, many Polish immigrants talk about their experiences picking mushrooms in the older national parks of Australia. Growing amongst the trees are different varieties of fungi, herbs and other plants that are supported by the partial European eco-system. The rituals of picking these plants in season and preparing them in dishes from 'home' provides many individuals and communities with powerful ongoing connections and happy attachments to other places that are important to their identities. For some migrant groups national parks are community gathering places. Large numbers of the Australian–Macedonian community have been coming to Royal National Park in New South Wales on Christmas Day since the 1970s. The Migration Heritage Centre study of this event quotes one woman as saying that they come to the park as a form of reunion:

> To come from such a far away country to meet again, that was a big thing, a really big thing, like in this beautiful country, you'd see these people you hadn't seen for five or six years. It was like a reunion. That's it: it's a reunion every Christmas (MHC 2003).

By the late 1990s the reunion was so extensive the park filled to capacity—the car parks were full and the gates closed. Interestingly, there was some worry from the park staff about this lively and large-scale use of the park. When the staff were interviewed about ideal national park use they acknowledged they:

> shared certain expectations about what visitors should be looking for in a National Park visit. They mentioned quietness, tranquillity, a preference for passive recreation over organised games. But they also recognised that these expectations were due to their own experience and preferences—often a background in bushwalking and direct involvement in conservation issues (MHC 2003).

The more rowdy use of the park did not fit with this expected use. There was a certain understanding about how this national space should be used and that use fitted more closely with Anglo–Australian use patterns (MHC 2003). But if national parks are understood as places where the values of the nation are captured, what weighting should be given to citizens who value the park as meeting place for a geographically diverse community rather than a tranquil walk?

Saving wilderness

The idea of wilderness space is not quite the same as national parks (though physically they often overlap). National stories of Australia include narratives of wilderness and its conquest. They also include a sense of wilderness needing to be protected. One of the ways in which Australia is understood internationally is as a pristine place—the Barrier Reef, the outback and the whole island of Tasmania. Yet gaining protection for wilderness areas is a difficult process. It can contradict other ideas of Australian-ness—especially those associated with economic growth and work. The example used to demonstrate some of the complexities here is the campaign to save the Franklin River in Tasmania in the early 1980s, although this scenario has been and continues to be replayed up until the present.

In October 1979, under a state Liberal government, the Tasmanian Hydroelectric Commission, a very powerful and politically astute body, announced a three-stage, billion dollar hydro-electric scheme on the Lower Gordon, Franklin and King rivers. The plan was to harness the power of the Franklin River. As one of the smaller Australian states, Tasmania's economic performance has for many decades been unexceptional. What Tasmania has no shortage of, however, is natural resources—forests and rivers. This was a key area for improving employment and income potential for Tasmanians. However, the idea of providing jobs for locals was important but the Franklin River was also known nationally and internationally for its beauty and majesty, so the plan for the Franklin–Gordon–King scheme was not immediately taken up by the new state Labor government when it came to power in 1980. In May 1982, a Liberal government again gained office and immediately passed the *Gordon River Power Hydro Electric Development Act*, giving the project the go-ahead.

An environmental campaign to save the rivers immediately swung into action (see Figure 8.4). Local environmentalists had earlier fought unsuccessfully to stop another dam project, so they were prepared. The campaign to save the Franklin River was also supported by the federal Liberal government and the federal opposition. In November 1981, Prime Minister Malcolm Fraser had lodged an application with the United Nations to have the Franklin River granted World Heritage status. The move was successful. However, the Liberal Fraser government—with its belief in state's rights—would not act to override the Tasmanian government's 1982 legislation with its own legislation forbidding the dam. It was hoping that the new world heritage status, along with a $500 million compensation offer, would be enough to convince the state Liberal government to stop the project. It was not. In March 1983, Fraser's Liberal government lost the election and the Hawke Labor government came to power on a promise, among many others, to save the river. In 1983, this new government introduced the

Figure 8.4 The famous Peter Dombrovskis photograph used in the Save the Franklin River campaign of the 1980s. (*Image courtesy of The Wilderness Society Collection and the Peter Dombrovskis Estate*)

World Heritage Properties Conservation Act to stop the Tasmanian government from going ahead with the project. The 1983 legislation drew its power from the 1972 (international) *Convention for the Protection of the World Cultural and Natural Heritage.* The Tasmanian state government took the case to the High Court, but lost. The river was saved.

The Franklin campaign was fought on a variety of grounds. The framework was based on the double argument of the pristine nature of the place and the uniqueness of this ecosystem in the global context. One part of the strategy was to get the Franklin River listed as a heritage site of significance to the world as a whole, as its global significance was seen to outweigh the regional significance or need for the site as an economic resource. The idea of the Franklin River as a wilderness space was the second powerful part of the argument used to save the river. It worked very effectively. In a nation that was just beginning to have discussions about the impact of humans on the land, this was a highly symbolic way in which to begin to give value to Australia as delicate and fragile environment needing to be treasured rather than trashed. However, the deployment of the wilderness argument made the presence of Indigenous peoples in this area invisible. Tasmania is the state in Australia where the idea of the total eradication of Indigenous peoples as a result of British colonialism still has credence. The notion of the 'last' Tasmanian Indigenous person being Truganini, a woman who died in 1876, was an everyday popular non-Indigenous understanding in the 1980s. In this context, representing the Franklin River area as a wilderness unspoiled by humans was easy to do. There was no large Indigenous group to disagree.

Yet interestingly, there was within the campaign to save the Franklin an argument about the need to protect evidence of Indigenous occupation—camp fires, stone tools and animal bones dating back to approximately 24 000 BP—in the area that would be flooded if the dam went ahead. In some ways, what the wilderness argument—in conjunction with the acknowledgement of Indigenous artefacts—does is reinforce an understanding of Indigenous people as outside of history and culture. Here Indigenous Tasmanians' (long gone) presence is understood as not making a place 'touched' or developed. It gives the area value, but it does not make it theirs. By this logic, the contemporary Tasmanian Indigenous community does not need to be consulted in detail. The Franklin River area was being saved as a precious generic Australian place, not one attached to either historical or ongoing Indigenous cultures and histories. What the Franklin campaign did was keep the space outside 'history'.

Stories of being Australian are formed in relation to land. Indigenous stories of belonging are often framed in terms of the Dreaming. These stories provide a complex and comprehensive map of country; one that explains the law, spirituality, geography, economics and familial relations pertaining to particular areas. For many non-Indigenous people this map is intriguing and they seek to have access to it as a way of thinking about their relation to the land. For these Australians accessing Indigenous understandings of land is how they represent themselves as belonging. One of the key spaces where the logic of the Dreaming is seen to make sense for non-Indigenous peoples is the outback, the centre. Whereas non-Indigenous people once understood this space as empty it is now more frequently understood as the key place where Indigenous knowledges are accessible to them. Each year thousands of tourists travel to the centre to hear Anangu or Walpiri peoples tell them the stories of their country. Other spaces are less likely to be understood in terms of the Dreaming of the Indigenous custodians. City spaces in particular are understood as erased of Indigenous meaning by non-Indigenous people. Obviously the obliteration of markers of the Dreaming over time along with the disturbance to Indigenous cultures through colonialism has made this land harder to read as Indigenous—yet it still is.

Marking land as *Australian* is a complex process that can at times draw on Indigenous spiritual systems, and it can at others depend on the erasure of Indigenous meanings. Marking land as *Australian* also works by representing particular peoples as belonging in the space—again this can sometimes be Indigenous peoples; at other times it is non-Indigenous people, in particular the bush bloke, the pioneer or the 'dinkum' Aussie who is seen to belong. Presently, Antarctica is uninhabitable yet Australian government claims 40 per cent of the continent. To mark the land as Australian it is being represented as a place for Australians—explorers, scientists, and intrepid tourists, all pioneers of a sort—and as a result is being mapped as belonging to Australia in a way that reinforces the legal claim. How land is represented as Australian; how it comes to be seen as Australian reveals some of the key forms of nationalism.

FURTHER READING

Griffiths, Tom 2007, *Slicing the Silence: Voyaging to Antarctica*, University of New South Wales Press, Sydney.

Hains, Brigid 2002, *The Ice and the Inland: Mawson, Flynn, and the Myth of the Frontier*, Melbourne University Press, Melbourne.

Haynes, Roslyn 1998, *Seeking the Centre: The Australian Desert in Literature, Art and Film*, Cambridge University Press, Melbourne.

Hill, Barry 1994, *The Rock: Travelling to Uluru*, Allen & Unwin, Sydney.

Horne, Julia 2005, *The Pursuit of Wonder: How Australia's Landscape was Explained, Nature Discovered and Tourism Unleashed*, Miegunyah Press, Melbourne.

Main, George 2005, *Heartland*, University of New South Wales Press, Sydney.

Rose, Deborah Bird 1996, *Nourishing Terrains: Australian Aboriginal Views of Landscape and Wilderness*, Australian Heritage Commission, Canberra.

Thomas, Mandy 2002, *Moving Landscapes: National Parks and the Vietnamese Experience*, NSW National Parks and Wildlife Service, Sydney.

9

THE LAND OF THE LONG WEEKEND

Public holidays and national events

IN THE WORLD of popular culture and the arts, the help governments might provide to support people producing stories of being
Australian is not very visible. It usually only appears as a discrete logo
at the end of a film or on the acknowledgements page of a novel
where a government body is thanked for financial support. Artistic
projects—even if they produce a story that fits with the dominant
national story—are understood as the outcomes of individual
endeavour and achievement. However, government influence is
much stronger in the production of some stories of Australian-ness.
This chapter focuses on official commemorations or rituals in the
Australian national calendar. The three rituals analysed are Australia
Day, Anzac Day, and the reconciliation process that culminated in
Corroboree 2000 and the bridge walks in 2000. First, the chapter
sets out the official or normative understandings of these rituals,
exploring how they relate to or reproduce particular understandings
of being Australian. It then analyses the critiques that have always
accompanied these moments of national 'unification', highlighting
some of the repressed stories that are ignored or marginalised in the
performances of these national rituals.

Australia Day

Australia Day is celebrated on 26 January each year. This holiday
commemorates the arrival of the First Fleet in Botany Bay in 1788,
and is designed to celebrate the founding of Australia as a nation.

The arrival of Captain Arthur Phillip on the east coast of Australia has been commemorated in some way from the very first anniversary in 1789, but it has only been known as Australia Day since 1946. Colonial and state governments argued the merits of a variety of days and events being recognised as *the* national day for over 150 years. Colonies and states in the west of the continent considered the choice of 26 January as the national day to privilege the history of the east coast. It was only in 1946 that all states finally agreed that this day should be the Australian national day. The fact that it took so long for Australians to choose a national day makes it clear there was nothing intrinsic to 26 January that made it obvious as the only choice for the national day. Therefore, in exploring the meanings of Australia Day one of the questions that arises is what stories are opened up and supported by the choice of 26 January as the national day and what stories are marginalised or disavowed?

The choice of 26 January obviously brings to the fore the arrival of the British in Australia as the event setting in motion the eventual emergence of a sovereign Australian state. Choosing 26 January to represent the story of the Australian nation is a powerful reinforcement of the view that the arrival of the British was a good thing. It makes an important link between this event and the eventual new nation. The choice of 26 January reinforces a particular understanding of the place of Indigenous peoples of Australia in the nation. Many Indigenous peoples understand the day as commemorating a trauma—the invasion of their countries. So to nominate this day as the national day is to marginalise their place in the nation. Indigenous peoples have pointed out the insensitivity of celebrating 26 January. They have also made sure non-Indigenous peoples are aware of the rich cultures that their arrival disturbed. Indigenous peoples reinforce the understanding that Australian-ness does not simply emerge from this British arrival, but is dependent on an originary and ongoing Indigenous presence. For example, when Murri songwriter Kev Carmody (1995) was asked for his perspective of Australia Day, he started by pointing out that: 'Victors recall history from a different standpoint from the vanquished.' He went on to express his feelings about the day by quoting from a song of his called 'Bloodlines':

We walked this land from the time of the Dreaming
　our spirit
　is forever
　this is
　our bloodline.

Carmody ends his article by asking the question: 'And so, as a non-Indigenous person celebrating "Australia Day", what is your bloodline?' Through his music, Kev Carmody wants to get non-Indigenous Australians to consider how they might fit into Indigenous stories of being Australian. He is not suggesting that other stories of being Australian are invalid, but that they need to be considered alongside the powerful and originary story of Indigenous peoples and their belonging. The celebration of Australia Day often erases this ongoing presence.

1938 and 1988

As Kev Carmody's media piece suggests, Indigenous peoples have used Australia Day to draw attention to their plight and to make known their political demands. A very famous example is 26 January 1938. On this day, non-Indigenous Australians celebrated the 150th anniversary of the arrival of the British in Australia. There were festivities all over the country, but particularly in Sydney, where Arthur Phillip and the convicts had landed in 1788. One event was the re-enactment of the arrival. In the recreation of the arrival on the beach, various actors played the roles of Arthur Phillip and his men, but there were also Indigenous people taking the roles of the Eora men who greeted the English colonisers when they stepped on to land. The Indigenous men who played the role of the Eora greeters were men from rural New South Wales. They had been brought in from the Indigenous reserves where they lived and accommodated in police lock-ups while they waited for their performance. On the day, they were dressed in loincloths for their parts in the play. The story, captured in grainy film footage, shows white-trousered, gold-braided Englishmen stepping out of their longboats and on to the sand to be greeted by spear-wielding Indigenous men who melted away as the Englishmen advanced up the beach to raise the British flag. The tableau was a perfect recreation of *terra nullius*, and reinforced the understanding of the arrival of the British as worthy of celebration.

Away from this (re)production, another group of Indigenous peoples, along with their non-Indigenous supporters, were enacting a different story of the day, one they called the Aboriginal Day of Mourning. Indigenous people here deliberately contrasted the non-Indigenous day of celebration with their own understanding of the day as one of remembering trauma. Jack Patten of the Aborigines Progressive Association gave a radio interview explaining the Day of Mourning:

You [white Australians] are going to celebrate your 150th Anniversary of 26th January next, but that day will be a day of mourning for us! . . . [W]e have no reason to rejoice. You have taken our land away from us, polluted us with disease, employed us at starvation wages, and treated many of our women dishonourably . . . [Y]ou have refused to educate Aborigines and half-castes up to your own standards of citizenship. You have never extended the hand of real friendship to us (Attwood and Markus 1999: 80).

When asked what Indigenous people wanted, Jack Patten replied:

We want to be regarded as normal, average human beings, the same as yourselves. We ask you not to treat us as outcasts, but to give us education and equal opportunity, which is our birth-right. Don't forget this, we are the real Australians, and we ask the invaders of this country, who brought new ideas to our land, to give us the chance to share in modern progress . . . I repeat we do not ask for charity, we only ask for equal opportunity (Attwood and Markus 1999: 81).

Jack Patten's story of the nation is one that asks non-Indigenous Australians to acknowledge the impact of their invasion on 26 January 1788. It asks non-Indigenous Australians to rectify the negative impacts this invasion has had on Indigenous peoples by changing their treatment of Indigenous peoples—changes that could be brought about, Patten suggests, through 'friendship' and 'equal opportunity'.

Many of the points made on the Day of Mourning were made again 50 years later, on 26 January 1988, when Indigenous people were still asking for justice. The government-sponsored bicentennial celebrations of 1988 were staged on an even grander scale than the 150th anniversary. The various federal governments of the 1980s set up high-level organising committees to oversee the development of a coherent theme for the year, to decide the form of the year-long celebrations, and also to plan the grand-scale events for the day itself—which included a royal visit.

One of the key tasks was to choose a theme. The year needed a slogan and a logo; it needed a story. However, the choice of a theme and focus for the bicentenary was fraught. The makeup of the committee changed over the years, as did the political persuasion of the federal government. One committee decided the theme needed to recognise the continual influx of people to the continent, not just the 1788 arrival. They decided the theme was to be: 'we are all immigrants'—making the point all Australians have come from somewhere else and have chosen to love Australia. Their theme emphasised that all Australians had an equal claim to being part of Australia. It asserted that any claim to Australian-ness should not depend on length of stay in Australia, but on a commitment to the country. The logic was that the different communities—whether they had been in Australia 10 000 years, 200 years or ten years—were all equal. The committee wanted to include the millions of non-British migrants who had come to Australia since 1788, but especially since 1945. This attempted to remove the focus from the particular community linked to the arrival of the First Fleet, which emphasised Sydney Harbour as the originary space of the nation and the British as the key future citizens.

The we are all immigrants theme certainly does work to open up opportunities for more inclusive alternative narratives of the nation. It makes differences in stories of belonging invisible. However, in this narrative, the tradeoff is that if Anglo–Australians give up their claim to being special, Indigenous peoples are also removed from any claim to being special as well. The claims by Indigenous peoples that their Indigeneity gives them a different right to the land and belonging is erased—because we are all immigrants together. The specificity of Indigenous peoples' original and ongoing connection with the land is reduced to a walk across an ancient land bridge millennia ago, and this is seen to be the equivalent of arriving by a Qantas jumbo jet thousands of years later. The government did not accept we are all immigrants as the bicentenary theme, but it still operates as a popular way of understanding Australian-ness.

The Aboriginal Year of mourning

Indigenous peoples, as well as many non-Indigenous peoples, were quite aware of the incongruity of spending millions of dollars on the bicentennial celebrations when those displaced by the colonisation process—Indigenous peoples—were often living in significantly disadvantaged communities. Indigenous community and political groups were very active during this period, even though the origin of this activism was decades earlier. It was in the mid 1970s that the federal government began to promise significant political and social changes for Indigenous peoples. The 1976 *Northern Territory Land Rights Act* was supposed to herald a national land rights scheme. Promises of a treaty were also given. These promises were responses to, as well as fuelled by, Indigenous activism in this decade. By the mid 1980s, when it was becoming obvious that these promises were not going to be kept, a large and diverse Indigenous activist community made the recognition of 1988 as an Aboriginal Year of Mourning a priority.

There were significant differences between 1938 and 1988. Many of the Indigenous participants in the 1938 re-enactment were 'living under the Act'. This meant they were classified as Aboriginal by the New South Wales government and their lives were regulated by the *Aborigines Protection Act*. To come to Sydney, they needed permission from the manager to leave the Aboriginal reserves where they lived. If they knew about the Day of Mourning meeting, they could not just turn up. Similarly, for many of the performers, the choice to be part of the re-enactment was not entirely theirs. Further, Indigenous people who were not 'living under the Act' were not allowed to freely fraternise with Indigenous people who were. Indigenous people's lives, as the participants in the meeting passionately argued, were highly regulated by the government.

In 1988, Indigenous peoples could no longer be dragooned into Australia Day events by government-appointed protectors. All Indigenous peoples could choose what they wanted to do on this day. They were now legally recognised as equal citizens—a significant change since 1938. A key marker of the Aboriginal Year of Mourning was the March for Justice, Freedom and Hope through the streets of Sydney on 26 January. As they had 50 years earlier, Indigenous peoples would again challenge the dominant story of Australia's national day. In the days before 26 January 1988, thousands and thousands of Indigenous people and their supporters streamed into Sydney from all over the country. The march was the largest gathering of Indigenous peoples in the history of the nation. As with the original Day of Mourning in 1938, the day was marked by two marches—one that was solely for Indigenous peoples followed by one where non-Indigenous supporters joined them.

However large the Indigenous presence was in the city of Sydney that day, it was more than matched by hundreds of thousands of non-Indigenous celebrators who may have had little interest in the protest. These two different realisations of Australia Day sat together in the same space, occasionally rubbing up against each other. When the replica of the First Fleet came into Sydney Harbour, it was greeted by thousands of waving fans on foreshore, but also by thousands of hissing protesters who entreated it to go home or, even better, to recognise the sovereignty of the Indigenous owners of the land to which it (re)came.

Showcasing Indigenous survival and empowerment

In the years following the bicentenary celebrations/protests, there has been increasing recognition of the multiple meanings of Australia Day. Indigenous communities have continued to challenge understanding of this holiday as being solely about the celebration of British achievement. Many refer to the day as 'Invasion Day' or 'Survival Day' rather than Australia Day. Calling the day Survival Day is recognition of the ongoing and proud tradition of Indigenous peoples in Australia. Indigenous peoples also organise alternative ways of marking the public holiday—particularly with concerts and festivals. For example, in Perth, the 2005 Survival Day concert took place in Supreme Court Gardens and was called 'Healing Without Violence'. Sydney's Survival Day Concert 'is a celebration of the cultural, physical and spiritual survival of Indigenous Australians . . . highlighting the energy and diversity of Indigenous music and dance'. The Yabun concert, also in Sydney, celebrates 'self-empowerment within Sydney's Indigenous community'. These festivals and concerts showcase the continuity and dynamism of the Indigenous cultures. They also demonstrate the diversity of Indigenous communities. Different concerts have different aims and desires. The proliferation and popularity of these festivals, with both Indigenous and non-Indigenous peoples, shows that Indigenous peoples' stories are beginning to occupy more space in the nation.

In the twenty-first century, it has become difficult for many Australians to celebrate Australia Day without some acknowledgement of the mixed meanings of the day. In the decades since 1988, there have been more efforts to broaden the day to include more recently arrived Australians. The emphasis on mass citizenship ceremonies on this special day encourages another story of Australian-ness. The day is represented in the media as a complex day where some people celebrate the arrival of the First Fleet with a visit to Sydney Harbour, while others celebrate with a street or community barbecue, not really linking the day to an event over 200 years ago. Others quite specifically acknowledge the Indigenous meanings of the day by attending Indigenous-organised events in their community. For many young Australians, the tainted nature of 26 January as Australia Day is too obvious to ignore; many suggest another day should be chosen as Australia's national day. One of the most popular alternatives suggested in recent years has been Anzac Day.

Anzac Day

Like Australia Day, Anzac Day has a long and complex history as a day of national remembrance. The day commemorates the landing of Australian soldiers on the Gallipoli peninsula in Turkey during World War I. The soldiers landed on 25 April 1915, undertaking the first major Australian military campaign of the war: a drawn-out and costly series of battles ending in withdrawal and defeat in December of that year. The first anniversary of the landing, in 1916, was marked by ceremonies in Australia and London. The commemoration was officially named Anzac Day in that year, and has been marked in Australia ever since. During World War II, the meaning of the day expanded to commemorate Australian soldiers who died in the 1939–45 war, and as Australia participated in more military actions, right up to the twenty-first century War on Terror, these wars were also added and acknowledged. The contemporary Anzac Day begins with commemorative Dawn Services and then moves on to parades of returned service personnel and ancillary services. It concludes with visits to the pub by the parade participants and spectators and hours of drinking, gambling and catching up. These services, parades and drinking sessions take place in cities and towns all over Australia.

Anzac Day, and the idea of Anzac, form a significant story of Australian-ness. It is through the remembrance of Anzac that a powerful story of the birth and development of a nation, as well as sacrifice and service to the nation, has been created and reproduced. As Ann Curthoys (1998: 174–76) notes: 'In the story of Anzac lies the emotional locus of Australian narratives of nation.' This emotional locus is sometimes represented in terms of grief—individual and national. However, the emotional weight of the narrative also makes it effective in terms of pedagogy and as a site for instilling disciplining practices of good citizenship. For example the Anzac Day Commemoration Committee (Queensland) Incorporated sponsors a website www.anzacday.org.au which provides materials for school children about Anzac Day. They argue: 'Learning about ANZAC Day helps young children to understand the life and times of Australia and its people.' Similarly a Victorian government report on Anzac Day laws had a chapter on education:

> The Committee received overwhelming endorsement for the need to develop appropriate strategies to ensure that school children are

educated about ANZAC Day and the ANZAC spirit. (Scrutiny of Acts and Regulations Committee 2002)

The role of Anzac Day is both commemorative but also educative—to teach Australians about something called 'Anzac spirit'.

Anzac innocence

At the centre of the story of Anzac is the individual Australian serviceman, emblematised as the Aussie digger. The most prevalent image of this figure is of the World War I Australian Imperial Force, or AIF, recruits. These recruits are remembered as young, beautiful men sent to needless sacrifice, but still men who were willing to sacrifice their lives for their nation.

Extending on this image of the young soldier is a more general representation of the meaning of Anzac Day in terms of innocence—both individual and national. A common cliché when representing the Gallipoli campaign, and World War I generally, is to perceive it as the moment when the Australian nation lost its innocence. One of the most popular and powerful renditions of this narrative of innocence is Peter Weir's film *Gallipoli* (1981). As Dermody and Jacka (1988: 159) write: 'the location of much of the film in the Australian outback sets it up as "the place where bodies are toughened and perfected, practical skills of survival and initiative are learnt, and a peculiarly Australian innocence is bred".' The film, with its beautiful young stars—especially the breathless innocence of Archie, the young athlete who dies in the film's last shot—produces a story of naive or unworldly young men caught up in an event that betrayed their value system.

The increasing popularity for young Australians to visit Gallipoli in Turkey as part of a European holiday tour has also reinforced the idea of Anzac innocence. Photographs of the silhouettes of young Australian visitors, with their packs on their backs, climbing the cliffs and hills of the area, sometimes appear on newspaper front pages around the time of Anzac Day. The media images invite a comparison to be made between the young visitors of the early twenty-first century and those young men, almost a century earlier, whose packs were not loaded with travel guides and spare jumpers but with supplies and ammunition. The conflation of backpacker and soldier empties the Gallipoli digger icon of its specific meaning—a member of a military force at war in another country—and makes it a lyrical figure signifying some mix of youthful naivete and antipodean thrill at seeing the world. This innocence abroad image also invites an over-identification with the diggers. Such representations encourage young Australian visitors to ignore the difference between the experiences of the soldiers, who suffered unimaginably in the filthy, dangerous trenches, and their own experience of the Gallipoli peninsula. Rather, roughing it, sleeping overnight under the stars and climbing the cliffs are represented as allowing the Australian tourist to experience what the men did. It suggests a reality when the tourist is actually participating in national myth-making.

The increasing practice in the Anzac Day marches of substituting grandchildren for their now-dead grandfathers, who were returned service men, also reinforces the idea of the innocence of the original Anzacs, and by association all Australian military personnel. The sight of very old soldiers walking along with very young children, especially young girls, proudly wearing their grandfathers' medals, creates a scene where it is difficult to understand war and war commemoration as anything other than the remembrance of innocence lost. It makes it difficult for those who are dissenters to question the validity of Australian military participation as criticism gets translated into a refusal to acknowledge the sacrifice of young and good men.

Over the decades, the Anzac Day rituals and stories have mythologised the experience of the Australian soldier at war. This has worked to create a powerful story of an homogenous Anzac. More than this, the mythologising 'replaces the complexity of human acts with the simplicity of essences' (Buchanan 1999: 27). It is this mythical and homogenous 'essence' that is seen at so many memorials and cenotaphs around the country—a tall, lean, muscular, larger-than-life masculine figure represents the digger. Also created is an homogenous experience of being an Australian soldier. This story, as encapsulated by a governor general, is said to be about 'courage, and endurance, and duty, and mateship, and good humour, and the survival of a sense of self-worth' (Buchanan 1999: 27). For many thousands of men and women, this is their story. And each person who has gone to war requires recognition of what they have been willing to sacrifice. However, the endless recitation of the 'commentary' of a singular military experience that is seen to derive from 'the sum of those human and national values which our pioneers found in the raw bush of a new world and tested in the old world for the first time at Gallipoli' (Buchanan 1999: 27) erases the variety of experiences of the people who have been to war. Other experiences are silenced by the dominant story (Thompson 1994). Indeed, the empty national 'commentary' stands in for the multiple stories of war. The complex reasons why men join up to fight in a war, their experiences of war, their different reactions to combat and death, and their myriad understandings of what their actions might or might not achieve are ignored in favour of the myth.

Other stories of being an Anzac

If these other stories were acknowledged it would result in a very different Anzac commemoration than presently exists. Mental illness is a significant part of landscape of war (Garton 1996, Mant 2002). In both World War I and World War II and right through to the Vietnam War, Australian governments tried to refuse to recognise that many soldiers have suffered Post Traumatic Stress Disorder as a result of combat. The prevailing belief was that it was a predisposition (Muir 2002). As a result ex-military personnel suffering mental illnesses and their advocates have had to fight hard for recognition of, and compensation for, their war injuries. What would happen if the cost to individual men and their families of these injuries and their neglect was included in Anzac mythology? Other aspects of people's experience of war could also be added to the Anzac story. What if the meaning of Anzac was opened up to include wars fought on Australian soil, or the experiences of women raped in war (Elder 2005)? What if the domestic violence that many men enact on their families after the violence of their war experience was talked about openly (Allen 1990: 130–56)? What would be gained and what would be lost? How would ideas of Australian-ness be changed? These stories are told in some places, but they are never put in the centre of the public story. If they were, a more nuanced and representative story of the experiences of war would be available. What would be lost, however, would be the usefulness of Anzac Day as an uncomplicated nationalistic story that can be deployed to reinforce a very narrow sense of shared history and future.

As seductive and as powerful as the homogenous cult of the Anzac has been since 1915, the desire to produce an 'inclusive national narrative' of 'harmony and unity' has always been 'deeply fractured and constantly contested' (Curthoys 1998: 174). As Ann Curthoys suggests: 'These white national narratives are not altogether straightforward . . . they have their shadow, their dangerous supplement, which lie inside the story, threatening to undo them' (1998: 178). Some of the 'shadows' threatening the coherence of the Anzac story are those that include women.

In the early 1980s, radical feminists in different major cities in Australia organised protests and set up alternative remembrance ceremonies on 25 April to recognise women who had been raped in war. For example, in 1981 approximately 300 women belonging to a group called Women Against Rape (WAR) attempted to join the end of the Canberra Anzac parade. Sixty-five people—mostly women— were arrested. News stories reporting on the day represented the actions as the protests of 'lesbian Marxists' who had disrupted the parades by lying down in the middle of the road and taking off their clothes. (The first claim was probably true for a few members of the march; the second was a fantasy.) The magistrate who heard the cases of the Canberra women arrested used the idea of terrorism and mutiny to refer to the women's actions, and sentenced three of the women to one month's gaol—for coming within 400 metres of the tail end of an Anzac Day parade (Elder 2005). The feminists told an alternative story about Anzac, one that challenged the innocence, duty and courage narrative. It was shut down immediately by the state. These alternative experiences of what war might mean to Australian women in particular were not given any space.

Though the threat to the parade and the day made by the women's protest was never significant, the violence and outrage the presence of the women elicited signifies the effort required in silencing alternative configurations to the national story of innocent military endeavour. The women were never invited to come into the march but their challenge opened up the march and the day to scrutiny. Over time their challenge provided a space within which to renegotiate the meaning of the day. The march was in many ways sanitised and demilitarised. Anzac Day has opened up even more to include a broader range of sacrifices. Other women—nurses in particular—were invited to be part of the march. A less threatening feminine 'other' was included.

The centralising of the national soldier rather than the victims of war is also demonstrated in another repressed aspect of the Anzac story—that of the wars fought between colonisers and Indigenous peoples in this land. Anzac Day, for all its rhetoric of inclusiveness, does not stretch to cover Indigenous people dying for their country against a British invader. Of course, there is room in the Anzac Day commemorations for Indigenous soldiers in the context of their participation in the Australian Defence Forces. Indigenous men and women march in the parades as ex-members of different regiments, medical and support groups. Given that Anzac Day and the rituals and monuments that accompany it can be any shape the community desires, why is there such a lack of interest in recognising the Indigenous military endeavour in defending their country? Perhaps because of the 'shadow' of another story—a story where non-Indigenous peoples are less heroically and less innocently positioned—worries many non-Indigenous Australians. To acknowledge Indigenous peoples' military actions to protect their land also opens up the possibility of recognition of Indigenous peoples' sovereign status as owners of this land.

A more complex story of the way in which Australians have achieved the present state of their nation would have to include less palatable elements. It could be argued that it would be churlish to embarrass those who are in the Anzac Day parades or who attend the museums to show their children or grandchildren what it was that they did in the war with confronting other stories. It would be uncomfortable for many Australians to find stories such as rape, racism and Australia as the aggressor in war alongside the more traditional stories of heroism. Yet, if the dominant story chosen as the national story is a sanitised one, then it needs to be acknowledged that someone is bearing the pain of exclusion. To protect the story of the digger, the stories of the women raped in war, the pacifists, and Indigenous peoples' experience of dispossession have all been sacrificed.

Anzac overseas

It has become increasingly popular for Australians, especially young Australians, to travel to Turkey for Anzac Day commemoration services at Gallipoli. Thousands of Australian visitors make the trip to Gallipoli every year. In 2005, Anzac Day commemorations at Anzac Cove in Turkey were seen as very special. It was the 90th anniversary of the original campaign. It was also understood that it was likely to be the last Anzac Day when veterans of World War I would be alive. Yet these commemorations were more controversial than usual. The first controversy was that to cope with the increasing numbers of visitors to Gallipoli, the Turkish government had built a new road to deal with the traffic. In doing this, the bones of some of the war dead whose remains still lie where they died in battle were disturbed. For many Australians, this was an unconscionable action on the part of the Turkish government. Others saw it as a side effect of the increasing popularity of Gallipoli for Australians. They asked how else the thousands of visitors were to be moved efficiently and carefully along the peninsula, which is both environmentally delicate and a massive war cemetery.

Some Australians mentioned that Australia regularly desecrates 'sacred sites' in Australia, but the outcry from non-Indigenous peoples about Indigenous sacred sites being disturbed is never so loud. Others noted that Gallipoli is not Australian soil—it is Turkish. Given this, the Turkish government could do what it wished. This aspect of the discussions foregrounded the fact that this important part of Australian national iconography is in fact overseas. It is not controlled by Australia. Indeed Prime Minister John Howard had discussions with the Turkish government at this time about the possibility of Gallipoli being placed on the Australian National heritage list (Davis 2005). The request was refused on the grounds that it could compromise Turkish sovereignty. These issues reinforce the invasive nature of the original Australia's presence at Gallipoli as part of a military endeavour attacking another nation.

On the night before Anzac Day 2005, there were some young people, amongst the thousands attending the Gallipoli services, who behaved badly—in particular, getting drunk and lounging on the gravestones. They also left their rubbish behind when they departed the peninsula the next day. Again, this set off a heated discussion in Australia about the meaning of such behaviour and Anzac traditions. Some letters to newspaper editors on the issue of these rowdy, irreverent partygoers argued this was an affront to the memory of the men who had fought at Gallipoli for future generations of Australians. The writers suggested that the original Anzacs would have never acted this way, that they were serious men who had a serious job to do. They believed that those who were visiting their graves should respect this and behave accordingly. Other letter writers claimed that such maverick behaviour was as typical of the Aussie digger then as it was of the Australian youth of today. They argued that those young men in 1915 would understand youthful hijinks and not mind if a young Aussie vomited behind their headstone. What united the letter-writers was the belief that the behaviour of the Australian tourists could be attributed to their Australian-ness and that Anzac Day was a central plank of being Australian. The actions of the visitors to Gallipoli were understood in terms of values that are reproduced in the very myth the young Australians were participating.

Reconciliation

In the discussion in 2005 about the disturbance of the bones of the long-dead soldiers at Gallipoli, some Australians drew on the experiences of Indigenous peoples to try to understand what the incident meant. This entailed an acknowledgement of the historical disregard for Indigenous peoples' lives by non-Indigenous peoples. Since the early 1990s, many of the issues of exclusion and second-class treatment of Indigenous peoples have begun to be acknowledged at a broader level by increasing numbers of non-Indigenous Australians. The 1990s was a period of intense rethinking and upheaval for many non-Indigenous peoples about their relationship with Indigenous peoples. This was not just about personal relationships, but also about the relationship of Indigenous peoples to the story of the nation. Many non-Indigenous people began to recognise that the dominant story only reflected their experiences rather than Indigenous peoples' lives. In that decade, a series of major challenges and shifts in government and legal understanding of the place of Indigenous peoples in the nation took place. The land claim case brought by Edward Koiki Mabo, a Torres Strait Islander man from the Island of Mer, reached the High Court and the judges found in favour of Mabo (see chapter 6). This meant the way in which non-Indigenous peoples placed Indigenous peoples in their legal stories about land were challenged. It was no longer possible to imagine that the exclusion of Indigenous people from the land over the last 200 years had been a just or even legal act. The passing of the *Native Title Act* in 1993 meant this exclusion could be challenged by Indigenous peoples and crown land returned to them. In 1997, another federal government inquiry, this one into the policy and practices of removing Indigenous children from their families was released (see chapter 6). The Human Rights and Equal Opportunity Commission report, *Bringing Them Home*, highlighted the extent of the practice of child removal across mainland Australia and detailed the devastating impact it had on Indigenous communities all over the country. This was obviously a decade where, at the government level, there was a focus on Indigenous peoples and their needs.

The whole decade was framed by a government and community project of reconciliation. In 1991, the federal parliament unanimously passed the *Council for Aboriginal Reconciliation Act* and a ten-year reconciliation period began. It aimed to:

promote a process of reconciliation between Aborigines and Torres Strait Islanders and the wider Australian community, based on an appreciation by the Australian community as a whole of Aboriginal and Torres Strait Islander cultures and achievements and of the unique position of Aborigines and Torres Strait Islanders as the indigenous peoples of Australia (*Council for Aboriginal Reconciliation Act* 1991: section 5).

The legislation convened a council which would work with the community and government to map out ways in which reconciliation could be achieved at both the local and the national level. The council was to be in existence for ten years, and in 2000 would hand over to the government a document of reconciliation. This was to be its 'road map' for Australians, setting out the basic principles that needed to be heeded for the reconciliation process to continue. For the first five or so years of its existence, the council had quite a low profile amongst the broader community in Australia. It undertook educational work and sponsored a series of scholarly publications setting out the main issues that needed to be addressed by governments, educational institutions and the general community in achieving reconciliation. The Council for Aboriginal Reconciliation and the idea of reconciliation really came into the national imaginary in the mid 1990s when changes to the *Native Title Act* were suggested by the federal government and *Bringing Them Home* was published. These two quite different events saw the meteoric growth of non-Indigenous groups in support of Indigenous rights.

However, the pivotal issue that put reconciliation on everyone's lips was the issue of apology. The *Bringing Them Home* report had within it a series of recommendations, ranging from the need to financially compensate and support Indigenous adults who had been removed as children, the establishment of a national archive, to the call for an apology to be extended to the 'stolen generations' by the prime minister on behalf of the non-Indigenous community. Prime Minister Howard refused to make this apology and an extended debate ensued. This refusal, and the publicity that surrounded it, had the effect of highlighting the process of reconciliation. The refusal to apologise was seen by many people—both Indigenous and non-Indigenous—as an act that stopped the reconciliation process from moving forward. Over the next year, many other members of government, different churches and religious groups, educational institutions and individuals said sorry to the members of the stolen generations. Formal apologies took place in the state houses of parliament. Many individuals signed 'sorry books'. This initiative, undertaken by a group called Australians for Native Title and Reconciliation (AnTAR), gave individuals or community groups the opportunity to write a personal message of apology for the policies of child removal.

All this time, the prime minister refused to apologise, arguing that it was not the responsibility of the present generation to apologise for the actions of those from an earlier generation. This ignited another set of community and scholarly discussions about Australian history. The prime minister and his followers argued that the way Australian history was being written ignored the fine achievements of non-Indigenous Australians in favour of a litany of accusations of violence and racism. The historians who wrote this history, including Henry Reynolds, Lyndall Ryan and Bain Attwood, and those who read it and found it relevant became known as the 'black armband' historians. Their response to the 'white blindfold' contingent (principally Keith Windshuttle) was to argue that only one side of the story had been told so far, and that the other side of the story of the formation of the nation had to be heard. The different groups highlighted the gulf that exists between different Australians and the enormity of any project of reconciliation.

The Bridge walk and Corroboree 2000

The Council for Aboriginal Reconciliation was in charge of organising Reconciliation Week in 2000 (the final year of its ten-year existence). One of its activities included a highly visible 'people's walk' over the Sydney Harbour Bridge. On 28 May 2000, somewhere between a quarter and a half a million people took up the Council's invitation, and the Harbour Bridge was closed for hours as Indigenous and non-Indigenous people from all over New South Wales and Australia streamed across it in a show of reconciliation. At some point in the morning a skywriter wrote the word Sorry several times in huge white letters in the blue autumn sky. When they had completed the walk, people were encouraged to move on to Darling Harbour where there were bands, musicians and a carnival-like atmosphere. The newspapers the next day carried banner headlines exclaiming 'Marchers bridge reconciliation gap', and 'Hands across the water'. In the weeks after the Sydney Bridge walk similar events took place in cities and towns across Australia. And again large numbers of Australians participated wherever the walks took place. The bridge walks were a potent symbol for signifying a wish for change.

The Sydney Harbour Bridge walk contrasted with a more formal ceremony that was also part of Reconciliation Week. This ceremony—Corroboree 2000—took place on the same weekend at the nearby Sydney Opera House. This ceremony had been organised so the Council for Aboriginal Reconciliation could hand over to the federal government (via the prime minister) its document of reconciliation. This document was the culmination of ten years' work and outlined the principles the council believed needed to underpin the understanding and the further pursuit of reconciliation.

The draft document of reconciliation, titled *The Declaration Towards Reconciliation*, was shown to the federal government for comment and discussion a few weeks before the Corroboree 2000 ceremony. The government did not agree with it, and so it was not accepted. Days of intense negotiation followed. As a media release from the prime minister's office at the time noted, the areas of disagreement were customary law, a national apology (compared with an expression of sorrow) and self-determination (Howard 2000). The document proposed by the Council for Aboriginal Reconciliation suggested:

> As we walk the journey of healing, one part of the nation apologises and expresses its sorrow and sincere regret for the injustices of the past, so the other part accepts the apologies and forgives.

The federal government's suggestion was:

> As we walk the journey of healing, Australians express their sorrow and profoundly regret the injustices of the past and recognise the continuing trauma and hurt still suffered by many Aboriginals and Torres Strait Islanders.

Besides stopping short of an apology, this particular phrasing deploys a common phrasing contrasting 'Australians' with 'Aboriginals and Torres Strait Islanders' as if the latter were not a part of the initial category. No compromise could be reached, so the document of reconciliation presented to the prime minister in the Opera House ceremony was that drafted by the Council for Aboriginal Reconciliation, including its commitment to self-determination and apology.

Though they were both part of Reconciliation Week in 2000, the contrast between the bridge walks and Corroboree 2000 is striking. At the bridge walks, the feeling of goodwill and joy was palpable. Indigenous people interviewed in vox pops at the Sydney Harbour Bridge walk expressed feelings of happiness, many saying that they had never felt such a strong tide of goodwill directed towards them. Non-Indigenous people expressed similar feelings of happiness, and suggested that a high point in race relations had been reached. Corroboree 2000 was a much more tense event. It was formally choreographed, and there was an invited audience including all leaders of

Australian governments. The event was tied to a very specific agenda: the completion of a report underpinned by national legislation.

In the Sydney Opera House, a very carefully worded statement was being handed over to a government whose political hopes were not the same as those of the Council for Aboriginal Reconciliation. The declaration was precise in what it said reconciliation was and what was required to achieve it. The bridge walks were amorphous sites and there were thousands of different ideas about what was required to achieve reconciliation (Pratt et al. 2001). While not dismissing the participants' feelings of connection and goodwill it is interesting to note that in many ways it was the emphasis on emotions rather than precise plans that made the bridge walks such feel-good events. The central word 'reconciliation' appeared everywhere—typed on badges, scrawled on banners, emblazoned on t-shirts. What reconciliation actually meant was not the same for everyone. Some declared that a treaty was required; others wanted land rights; while still others stated that 'love is all we need'. The open nature of the walks allowed space for myriad approaches to reconciliation, but it also meant that the crowd did not have to agree on a plan for the future. Though the idea of a group of dog owners in the Sydney event walking with their pets under the banner of 'Kelpies for Reconciliation' is cute, one can also ask what it really means. Obviously, walking over the Harbour Bridge was a powerful symbol of energy directed towards the project of reconciliation, but what were Australians going to do after they returned home from the walk? Did the walk seal reconciliation as achieved in Australia? Was it just the beginning, or was it an easy way to say 'I've done something' without having to consider the nitty-gritty issues of dispossession, child removal, cultural and economic loss and sovereignty? At Corroboree 2000, the *Declaration Towards Reconciliation* outlined the specific issues that had to be faced head on for a meaningful reconciliation to take place. The cautious approach of the government (as elected representative of the community) in accepting even these basic principles reflected the problems at the centre of the idea of reconciliation.

Interestingly, later that year the City of Sydney hosted the Olympic Games. Given the location, Australia was able to field a large team and was expected to do well in the medal tally. One of Australia's big hopes for a gold medal was the young Indigenous runner Cathy Freeman. Sure enough, she was in the 400 metres final. In the lead-up, Freeman (unusually so for her) had been quite vocal about the issue of apologising to the stolen generations, revealing that her grandmother had been taken from her family. In the weeks before the Games, there was much discussion about protests being held at the Olympics in response to the federal government's intransigence on a series of Indigenous issues. Freeman's attitude was that she would best make her presence felt by winning (Freeman 2000).

As it grew closer to the final of the 400-metre event, the hype about Freeman increased. In particular, the race began to be seen as a moment where reconciliation could be achieved. When Freeman won, the nation went wild. Neville Roach, writing for the *Sydney Morning Herald*, declared:

> when Cathy Freeman . . . won a gold medal, she united indigenous and non-indigenous Australians in the most inclusive celebrations in our nation's history. Reconciliation is a much longer, more complex and arduous race than the 400 metres, but its prize is far more valuable than all the gold medals of all the Olympics (2000: 10).

As with the bridge walks, the symbolism of Freeman's win was used to create a feeling of togetherness—although it was acknowledged that more had to be done. Again, as with the bridge walks, what this entailed was not specified: it was simply rhetorically represented as more precious than gold (Elder et al. 2007).

For many Indigenous and non-Indigenous people, reconciliation was a chance to right wrongs that had taken place over the 200-plus years of non-Indigenous occupation of the continent. Central to making things right was the need to recognise that Indigenous peoples had been dispossessed (their land stolen) and that they had lost their right to self-governance (they were part of the new regime, whether they liked it or not).

There are many different Indigenous viewpoints on how these wrongs may be righted, and there is near-universal agreement amongst Indigenous communities that the wrongs need to be properly acknowledged as having taken place, that they were unfair, and that they require some sort of action to change the unacceptable status quo. Fiona Nicoll (1993: 707) explains that reconciliation has two different meanings. One is to become reconciled *to* something, in the sense of not being able to change it; the other is to be reconciled *with* another. The slow-moving acknowledgement by many Australians of the original disadvantage suffered by Indigenous people means many non-Indigenous peoples do seem to expect Indigenous people to become reconciled *to* their ongoing ill-treatment. Reconciling *with* each other has to mean something more than getting excited when Cathy Freeman wins gold.

The *Declaration Towards Reconciliation* was one attempt to achieve such a change. It asserted principles all Australians can work towards in trying to achieve justice for all. Similarly, the banners unfurled on the bridge walks that declared the next step was a treaty suggested a path forward in the move towards acknowledging ongoing injustice. Yet, for many Australians—even those who enthusiastically stepped out on bridges across the country—the idea of changes such as self-determination, land rights and a treaty was threatening and went well beyond their understanding of what reconciliation entailed. These more extravagant notions of what reconciliation might mean suggested to many non-Indigenous peoples that they might have to give up something in the reconciliation process—perhaps their mostly unacknowledged place as the privileged group of the nation.

The popular calls for a treaty have not been followed up by most non-Indigenous peoples. It is easier to chant this as a slogan than it is to bring into being. Even if every Australian wanted a treaty between Indigenous and non-Indigenous peoples the negotiations would be a complex and fraught process. First, to establish a treaty requires 'nation to nation' discussions (Tully 1998: 151). Many Australians baulk at this initial step. 'Nation to nation' means the recognition by the Australian state of Indigenous peoples' sovereignty—the right to self-government. Establishing Indigenous self-government is inter- preted by some citizens as meaning the dissolution of the singular Australian state and the formation of a separate, or separatist, Indigenous state. For some Australians this is positive (Mansell 2002) for others it is negative (Windschuttle 2001b). So powerful is the pleasurable story of a united Australia that even at an emotional, rather than a practical level, a treaty is understood by many people as divisive for the nation, rather than a just recognition of Indigenous peoples' rights (Kirk 2000).

Scholars such as James Tully (1998) and Fiona Nicoll (2000) point out that Indigenous peoples already possess a sovereignty, and the right to self-government does not come into being only if it is recognised by non-Indigenous peoples. Therefore, the failure to recognise this sovereignty continues a longstanding system of inequality. So the call for a treaty is an implicit recognition of this sovereignty; the failure to act on it reflects the practical and emotional work that would follow this non-Indigenous recognition. One part of this work would be the process of giving up the story of the singular Australian nation.

In sacrificing something in the process of reconciliation, non- Indigenous people would also have to give up their long-held understanding of themselves as 'good'—a vision that is reinforced repeatedly in national discourse and, in particular, in war commemoration. In these stories, Australians are the innocents abroad, the ones who fight for what is right against aggressors who desire that which is not theirs. The process of reconciliation, requires non-Indigenous peoples to acknowledge that the British colonisers were the aggressors in a process that led to the Indigenous peoples of Australia being dispossessed, and that they are the ongoing benefactors of that long-ago process. This shift from innocent to 'bad' or 'compromised' can be painful, especially for a group of people so heavily invested in themselves as good. Yet again, a failure to acknowledge this means someone else has to pay the price. Here it is the Indigenous peoples who must bear the burden.

As suggested earlier in this book, national stories or feelings of belonging to a nation must be continually reinforced. The idea of being Australian is not an innate feeling. For the idea of being Australian to have particular meanings, these meaning must be produced against all other possible meanings. National days are important events in the production of these meanings. Australia Day and Anzac Day are central stories in creating feelings of loyalty and love of country. Yet they are never uncontested. Many citizens engage with the spectacle of these days—parades, fireworks, even the sadness of the Anzac dawn services—yet they are still contested and open to critique because there are always other ways of understanding citizenship and belonging. The critiques made by Indigenous peoples to the choice of 26 January as Australia's national day have been particularly effective and the stories told about Australia Day have changed. More citizens are aware of the limits of the day as one of simple celebration and understand the criticisms made by citizens who have suffered as a result of colonialism. For many citizens the solution has been to think about other meaningful commemorations as Australia Day. Anzac Day often seems like the logical choice. The critiques made of Anzac Day in the 1970s and 1980s have faded and in the twenty-first century the day is the focus of both government and community campaigns that centralise Australian war experiences and military sacrifice as emblematic of Australian-ness. However, Anzac Day is a holiday that does work producing particular stories of the nation. Though it has a powerful mystique about it, it can also work to produce quite conservative stories of the nation.

In thinking about national days and their meanings when one day becomes problematic, as Australia Day has for some citizens, the solution is not to simply find another day or event to celebrate, but to explore what the criticisms say about the story of the nation told by that particular holiday.

FURTHER READING

Australian Declaration Towards Reconciliation 2000, cited at <www.austlii.edu.au/au/other/IndigLRes/car/2000/12/pg3.htm>, accessed on 11 March 2007.

Bennett, Tony, Buckridge, Pat, Carter, David and Mercer, Colin (eds) 1992, *Celebrating the Nation: A Critical Study of Australia's Bicentenary*, Allen & Unwin, Sydney.

Corroboree Speeches 2000, cited at <www.austlii.edu.au/au/other/IndigLRes/car/2000/14/speeches.htm>, accessed on 11 March 2007.

Dodson, Pat 1999, *Until the Chains are Broken*, Fourth Vincent Lingiari Lecture, cited at <www.austlii.edu.au/au/other/IndigLRes/car/pubs.html#publish>, accessed on 11 March 2007.

Human Rights and Equal Opportunity Commission 1997, *Bringing Them Home: Report of the National Inquiry in the Separation of Aboriginal and Torres Strait Islander Children from their Families*, HREOC, Canberra.

Inglis, Ken 1998, *Sacred Places: War Memorials in the Australian Landscape*, The Miegunyah Press, Melbourne.

Kalantzis, Mary and Cope, Bill (eds) 2001, *Reconciliation, Multiculturalism, Identities: Difficult Dialogues, Sensible Solutions*, Common Ground, Altona.

Moreton-Robinson, Aileen (ed.) 2004, *Whitening Race: Essays in Social and Critical Criticism*, Aboriginal Studies Press, Canberra.

Pratt, Angela 2005, *Practising Reconciliation? The Politics of Reconciliation in the Australian Parliament, 1991–2000*, Parliament of Australia, Canberra.

Reconciliation Australia, cited at <www.reconciliationaustralia.org>, accessed on 11 March 2007.

Road Map for Reconciliation: cited at <www.austlii.edu.au/au/other/IndigLRes/car/2000/10>, accessed on 11 March 2007.

Spillman, Lyn 1997, *Nation and Commemoration: Creating National Identities in the United States and Australia*, Cambridge University Press, Cambridge.

Stocks, Jenni (ed.) 1998, *Images and Language '88: Aboriginal Perspectives on a Celebration*, Inner City Education Centre, Sydney.

10

TAKING TO THE STREETS

(non) National uses of public spaces

Not all those Australians who take to the streets for parades and ceremonies are doing so to explicitly mark or even contest national stories. In this chapter, the focus is on the use of public spaces by groups whose claims or demands are not understood generally as national. However, these street-based events can still be about the nation because they may produce or contest stories of the nation. The three very disparate examples of street action chosen are labour protests, flashmobs and the Sydney Gay and Lesbian Mardi Gras parade. For many Australians, the era of the large street protest is associated with the huge anti-Vietnam War rallies of the late 1960s. This is often accompanied by a suggestion that Australians, especially contemporary Australian youth, are post-political (Evans and Sternberg 1999, Mendes 1999, Vromen 2004). The numbers of people attending reconciliation walks, labour protests and anti-war rallies in the early 2000s suggests this is not exactly the case; however, it is worth investigating the reasons people do take to the streets these days, to see how they fill that street space and how it relates to the idea of the Australian nation.

Everyday understandings of public space are premised on the notion that it is equally open and accessible to all. Public space is understood as part of the public sphere. Public spaces are places where individuals come together to discuss issues of common concern. The public sphere is not equitable space. Indigenous peoples, women, gay men and lesbians, people with disabilities—these groups are all, at one time or another, marginalised in this sphere.

And when groups are sidelined in the public sphere, 'counterpublics' develop. A counterpublic is 'an arena of alternative value formation "where members of subordinated social groups invent and circulate counter-discourses to formulate oppositional interpretations of their identities, interests and needs"' (Bailey and Iveson 2000: 519). So a counterpublic (perhaps a trade union meeting in the lunchroom or a gay social club gathering in a local pub) is a place where groups who feel isolated from the public sphere figure out ways of inserting themselves and their messages and values into that sphere. This often involves taking up public space.

Janis Bailey and Kurt Iveson (2000) note that the entry of subordinated groups into public space is not seamless. They generally do not enter the public sphere with their values, ideas and claims organised and ready to 'deliver' to the dominant society. Bailey and Iveson argue that the process of marginalised groups entering the public sphere is a multifaceted one. On one hand, it works to represent the alternative values held by the subordinate group, but on the other it actually helps form those values. Participants or members of a marginal group use the public events they have organised to 'negotiate their relationships with each other, even to debate the very political points they wish to make' (Bailey and Iveson 2000: 530). So, during a protest event, a pre-determined message is not simply delivered to the general citizenry (usually via the media), following which the participants return home. Rather, the participation in a protest involves the coming together of multiple stories—and this can mean clashes, interactions and exchanges between different individuals and groups *within* the protest. Think how many people there are at a protest—often hundreds, sometimes tens of thousands—most of whom do not know each other. It is unlikely that everyone there has exactly the same take on the issue.

Actions in public spaces—the streets, in front of parliament houses—are ways in which groups assert their values and understandings of how an aspect of the nation should work; however, they are also ways in which groups become aware of how others, who are out there in the streets with them, view the situation. So, for example, on a picket line the value espoused by the participants might be justice for workers. Being on the picket and interacting with others—both supporters and opponents—help to define what that justice is. A parent–worker on the picket may make different points to those made by a single person. A person in a wheelchair may suggest issues that others have not thought of. So what constitutes justice for Australian workers is being figured out by the members of the group as they protest. And of course, just because a group is marginalised does not mean its members are saints—factions within groups may very well come to blows or splinter in the face of differences of interpretation.

Labour protests

As discussed in chapter 2 there is a history of labour protest in Australia. In fact, the commemoration of labour agitation is integrated into the national story as a holiday. Most states have a Labour Day public holiday at some stage during the year—though in the twenty-first century it is in serious competition with the Queen's Birthday as the least-noticed and most underwhelming public holiday in terms of pomp and circumstance, and community participation. Compared with the build-up to days such as Anzac Day and Australia Day, Labour Days pass almost uncommented on. This was not always the case. Labour Day—which recognises the eight-hour day movement of the 1850s—was once a huge affair. Celebrating Labour Day in the early parts of the twentieth century was not understood in terms of protest, but as an integral part of the fabric of the nation. Labour Day was a day when men and women could celebrate and have acknowledged their contribution to the nation. Over time, the street marches that marked Labour Day disappeared or dwindled as trade union membership dropped and the shape of work life changed. However, as will be demonstrated, there are still labour protests that contest ideas of what it means to be Australian in the workplace.

The Gurindji walkout

Before discussing more recent protests, it is important to focus on an older protest that changed the landscape of Australian national stories of work and protest. It is the story of the Gurindji people of Dagaragu in the Northern Territory. The working conditions of Indigenous peoples in both the cattle industry and more broadly across the economy were appalling for most of the twentieth century. Pay rates were low and there were even situations where Indigenous peoples were not paid wages at all. In addition, there were high levels of maltreatment of Indigenous peoples—especially in isolated or private workplaces. Yet in the public sphere (parliaments, media, the law courts) the level of discussion about this unjust situation was not significant. Though there were a number of groups—both Indigenous and non-Indigenous—working on campaigns for full civil rights and better working conditions for Indigenous peoples, they were not central to national discussions about justice. The Gurindji protest and strike established a counterpublic that centred the story of the lives and living conditions of Indigenous peoples in the national narrative of work. This centring was hard-won. The physical location of the protesters on a piece of land in the Northern Territory and the marginal place of Indigenous peoples in the public sphere perhaps explain why it took over eight years for the protest to fully register and to be resolved.

In August 1966, Vincent Lingiari, a Gurindji man who was working on the huge Wave Hill cattle station, a property that was laid over his own country, approached the station manager and asked, on behalf of other Indigenous workers, for their pay to increase to $25 a week. Though a rise of this amount would still leave Indigenous workers' wages well below those of non-Indigenous workers, the request was rejected. The issue of pay was the last in a long line of requests Lingiari had put forward to improve Indigenous people's conditions on the station. Over time, he had also brought to the manager's attention the use of Indigenous child labour and the sexual abuse of Indigenous women (Attwood and Markus 1999: 225). So, when the pay rise was rejected, it was the last straw: Lingiari told his employer that he was no longer working for the manager. Lingiari consulted with the full community, and he and all the other Indigenous people on the station stopped work and moved to Dagaragu, or Wattie Creek as it is also known, a site on the Wave Hill property that is very special to the Gurindji. At this spot, the Gurindji protesters and workers sat down and waited for justice. So began one of the longest strikes in the history of Australia. It is important to note here that the Gurindji workers did not walk *off* the property, and also the strike was never simply a labour strike. As Lingiari explained: 'the issues on which we are protesting is neither purely economic nor political but moral . . . on August 22 1996 the Gurindji tribe decided to cease living like dogs' (Broome 1994: 141). The walk out also marked the beginning of a formal claim for the return of their country. This is made clear in the 1967 petition the Gurindji sent the governor general:

> We, the leaders of the Gurindji people, write to you about our earnest desire to regain tenure of our tribal lands in the Wave Hill–Limbunya area of the Northern Territory, of which we were dispossessed in time past and for which we received no recompense. . . . (In August last year, we walked away from the Wave Hill Cattle Station. It was said that we did this because wages were very poor (only six dollars per week),

living conditions fit only for dogs, and rations consisting mainly of salt beef and bread. True enough. But we walked away for other reasons as well. To protect our women and our tribe, to try to stand on our own feet. We will never go back there) (Attwood and Markus 1999: 224–25).

The Gurindji made the point that for years and years they had worked on *their* land without pay and without the recognition that it was *their* country. So the original strike, which was framed in terms of work conditions and treatment, was additionally formulated in terms of land rights.

The owners of Wave Hill (Vestey, an overseas company) were in no mood to negotiate. Instead, the Gurindji workers were replaced and life went on. However, the strike and search for justice never faltered. As well as petitioning the governor general, Lingiari travelled to the east coast of Australia and spoke with both Vestey officials and the federal government. Though very little was offered to the strikers by either of these groups, there was a significant amount of publicity and support for the strikers. This strike and protest had highlighted the appalling conditions in which Indigenous people across the Northern Territory lived, and it tied in with other civil rights actions in the same period. As a result, many people from all around Australia contributed to fighting funds for the strikers.

The staying power of the Gurindji and the national momentum that their strike gathered is captured in Paul Kelly and Kev Carmody's well-known song 'From Little Things Big Things Grow' (1994) which tells the story of the strike:

> Vestey man said I'll double your wages
> Seven quid a week you'll have in your hand
> Vincent said uhuh we're not talking about wages
> We're sitting right here till we get our land
> Vestey man roared and Vestey man thundered
> You don't stand the chance of a cinder in snow
> Vince said if we fall others are rising

Over the years, efforts were made to end the strike, but they did not meet the requirements and needs of the strikers. As Kelly's and Carmody's song says, Vestey's management offered more money. The government offered to move the strikers to a more convenient spot closer to welfare amenities. None of these offers addressed the issue of land and justice, so the Gurindji refused them. It was only in the early 1970s that progress began to be made. Vestey offered the

Gurindji title over a small portion of the land they were demanding. More importantly, in 1972 a new government came to power that was far more sympathetic to Indigenous peoples' demands for land rights. Finally, genuine negotiation took place. The outcome was a splitting of the lease of the land—half became Gurindji land, the other half remained with Vestey. An eight-year long protest carried out thousands and thousands of kilometres from the nearest big city was successful.

Over that eight or so years, the identities claimed by the Gurindji—as workers and as Indigenous people with a sovereign claim to land—were heard by members of the wider public sphere. The strike took place at a time when understandings held by non-Indigenous peoples of the status and rights of Indigenous peoples were being challenged and changed. The protest by the Indigenous people at the Wave Hill station constructed a counterpublic that began to resonate in governments, unions and community organisations around the nation. The broader protest allowed people from a variety of public spheres (Indigenous, labour, feminist) to talk to each other and work out ways in which their concerns about work and justice were linked in terms of rights. The protest also connected with other parts of the Indigenous justice story and worked to reshape the idea of being Australian in terms of being both Indigenous and a worker.

The maritime union strike

In the contemporary period, the counterpublic developed by labour unions and workers is often presumed to be antithetical to that of a wider public. As Shaun Wilson (1998) notes, in Australia the mainstream media generally represent the trade union movement as acting against the good of the nation. For example, the suggestion is that their protests will cause 'economic damage' to the economy or breach the 'national duty' of the labour force to increase productivity (Wilson 1998: 26). Though this narrative of the sectional and divisive demands of the union movement today is a powerful story of Australian-ness, it is not totalising. Sometimes the values developed or highlighted in a counterpublic space produced by unions *do* resonate with a wider public, which challenges the story of trade union protest as un-Australian selfishness.

A good example is the Maritime Union of Australian (MUA) strike which took place in 1998. A shipping company—Patricks— wanted to replace its unionised workforce with one that was not unionised. Having trained replacement workers overseas, the company sacked 1400 workers one morning. The workers, supported by the MUA, went on strike claiming a lack of justice and the illegality of this decision. A number of industrial commentators have analysed the strike and suggested that Patricks and the federal government probably imagined the media would run the story of the strike in terms of 'wharfies' as un-Australian 'bludgers' who would not know a fair day's work if it bit them on the nose (Wilson 1998, Trinca 2000, Vandenberg 2001). As Helen Trinca writes: 'Who would have thought that the wharfies could win the media battle at the end of the 1990s, at a time when unions generally were losing their clout and when many Australians had negative ideas about the waterfront union in particular' (2000: 107).

The support for the strike was substantial. The story of the legitimacy of the strike, as imagined and presented by the unions, in concert with favourable legal judgments for the MUA, meant the values of the trade union counterpublic resonated with a larger group of people than perhaps was expected. The union story of the likely possibility of this type of industrial action (sacking and replacement with non-union labour) becoming more common seemed to make sense to other workers. It may have resonated in particular with white- and blue-collar workers who had felt the cool wind of neo-liberal downsizing. Those workers, who were not happy with the rationalisation of work life that had been taking place over the previous decade, perhaps also saw the need for strike action.

Added to this broad worker support, the usual media stories of union 'thuggery', violence and so-called unrepresentative strike actions did not fit with what was actually happening in the MUA dispute. Again citing Shaun Wilson (1998), the protest sites—which were the picket lines—were organised around peaceful protest (drawing on the tactics of non-violent green protests). The protesters were mixed—including well-known Australian actors, children, right-wing or more conservative unions and women's support groups for the maritime workers (Baker and Oakham 1999: 132). More than this, the MUA received international support that further legitimated its cause. All of this countered the story that was being narrated by the company and the federal government. It was hard for Australians who watched the news or attended the picket to see peacefully protesting Australians being menaced by dogs hired by the company as union violence. In this atmosphere, the usual story of hard-line unionists as un-Australian because they did not play by the rules of a fair day's work for a fair day's pay did not make sense. Another story of the right to be a worker and a unionist, as well as the one about a 'fair go', dominated and, though not all were happy with the outcome in this instance, the dominant story produced in this space was that, in the twenty-first century, Australian-ness *could* be about being a unionist.

In 2005, the federal Liberal–National coalition government passed legislation to change industrial relations in Australia. This legislation *Workplace Relations Amendment (Work Choices) Act* 2005 is regarded by most experts as initiating the most wide-reaching changes to labour laws in Australia in over 100 years (Bamber et al. 2005). The legislation saw the dissolution of the Arbitration Commission, the consolidation of a federal industrial system, the eradication of many basic workers' rights such as overtime, and the support of individual bargaining over collective (trade union) bargaining. The response to the release of the detail of these changes led to significant street protests—in March 2006, tens of thousands of workers gathered in the larger capital cities as did substantial numbers in regional centres all over the country. As suggested earlier, the language of class—including the vocabulary of workers' rights in a capitalist system—has lost much of its cachet in contemporary Australia. In protesting the changes, it is interesting to note the deployment of notions of being Australian or un-Australian. The eradication of weekend penalty rates in concert with an emphasis on more flexible working weeks has seen many union leaders declare the great Aussie tradition of a Sunday barbecue to be dead. A story of being Australian—here, one about community and family time—is used to protest changes that are transnational in their origins. In response, the federal government has used the idea of the 'common decency' of Australian bosses to reassure Australians about the 'benign' nature of the changes. In an uncertain world, where the changes wrought by the new forms of global capitalism are unknown, many Australians still cling to a familiar story of Australian-ness, that of the Arbitration system to explain how they should act and what they accept.

Flashmobs

In labour protest, engagement with a wider public as well as the stability and coherence of a protest are what helps it succeed. The long-term or intimate connections set up between protesters, as a result of sitting on a picket or handing out leaflets to others, are seen to help reinforce or develop the values associated with a particular counterpublic. They are also understood to introduce these values to a wider public. As the maritime strike of 1998 and other large antiglobalisation protests suggests, this type of protest still plays an important role in shaping the story of Australian-ness, especially in terms of social movements organised around labour, peace activism and the environment. But other types of street protest or presence have emerged in the last few years that draw on very different ways of making a point.

Flashmobbing is one of these. Flashmobbing is a form of street theatre or action. An oft-quoted definition goes: '(FLASH mawb) n. A large group of people who gather in a usually predetermined location, perform some brief action, and then quickly disperse' (Marchbank 2004). More specifically:

> Flashmobs are organised through loosely affiliated, non-hierarchical networks of people using . . . mobile phones, the Web and email. They are orchestrated to bring as many bodies as possible together at a pre-arranged time and place to enact a publicly disruptive and spectacular act of ludicrousness (in the Latinate sense of something playful, a game) (Marchbank 2004).

A typical flashmobbing event, according to Thomas Marchbank—and perhaps the most well-known such event staged in Australia—involved over 100 people gathering on the steps of Flinders Street Station in Melbourne, each donning a yellow rubber glove and pointing to the sky (see Figure 10.1). Then, in true flashmob style, they melted away into the crowd. More recently, 80 or so Sydneysiders gathered at the large intersection near the Sydney Town Hall. When the lights turned green, flashmobbers began to cross the street with the other pedestrians, only to find their feet were 'sticking' to the road. They began frantically trying to move or get help. As the 'don't walk' sign started to flash, the flashmobbers suddenly began to move back to the kerb. Again they then disappeared into the crowd. When curious bystanders ask flashmobbers what is going on, their typical answer is that they don't know. Contrast this with a question put to a participant in the Gurindji strike or the maritime union strike, or a *Socialist Alternative* newspaper seller, or a participant in a Women in Black protest. In these cases, sharing the meaning of the event with others is part of the intention. For the flashmobbers, it is not. The flashmob crowd is already a community: its purpose is not to convert more people to the cause through the event.

Is flashmobbing pointless protest? Is it protest at all? There is no agreement, as you might imagine, amongst flashmobbers about whether the acts are political or not. One Melbourne organiser told

Figure 10.1 Flashmobbers take part in an 'action' on the steps of Flinders Street Station in Melbourne in 2003. (*Photograph: John Englart <www.takver.com>*)

a news reporter: the events are 'non-confrontational and apolitical; more bizarre. Melbourne people can get a little bit sick of the whole politics and corporate thing, the hustle and bustle' (Lisa Mitchell 2003). Yet another Melbourne organiser said:

> I think it's inherently political because people are gathering. It's like a human art exhibition . . . It's also drawing on the idea of reclaiming public spaces. There's so much rigmarole with permits and things, whereas flashmobbing is all about spontaneity. It's organised spontaneity (Creagh 2004).

Unlike most other groups who gather in the street, flashmobbers may not be overtly seeking to make social or political change. Or perhaps the political point they are making may simply be less overt.

Thomas Marchbank (2004) notes that even though many flash-mobbers reinforce the 'random acts of silliness' aspect of their street actions, 'there is a distinct and recurrent theme of the comic disruption of commercial and economic space' in flashmob events. That is, apolitical flashmobbers often end up in the offices of multi-national corporations and fast-food restaurants, sites associated in a global world with so much that is problematic in contemporary society. So, although the reason for the protest may not specifically be spelt out and, as Kurt Iveson (2001) suggests, the whole meaning of the action may not be fully understood before it takes place, this is not to say that, in enacting a performance where people undertake a seemingly foolish ritual, there is no meaning. Perhaps, in the hectic globally connected world in which we live, to organise an act where others stop and slow down for a moment to observe a group of people staring skyward is politics enough. However, the flashmob should not be understood as a utopic space of anarchic social improvement. Howard Rheingold (2002), an American academic interested in new forms of community and protest, writes that flashmobs—or smart mobs, as he calls them—are neither inherently good nor bad.

Flashmobs have congregated in Australia to walk across a street in a comical fashion. They come together as a mob through the sending of a message via new technologies—primarily their mobile phones. (By way of contrast, there was much consternation when it was found that the Cronulla riots of 2005 had been organised by the circulation of SMS messages via mobile phones. Here the calling together of a mob for racist ends using new technologies was unsettling.) But flash-mobbing and smartmobbing are not locally derived counterpublics: Australian adherents are copying overseas groups. But then Socialist Alternative and Women in Black are not locally derived products either. Flashmobbing and smartmobbing are global phenomena, which prevail in countries that share many of the same conditions as Australia—an angst about the future, a cynicism about possibilities for change, a melancholy about a refusal to see any meaning beyond consumption. Again quoting Marchbank (2004), mobilising people and resources for 'fun that does not require a deep commitment of time or engagement, plays directly into the depoliticised, media-saturated moment of the present'.

Flashmobbing tends to attract young people (though some flash-mobbing groups have members who are in their eighties). It engages with groups who are typically represented as apolitical or 'out of it' when it comes to thinking about issues. Is this type of street perform-ance a funky way in which some people can re-engage with a world in which they may feel disenfranchised or whose dominant protest methods make no sense to them (Luckman 2001: 218)? For lots of flashmobbers, the street action is just about the giggle and then the debrief in the pub afterwards where you giggle even more as you rehash what happened. But there are aspects of the flashmobbing approach that do 'mark a renewed visibility for and popularity for direct action which never actually went away', but which in the 1990s in countries such as Australia were mainly identified as the sole province of 'extremist' environmental and/or anti-militarist—'single issue—campaigns' (Luckman 2001: 218).

Critical Mass

One of the most long-standing and effective overtly political flash-mobbing events is the cyclists' rights movement, Critical Mass. As with most flashmobbing groups, there is no structured organisation for Critical Mass. In fact, its organisation (and in some ways, its purpose) are deliberately vague. As one Critical Mass website notes: 'Critical Mass is anything ranging from a group of cyclists riding home together, to a massive eco-social movement of global proportions, that is limited by no set boundaries' (<www.criticalmass.org.au/melbourne/whatis. html>). Another 'member' states: 'According to its own propaganda, CM just "is". It is "about" anything the people who join in choose to make it about, that's what "xerocracy" means: putting out your own agenda/political statement/route map' (<www.criticalmass.org.au/ melbourne/xerox.html>). Another 'member' goes on to explain that:

> A 'xerocracy' is where YOU choose. Like a democracy, but no leaders are elected. Like a collective, but everybody's involved. EVERYBODY chooses and then the MASS DECIDES. So how does it work? If you have an idea, put it on a piece of paper and photocopy it. Pass it around at Critical Mass and if enough people think it is a good idea, then it will happen, if people think its a bad idea, then it won't happen, but at least people have had the choice to think about it for themselves rather than having never heard the idea in the first place (<www.criticalmass.org.au/melbourne/xerox.html>).

Critical Mass flashmobs coalesce around cycling. The events take place at 5 p.m. on the last Friday of the month. The participants are people who usually cycle home. They will receive a message telling them where to meet on the designated evening. If enough people turn up, you have 'critical mass' and route maps are distributed for a ride. On these evenings, hundreds of cyclists, who seemingly appear out of nowhere, make their way across town.

As was suggested about flashmobbing generally, Critical Mass is part of a global phenomenon. It began in the United States in 1992, but countries all round the world have Critical Mass groups. Critical Mass is more overtly political than many flashmobs and is more of a western phenomenon. Critical Mass is about making people notice how choked with cars some cities are. In their events, the cyclists of

Critical Mass fill a space that is usually the provenance of petrol-guzzling cars, not pedal power. Not all cities need Critical Mass groups: if the public transport infrastructure and provisions for cyclists are in place, then there is no point. The protest does not work around the logic of a nation but around much smaller spaces. Some cities in Australia share with other large cities in the Untied States and Europe global problems such as pollution and the dependence on fossil fuels, while other Australian cities are more environmentally friendly.

Not surprisingly, Critical Mass events irritate many car drivers. When a critical mass of cyclists is in front of you, Friday night traffic seems to slow from its usual crawl to a snail's pace. Not only can the events be understood as irritating, but aspects of them are also illegal. Obviously being a cyclist is not illegal: it is simply another way of being in the street. What makes the ride illegal is the massed aspect of the ride. The cyclists stick together as a single entity. So they all cross an intersection *en masse*. If the lights change halfway, then some cyclists do what is known as 'corking' and block the way of cars so the rest of the cyclists can cross the intersection. Obviously, in terms of the status quo, the way in which the cyclists should make their needs and concerns heard is in the public sphere—where all citizens can discuss issues of common concern. Yet the needs of a marginalised group such as bike-riders hardly ever make their way onto a national agenda; instead, Critical Mass forces its way into public space and so gains visibility.

Reclaim the Streets

A group similar to Critical Mass is Reclaim the Streets, which is devoted to 'challeng[ing] and question[ing] the ordering of societies priorities by presenting, what for the participants at least, is one possibility of a more pleasurable alternative: a society which embodies the freedom and shared sense of community' (Luckman 2001: 208). As with Critical Mass—and, indeed, as with the implicit aims of flash-mobbing—the focus is on encouraging a world that is less centred on the car and consumption—influences seen as breaking down communities and privatising public space. As someone who took part in a Reclaim the Street Party in Melbourne wrote:

> Reclaim the Streets is a party with a purpose, a celebratory taking back of the street space, normally off limits to anyone who values their safety . . . Unlike demonstrations or rallies RTS is all about having fun, it is an experiment in what the world would be like without the

omnipresent automobile that fills the air with fumes, fills our media with its image, warps our economy with its hunger for resources . . . (Luckman 2001: 208).

In these street reclamations, people come out into the street to dance to the techno beat of sound systems that seem to appear out of nowhere. The participants are united by a commitment or interest in imagining another type of community (even if it is just for the duration of the party). And, as Kurt Iveson (2001) argues, the party or protest is not necessarily the end-point: it can be the beginning of discussions and formations of new identities.

As with aspects of Critical Mass, Reclaim the Streets parties are illegal. Just as a group of cyclists cannot legally ride through red lights, a group of people cannot just close off a street of their own volition and fill the space with potted plants, chill-out tents, DJs and sofas. Yet it happens. Sometimes the values of the counterpublic resonate with sufficient numbers of people that even the police agree to a compromise. (Interestingly, these deals between participants and police also happen quite frequently on labour picket lines.) At other times, the inconvenience to the general public is seen to be too great and sound systems are confiscated. However, as with the 1998 maritime workers' strike, participants often draw on successful green non-violent protest tactics to slow down the packing up of the party. It needs to be noted that most flashmobbing events are organised so that they are legal. For example, if you are one of the 80 people trying to cross the road and found your feet sticking to the road when the pedestrian light is green, they unstick pretty quickly when the amber light appears. This reflects the multiple ways in which individuals and groups contest dominant narratives—some within the law, others not—and also perhaps reflects the different levels of power and control different groups have in public space.

The dominant story of protest is that there is legitimate protest, but also forms of protest that are illegitimate (which is not the same as illegal). Legitimate protest is posited as that which does not interrupt those who are going about their 'legitimate' business. So, in the maritime union dispute and other labour protests, the concern is that the workers do not disturb the smooth running of the national economy. In legitimate protest, the participants agree to abide by rules set out by the state. For example, there are guidelines for protest at Parliament House in Canberra. The guidelines are organised so as to locate any protest in a place where it does not hinder those who are going about their business in the parliament—this includes tourists, workers and parliamentarians. But a protest cannot be successful if the protesters are so marginalised that they do not have an impact on others. The very idea of protest is to get people to think about an alternative to the present story. It is about getting people to pause and reflect. So, just as a minute's silence is enacted every year to encourage Australians to think about the price of war, so protests also seek to slow people down and get them to think about issues of justice, rights and equality.

The Sydney Gay and Lesbian Mardi Gras

The Sydney Gay and Lesbian Mardi Gras is a street protest that has morphed into a giant parade (with protests still located within it). In terms of counterpublics, the Mardi Gras, which takes place every March in Oxford Street in Sydney, is a good example of the ways in which counterpublics can set up conversations between different participants within a protest. The mardi gras as a spectacle attracts international, interstate and regional visitors every year. Those who are in the parade, and its associated workshops and gala events, are also mixed. There are Oxford Street locals, people from the Sydney suburbs, and visitors from regional New South Wales towns and cities, from interstate and from overseas. So, within the bounds of the whole mardi gras or 'gay pride' space, a very heterogeneous group of people come into contact with each other: people from different classes and ethnicities, and people with different genders and sexual identities all come together for a mardi gras event in a party/protest space that seeks to achieve gay, lesbian trans-gender, bisexual and queer people's rights; however, what that means may vary for different people. As such, the mardi gras is a good site to explore the complexity of the negotiations about identity that go on *within* groups who are marginalised in the nation.

The first mardi gras took place on 24 June 1978 and was held to commemorate the Stonewall riots in New York. These riots took place when the gay men and women who frequented the Stonewall Inn stood up and protested about the police harassment they routinely experienced. June 1978 was the ninth anniversary of these famous riots and, with encouragement from American gay groups, a series of international solidarity marches were held in cities around the world, including Sydney. Australian gay men and lesbians had been taking to the streets for years. What was different about the 1978 gay rights protest for many of the participants was that it was to end with a street party. As Lance Gowland remembers:

Traditionally we'd marched with banners and around issues of discrimination or international solidarity, and the idea of having music in the street and dancing and everything was outside of our experience or anybody's else's experience about political activities (Carbery 1995: 9).

The celebrations and commemorations that took place during the day of 24 June 1978 went well; it was at the night-time street party when things went awry. There was a mix-up about the parade's route, and the marchers started heading in a direction that the police argued was not on their route. The result was a violent confrontation between the marchers and the police. Lee Franklyn remembers: 'Police kicked and punched demonstrators who struggled to get free as bystanders hurled garbage bins, bottles and cans at the melee' (Carbery 1995: 12). The police rounded up and arrested 53 people and drove them to Darlinghurst Police Station as the rest of the furious crowd followed. Eventually the charges against the arrested marchers were dropped. And there was, of course, a mardi gras the next year—if for no other reason than to celebrate the successful outcomes of the first. There has been a mardi gras every year since.

During the almost 30 years the Sydney Gay and Lesbian Mardi Gras has existed, it has expanded: the parade has grown bigger, the costumes and floats have become more spectacular, the spectators have become more numerous. The number of activities around the parade has also grown. A festival with a big opening event on the steps of the Sydney Opera House, a fair day with drag queens, dog shows and celebrities, a film festival and sports carnivals were all added, as well as a mardi gras workshop where groups who were going to participate in the parade could get help to produce their floats and costumes. And after the parade there is always a huge party with multiple stages and rooms, surprise international guests and elaborate stage shows. Given the magnitude of this story of gay and lesbian pride, it would be impossible for it to comprise one coherent narrative.

One of the first debates within mardi gras was whether it was 'a political demonstration to demand Gay Rights or . . . a celebration of COMING OUT, with its only political goals being to demonstrate the size and variety of the gay community and to establish its right to be' (Carbery 1995: 29). The 1981 decision to shift the mardi gras parade from 28 June—a meaningful date in the International gay civil rights calendar—to a convenient Saturday in late summer sparked debate about the commitment of some participants and organisers to the cause of gay rights as opposed to a party. This debate took on another meaning as the impact of HIV/AIDS shook the gay and lesbian community to its core around 1983. Its impact was devastating. For many gay men, their energy was now directed towards staying alive, supporting their friends and dealing with the daily barrage of prejudice the disease unleashed. In the light of this, there was debate about whether—in the face of so much death—it was appropriate to have mardi gras at all. One parade organiser from that time, Brian Hobday, argued that the parade was a 'much needed show of strength and support within the gay community' (Carbery 1995: 73). Other groups suggested that, at a time when the civil liberties of gay men were being threatened, a political presence was even more important than usual (Carbery 1995: 73). Heterosexual opponents of mardi gras also raised questions about the appropriateness of the event taking place. In 1985, media-driven hysteria about the parade and party as sites for 'orgies' of unsafe sex suggested that the parade only encouraged the spread of HIV/AIDS. This led to suggestions that it should not continue (Carbery 1995: 73). Of course, the parade did continue and, by the mid 1980s, a remembrance section for those who died of HIV/AIDS had been incorporated. A special float is commissioned every year by the AIDS Council of New South Wales (ACON) to highlight the lives lost, the memories that remain, and the support provided for those whose friends, family members or lovers have died.

A gay Anzac Day

Gay men who have lost many friends and lovers to the illness comment that for them mardi gras is the equivalent of the Anzac Day commemorations. Ron Muncaster, a long-time participant and one of the chief costume-makers for the parade, notes: 'Mardi Gras is a night when I remember all of my dead friends . . . For me, it's a bit like Anzac Day' (Dennis 2003: 5). In 1997, an art installation by artist Gary Carsley was included as part of the arts festival (see Figure 10.2). The sculpture, which was to be placed on Oxford Street at Taylor Square, the centre of the Mardi Gras Parade, was designed as a replica of the war memorial in Hyde Park, which sits at the other end of Oxford Street. This MEMORIAL project was intended to inversely mirror the Hyde Park Anzac War Memorial as a site of national mourning. Remembering gay men who have died of HIV/AIDS was the same as, but also very different to, mourning the war dead.

Figure 10.2 MEMORIAL, part of the 1997 Sydney Gay and Lesbian Mardi Gras. The model both mimicked and moved beyond the Hyde Park War Memorial. (*M.O.P.W., 1996—cardboard, bronze roses, gouache, electric cord and light; 75 x 40 x 40 cms—to scale ANZAC Memorial, Hyde Park. M.O.P.W. for this project was Gary Carsley, Grahame Rowe, Peter Todd and Rafael von Uslar. Image courtesy of TORCH Gallery, Amsterdam and Sabine Schmidt Gallery, Cologne.*)

So, where the central Hall of Silence, with its beautiful sculpture representing youthful death, is entered by descending, the key parts of the MEMORIAL are entered by ascending. Whereas the Anzac War Memorial is austere, MEMORIAL is colourful:

> The artists have mimicked its architectural lines—but theirs is no grim commandment to 'remember the dead'—rather, MEMORIAL is a living sculpture, spectacle, adorned with lavish bronze roses, translucent windows of colour light (Sydney Gay and Lesbian Mardi Gras 1997: 19).

The artists also insisted that the juxtaposition between the two memorials should be read as asking questions: 'What are we doing? Are we setting up structures which merely mimic those of heterosexual culture?' (1997: 19). This MEMORIAL complicated the simple national mourning story of what it means to die for or within one's nation. There was some agitation from non-gay men at the appropriation of the form of the Hyde Park war memorial—a memorial they suggested represented a national mourning—to make a point about homosexual mourning, something they saw as unrelated. Tying national war mourning to gay men's grief linked the ideas of the military and being gay too closely together for some heterosexual men's comfort. In the end, the gay men's memorial was moved somewhere less visible. It was not seen as needing to be in the streets.

Excluding others

As well as contesting many understandings of what constitutes a real Australian identity, the community whose members make up the mardi gras counterpublic can reflect and reinforce other prejudices. For example, Graham Willett (2000) discusses the debates that took place in the 1990s about whether straights should be allowed to attend mardi gras parties. These discussions were couched in terms of heterosexual people taking over the parties and changing the feeling of the space. As Willett points out, some of this concern about keeping out straights was actually a concern about keeping out people from the western suburbs of Sydney. Some of the middle-class demographic that makes up the bulk of party participants was appalled by the flannel-shirted 'westies' who turned up. Some—or even many—of these attendees may have been straight; however, the criticism about their presence was often couched in class terms. These straights were not made visible because of their ogling of the gay scene or their passionate kissing of people of the opposite sex, but by their costumes and clothing—which marked them as suburban.

The counterpublic that makes up the mardi gras has always been open to men and women. By the late 1980s, the presence of increasing numbers of lesbians in the parade led to much discussion about the balance between men and women in organising, managing and participating in the parade. In some ways, the core of these issues can be seen in the discussions about the name of the parade. There was a move amongst many lesbians to break out from under the umbrella title of 'gay' and claim their own identity as 'lesbian'. For many, this meant a change in the name of the parade from the Sydney Gay Mardi Gras to the Sydney Gay and Lesbian Mardi Gras—a change instituted in 1988. What happened here was that aspects of feminism intersected with and challenged the shape of the gay rights movement. As in other areas of national life, women began to challenge male-dominated institutions. Though in many ways the mardi gras is marginalised from any mainstream understanding of being Australian, it still mimicked some aspects of male-dominated national culture. Along with the demand for a name change came a demand that the organising committees and boards be more reflective of the makeup of the community, rather than being mostly male. Discussions within this counterpublic continue today. Other groups who feel the mardi gras space does not accommodate their needs or reflect their desires—bisexual and trans-gender individuals and groups, for example—challenge the make-up of the parade and the committee. Discussions take place between younger people who use the term 'queer' to describe their sexual identity and older Australians who prefer gay or lesbian.

It is not only in terms of class and gender that the mardi gras has had to consider its politics. Over the decades, issues of ethnicity and Indigeneity have also been discussion points in the evolution of the idea of gay and lesbian communities. For many non-Anglo–Australian gay men and lesbians, the issues that arise from being part of the parade are different from those faced by Anglo–Australian participants. Levels of homophobia may differ in different individuals' families and communities, but for people who are part of ethnic minority communities the idea of coming out and perhaps being excluded from their family and community is sometimes more difficult than it is for those in the dominant Anglo–Australian community. For example, if you are a member of a minority ethnic community, and within the larger (and slightly alien) world of Anglo-Australia your family provides support and connection to important parts of your identity, then to be isolated from that community when you come out may have a higher cost than for those whose ethnic community is the dominant one.

For many gay, lesbian and queer people of Asian heritage their participation in mardi gras is also complex. They are members of communities that have been on the receiving end of racism in Australia for centuries. For many gay Asian–Australian men this is still a part of how they experience their place in the gay community. As Tony Ayres (1998) writes of the gay 'scene' (which he distinguishes from the gay community): 'Caucasians have a preconception of what an "Asian" looks like. It's this preconception that puts us near the bottom of their sexual hierarchy' (1998: 112). Many Asian men and women have formed community groups to talk about issues and frame approaches to this problem. One of the outcomes, specific to the mardi gras, is get support for and to design events that are organised around gay scenes other than hyper-masculine, broad-shouldered white stereotype made famous by artists such as Tom of Finland. As a result, there are now events designed and organised by Asian–Australian gay men and lesbians.

Gay, lesbian and queer Indigenous people often find it difficult to negotiate their place as homosexual and black. For them, the simple equation that their community equals their gay and lesbian friends does not compute. For many gay, lesbian and queer Indigenous people, it is important that, within the gay, lesbian and queer community (or the mardi gras in particular), there is an understanding of the very different form of their marginalisation. They ask that the difference between Indigenous peoples as sovereign owners of the land (including the parade route) and the marginalisation of the gay and lesbian community be acknowledged. This difference has been integrated into the idea of mardi gras. For example, in 1988 an Indigenous actor, Malcolm Cole, dressed as Captain Cook, led the parade. The intention was to satirise the bicentenary. There have been large contingents of gay, lesbian and queer Australians participating in the parade under the banner of reconciliation. In 2000, the parade was led by a group of gay, lesbian and queer Indigenous people acknowledging that the parade takes place on Eora land. Within the counterpublic of gay and lesbian rights, negotiations took place that saw other identities and issues considered and the meaning of being queer, gay or lesbian in Australia changed in relation to Indigenous rights.

Global/local queer

The Sydney mardi gras figures as a date in a global queer calendar. There are thousands of gay men and lesbians who travel to Sydney (and then on to the resorts of Queensland to recover) every year. Some are spectators; others are participants in the parade. The financial contribution that the mardi gras makes to the economies of a number of states through tourism operates to centre this event in the national story. Some—not all—state premiers, and federal leaders and their equivalents in opposition, have publicly declared their support for the event. Yet the mardi gras is never reduced to, or solely understood in, national terms. In 1998, the *Sydney Star Observer*—a queer newspaper—had a cover story in the week before the parade about the number of gay American men who were in Sydney for the mardi gras (not enough, it seemed). The article was cheekily subtitled: 'They're over-sexed over-paid and supposed to be over here'—a satirical reference to the panic during World War II about the presence of so many American soldiers in Australia. The worry in the 1940s was that, with Australian blokes away, who knew what Australian women would do in the face of so much masculine Hollywood glamour? The national resentment towards American soldiers by their Australian counterparts in World War II does not resonate in terms of the mardi gras, where global sex rather than national sex organises the libidinal economy. In this story, more American men were wanted.

Mardi gras encountered a substantial financial crisis in 2003. In the early 2000s, the Sydney Gay and Lesbian Mardi Gras Incorporation was in serious debt, and in 2002 it entered voluntary administration. There was much speculation that mardi gras had come to an end. However, the end of the incorporated business entity was not the end of the parade. For many queer, gay and lesbian Australians, this was an opportunity to bring the parade back to the community. There was a large group of gay and lesbians for whom the commercialisation of Sydney's mardi gras—especially the parade and the parties—had created a sense of estrangement from the event. They felt that the original political/community feel had been overridden with commercial floats sponsored by multinational alcohol and telecommunications companies. For these people, there seemed to be a tension between the increasing popularity, the attendant commercial success of the parade, and the needs of a local or minority population to join together and celebrate.

This tension between commercial success and alienation can be illustrated in a number of ways. First, it can be demonstrated in terms of the spatial arrangement of the parade. In the early parades, there was no real separation between the audience and the marchers. Everyone was both. Obviously, as the size of the parade grew and more and more people came simply to watch, a spectator/participant division became more pronounced. In time, it became necessary for people to register their intention to participate in the parade, and barriers were erected to provide crowd control as the number of spectators rose to the tens of thousands. By the late 1990s, there was a very obvious distinction between participant and spectator. Further, the success of the mardi gras meant that a mainstream audience was coming to see the parade so the makeup of the audience was increasingly heterosexual, but also more diverse.

If you have ever been a participant in the Sydney Gay and Lesbian Mardi Gras parade, you will know that as the parade wends its way along the route the feeling from the crowd changes, reflecting its diverse makeup. At the beginning of the parade route, the participants pass by a large gathering of Christians, usually led by New

South Wales parliamentarian Fred Nile, who are openly anti-gay and anti-lesbian. Their presence is a long-standing part of the parade. They are the openly antagonistic group whose members clearly find the idea of an Australian nation celebrating sexual diversity unacceptable. The passing of a Bill in federal parliament in 2004 forbidding same-sex marriage suggests this feeling is not isolated to these few dozen protesters. However, after passing through this 'baptism of fire', participants enter Oxford Street and encounter a completely different atmosphere. Here the crowd is made up of visitors, first-timers and diehards. The crowd is ten deep, and people stand on platforms rigged up with ladders, wood and milk crates. The enthusiasm of the crowd is overwhelming. Anything a participant does leads to whoops of delight. A bevy of marching boys wiggling their bottoms will result in howls of approval, but equally a mum in a cardigan and sensible shoes, walking next to her gay son or daughter, elicits the same reaction.

Further along the parade route, there is the Bobby Goldsmith Stand. It is here that many parade participants feel at home. The crowd in this pre-paid seating area, the profits of which go to support HIV/AIDS charities, is mostly gay and lesbian and the feeling is of mutual recognition. On other parts of the route, marching can be an odd experience. A wave to the crowd can be met with a blank stare. The extravagant gesture of a drag queen might be met with bewilderment or a sneer. Here the feeling of being a freaky minority on display to a straight majority can be strong. The fence dividing the crowd from the participants can feel like a necessary safety measure—or worse, like the fence in a zoo designed to keep the exotic animals caged for inspection by the locals.

Since 1994, the mardi gras has been broadcast on television. Originally it was broadcast by the ABC, and more recently it has been aired by a commercial broadcaster. The original decision to broadcast the parade was met with a vigorous discussion about the pros and cons of such a step. As with the protesters who stand at the beginning of the parade, there was a chorus claiming the parade displayed an aspect of Australian life that was not acceptable, especially for young eyes. In time, the ratings for the parade were high enough for a commercial entity to be enticed. The parade is not shown live, but is packaged and shown as highlights. It is this process that disappoints many participants and fuels their arguments that the parade is no longer about the gay and lesbian community but about what straight audiences want in terms of an experience of *watching* gay and lesbians.

This is easily illustrated with an anecdote from participating in the parade. As those who have watched the parade from behind the barriers in Oxford Street will know, the mix of participants is varied. There are the 'Dykes on Bikes', the marching boys and girls in their skimpy outfits, and drag queens in extravagant costumes. But there are also dozens of community groups such as gay and lesbian teachers' organisations, HIV/AIDS organisations, religious and cultural groups. Many a marcher from the latter group of partici-pants—especially those marching for the first time—will tell the story of the fun of walking up the first part of the parade route—that intox-icating part of Oxford Street. As you get to the top of the street, you can see the camera lights blazing at Taylor Square. It is here that the television cameras are fixed and that the story of the parade goes out to the broader national community. For many participants, rounding that corner is an odd experience. As your group comes into camera range, the lights seem to dim. The cameras are not filming you or your part of the parade.

It is not the personal disappointment for all those participants deprived of their fifteen minutes of fame that is important here. It is the issue of what constitutes the Sydney Gay and Lesbian Mardi Gras. The version of the parade that is packaged for national television tends to focus on gay and lesbianism as outrageous spectacle. The other parts—of living a family life, of supporting friends who are gay, of parents loving lesbian daughters, of supporting HIV-positive mates, of mourning lovers who have died, of demanding equal rights—many of these parts fade into the background. The story of the mardi gras beamed to the nation is not one that helps build a sense of the complexity of gay and lesbian life, but of stereotyping and marketing. For many participants, the end of Mardi Gras Inc. marked the possibility of new beginnings: the possibility of telling stories to each other that encourage understanding and mutual respect, as well as translating this story so it can be understood by straight Australia.

Taking to the streets is a common way in which communities connect, protest and celebrate. Given the streets are public spaces it is interest-ing to explore for whom and when the streets are shut down and clearways created. And it is also important to analyse who uses the streets without permission and why. Flashmobs use the streets in ways that are not organised around getting council permission or making clearly expressed political points—they are having fun. Not many observers of a flashmob event would see it as anything to do with being Australian. Indeed the phenomenon is more about the identity of globally connected middle-class youth than national citizens. Critical Mass and street parties also derive from broad western social action groups where information circulates via the internet and groups are local not national. Labour protests have a long history of being connected to international movements of workers' rights, though they often use stories of being Australian as very effective means of making their point. For example, it is the low wages paid to manufacturing workers in the Asian region that are drawn on in arguments about Australian workers' rights. The Sydney Gay and Lesbian Mardi Gras also has a international history and is part of a western phenomenon of gay and lesbian pride street marches. Yet it also engages with the national. For example, the place of Indigenous peoples in the march is about the specificity of gay, lesbian and queer Australians relationship to the history of colonialism. In each year's parade there are floats making points about legal rights—for example the right to marry—though these are issues gay, lesbian and queer people around the world grapple with, in the context of the mardi gras they are also very specific stories about how some Australians are experiencing their citizenship.

FURTHER READING

Burgmann, Verity 2003, *Power, Profit and Protest: Australian Social Movements and Globalization*, Allen & Unwin, Sydney.

Carbery, Graham 1995, *A History of the Sydney Gay and Lesbian Mardi Gras*, Australian Lesbian and Gay Archives, Melbourne.

McKnight, David 2005, *Beyond Right and Left: New Politics and the Culture Wars*, Allen & Unwin, Sydney.

Nicoll, Fiona 2001, *From Diggers to Drag Queens: Configurations of Australian National Identity*, Pluto Press, Sydney.

Scalmer, Sean 2006, *The Little History of Australian Unionism*, Vulgar Press, Melbourne.

Willett, Graham 2000, *Living Out Loud: A History of Gay and Lesbian Activism in Australia*, Allen & Unwin, Sydney.

11

BACKYARDS AND BARRACKING

The everyday in Australia

THIS CHAPTER ANALYSES some unremarkable sites where stories of being Australian are played out. The sites explored are the sporting event, the often-maligned suburban space, and non-city places such as country towns. As with the previous chapter, these unremarkable sites will be explored in terms of the pleasures and tensions that surround ideas of national identity in these places. In particular, the chapter will look at the ways in which sport is represented as a national endeavour and yet works in other ways for many people. The space of the suburb will be analysed in terms of its frequent absence in national stories. The non-city space will be analysed in terms of the view of country towns as dying and representations of their revitalisation as linked to the health of the national community.

Sport

As the earlier discussion of the 2000 Sydney Olympic Games demonstrated, Australian governments are willing to spend extremely large amounts of money on events showcasing national sports teams and individuals. They are, of course, not alone in this endeavour. Nations around the world vie for what is often seen as the privilege of hosting international sporting events, and most governments in developed nations dedicate large amounts of money to support and train elite sportspeople. However, in the pantheon of big public spenders for elite sport, Australia is in a league of its own. Though Australia has a population of only 20 million, it sent one of the largest teams to the Athens Olympic Games. What is it about international sporting events that makes it uncontroversial to spend millions of dollars to support them? And is there something particular about Australia that explains why governments commit these extra dollars to elite sport?

One argument that has been put forward by popular and scholarly commentators to explain the high level of government spending on sports in Australia is that Australians are sports-mad. Craig McGregor wrote in 1966: 'it would be surprising indeed, if there were any other country in the world in which two-fifths of the population played sport regularly and three-quarters watched it' (1966: 139). The argument is that, as sports-mad people, Australians expect a similar level of commitment to sport from their government. Yet, as McGregor's old 1960s statistics suggest and more recent studies confirm, there are millions of Australians who do not play or watch sport. Even if an event such as the Olympics means more Australians get excited about playing sport after watching the elite swimmers and runners, that spike of activity subsides quickly and most Australians go back to a more sedentary life. However, even though being sports-mad is an insufficient explanation for the national spending on sports, the spending still takes place.

In fact, despite the evidence that there is a more complex relationship between sport, Australians and the idea of being Australian than the simplistic argument that 'all Australians love their sport', sport still works as a central way in which Australian-ness is produced and marketed. One important reason for this is the sheer scale of the contemporary sports event. National or inter-national sports attract large numbers of people to one place at one time. This makes them dramatic spectacles. Mass spectacles such as large-scale sports events, with their substantial budgets for opening ceremonies, high-profile guests, huge noisy crowds and elaborate rituals such as crowd waves, chants and anthems, are effective spaces in which to promote a story of the nation. The international or national sports event is actually a very effective advertisement for nationalism. This nationalistic advertisement features tens of thousands of fellow Australians, clad in green and gold, converging in a single place to support their national team in its endeavour to beat a 'mortal enemy'. That is, the advertisement sells Australian-ness as the simple but powerful pleasure that comes from being part of a national sports team's victory.

National sport

The link between Australian-ness and sport is sometimes represented as so intimate that the Australian national sporting team is understood to stand for the nation. The selected team members are not simply the ten, eleven or twelve individuals who most excel in their particular sport, they are represented *as* 'Australia'—so much so that when a national sports team or individual wins a race, a match or a game, news headlines scream 'Australia triumphant' rather than 'Australian sports team wins'. In this conflation of team or player and nation, the particular skills or qualities of a team are being attributed to the nation as a whole. As Peter Kell explains:

> Virtues accorded to sportsmen such as selflessness and sacrifice on behalf of the interests of the team and the collective interests of the game itself are particularly self-identified by many Australians as 'Aussie' communal values (2000: 26).

For example, this conflation of sport and national values is seen in the annual Anzac Day Rugby League test match between Australia and New Zealand. In representations of this match, there is a sense that the men of the game are somehow exhibiting—through sport—the values of the Anzac tradition. However, there is often a tension between a national team as a professional body, made up of a variety of individuals, and the team as exemplary representatives of the Australian people. This can mean that, when the team loses or individuals behave poorly, 'Australia' is disgraced rather than just the team or person.

A good example would be the news and media discussions about the Australian cricket team in the summer and autumn of 2003 when they played England and Sri Lanka in Australia and then travelled to the West Indies for a test series. The behaviour of the team—which included incidents of misconduct (slamming a dressing room door so hard that the glass broke), the use of racial slurs and a positive drug test for one of the players—was read as bringing shame on Australia. In this period, bowler Shane Warne was chastised because he failed to be a role model for young Australians; batsmen Darren Lehmann was rebuked for behaviour reflecting badly on a nation trying hard to move away from a past that is understood to be racist; and bowler Glenn McGrath was the subject of dozens of letters to the editor complaining that homophobic comments and racism attributed to him were not worthy of the great game of Australian cricket. Here the team was understood to be more than simply a group of talented individuals who played overseas and domestic cricket. They were understood as representing Australians, and so they needed to reflect values that were seen as good—that is, 'Australian'.

Un-national sport

Interestingly, not all teams involved in international sports are understood to be representing the nation in the same way. Not surprisingly, this differentiation between national teams who are represented as truly Australian and those who are not is inflected in terms of gender and ethnicity. Most Australian readers of a front-page story about *the* Australian cricket team would know the story was referring to the men's team, not the Australian women's cricket team. Sports with a history attached to Anglo–Australian heritage are also more likely to be understood as national sports. Again, cricket is a good example: it is often espoused as *the* Australian sport. The different codes of football—Rugby League, Rugby Union and Australian Rules (AFL)—are also claimed as truly Australian sports. Compare these three with another code of football—soccer. Soccer is played by millions of Australians, yet it has only recently been represented as 'Australian' and taken up by media and marketers as something to sell to Australians as a game in which they need to support their national team. For years, the dominant representation of soccer was as 'wog ball'—an 'ethnic' game associated with marginal groups of citizens rather than the nation as a whole. Today, as Australian teams consistently do better in World Cup qualifying soccer matches, and actually qualifying in 2006, the game is gaining Anglo–Australian credibility.

Sport plays a role in establishing and cohering many local communities. Philip Mosely has demonstrated how soccer clubs 'enabled newly arrived European migrants to Australia after World War Two . . . to preserve both their roots and a sense of continuity' (1994: 200). Soccer also operated as a way in which individuals dealt with the social isolation associated with migration. By joining clubs, they created a social network. The desire on the part of many migrants to create a sense of continuity can be seen in the naming of the clubs after the places left behind—flags and kits were also in the regional or national colours of the departed land. This reinforced the links to cultures left behind for those who had migrated and for the next generation born in Australia. Many Anglo–Australians saw this fidelity to departed homelands as distasteful and unpatriotic to Australia. There are many stories of soccer clubs being asked to change their names to something more neutral, and to do away with waving flags that were not Australian. When amateur soccer clubs in Australia changed their names from those referring to previous national affiliations, it was seen as a positive step by many Anglo–Australians in the process of becoming Australian.

In the last decade or so, there has been a concerted effort from sports marketers to position soccer as a national or 'Australian' game. Interestingly, to make soccer 'Australian' it had to be de-ethnicised. As suggested above, one of the key steps taken in remaking soccer 'Australian' was changing the names of some teams. For example, in 1994 Sydney Croatia became Sydney United and Melbourne Croatia became the Melbourne Knights, because the original names were seen as too partisan—too 'ethnic'. These names were seen as not quite Australian and as creating an atmosphere that encouraged citizens/fans to maintain a loyalty outside Australia. It is interesting to note that these name changes were only considered necessary in the 'foreign' game of soccer. The Rugby League and Union codes, which were seen as much more 'Australian'—their fan base was more solidly Australians of Anglo–Celtic heritage—did not get asked to change the names of teams alluding to foreign people and places. So St George (patron saint of England) did not have to change its name from an 'ethnic' one to an 'Australian' one. The Brisbane Broncos were not considered foreign because they had an American allusion in their name.

Yet it would be too simplistic to equate the feelings attached by some soccer fans to their team's 'ethnic' names with those of fans in codes such as Rugby League. The role of soccer in the lives of fans is often different from the role of the state or national Rugby or AFL football teams. For many soccer fans, their clubs are part of a broader community with links both inside and outside Australia. Supporting, say, Juventas Soccer Club, may be a way in which Italian–Australians can maintain connections with aspects of Italian culture and their homeland that may not be supported in dominant Australian life. The maintenance of such connections may be less important for sports fans whose cultural affiliation is part of the dominant social and sporting cultures of Australia. So St George seems to be a culturally neutral team with culturally neutral fans because the culture of many of the fans of this team is seen to be everywhere.

The 'Australianisation' of soccer was not just about erasing club names that marked the specificity of soccer as a game dominated by teams whose links were outside the Anglo–Australian sphere. It was also about trying to broaden the support base for the game. Soccer is played by millions of Australians as both a junior and senior amateur code. However, the dominant perception was that professional soccer clubs in Australia were not Anglo–Australian. The high proportion of teams, fans and players from suburbs and regions that were not dominated by Anglo–Australians was understood as making the code unrepresentative—that is, not national. By this logic, to make soccer Australian it had to be watched and played at a professional level by Anglo–Australians. In 1998, the National Soccer League approved the establishment of a new team (called Northern Spirit) in the Anglo–Australian enclave of North Sydney. One outcome of this approval was that this team would help mark the game as an Australian game because it helped to make the league more 'multicultural'. By comparison, the Anglo–Australian nature of the Australian cricket team has never been a problem, and a concerted campaign to 'de-ethnicise' it has never been mooted. This is obviously because what is 'ethnic' in Australia is not seen as that which is British-derived. So the Australian cricket team is neutrally 'Australian'; the teams of the national soccer league are 'ethnic' because they often comprise Australians who are not of Anglo–Australian heritage.

More recently, dominant representations of soccer have also shifted from being understood as a game that is now played by 'Australians' (rather than 'wogs') to one that has found a place in the national sporting calendar. In 2005, a new national soccer league—A League—was established. The Australian soccer team is now becoming understood as national. Now, when the Australian team plays qualifying matches for the Soccer World Cup or participate in the World Cup as they did in 2006, it is a 'mainstream' nationalist sports spectacle—gold and green-clad crowds watch the match on televisions in pubs. There is high-level media coverage, and politicians comment about the outcome. The long-standing popularity of the game in Australia amongst a wide range of citizens, in combination with the growing awareness of soccer as a game with a worldwide commercial and cultural profile, has meant the code is now on the calendar of sports events that require the media and politicians' attention.

Interestingly, being a soccer fan now also operates to link Australia and Australian fans with a new transnational bourgeois culture. Here, soccer is understood as something more than a game played by homesick migrants. It is viewed as a game that is more cosmopolitan than the parochial national games of cricket and football. Given the truly international scope of soccer—played in Europe, the Middle East, Africa, Asia and South America—it has come to be understood as a global and cosmopolitan game. Jason Wilson (2002) argues that this cosmopolitanism has changed the way many Anglo–Australians identify with the game:

> the emerging preference for [soccer] can be linked with an emerging class-formation. In Australia . . . being a football fan can indicate membership in the class of networked, metropolitan, media- and information-rich, well-heeled, well-educated, pluralistic and mobile globalists; those whom McKenzie Wark refers to as the 'urbane'.

The soccer fans Wilson refers to like soccer because it is watched by people around the world who seem to be the same as them. Sport here is global rather than international. The links are established via the new technologies that make it possible for citizens to see themselves not as Australian, but as refined and well-heeled corporate players who have more in common with other corporate players around the world than with their fellow national citizens.

Sport and community

Not all sports fans want to be cosmopolitan and global. A good case is found in the attempts made in the late 1990s in New South Wales and Queensland to internationalise the state Rugby League. In undertaking this huge reshuffle of teams, the league management came up against a type of fan who only wanted to be local. When the east coast Rugby League world reformed as two leagues (Australian Rugby League and Super League) and then one (National Rugby League), the meaning of club sport changed irrevocably for many supporters and their clubs. Clubs were now regarded by many fans as existing to please a national or international television audience, rather than being about a community of loyal and local members, players and fans. This new approach to Rugby League was seen as rationalising the teams to please a large multinational company, not supporting the teams who actually made up the league. In 1997, when the Australian Rugby League (ARL) and Super League decided to merge the ten Super League teams and the twelve ARL clubs, the outcome was to be one league and fourteen teams by 2000. In the formation of the National Rugby League (NRL), there were voluntary and forced mergers of teams. In 1999, fifteen teams presented for the 2000 seasons: one had to go. The team chosen was the South Sydney team the Rabbitohs.

The criteria used by the NRL to decide which teams were viable and which were not was financial. Using financial criteria to decide whether a Rugby League team should live or die did not fit with the fans', members' and supporters' understanding of the value of a team. In 1999, fans took the NRL to court, challenging the corporate story of the value of sport. The legal argument had to be framed differently, but in the streets the story was about community and loyalty versus business values (Bullock 2000). In a large October 1999 Sydney rally to 'Reclaim the Game', the distinction was drawn between Rugby League as being about 'business values and community traditions'. As the publicity for Alana Valentine's (2004) book *Run Rabbit Run* suggests, 'when South Sydney came out fighting they showed the importance of community and the power of momentum'. Television presenter, Andrew Denton, a well-known participants in the 'Save Souths' campaign, said the fight was about: '[the] people versus the juggernaut'.

The loyalty and long-term commitment of the fans to the club was also an important motif used by supporters to explain why the Rabbitohs should not be obliterated. It was the historical association of the team with the community, along with its local roots, that were seen as important to the fans—not the idea of an (inter)national league. For example, in media representations of the court dispute, the story of South Sydney's working class community origins was often referred to. For many fans, being a Souths' fan was a central part of a class identity located in a particular neighbourhood and associated with a specific and long sporting history. Radio presenter Chris Bullock (2000) interviewed Souths' supporter Myra Hagarty:

> I just worry about it, like not being in it, because it was so much a part of us all the time. You've got to be a Souths' person to understand fully how it's hurt us all. A lot of my friends, they're all old and they're dying, and they're dying with a broken heart because of what they've done to Souths; they've followed them for much more longer than me, like years longer than me, and mine's over 50 years.

For Myra Hagarty and her friends, their identity as local Souths' supporters was important to their understanding of who they were in an everyday, but powerful, sense. The global soccer fans referred to earlier created their identities via class affiliations spanning nations and continents. For the Souths' fans, the affiliations were long-standing and tied to specific local neighbourhoods.

Other fans described Rugby League as a thread that held their life together. As Chris Bullock (2000) suggests, the grief at the loss of the team was 'about the loss of something that brings a lot of very different people together . . . [it registered as] a very personal loss'.

South Sydney was readmitted to the NRL in 2002. In this case, the power of the fans trumped the powerful media interests that sought to make sport about watching games on subscription cable television rather than about local fans turning up to the game and then going back home or to the pub for a dissection of the boys' performance.

Sport and egalitarianism

If the South Sydney Rabbitohs' victory can be seen as a win for people power, then it suggests that, within sport, the mighty boardroom lawyers are no better than the loyal working-class supporters. Within the story of sport in Australia, the idea of egalitarianism is very powerful. In fact, in the Australian story of egalitarianism, sport features as the key place where equality is practised. As Peter Kell states: 'There is [in sport] an assumption that merit will win out against social cultural and economic barriers to participation and prosperity' (2000: 37). There are many examples of this egalitarian myth of sport as the great leveller. Kell writes: 'Sport has long been sustained by images of all those working-class poor boys and girls who have made good' (2000: 37). He cites the way in which working-class Balmain-born Olympic swimmer Dawn Fraser stands as evidence of this egalitarianism. Australian Rules football and Rugby League are also represented as sports where boys from the wrong side of the tracks can make good. Similarly, Australian Rules and Rugby League are codes seen as offering Indigenous and Pacific Islander men the experience of being Australian without the racism and prejudice found in the wider society.

The issue of equality and sport is, of course, much more complex. The series of scandals about racism in the AFL in the mid 1990s demonstrated that being part of a team did not necessarily mean equality. Players can be well-paid, well-respected and great sportsmen, yet still be on the receiving end of racism—not only from opposition players or fans, but from within their own team or club (see Figure 11.1). The opportunities offered by sport to men and women from poorer or marginalised groups must be contextualised. The sport of boxing is a good example. Professional boxing is a sport in which Indigenous men have been over-represented in terms of their numbers in the general population. Particular Indigenous communities have produced more than their fair share of local, national and international boxing champions. Boxing was for many Indigenous men their way out of poverty and marginalisation. They took this opportunity and made the most of it. For many Indigenous

Figure 11.1 St. Kilda player Nicky Winmar in a now famous display of Aboriginal
pride, pointing to his black skin and telling the crowd taunting him
with racial insults that he is proud to be Aboriginal. (© *Newspix/News Ltd/
3rd Party Managed Reproduction & Supply Rights; Photographer John Feder*)

boxers, it was not only the thrill of being a state or national champion
that inspired them, but the pride their success created in their
Indigenous communities.

Yet it needs to be remembered that, for the first half of the
twentieth century, the world of boxing was often framed in terms of
a battle between the races. For example, the 1908 bout in Sydney
between Tommy Burns and the African American Jack Johnson was
regarded in terms of the Australian boxer as the 'great white hope'
pitted against not only an outsider, but a black man. This trope of
black versus white framed American boxing for most of the twentieth
century, and Australia was not immune—in fact, it sometimes drew
on the same discourse. In this context, sport replicated the racism of
the everyday world rather than challenging it. As Richard Broome
and Alick Jackamos (1998) argue, some aspects of Australian boxing

can be understood as reprising the wars of the frontier, where Indigenous men fought non-Indigenous men for the land.

This 'war' was most obvious in boxing tents. Another way Indigenous men participated in boxing was as workers in boxing tents, or troupes, that travelled the Australian countryside throughout the twentieth century. These tents were made up of an owner and his team of boxers, who moved from town to town. When they arrived in a town, the owner would set up a stage and spruik to the townsfolk, letting them know the troupe was in town and ready to challenge any of the local men to a bout, with a nice winner's purse for anyone who beat a member of the troupe. By nightfall, when the matches got underway, there were plenty of half-drunk men willing to have a go. They were often inspired by a dummy match where a plant in the audience easily beat one of the troupe. The evening often ended with plenty of battered bodies and a professional bout between an overseas boxer and a well-known national fighter.

Many Indigenous men remember their stints in the boxing tents as times of great freedom. While other members of their community had to get permission to leave the reserve or were earning a pittance, these men had the chance to travel the country and were reasonably well paid. They were also recognised as skilled and talented sports-people. However, just because you were paid to punch white men (something Indigenous men were not often invited to do) did not mean all-round equality. The experience of being a boxer in the troupe took place in the context of Indigenous peoples generally being regarded as second-class citizens. As some boxers remember, when they arrived in town with the troupe, and were perhaps walking down the main street during the day, they were sometimes spat at. It was only at night as a sportsperson that they had the opportunity to make right this wrong. Even so, the next day in the street they were second-class citizens again.

Sport operates as a pivot around which many stories of being Australian are created. These may be stories locating a person in a national frame or a more local one. For many Australians, sport is marginal in their lives—they do not play it and do not watch it. Yet it is hard to get away from it. When Sally Robbins suddenly stopped rowing in an Athens Olympics rowing final in August 2004, it was a major media event. Though a similar incident took place during the same Games—a Canadian rower stopped rowing in his team's final—it did not similarly register in the Canadian press and current affairs. In Australia, politicians were asked for (and gave) their opinions;

Hollywood actor Matt Damon was in town and was asked to give his response. After the initial round of reports about what had actually happened (had she given up or was she paralysed with exhaustion?) the next round of opinion pieces emerged responding to the responses to the incident—why did Australians care so much? Why was the discourse of the Anzac and mateship invoked to help clarify the issue? Why did the epitaph 'un-Australian' spring to mind? Though the incident faded in time and the notion of 'doing a Sally Robbins' did not enter the lexicon, the fact a sporting incident—mostly concerning eight heartbroken women—became a national incident says much about how Australian-ness is produced through sport. You do not have to row or even compete in sport to be affected. The saturation coverage still works to actively invite Australians to ask 'should she have done it?' 'Would I want her on my team?' 'Did she let the side down?' And the side is not just her and those other seven women, but 'Australia'.

The suburbs

Craig McGregor (1966) cited the statistic of 75 per cent of Australians watching sport to demonstrate that they were sports mad. Eighty-five per cent of Australians live in the suburbs, so does this make them suburbs mad? If sport is proudly quoted as a quintessential aspect of being Australian, then suburban life sits at the other end of the spectrum, as something that is often actively ignored and certainly not something to boast about as being typically Australian. Architect Robin Boyd characterised Australian suburbs in the 1950s as 'bald, raw, sunbeaten' and with a certain 'drabness' (Murphy and Probert 2004: 275). Still, much has been written about the suburban nature of Australian community living. Graeme Davison (1994) argues that Governor Arthur Phillip's 1789 plans for Sydney already suggest a suburban vision of Australia—sprawling geography with 'aspirations to decency, good order, health and domestic privacy' (Davison 1994: 100). The suburbs have been vilified, lampooned, eulogised and idealised. As Kimberley Weber puts it, for Australians 'the suburb is both their greatest aspiration and their worst nightmare' (1992: 24). Trevor Hogan suggests, suburban life is 'tied directly to the nation-state project and the cultural self-understandings of the Australian people' (2003: 60). So whether we like it or not, the suburbs and suburban life reflect and reproduce stories of being Australian.

Suburban existence emerged in Australia around the 1880s. From this time, increasing numbers of people were living in housing arrangements that involved a free-standing house on a small block of land surrounded by other houses of the same type. Not all Australians had access to the suburban existence: it was a bourgeois lifestyle. Buying a block of land in the suburbs from the turn into the twentieth century was something only the middle classes could afford. Less well-off citizens remained living in the less desirable and often run-down inner-city areas. The long boom of the post-1945 period saw a rise in many workers' standard of living, and hence their ability to become suburban house-owners. Further, the large immigration population who arrived after 1945 often could not afford houses in the suburbs and so moved into the inner city. Continuing the earlier pattern, as they grew wealthier they also moved to the suburbs. It was not until the 1970s that, in most big cities in Australia, there was a move back into the inner city by younger middle-class couples and families. The idea of living close to a city again became desirable.

Suburban life described not just a particular type and organisation of housing, but also implied a particular type of Australian family and family life. It suggested a particular relationship between the adults in the household and the paid workplace. The process of suburbanisation in Australia reflected the gradual shift from a society organised around single men undertaking itinerant work in the rural sector to a society made up of a disciplined workforce, living in nuclear hetero-sexual units and undertaking an increasing amount of work in factories and the tertiary industries of the city (Murphy and Probert 2004: 279). Ideas of Australian-ness do not simply derive from a majority of people engaged in a particular way of life (say, living in the bush); they derive more from representations of particular values being associated with the Australian way of life. So, no matter what a person's circumstances, by virtue of being Australian they are associated with those values. Although the reality was that more and more people over the twentieth century were living suburban lives, the idea that Australian-ness was located in the bush or the life of the bushman lingered. The non-Indigenous Australian suburban habitus was occluded from the Australian story (Hogan 2003: 60). This distaste for the suburbs is not unique to Australia. The form of indus-trialisation taking place in Europe and the United States at the same time produced similarly ambivalent feelings (Kirkby 1998: 3).

Suburban alienation

Of course, the existence of the suburbs and being Australian was not completely denied, but it often emerged as a form of dark and savage humour (see Figure 11.2). The shift from the story of Australia where blokes wielded axes to clear land for a new nation to one where these same blokes were pushing a lawnmower around a patch of grass was distinctly uncomfortable as a vision of Australian manhood. In the early 1960s, Max Harris asked a sarcastic question:

> Sunday mornings in the suburbs, when the high decibel drone of the motor-mower is calling the faithful to worship. A block of land, a brick veneer, and the motor-mower beside him in the wilderness—what more does he want to sustain him . . . ? (Murphy 1995: 545).

Satirist Barry Humphries created a number of characters—including Dame Edna Everage—who dwelled in the suburbs. These comic characters expressed Humphries' understandings of some of the deadening and isolating effects of suburban life. Sandy Stone writes a letter to his wife Beryl while she is away on a *Woman's Weekly* World Discovery Tour, filling her in on his life:

> Just a note to let you know I am in the land of the living . . . Things on the home front are much of a muchness . . . Nora Manly dropped

Figure 11.2 James Mellon's *Gene @ Home* (2003) illustrates another side of suburban life from that of the cheerful nuclear family. (*Image courtesy of the artist*)

in today to borrow a cup of castor sugar, I was watering your mother-in-law's tongue (Humphries 1990: 71–72).

Poet Bruce Dawe enunciates an even bleaker picture:

'Kids make a home,' he said, the family man
speaking from long experience. That was on Thursday
evening. On Saturday he lay dead
in his own wood shed, having blown away
all qualifications with a trigger touch (Dawe 2006).

More recently, the ABC comedy *Kath and Kim* has offered an updated satirisation of the suburbs. In this manifestation, mother and daughter, and their respective partners and 'second best friends' provide comedy for viewers as they trundle the Fountain Gate shopping centre in outer suburban Melbourne, spouting a 'barrage of witless clichés [reinforcing] the supposed cluelessness of outer suburbanites' (*The Age* 2002). As Joy Hooton, citing Barry Humphries expresses it: 'the robust awfulness' of characters who inhabit suburban life 'serve to defeat the fear of nothingness, the fear of "the desert inside Australia, of the vacuum in the heart of it"' (Hooton 1995: 66).

Desiring suburbs

The suburbs were seen as distinct from both inner city and rural living—as Hogan explains, a '"third space" that mediates urbanism and nature' (2003: 56). The layout of the suburbs reinforces a sense of 'status and class' (Wood 2002: 1). Take, for example, the names of outer Perth suburban estates—'Killarney Gardens', 'Henley Rise' and 'Settlers Hills'. They all suggest a link to bourgeois Britishness and nature (Wood 2002: 1). More recently, 'enclave estates', or gated communities, have appeared in Australian suburbia. These single-entrance, walled communities are designed to reinforce a sense of community cohesion, with the walls locating 'the dangerousness of difference . . . outside the enclave walls' (Wood 2002: 10). These suburbs are filled with the owners' dream houses—derided by detractors as 'McMansions'—reflecting both an ecologically unsustainable use of resources and excessive consumption, but loved by their owners as spacious, modern and family friendly.

Though not about a family living in a McMansion, one of the most affectionate representations of the love of the suburban dweller for their home was the film *The Castle* (1997). In this story the Kerrigan family fight to keep their home from being compulsorily acquired as part of an airport expansion. The early images of the house, located adjacent to a noisy international airport, suggest that no-one would want to live there, but the film creates an affectionate portrait of the Kerrigan family's life that many Australians identified with. A contrast was drawn between the unfashionable house and the love associated with a suburban family home. In the last decade, the 'drabness' of suburban identity has also been reworked in popular culture as a desirable—or even sexy—identity of which to be proud. This has mostly worked through the confluence of television and consumerism. Through television shows—beginning with *Burke's Backyard*, and followed by *Auction Squad* and *The Block*—the suburb has become a space where (mostly) young, coupled, middle-class and desirable Australians are represented as creating an enviable suburban lifestyle organised around over-valued real estate, DIY and product purchase.

Yet suburbs are not always well-organised communities. They have not always provided the facilities and resources the inhabitants have required. For example, suburban public transport systems often cater for people who leave the suburbs for work in the city each morning, rather than for the person who stays in the suburbs and needs to negotiate their way around them. They have also often lacked the facilities that make life workable—including leisure, commercial and governmental support facilities. For people—mostly women and children—who have inhabited the suburbs, getting around them, but also out of them, to vital services has often been difficult. It was the phenomenon of western bourgeois women's suburban existence that was part of the impetus for the second wave of feminist action in the 1960s and 1970s. For so many women, the deadening effects of the suburbs reinforced how much more they could do with their lives if society was not ordered in terms of a breadwinner husband and a stay-at-home wife.

Urban policy expert Brendan Gleeson (2006) has argued that the failure to provide public services to suburbs in the past 20 years is again creating spaces where groups of Australians are caught in 'new "private" worlds of disadvantage' (Gleeson 2003: 62). He argues that the emphasis on the provision of privatised infrastructure—including health and education facilities—for new suburbs is creating a gap between the recipients of these publicly subsidised 'private' services and those left behind in the older suburbs where under funded public infrastructure are becoming degraded and neglected (2003: 62–63).

Contemporary youth subcultures are often figured around a flight from the suburbs. There is frequently nothing for teenagers to do in the suburbs. As Christos Tsiolkas (1995) puts it in his novel *Loaded*, the suburbs are places where the young are 'meant to buy a house, grow a garden, shop, watch TV and be buried'. Young Australians often spend their leisure time in the city rather than the suburbs, as the urban setting can provide 'an escape from the suburban and traditionally Australian—"strine"—modes of identification' (Alach 1997: 117). Felena Alach gives the example of ravers, many of whom reject the traditional, hard-drinking, macho Australian identity in favour of enacting a less straight version of masculinity. The escape into the cities from the suburbs also allows young people to achieve a level of anonymity. The habit of young people from the suburbs coming to the city and congregating in a mall or near the post office also allows them to define themselves against the conformity of the suburbs. Alach writes of the youth who congregate in Murray Street mall in Perth as creating a 'collective voice that set[s] itself apart from the culture of the mainstream' (1997: 119).

Suburban beaches

A significant part of Australian suburban life includes suburban beaches. Most Australian cities have beachside suburbs. These spaces have been represented in iconic films such as *Puberty Blues* (1981) or more recently the television soap *Home and Away*, set in the seaside town of Summer Bay. Here the suburban beach is a homely place filled with locals, in particular young people, who enjoy the freedom and ease of beach life. Yet *Puberty Blues*, based on a book by Kathy Lette and Gabrielle Carey (1979), was a controversial book that not only exposed the sexual activity of teenagers, but also the gendered dimension of the beach where boys surfed and girls watched and went to fetch fast food when required. At this time the freedom of the beach was restricted for women who had very narrow roles to play—to sit and look good. The young women represented in this coming-of-age film had limited options in terms of sexual behaviour as well. Whereas the men could be sexually active without being seen negatively, for women the chance of being read as a 'moll' or a 'scrubber' if they were sexually active was a constant threat. *Puberty Blues* ends with two of the young women taking up surfing rather than just watching. In Australia in the twenty-first century the gender dynamics of the beach is not as sexist, many more women surf and boogie board, but the majority of people 'out the back' are men.

The suburban beach space is also a predominantly white Australian space. This is often represented in terms of the beach as a place for locals. Non-suburban beach spaces in Australia are understood to be filled with out-of-towners during the summer, but the suburban beaches are constantly available to other city dwellers. The arrival of non-locals is sometimes represented as an unwelcome invasion. When explaining the Cronulla riots in December 2005 many residents of the area emphasised the insular and village-like atmosphere of 'the Shire' (the local name for the local government area where the beach is located). Long-time residents explained that people knew each other and loved the family atmosphere of the place. The Cronulla Beach area has always been a popular spot for people living outside 'the Shire' to visit on weekends. In more recent times many of these beach users are non-Anglo–Australians. They come to the beach not only in family units but as groups of young men and women who use the beach in ways that are different from the Anglo–Australian norm. For example they may play rowdy games of soccer, and occasionally there were also incidents of bad behaviour and violence. The normative status of the beach as a white space makes these Australians visible in the landscape. They are represented as ethnic gangs in opposition to the Anglo–Australian family beach users. The story of white women and children being in danger is also deployed. The locals are seen as protecting the beach, women and children from an external threat. The idea of the non-Anglo beach users as being outsiders is made clear in the slogan one Cronulla protester wrote on his chest: 'We Grew Here! You Flew Here!' (see Figure 11.3). The slogan represents the non-Anglo youth not only as from outside the local area but as from outside Australia.

When the riots broke out in Cronulla and nearby Maroubra there was a concerted effort on the part of some politicians and conservative commentators not to read the behaviour of the mob as racist. For example, it was identified in an editorial in *The Weekend Australian* newspaper as 'disgraceful behaviour' (Editorial 2005: 16) and Prime Minister John Howard insisted: 'The thing has to be dealt with strongly from the law and order point of view' ('Australians Not Racist: PM' 2005). Yet as seen above, many of the participants and people caught up in the violence, placed issues of ethnicity and difference at the centre of their stories. One letter writer to *The Australian* suggested the only 'real answer is the prohibition of any further Islamic immigration' (Congram 2005: 16). Many participants in the riots also framed their actions in terms of race: 'It's a lesson for the wogs. We smashed them. They came to our territory; they cop it' (Cubby 2006: 83). Commentators viewing the riots from other countries read them as race based. *The Globe and Mail*, Toronto in

Figure 11.3 A young Australian, with an Australian flag worn as a cape, draws a
distintion with a slogan written on his chest between Australian citizens
born in the country and those born overseas. (© *Newspix/News Ltd/
3rd Party Managed Reproduction & Supply Rights; Photographer Noel Kessel*)

Canada used the image of the Klu Klux Klan in one cartoon to
represent the violence (see Figure 11.4).

There was significant retaliation from groups of non-
Anglo–Australians in response to the attacks on them. Ben Cubby
(2006), who spoke to some of those who participated in the riots
and the revenge attacks, quotes one man as explaining the response
this way: 'We didn't know what lengths they would go to, what they
were capable of. I seen what they done on TV, at Cronulla. There was
thousands of them. Everyone wanted to get together, to protect
themselves. Because we knew the cops wouldn't' (Cubby 2006: 80).
Part of the anger is linked to feelings of 'alienation': 'When we were
growing up, we were just dealing with people calling us wogs.
Now young Muslims have to deal with getting called terrorists and
rapists' (Cubby 2006: 81). Similarly all Anglo–Australian beach users
are not racists. However, the suburban beach space is racialised and the

Figure 11.4 Cartoon from Canada's *Globe and Mail* lampooning the racist riots in Cronulla in December 2005. *(Reprinted with permission from* Globe and Mail*)*

Anglo–Australian group has the most power to shape how the space is used and to monitor the boundaries of the space. This means the beach is read in terms of particular bodies belonging and other bodies as invaders. In some discussion about the reasons for the riot the explanation put forward was that it was in response to 'young Lebanese males [who] have acted in ways outside the pattern of normal behaviour' (Barclay and West 2006: 77): in particular sexually insulting young Anglo–Australian women. This behaviour is understood as part of a larger phenomenon of 'an Anglo–Australian community under threat' from 'a criminal, violent and sexually voracious underclass' (Perera 2006: 26). As Suvendrini Perera notes this threat is represented as *demanding* a 'response' of 'retaliatory violence'. So for example one academic explanation of the riot notes that the 4 December 2005 attack at Cronulla of two volunteer lifesavers by Lebanese–Australian men, which is understood as the catalyst for the riot, was 'provocative' and in some way invited a violent response: 'People know that lifesavers do literally save lives. The weekend volunteers are not paid for what they do. For someone to attack lifesavers was to commit a very provocative act which was likely to cause an angry reaction' (Barclay and West 2006: 77). Though the authors are not defending the rioters' behaviour their explanation replays a common story of sexually malevolent and aggressive outsiders who are seen to threaten the 'local' community and as such invite or demand retaliation. In fact what the Anglo–Australian violence does is re-assert white power. The Lebanese–Australian men are understood to threaten not only the individual women they insult but the local Australian male who '[feels] displaced by all the immigrants who had arrived in Australia' (Barclay and West 2006: 83). The violent response directed at the 'wogs' or 'lebs' does not work to end the sexually threatening behaviour but reasserts the place of particular Australians as at home at the beach.

The suburban beach is a place continuous with the 19 000 kilometre coastline of Australia. The Australian coast has been represented as uniquely vulnerable in dominant Australian narratives of nation. In the twenty-first century it has been read as being invaded from both sides—by both asylum seekers and also non-Anglo–Australians. Not many 'locals' represented the need to protect their beach in terms of an earlier invasion of the beach by the British. The proximity of Cronulla Beach to the place of original colonial invasion in 1788 makes it easy for many Indigenous peoples to wonder how this invasion is erased from non-Indigenous memory and re-presented as their place. For many Australians the desire to see Australia as the 'good neighbour' (Rutherford 2000) precludes the possibility of reading the behaviour of the mob in 2005 as racist. It also precludes the possibility of remembering the British invasion as unjust. Indeed the long history of white Australian refusal to let neighbours visit or play on their beaches and the exclusion of Indigenous peoples from this space has to be repressed and the loutish behaviour seen simply as a law and order issue.

Belonging

The house in the suburbs also signifies ownership of and belonging to Australia. Early suburban subdivision reproduced the British colonial imperative. Land developers purchased land from the government and razed it of all that was native (plants, grasses, inclines and natural features), then sold the 'empty' quarter-acre block to buyers to be re-formed as domesticated space in the British or European tradition. Further:

> the contemporary suburban Australian home could in fact be seen as a shrunken version of the free selector's dream; the quarter acre block is a satisfyingly compromised metonym for 'our selection', continuing to assert everyone's right to acquire property in our egalitarian society (Fiske et al. 1987: 27).

Of course, the 'everyone' here refers to non-Indigenous people. The sale of newly acquired crown land to selectors came about as a result of the dispossession of Indigenous peoples. Yet Indigenous peoples have sometimes been selectors. They have bought freehold land over the centuries, but the recognition they are buying back their own property is not often even symbolically acknowledged.

Obtaining a suburban block did not complete the act of belonging. Katie Holmes (1999), in her work on gardens in Australia, demonstrates how the practice of domestic (and large-scale) gardening was a way in which British colonisers 'established themselves in a foreign landscape':

> Through planting, tending and harvesting, settlers transformed alien spaces into images of their own making. A stolen land became claimed and 'owned' through this central 'ritual of habitation' (1999: 1).

This tending still takes place on a large scale, as well as at the micro-scale of individual gardens surrounding homes. The ritual of occupying and reshaping is effectively a reterritorialisation of land to be part of the Australian nation (Cerwonka 2004: 4).

Front and back yards

The basic unit of life in the suburbs—the quarter-acre block—is traditionally filled with the house, but also the yards or gardens. The front garden, with its low fence, welcoming gate, letterbox and occasional gnome or tyre-swan, is where home occupiers show off to and connect with the outside world. In some newer suburbs, front gardens are not fenced at all, encouraging a feeling of the link between the public space of the street, the nearby parks and the footpaths and the private space of the home. The visual link between the front garden and public space means the way residents use or tend their front gardens is often understood as reflecting 'the moral order of modern suburbia' (Hogan 2003: 55). It is seen to reflect their status as Australians. Long unkempt grass and cars on blocks in the front yard are understood to lower the tone of the neighbour-hood. When some non-Anglo–Australian families moved to the suburbs and started using their front gardens for growing vegetables rather than as display areas for neatly arranged hoses, Anglo–Australian residents often saw this as lowering the tone. There was often a collective neighbourly frown. More recently, there have been cases where some house owners have been building largish religious shrines in their front yards and have been confronted by their local councils; who have argued that building permits are needed and that the shrines may not be appropriate decoration in a semi-public space—again, a frown for the ethnic 'other' from the Anglo–Australian majority.

The back yard is the part of the quarter-acre block that is totally fenced off and available only to the family. Mostly out of view of neighbours, the back yard is seen as the resident's private space. It is here that the iconic Hills Hoist clothesline is planted and underwear can be dried in privacy. More than this, the back yard is drawn on to produce one of the most potent narratives of non-Indigenous belonging. When the High Court of Australia found in the *Mabo* case that native title still existed for the Meriam people of the Torres Strait, it set off a phenomenon the Turrbal peoples of Brisbane call 'back yard syndrome' (Turrbal Traditional Owners 2005). The 1992 decision recognising this specifically Indigenous form of land title was interpreted by some non-Indigenous people as a legal decision that enabled Indigenous peoples to take the near-sacred back yards of non-Indigenous peoples as they desired. Jeff Kennett, premier of Victoria, and Peter Cochran, Western Australian parliamentarian, both suggested at the time that back yards were in danger. John Howard, when asked in a 1997 interview whether it was clear that 'native title [had] no chance of affecting suburban back yards', answered, 'I think that is the law' and, when prompted with the follow-up question, replied: 'Well I am not certain because there has been no specific test case on that proposition' (Howard 1997). Within this fear campaign (which in no way reflected the very limited capacity of the *Mabo* decision to deliver land to Indigenous peoples), there was little recognition of how non-Indigenous people had acquired their quarter-acre blocks, their 'selections' or their back yards in the first place.

The anxiety about the threat of the loss of one's back yard to Indigenous land claims was based not on a genuine fear of this happening (because it clearly could not), but on the barely acknowledged understanding that any land non-Indigenous people have directly correlates to land that Indigenous people have lost. Suburbia in Australia is built on Indigenous land—land that was confiscated, sold to non-Indigenous people, cleared of the 'native' (people, flora and fauna). It was then reconfigured with fences and roads, subdivided and sold to individuals, who then remade the land—first in homage to a British homeland and later to a native land of which they were the centre. Yet all this remaking could not undo the knowledge that at some level the land did and does belong to Indigenous peoples, and that it was taken from them without compensation. The ubiquity of the myth of the loss of the back yard through native title in no way reflects reality—the reality is that Indigenous peoples, especially those from the heavily populated east coast and intensely farmed hinterlands of all states, are the group in Australia who have lost out when it comes to land ownership and access.

The national back yard

The story of the back yard also works in relation to the region in which Australia is located. Historically a powerful way of imagining Australia was as a lone white bastion of Britishness in a region mostly made up of 'backward' Asian nations. Today this story has been reframed in terms of a democratic and developed Australia surrounded by nations struggling to achieve these goals. In this story the region to the north of Australia is sometimes imagined as 'our back yard'.

Australian space is seen to extend beyond national boundaries. Ruth Balint (2005) has pointed out that Australian territorial waters have extended hundreds of miles out to sea in the last few decades and now encompass spaces that are the traditional fishing grounds of West Timorese fishing communities. Having read this ocean as *mare nullius* (sea belonging to no-one) it has been incorporated into Australian territory and is now Australia's back yard. The West Timorese fishermen who continue to fish here are seen as trespassing and arrested and their boats burned. Fiona Nicoll (2001) gives another example. She writes of the episode when ex-Australian Prime Minister Keating walked the Kakoda Track in Papua New Guinea. The Kakoda Track is a significant part of the Australian military story of World War II. Nicoll argues that Keating's visit, which included the gesture of kissing the ground, relocated the story of Australian 'digger' values from Europe to somewhere closer to home. However, as Nicoll points out, it also reinforces Australia's historical role as a colonising state and its continued dominance. Kissing the ground is usually what a citizen does when they return to their homeland. In enacting this gesture on the Kakoda Track the prime minister reinforced the sense of this area as part of the national back yard.

A last example can be found in the use the Howard government made of Pacific Islands as a holding space for unauthorised arrivals seeking refugee status in Australia. When the ship the MV *Tampa* took on board the 300 or so people seeking asylum in Australia in 2002, the federal government would not let them enter Australian territory. Instead they paid the government of Nauru to hold asylum seekers in detention while Australian immigration officials processed them. These desperate people, most of whom were given refugee status, were kept in the back yard out of sight. These 'new forms of self assertion throughout the region' represent 'the triumphant performance of Australian sovereignty abroad' (Perera 2005: 30). Non-Indigenous Australia is at home even overseas. However as Suvendrini Perera (2005) points out, drawing on work by Aileen Moreton-Robinson, these assertions of sovereignty, of being at home outside the territorial boundaries of the nation, depend on the 'Australian state's appropriation of Aboriginal sovereignty'. The legal move that makes Indigenous peoples' country into non-Indigenous peoples back yards can be extended overseas. This certainty of being at home and being the most developed state in the region means the Australian state extends its back yard as far as it sees fit.

Rural life

If suburban spaces are often understood as ambivalent spaces—both a feminised ghetto and a bulwark against the anonymity of the city—then by contrast the bush and the country towns servicing it have long been represented unequivocally as the soul of Australia. Indeed, the health of the nation is still metaphorically measured by life in the bush or country town. For example, in times of regional drought, formulaic media stories are often framed in terms of the proportion of land that is in drought. The health of the state or the nation is then calculated from this percentage. It would be most unusual to see similar mappings of, say, the number of homeless people in a city, and have parallels drawn about what this meant for Australia. The health index of the nation is in the bush.

Australian-ness has long been associated with the bush and the characters that are understood to inhabit it. Country towns are represented as the places where these characters—or real Australians—congregate. The notion of the country town as the quintessential Australian space still has power in the twenty-first century. For example, during a visit to the New South Wales town of Gunnedah in August 2004, Prime Minister John Howard was reported as saying:

> Despite the fact that he had grown up in the southwestern suburbs of Sydney, he loved getting out into the bush and meeting country

people. The bush was essential to the character of Australian, he said (Maher 2004: 2).

Yet, as Graeme Davison (1982) was arguing back in the 1980s, this 'Australian character' did not emerge from 'the transmission to the city of values nurtured on the bush frontier, so much as the projection onto the outback of values revered by an alienated urban intelligentsia' (1982: 129).

Representing bush life or country towns as the centre of stories of Australia-ness is a long-standing habit. The poets and painters of the 1890s were the most influential group to do this. Yet it continued through the twentieth century and, as Prime Minister John Howard's quote suggests, into the twenty-first. As discussed in chapter 8, many popular representations of life in outback towns suggest that in these spaces individuals can access the real or the authentic Australian life or person. To take a popular media example, television shows that are set in country towns are peopled with adorable characters who, though they are outside the everyday experience of most Australians, are instantly recognisable (for example, grumpy farmers with hearts of gold, larrikin blokes, handsome shearers, young women 'wed' to the land they have inherited). The stories of these television serials reinforce the perceptions of city folk about the ideal Australian type. These are fantasies of the ideal Australian community, seen as missing in the fast-paced city but as still available in the bush.

From the 1980s on, significant economic shifts connected to the phenomenon of globalisation had a sustained negative effect on Australian regional centres. The site of economic growth in the nation shifted from the land and regional centres to the big cities. This shrinkage in regional economies led to a decline in infrastructure in the towns. For example, in the 1980s many banks shut down their local branches, while other service providers also slowly drifted from the towns. Federal and state governments have spent much time and money over the past few years trying to encourage companies, industries, even individual professionals—especially medical professionals—to move away from the big cities to the bush. However, the smaller centres often cannot compete with the cities as the place to be for work and for services. For the last few years, Australians have been encouraged to take out private health insurance. For many rural dwellers, this is a problem as many of the basic services provided with insurance—physiotherapy, cosmetic dental work—cannot be accessed in their region. So the story for many towns has been that, as factories closed, no new or replacement industries have opened and young people have left the towns to work in bigger cities. As professionals such as doctors leave, no replacements can be found.

Hippies and sea changers

It is important to note that there have been significant demographic shifts of population to regional centres or towns from the city— though not all newcomers from the city fit the stereotype of thetypical Australian bush dweller. One group whose members have provided new life for regional centres since the 1960s have been alternative lifestylers and hippies. This mixed group has been more significant for capturing the social imagination than as an actual demographic phenomenon (Murphy and Burnley 2002: 6). These alternative lifestylers came to signify a group of people who wanted to get out of the rat-race of city life and live a life based around a different set of principles. The communes of Nimbin in northern New South Wales are probably the most well-known alternative communities in Australia. The town of Nimbin is a tourist spot in its own right, with a local museum dedicated to displaying the alternative ideas of the residents. Nearby Byron Bay is probably one of the most famous alternative country towns in Australia. It was originally a whaling town and it once supported a local dairy industry. The 1973 Aquarius Festival in Nimbin saw hundreds of students converge on the town for a celebration of alternative lifestyles. Many never left. Around this original population, other alternative communities— including surfers and musicians—have gathered, establishing Byron Bay as *the* alternative country/coastal destination.

In the past few years, a new group of alternative lifestylers has joined the outflow of people from the city. These 'sea changers' or 'tree changers' are professional people who move out of large cities and into coastal towns (the sea change phenomenon was amusingly portrayed in the ABC television series of the same name), and more recently to country towns (the tree change version). These newcomers overcome the infrastructural shortcomings of the towns by bringing their own services with them. They are usually older professional couples with well-established businesses that can be run via internet technologies. They get the benefit of country life while making use of the technologies of globalisation to connect themselves to well-paid industries and jobs. As with the original alternative lifestylers, this group lives very differently from the majority of town dwellers. The typical economic prospects for local workers in regional centres are much less well paid than they are for the sea and tree changers. As Peter Murphy and Ian Burnley (2002) explain, the economies of rural centres are not strong, and the jobs that are available are most likely to be in the tourism or service sectors that support the tree or sea changers who flow into town.

Interestingly, one of the ways in which the new and revived coastal and bush towns are represented in the metropolitan centres is that when the city-folk arrive the non-urban spaces tend to become more cosmopolitan. The suggestion is that, in moving to the country (or non-city) environment, sea or tree changers bring with them some of the better aspects of the city—a touch of 'urban chic' (Pryor and Lewis 2004: 25). Good country towns are viewed by these groups as the ones that have fine restaurants, nice shops and a barista who can make the perfect short black. Not all locals would agree. By way of contrast, various representations of moving from the city to the country or coast are based on a familiar dichotomy of real/fake, fulfilling/unfulfilling or even good/bad. The city is associated with the lesser term—dirty, shallow, unhealthy—and the country town is associated with authenticity, truth and sustainable values. There is obviously some truth to this idea. For example, recent statistics on the number of deaths per year related to pollution demonstrate it is about the same as the national road toll. Yet the country town as bucolic space or utopia is perhaps an over-simplification.

Rural lack

One of the significant difficulties of non-city life is the lack of services. The share of government services (from taxes) delivered to the country is less than is required to actually provide sufficient services to Australian citizens living outside the city. Services city-dwellers take for granted—counselling services, medical services providing bulk billing or late-night medical clinics—are often non-existent in the country. The specific pressures of non-city living—such as isolation and small communities—mean youth suicide and domestic violence have become significant problems. Again there are not enough support services for people at risk in the bush. The general lack of services can make life more difficult in a country space than in the city. For example, retirees make up a significant flow of population to smaller centres. Members of this group sell-up houses worth a significant amount in the city and buy a cheaper place in a slower, friendlier coastal town. Citizens on welfare benefits—especially sole parents—also frequently relocate to towns outside capital cities because they are cheaper and easier to get around. The newcomers arrive not knowing that services that are basics in the city are special in the country. Further, this higher density of people requiring extra or specialised medical and social welfare support can put a strain on the resources of smaller towns.

It would be simplistic to suggest that the general popular understanding of country, coastal or bush towns is universally optimistic or without blemish. There is a long history of representations of the country town as a place of small-mindedness and violence. The book (and film) *Wake in Fright* is one such (extreme) example. The 1961 book by Kenneth Cook and the 1971 film made by Canadian director Ted Kotcheff tell the story of an indentured schoolteacher working in a small country town in the outback. When school breaks up for summer, his train trip back to the city is broken with an overnight stay in another country town known to the locals as 'The Yabba'. Going to the pub that night, he stumbles upon a two-up game. He loses all his money—including his fare back to the city—and is so drunk and broke he spends a long weekend in the ultra-masculine environment of 'The Yabba', binge drinking, 'roo-shooting, fighting and being raped. Here, the space outside the city is represented as masculine, alcohol-centred and organised around an oppressive and conformist mateship principle. *The Adventures of Priscilla, Queen of the Desert* (1994), a more recent film, has similar moments, though this film does not create such a totalising story of masculine violence. However, in one scene the local men take one of the non-straight visitors out into a dark alley for a bit of 'poofter bashing'—though, in this film, a tough-talking and hard-fighting transsexual saves the gay man. A more poignant portrayal of the deadening effect of small-town life comes in the film *Muriel's Wedding* (1994), where the downtrodden wife of a local property developer commits suicide. The wreck of her life is represented through her last gesture—a burnt-out back yard with its smouldering Hills Hoist.

Race and country living

Life in the country towns of Australia is, as Gillian Cowlishaw (2004) writes, frequently structured around intimate, though often fraught, relations between Indigenous and non-Indigenous peoples. The proximity of Indigenous and non-Indigenous peoples in rural towns shapes relationships in ways that the more segregated existence in cities and suburbs does not. There is a meshing of the lives of 'black-fellas' and 'whitefellas' in rural spaces that does not take place in the cities. Cowlishaw describes the ways in which race relations operate in rural towns in terms of the 'public secret'. She uses this phrase to describe two aspects of life in the towns: the race war and the intimacy that exists. The intimacy and racism of rural Australian town life can be demonstrated with the example of the town swimming pool. When the Freedom Riders went on their bus trip through western New South Wales in 1965, one of their tasks was to challenge the exclusion of Indigenous peoples from this public amenity. Australia has never had apartheid laws as strict as those of South Africa or the southern United States of America, yet Indigenous people were informally excluded from many public spaces. The racist logic of Indigenous peoples as dirty was used to justify their exclusion from public swimming pools. These spaces, where strangers frolicked in scanty clothing, were understood as intimate spaces that needed careful racial policing. Yet as Darlene Johnson's 1996 film *Two Bob Mermaid* demonstrates, these spaces could never be policed totally. In this film, set around the early 1960s, a young fair-skinned Indigenous woman who longs to be a famous cinematic swimmer (like Esther Williams) passes as white so she can use the swimming pool. As she practices her moves in the pool her darker skinned siblings and friends, who have not been able to, or do not desire to pass, watch from outside the pool fence. In policing the swimming pool space the sexual intimacy of the past, an intimacy that led to lighter skinned Indigenous children, is ignored and instead a belief about an unequivocal, and visible, divide between Indigenous and non-Indigenous peoples is used to decide who can enter.

Despite this intimacy, which sees 'evermore interwoven relationships between evermore varied ancestors', relationships are framed as an antagonistic binary. In this orthodoxy, non-Indigenous peoples are 'victims of disruptive and disreputable Aborigines' and Indigenous peoples are victims of 'dispossession, as well as white prejudice and racism' (Cowlishaw 2004: 31). Indigenous peoples in country towns also have to deal with representations and feelings that encompass both shame and pride. Their lives away from what are seen by so many people as traditional or authentic Indigenous lives can leave them feeling ashamed:

> A fact of life growing up in a small country town . . . We weren't quite up to the standard of an Aborigine. We were the outsiders in the setting. Not quite black and not quite white. We didn't fit in (Lockyer 1993).

Prejudice and disruption do, of course, mark parts of life in rural towns. Young Indigenous people in bush towns are over-represented in petty crime and illegal drug abuse is endemic in some communities. There are often limited opportunities for both Indigenous and non-Indigenous young people in country towns; however, leaving town is sometimes easier for non-Indigenous than Indigenous youth. More limited resources, community ties and fewer educational opportunities often come together to tie Indigenous young people to the rural area they grew up in. Boredom and anger can be a powerful combination in young adults. For Indigenous young people, these feelings are more likely to be pathologised by non-Indigenous commentators, and understood as destructive and dangerous.

Most of the representations of Indigenous/non-Indigenous relations in rural towns that enter national stories emerge from the urban media and general cosmopolitan rhetoric. These narratives are frequently cut adrift from reality, and often reflect a cosmopolitan non-Indigenous reading of rural life. In these stories, racism is something perpetrated by rednecks, and is roundly condemned. In its place, urban non-Indigenous Australians assert their goodwill. Such assertions often substitute for 'actual relationships' (Cowlishaw 2004: 24). In this way, the difficult and ambiguous ways in which racism and intimacy work in rural spaces are replaced in national stories with moral tales of good Indigenous people and bad non-Indigenous people.

Queer country

The complexity of the relationship between country and city can perhaps also be demonstrated through the stories of a group of gay men and women living in a medium-sized Queensland town. This group, whose members were interviewed for a documentary about life as a gay person in the country, spoke about the difficulties that they faced in smaller towns, where queer communities were also smaller and a cheek-by-jowl existence with all sorts (rather than the safety of a gay-friendly suburb) meant that abuse—including physical violence—was not unknown. However, none of the people interviewed wanted to leave their town. They liked the size of the community, the intimacy and the peace. Country life was not some sort of nirvana: some of the traits that are commonly represented as lovable in a country community—the boofy larrikins of the local football team—can make life impossible for those who do not fit the stereotype of the typical Australian. This is not to suggest that living in a gay-friendly suburb in a city is a perfect solution: homophobia is everywhere, and there are plenty of gay bashings in inner-city Sydney, both by locals and by lads who drive in from the outer suburbs for a bit of 'poofter bashing'. More to the point, fixing a place as the Australian place and pouring into it all the virtues imagined as needing to be in this place for it to be exemplary only exists in those nineteenth-century paintings Australians hang on their walls.

Being Australian is something citizens are called on to be everyday. Yet they are also experiencing themselves as many other things—as locals, 'Westies', farmers, Queenslanders or out-of-towners. At a particular moment—for example when the World Cup is being played in Germany—a citizen may see themself as an Australian who barracks for Italy or perhaps a Croatian–Australian who wants the Australian team to win. At other times, someone might see themselves as loyal to the Brisbane Lions though they remember them as the Fitzroy Lions, the team they grew up with down the road. And someone else may take up supporting the Fremantle Dockers because they are sick of supporting AFL teams from outside their state. Stories of Australian-ness intersect with stories of belonging to local communities, to regions, to a city or a country town. At times these stories fit neatly— for example when a citizen's rural identity seems to be reflected in popular cultural representations of being Australian. At other times they clash—for example when a suburb is represented as alien to Australia as sometimes happens to suburbs with large populations of newly arrived Australian residents or citizens.

FURTHER READING

Booth, Douglas and Tatz, Colin 2000, *One-eyed: A View of Australian Sport*, Allen & Unwin, Sydney.

Broome, Richard with Jackamos, Alick 1998, *Sideshow Alley*, Allen & Unwin, Sydney.

Cliff, Paul (ed.) 1999, *A Sporting Nation: Celebrating Australia's Sporting Life*, National Library of Australia, Canberra.

Gleeson, Brendan 2006, *Australian Heartlands: Making Space for Hope in the Suburbs*, Allen & Unwin, Sydney.

Johnson, Lesley (ed.) 1994, *Suburban Dreaming: An Interdisciplinary Approach to Australian Cities*, Deakin University Press, Melbourne.

Kell, Peter 2000, *Good Sports: Australian Sport and the Myth of the Fair Go*, Pluto Press, Sydney.

McCauliffe, Chris (ed.) 1994, *Beasts of Suburbia: Reinterpreting Cultures in Australian Suburbs*, Melbourne University Press, Melbourne.

Mangan, J.A. and Nauright, John (eds) 2000, *Sport in Australasian Society: Past and Present*, F. Cass, London.

Troy, P.N. 2000, *A History of European Housing in Australia*, Cambridge University Press, Melbourne.

Wells, Jeff 1998, *Boxing Day: The Fight that Changed the World*, Harper Sports, Sydney.

12

AUSTRALIA ON DISPLAY

Museums, heritage and the national capital

LOOKING AT WHAT new nations regard as vital to their status as nations, heritage scholar Patrick Boylan notes: 'many governments of new nations see the national museum as "one of four vital symbols of nationhood" along with a national defence force, a national broadcasting service and a national university' (Prystupa 2001: 42). These publicly funded institutions are considered by governments to be prime sites for the creation, narration and defence of stories of the nation. A national museum in particular is seen as a place where the best of a nation's arts and culture are displayed for the nation's citizens and international visitors. This chapter explores public sites where the material culture of Australia is displayed for consumption by international tourists and Australian citizens. The three types of sites examined here are: museums, heritage sites and the national capital, Canberra.

Museums

Citizens often see museums as dull places. Though governments may see them as important sites for the narration of national stories, this is not a universal feeling. Unlike a sports event, which brings a mass of citizens together in one spot and produces a pleasurable feeling of national togetherness with noise, light and massed bodies, museums do not create a national spectacle. Indeed, the national spectacle of the museum is often understood as the opposite of this type of populism. Traditionally, the museum was represented as a serious space for solemn learning: 'The nineteenth century museum combined its scientific role of collecting natural history, fauna, flora and human artifacts with the civic role of educating and enlightening its citizens' (Macintyre and Clark 2003: 198). National histories are frequently articulated through formal education processes. In many ways, museums are adjuncts to this education process—providing the evidence for the national history and ongoing access for all who need or want to hear the stories again. The key museums in Australia are the state (originally colonial) museums. The National Museum of Australia was only opened in 2002—more than a century after federation.

Generally the spectacle of the national museum is created through the architectural grandeur of the building, the sumptuousness of its galleries and the calibre of the treasures it holds. In a museum, the nation's 'loot' is on display for the people. The form of the Australian colonial museums was based on practices imported from Europe. One was the eighteenth-century aristocratic practice of collecting exotic and unusual objects whilst travelling; the other—more egalitarian—practice was the local fair, a place where people gathered to see the unusual, the strange, the exotic and the unimaginable (Bennett 1995). Publicly funded museums tended to follow the aristocratic form of the *objets d'art* kept in 'cabinets of curiosity'. However, they also contain the bizarre and unusual. The Museum of Victoria contains the hide of Australia's most famous racehorse, Phar Lap, while the National Museum has his heart, and his bones are in a museum in New Zealand.

Colonial museums

Colonial Australian museums were seen as spaces where the history of 'civilisation' was set out and a subject's or citizen's place in that great trajectory explained. They were places of education about the glory of British and European 'civilisations' and the place of Anglo–Australia in that project. Often materials were imported from overseas so a museum would have a range of exhibits that informed the visitor about the order of the world. For example, early Australian museums obtained Greco–Roman statuary or copies of the Magna Carta to educate viewers about the longer history into which they were being inserted. The building of many of the key museums in Australia coincided with the high point of British colonial endeavour and powerful ideas about the role of science in shaping national stories. The early private 'cabinets of curiosity' often included cultural artefacts from the colonies. Museums continued this practice—they were filled with exotic objects brought back by individuals who were part of the colonial endeavour. Australian museums were furnished with materials obtained from the colonial practices within Australia, but also from the region—including Papua New Guinea. These materials included the skeletal remains of Indigenous peoples of Australia. Over time, tens of thousands of body parts of Indigenous peoples entered museum and university collections in Australia and overseas.

Australian colonial museum practices were also linked to nineteenth-century scientific theories of classification and the possibility of total knowledge. The natural history museums sought to order the world and everything in it—from smallest to largest, from north to south, from amoeba to human. They ordered the world not only in the sense of sorting it, but also into a hierarchy. The objects brought back from the colonies helped to fashion this hierarchy. Australia's unique plant and animal world also excited museum collectors in Australia and overseas. These specimens were seen as filling in the knowledge map of the globe. Australian Indigenous peoples were also understood to fill a gap in knowledge. They were integral in bolstering beliefs in European superiority. Indigenous peoples were often categorised as part of the flora and fauna of the continent, and so collected and classified with these objects within museum collections. If Indigenous peoples were not exhibited as unique curiosities along with the platypus and lyrebird, they were often fitted into the imported European knowledge system as living examples of evolution and evidence of the story of human progress. Indigenous peoples and their cultures were often represented as 'stone age' and placed at the beginning of a chronology that posited Europeans as the most developed in the evolution of 'mankind'. This story placed Indigenous peoples at the bottom of a hierarchy of human development, and therefore in need of education and control. This story was a powerful adjunct to the physical presence and governmental authority displayed by the British colonisers over Indigenous peoples.

In more recent years, other types of museums and galleries have emerged in Australia. There was a desire not only for exhibitions demonstrating to Australians where they fitted in the world, but also exhibitions celebrating who they were. By the mid to late twentieth century, the popular private entertainment museums had emerged. These 'theme park' museums, such as Old Sydney Town near Gosford, or Sovereign Hill in Victoria, were nationally focused museums. They re-enacted stories from the 'heroic' past of Australia, but also told stories about some of the more distasteful elements. Old Sydney Town exhibited the convict past of Australia and included in its daily schedule realistic floggings. Most popular museums in Australia explore the heroism of the British colonial settlers—the fight against the harsh environment that greeted the first colonists and the fight against the injustices suffered by the average working man in the new colonies. For example, in 1988—the year of the bicentenary of colonisation in Australia—Queen Elizabeth II opened the Stockman's Hall of Fame at Longreach in western Queensland. This museum celebrates the everyday lives of Australian workers who were a vital part of the agricultural industries of the nation. Popular museums such as this are not often considered to have the *gravitas* that attaches to state or national museums. Yet it is interesting to consider who visits different museums. Research has indicated that citizens with higher levels of education tend to visit the public national museums, whereas 'theme park' museums have a broader visitor base.

National museums

Given the long absence of an official national museum, the Australian War Memorial in Canberra was often seen as the exemplary *national* Australian museum. This memorial functions as both a sacred space and an informative museum space. It is the most visited museum in Australia. The Australian War Memorial advertises itself as being the place citizens and visitors alike can go to see the essence of Australia: 'using film, sound, light and modern technology the Memorial offers to its visitors the opportunity to better understand what it means to be Australian' (Australian War Memorial [n.d.]). In this story, Australianness is located in war experiences. Visiting the Australian War Memorial does not only give a better understanding of war, but of Australian-ness. This is an enormously popular understanding of Australian-ness and yet it reflects a narrow range of experiences (even within the category of war experiences, the types of experiences represented are limited). For such a partial story to have such a dominant place in the pantheon of museums in Australia once again reinforces the limited nature of dominant stories of Australian-ness. Yet this does not stop this story being extremely popular.

There is now an official national museum: the National Museum of Australia in Canberra. This museum was first mooted in the very early twentieth century, but was never established. In 1975, a Committee of Inquiry on Museums and National Collections once again recommended that a national museum be established. They suggested that such a museum would be a fitting extension to the existing ones. Their proposal was for the museum to be located in Canberra and that it should be dedicated to Aboriginal and Torres Strait Islander culture, Australian society and its history since 1788, and the interaction of people with the environment (Casey 2001: 5). The recommendations were made at a time when museum practice and ideas about what belonged in museums and how viewers learn in museums were changing.

The development of Australian museums as adjuncts to colonial ventures was now being regarded as suspect. In earlier periods of museology, there was no question of non-Indigenous peoples negotiating with Indigenous peoples about what aspects of their cultures should be on display. It was simply a question of choosing what was seen to be edifying for the non-Indigenous citizen. In the world after the Holocaust, when new international anti-racism mechanisms existed and the decolonisation process was taking place, the stories of traditional natural history museums in Australia were often seen as outdated and offensive. The National Museum of Australia was developed in the light of this colonial history and postcolonial critique. As Graeme Davison (2001: 12) states: 'in a post-imperial era, when the colonisers are often on show to the formerly colonised, the museum becomes a prime site for a renegotiation of national identity'.

Unlike with earlier exhibitions of Indigenous peoples and cultures, from the outset Indigenous people were curators in the Gallery of Indigenous Australians in the National Museum. The National Museum's Indigenous Gallery represents Indigenous peoples as the original occupants of the continent, and their cultures and communities as complex, vital and ongoing. (State museums have also reworked their exhibitions in light of this critique.) These understandings of Indigenous cultures have always been available (it is not as if Indigenous peoples took up the story of themselves as 'primitive'), but to have the story as a central part of public museum narratives is a significant shift. To have Indigenous stories understood as part of history rather than pre-history or nature also represents a substantial change in understandings about the relationship between Indigenous peoples and non-Indigenous peoples in Australia. However, as Gaye Sculthorpe (2001: 81) notes, this rethinking is not universal: 'we paint Qantas jumbo jets with Aboriginal designs, yet accepting past treatment of Indigenous Australians as part of Australian history remains problematic for many.'

Dawn Casey (2001), the first director of the National Museum, suggests storytelling—especially national histories—is one of the missions of museums. However, she notes that in contemporary museums there is often a gap between the story governments see as needing to be told and that which the experts working in the field (historians, curators, directors) see as deserving space. Often the distinction comes down to telling a triumphant story versus telling more complex stories that demonstrate the mixed and multifaceted nature of nation-building. Given this, it is not surprising that the shifting of Indigenous histories to a central place in the National Museum of Australia and the shifting of Indigenous cultures into history has not been without its critics.

There have been specific criticisms of the National Museum as well as critiques of the state museums' reworked Indigenous galleries from more conservative Australian thinkers (Windschuttle 2001a). Their critiques fit with a broader distaste for the rewriting that took place at the end of the twentieth century in Australia of national histories of race relations (Windschuttle 2002a, Moran 2003). Conservative critics argue that the rethinking of histories of Indigenous and non-Indigenous relations has gone too far and that they present a world where non-Indigenous peoples were always bad and Indigenous people always good. The extreme version of this view suggests accounts of the ill-treatment of Indigenous people by non-Indigenous people are exaggerated, based on flimsy or non-existent evidence or just wrong (Windschuttle 2003). The often fiery debates between different Australian intellectuals on this topic have been dubbed the 'history wars' (Attwood 2005, Macintyre and Clark 2003).

One of the more contentious issues is the representation of massacres of Indigenous peoples in museum exhibits. Keith Windschuttle (2002b), who sparked the 'history wars' with his book on Tasmanian history, criticises the representation of the Bells Fall Gorge massacre in the National Museum. He writes: 'there is no contemporary evidence that anyone was killed there at the time' (2002b: 2). It is very important to note that most massacres were not formally reported or recorded by the perpetrators when they took place. Murdering Indigenous peoples was illegal, so large-scale murders were often coded as 'dispersals' in official reports or not noted at all. The group whose members did remember and record the occurrence of massacres was Indigenous people. They shared the stories with each other. Windschuttle's argument is that massacres can only be confirmed to have taken place if they were recorded in written documents at the time of the murders. As Bain Attwood (2004) points out, this argument privileges non-Indigenous written documents over Indigenous histories told via oral stories and only committed to paper some time after the event.

Complaints about museum exhibits representing Indigenous/ non-Indigenous relations also came from museum visitors. For example, when the Western Australian Museum's 'First Peoples of the West' Gallery used the term 'genocide' in a display outlining the policy of the removal of Indigenous children from their families, some non-Indigenous museum patrons were upset and lodged complaints. They were upset not because of the inhumanity of the process of child removal, but that the term 'genocide' could be associated with Australia. This is not what most patrons of Australian museums (and most museum patrons are non-Indigenous) were used to seeing. Many expected—and have been brought up on— more glorious stories about the nation. In these stories, Australia's non-Indigenous people are good, not bad. For non-Indigenous Australians who are deeply invested in stories of the 'good' Australia, there is frequently an immediate reaction that refuses to accept the possibility that an alternative experience might exist. Dawn Casey noted, even before the National Museum of Australia encountered its first dissension, that:

> Controversial exhibitions mark the sometimes painful steps towards proper discussion. While controversial exhibitions may be perceived to have failed on one level . . . they can also be instrumental in focusing attention upon matters of public importance (Casey 2001: 10).

In Casey's view, the shock registered by non-Indigenous patrons is useful in starting important discussions about the past. Dawn Casey was not reappointed after her first term as the National Museum director; however, her strong vision about the integrity of the national museum has assured that it is a place where 'visitors are both reassured by the familiar, and challenged by the new' (Casey 2001: 6).

Bain Attwood (2004: 284) puts the achievement of the National Museum and other museums such as the Western Australian Museum in another way. He suggests that their achievement lies in 'sharing histories'. He contrasts this achievement with the rather more conservative endeavour of producing a 'shared history'. In the last decades of the twentieth century, museums—and particularly their Indigenous galleries—have become spaces where the process of 'sharing histories' has taken place. They have become places where more radical dialogues between conflicting, complementary and contradictory stories can (and do) take place. These dialogues are not always easy: as already illustrated, non-Indigenous people sometimes find them threatening. Indigenous peoples also have issues with these dialogic and confronting exhibitions. Sometimes different Indigenous communities may have conflicting views on a story in an exhibition. Indigenous peoples are not always happy with the ways in which they are included in museums, and they often demand more active and higher levels of consultation in the creation of new exhibits featuring Indigenous cultures and histories. These difficulties are the pitfalls of 'sharing histories'. They won't go away—they mark the process of talking to each other. Controversies sometimes emerge if mistakes are made when new histories are aired; however, controversies also reflect the pain of facing difficult histories.

One of the key issues for many Indigenous communities in relation to museums is the repatriation to their communities of skeletal remains that have been part of exhibits or collections. The return of Indigenous skeletal remains has been a fraught aspect of national museology for some years. These body parts, reflecting colonial connections, are in institutions in both Britain and Australia. The return of these aspects of museum collections has been confronting for the museums. In Britain, the national public institutions initially refused calls for repatriation, claiming it was against their charter to dispose of portions of the public collection. There was also the worry that claims for Indigenous skeletal remains would be the beginning of more claims from around the world for plundered goods to be returned to the nation of origin (Peers 2004: 4). Other scientists have claimed Indigenous demands for repatriation were not in the interests of humankind (Stringer 2003). They argued that the remains were the property of a global community who would benefit from the scientific research that could be undertaken on the remains and provide more clues to the 'origin' of the human species. By this logic, the return of the bodily remains was a loss to the world, not a gain for Indigenous peoples who felt violated and saddened by the original theft. Interestingly, many museums in Australia have bodily remains in their collections, but it is Indigenous bodily remains that seem to cause the least comment when they are displayed. The Australian War Memorial has a collection of body parts preserved after medical operations on Australian soldiers during World War I. Even 90 years after the event, these are considered too controversial to show. This squeamishness was not so obvious when Indigenous bodily remains are the exhibits.

The process of 'sharing histories' can be difficult. For Indigenous peoples, telling many of their histories can be painful. For non-Indigenous people, such as those at the Western Australian museum, new histories can be shocking—seeing oneself represented as not good can be uncomfortable. Yet there are also pleasures to be had.

For Indigenous peoples to have their cultural knowledge showcased in the premier museum spaces of the nation, as an integral aspect of the life of the nation, can be gratifying. Perhaps non-Indigenous Australians have to accept being upset in the museum space, both because it is confronting and unfamiliar, if such feelings are matched by Indigenous peoples finding these spaces more familiar and as finally articulating some of their painful stories kept out of the public sphere for so long.

Heritage

The formal process of the framing of national stories in museums has a corollary in less formal modes of heritage and preservation. Alongside grand institutions such as state and national museums, there are smaller plaques, statues and signs reminding those who pass by of the significance of an area, a person or a day. There are whole towns, single buildings and natural features marked as significant to the heritage of Australia. Heritage is usually understood as being created at two levels—the family and the nation (Howard 2003: 4). Most people will have some experience of piecing together some aspect of a family history. This family story is often attached to the nation. For example, many Australians search to see whether they had any convicts forbears on the First Fleet. Others map their heritage by calculating the number of generations their family has been in a particular area. The feeling of attachment created through the nexus of family and national heritage builds a powerful sense of national belonging and being at home in a place. This is why it can be painful for citizens who are unable to trace their heritage. They are unable to locate themselves in a familial or national story.

Mapping heritage is not only about individuals or families locating themselves within a national story; it is also undertaken by the state. All around Australia, there are signs directing people to heritage spots. (Interestingly, in New South Wales these signs are marked with an icon resembling a castle turret—evidence of the British tradition that shapes some ideas of what heritage is.) Some sites are sponsored by the federal government and marked as part of a national heritage. State heritage groups, local governments or history groups have sponsored other sites. What counts as Australian heritage ranges from stately properties owned by wealthy families of the nineteenth and twentieth century to workers' cottages in inner-city suburbs. Heritage places can involve whole precincts such as Chinatown in Broome or the German migrant towns in the Barossa Valley in South Australia.

Heritage can also be captured with a mixture of authentic and replica buildings: the tourist town of York in Western Australia contains some older heritage buildings and features, but also modern replicas built to fit the heritage mood of the town.

Traditionally, there was a class dimension to heritage preservation. The emphasis was on the material culture of the rich and exceptional rather than the everyday and poor. This means some communities' history is more commonly represented in heritage registers than others. A mansion built by a wealthy pastoralist to memorialise his family for centuries is more likely be listed on a heritage register than a worker's cottage or a shanty-town probably seen as an 'eyesore' and deliberately removed. So one type of heritage is preserved while the other is lost. Similarly, during her lifetime, a bourgeois woman's clothing might be carefully washed and pressed and kept in a closet, whereas the maids in her kitchen, with fewer sets of clothing, would be more likely to wear their work clothes until they were no longer wearable and then convert them to cleaning rags. One group of women's heritage is more likely to be available, the other more likely to be lost.

Not surprisingly, there is also an ethnic dimension to heritage. For many years, the focus of preservation was Anglo–Australian cultures. Churches rather than mosques are more likely to be on a heritage register. Blue Mountains rose gardens appeared on the register long before the La Perouse Chinese market gardens. Similarly, Indigenous peoples' cultural life was often neglected in the heritage registers. Indigenous histories were mostly understood as located in the bush. Indigenous heritage was only understood as rock paintings and middens. Indeed, for many years, the only protection for Indigenous heritage was in legislation covering national parks, flora and fauna. Sites such as meeting halls where civil rights actions took place were ignored, as they did not fit the non-Indigenous definition of Indigenous heritage, which located it in national environment. Further, as physical and written heritage is privileged over oral and remembered history, again Indigenous heritage was less easily captured.

Over the past decade, state heritage offices have been increasing the recognition of non-Anglo–Australian communities in the heritage listings of the state. Through consultation with many different communities, the offices are increasing the cultural diversity of their registers. Some of the obvious sites and items of significance for the history of migrant groups are the places where they arrived in the country—for example, Albury railway station in New South Wales and Bonegilla Reception Centre in northeast Victoria, where many migrants were accommodated on their arrival in Australia, have been nominated as sites of significance. Other sites are specific to the cultural practices of the communities—for example, places of worship, or gathering places for the communities, such as clubhouses. The site of the 1938 Aboriginal Day of Mourning meeting in Sydney has also been recognised.

Heritage on the margins

In cataloguing and preserving the heritage of the nation, taboo or private aspects of life are also often missed. In Canberra in 2001, a group called the Eros Foundation opened a National Museum of Erotica. They argued that this was necessary because the newly opened National Museum of Australia omitted to include any reference to sex in its exhibits (Adams and Francis 2003: 19). Simon Adams and Rae Francis note that the markers of sex work (prostitution) are also generally missing from national heritage stories. Given the historical centrality of government policies that focus on national population growth, it is interesting that this vital component is missing from heritage registers. Yet, as Adams and Francis point out, sex is not always missing from the tourist's heritage route. In the Western Australian town of Kalgoorlie, a top tourist attraction is the historic 'Langtree 181 Bordello'. Three times a day, guides take tourists on tours through the rooms of the brothel and provide a history of sex work in the town. Adams and Frances note that the tours successfully convey to visitors a sense of how providing sex is gendered work in the social history of Australia.

If Kalgoorlie now provides evidence of the heritage of the Australian sex industry, then another vital aspect of Kalgoorlie life—mining—also has its own museum. Unlike the private brothel tours, mining heritage is partially government funded. The Australian Prospector's and Miner's Hall of Fame was mooted around the same time as the Stockman's Hall of Fame, and was provided with $5 million of federal government funding as well as commercial funding from the mining industry. This aspect of Australian heritage is explicitly linked to a major Australian commercial industry, which in turn allies itself to a story about the well-being of the nation:

> In sport, you know how important it is for your team to win. More importantly, if the mining team doesn't win, the whole nation suffers ... Through leadership our innovative, technologically advanced, responsible, and productive industry will continue to carry our nation forward (Australian Prospectors and Miners Hall of Fame 2005).

In 1998, when this museum received its government funding, the press release announcing it made a connection between the Prospectors and Miners Hall of Fame and the Stockman's Hall of Fame in Longreach—two museums dedicated to celebrating male-dominated industries. Donald Horne (1990) points out these two industries are much better represented by the figure of the wealthy capitalist 'corporate raider' than the rugged individual from the 'land' who is so often associated with the pastoral and mining industries. Obviously there is a distinction to be drawn between a historically illegal industry (sex work) and one that is at the centre of the Australian economy (mining). Still, what impact is there on ideas of being Australian if some central parts of life—sex—are left out of national narratives and others—men's work and capitalist endeavour—are made central though government funding.

Dispossession

The concept of heritage developed by some Australian sites suggests that the process of colonialism was unproblematic. Consider this quote from the website of the Australian Prospectors and Miners Hall of Fame:

> Australia's Prospecting and Mining industry has played a major part in the history of our nation. The industry was initiated within Australia by Aboriginal People prospecting, mining and using minerals long before the landing of the First Fleet in 1788. Australia's Mining Hall of Fame is dedicated to explaining to all Australians just how central our industry is to their continuing well-being (Australian Prospectors and Miners Hall of Fame 2005).

Similarly, the Stockman's Hall of Fame website sets the scene for its story:

> This gallery is all about the discovery, exploration and settlement of Australia by the various races, cultures, individuals and groups who call this continent their home.
>
> The Australian Aborigines were joined by explorers, settlers and fortune hunters, all eager to make a living on the land . . . Most were not native born but they all had the courage to venture into the unknown vastness of a strange land. They were often ill equipped for their adventure and completely unaware of what lay before them in the way of terrain, weather, water and hostile natives (Australian Stockman's Hall of Fame 2005).

In both cases, the setting for the story of national heritage is about the continuity and similarity in purpose between the Indigenous and the non-Indigenous occupation and use of the land that followed. These museums tell heritage stories suggesting non-Indigenous cultures existed peacefully and cooperatively alongside the original Indigenous cultures. The Prospectors and Miners Hall of Fame tells the visitor non-Indigenous peoples are part of a long and continuous mining industry that started with the Indigenous peoples. It is not explained that this mining industry is the same one the Yolngu people of Arnhem Land petitioned federal parliament to keep off their land in 1961. After they lost their appeal, their country was razed by Nabalco as it mined for bauxite.

In the Stockman's Hall of Fame story of heritage, Indigenous peoples are represented as just of one of many groups of people who 'discover' and use the land. Early in this story, the phrasing suggests a convivial 'joining' between Indigenous peoples and non-Indigenous peoples. Later in the story, it is only non-Indigenous people who encounter 'hostile' elements in this joint home. There is no recognition that Indigenous peoples also encountered 'hostile' colonisers. More importantly, there is no recognition of the prior Indigenous ownership and the fact one culture dispossessed the other. In acknowledging this heritage of non-Indigenous pioneers, Indigenous peoples first appear as joint occupiers of the land, and then reappear as 'hostile natives'. This is the ambivalence so often underling non-Indigenous stories of being Australian, of being at home.

The passing reference in the Stockman's Hall of Fame's display to 'hostile natives' obliquely and insensitively refers to the fact that Indigenous peoples resisted the occupation of their land by colonisers. The forms of resistance varied: some simply involved remaining aloof from British settlements; other resistance was specific retaliation for crimes committed by the British colonisers—for example, spearing non-Indigenous men who had raped Indigenous women. Other acts of resistance were organised guerrilla warfare designed to expel the invaders. The Aboriginal Memorial created by the Ramingining artists of Central Arnhem Land is a memorial to the Indigenous people who died in defence of their country (see Figure 12.1). Djon Mundine, the artistic adviser to the Ramingining, was inspired by John Pilger's film *The Secret Country* (1985). Pilger says in this film: '[I]n a land strewn with cenotaphs which honour the memory of Australian servicemen who have died in almost every corner of the earth, not one stands for those [first Australians] who fought and fell in defence of their own country.'

Figure 12.1 *The Aboriginal Memorial* (1987–88) by Ramingining Artists draws on the hollow burial log ceremony of Central Arnhem land—200 logs represent Indigenous suffering from 1788–1988. (© *Ramingining Artists* —all 'The Aboriginal Memorial' 1987–88 installation are natural pigments on wood, height 327 cm. Purchased with the assistance of funds from National Gallery admission charges and commissioned in 1987. National Gallery of Australia, Canberra.)

The Ramingining artists' project is a memorial to those people. Stories of Indigenous people resisting the invasion of their land often go unremarked in the national narrative of remembrance.

A good example of this is a memorial commemorating the death of explorers Frederick Panter, James Harding and William Goldwyer in 1864 in Boola Boola (La Grange Bay), Western Australia. The plaque reads:

> This monument was erected to the memories of . . . PANTER, HARDING AND GOLDWYER earliest explorers after Grey and Gregory of this Terra Incognita. Attacked at night by treacherous natives they were murdered at Boola Boola . . . Also as an appreciative token of remembrance of MAITLAND BROWN . . . intrepid leader of the government search and punitive party . . . Lest We Forget.

In an effort to counter the absence of Indigenous people's resistance and suffering, a supplementary plaque was commissioned to accompany this memorial. It tells a more comprehensive story:

This plaque was erected by people who found the monument before you offensive. The monument describes the events at La Grange from one perspective only: the viewpoint of the white 'settlers'.

No mention is made of the right of Aboriginal people to defend their land or of the history of provocation which led to the explorers' deaths. The 'punitive party' mentioned here ended in the death of somewhere around twenty Aboriginal people. The whites were well armed and equipped and none of their party was killed or wounded. The plaque is in memory of the Aboriginal people killed at La Grange. It also commemorates all other Aboriginal people who died during the invasion of their country. LEST WE FORGET (Council for Aboriginal Reconciliation 1994: 28).

Though there is yet to be national recognition of the resistance of Indigenous peoples to the occupation of their country, there are a growing number of memorials and plaques marking the prior occupation of Indigenous people in this land. A convict lumberyard in Newcastle that has been made into an historical tourist site includes a plaque naming the Indigenous people on whose country Newcastle was built:

For many thousands of years the Awabakal tribal people lived along the banks of the Hunter River . . . Excavations carried out on this site have revealed stone tool artifacts which predate the European industrial use of this site.

European invasion and occupation had drastic long-term conse-quences for the Awabakal. Disease, violence, the exploitation of their women and the disruption of tribal culture all devastated their way of life, but these people continued to adapt and survive, living and working in the Newcastle area to the present day.

The plaque notes the cost of progress for the Awabakal people, setting out the devastation brought by the arrival of the British. Importantly, though, this commemorative site acknowledges the continuous and ongoing occupation and cultures of the Awabakal in Newcastle. Many Indigenous heritage sites focus on the devastation of colonisation, creating the impression Indigenous people are gone. The plaques refer to Indigenous peoples' occupation of the land in the past tense—suggesting they no longer exist. This passing away story produces the same effect as the absence of a memorial—one erases Indigenous peoples from the past; the other erases Indigenous people from the future.

In the period after 1788, Indigenous peoples' history intersects with non-Indigenous history. There are also Indigenous histories that are separate. The Dreaming encompasses Indigenous histories before and after colonisation. These histories are marked all over the continent in Dreaming tracks and sites, sometimes referred to as sacred sites. Many sites of significance for non-Indigenous peoples are located on top of sites of importance for Indigenous peoples. It is slowly being acknowledged that in 1788 Australia was already marked by another group of people, and that the non-Indigenous built environment has often destroyed or disturbed Indigenous histories and cultures.

An example of this is the tomb of Reverend John Flynn, the man who began the Royal Flying Doctor Service. He was buried in 1951 in the Macdonnell Ranges, west of Alice Springs. His tomb was marked with a large stone brought from a sacred site of the Kaytetye and Warumungu people—Karlu Karlu (often referred to by non-Indigenous people as the Devil's Marbles)—near Tennant Creek. This stone was part of the Dreaming of the Kaytetye and Warumungu peoples, and its removal from their country to another area was distressing and disrupted their culture and history (Ensor 1999: 5). The Kaytetye and Warumungu people negotiated for many years to have the stone returned, and finally in the late 1990s it was moved from Flynn's grave and taken back to its place in Karlu Karlu. Another large stone from the local area now marks the grave of Flynn. This new memorial was undertaken in consultation with the Arrente people who are the custodians of the area where Flynn is buried. This time the memorial to an important non-Indigenous actor in Australian history does not disturb central aspects of an Indigenous culture. Further, through consultation, Indigenous people were also able to be part of the commemoration of this post-contact history of which they are also a part.

Suburban heritage

Suburbs are not often seen as key sites of Australian heritage, the exception is suburbs built in the nineteenth century which get significant recognition. In the post-1945 period, the migrants who arrived in Australia moved to the cheaper, older, inner suburbs of cities. Over the years, citizens renovated these old nineteenth-century houses—redesigning them to suit their needs and memories of home. For example, the original small wooden windows were often removed and replaced with large aluminium-framed windows. Front gardens were converted into vegetable patches where fruits, vegetables and herbs from their country of birth were grown. In the 1980s, there was a process of gentrification of many inner city suburbs. They became desirable yuppie housing stock. Often encouraged by local councils, there was a trend to re-renovate these houses back to Federation or Victorian style with cottage gardens to match. Streetscapes recreated a late-Victorian look. The changes that the previous generation of owners had made were eradicated.

There is nothing wrong with the renovation of a house. The point here is that encouraging owners of houses to renovate their property to regain the look of the houses when they were built required the erasure of the presence of the later occupants and their style. To suggest owners who had made their houses modern in the 1950s had somehow spoiled the house and ruined the look of a street is to valorise one particular culture (here Anglo–Australian) over another. The celebration of the federation moment as the best time (both for the houses and by inference for the neighbourhood) is to hark back to a time when Australia was predominantly Anglo–Australian. It erases non-Anglo–Australian peoples from the landscape of the national imagination. Federation houses are often given heritage listings by state governments in recognition of the fact that they capture a moment in Australian history and culture that it is seen as important not to lose. It is only more recently that houses from the 1950s and 1960s have been considered important enough to list. However, it is not often that the houses listed are those marking the style and contribution of non-British migrants. Even though these houses—renovated by their owners who had arrived from another country and made Australia their home, introduced new ideas and cultures, worked hard and remade Australia—marked an amazing moment in Australian history—one of the largest immigration programs in the world—their houses do not often get a heritage plaque in the front hallway.

The gentrification of the inner city areas of many Australian cities also has implications for the heritage of urban Indigenous peoples. In the early 1990s the Western Australian government in tandem with the federal government initiated a plan to redevelop East Perth, an inner city area of the city of Perth. This part of Perth had been made up of prosperous suburbs in the nineteenth century but since then had become highly industrialized and by the late twentieth century was home to mostly Indigenous and poorer new migrants. However, the area was especially important for the Nyungah and Noongar peoples both in terms of the Dreaming and as an urban community focus. It was the site of many services for Indigenous peoples but also the site for important parts of recent heritage, including the painful history of child removal. The Indigenous child removal policies of Western Australia meant Indigenous children and young people were continually being moved from reserves and missions in outlying areas of Western Australia to work places, institutions or foster homes in other areas. A site of significance in this movement was Bennett House. Established in the 1930s Bennett House was both a living quarters for Indigenous women who worked as domestic servants in Perth, a pre-birth waiting place for Indigenous women pregnant to white men and a holding place for girls en route to other institutions (Hillyer 2001: 49). Though the building held many painful memories for local Indigenous people it was also, as Nyungah elder Judy Jackson, said 'doing something'. It's a part of us' (Hillyer 2001: 58). However, in imagining the redevelopment of East Perth to a '"classy" urban village of the twenty-first century' (Morgan 2001: 718) Bennett House did not fit. Bennett House was a registered Aboriginal site of particular significance, but in the eyes of many non-Indigenous people its heritage value was compromised by 'numerous brick and asbestos additions' (Hillyer 2001: 51). Knocking it down was seen as 'presenting a "brilliant new opportunity to enhance the corner environment of the site"' (Hillyer 2001: 51). As a result of a series of complex planning determinations, decisions made by various Aboriginal bureaucracies under pressure, and insufficient consultation with Indigenous communities, Bennett House was demolished early one morning in 1998. Today East Perth is an area that most Indigenous people can no longer afford to live in and their presence has been reduced to the names of parks and artworks that dot the precinct. A rare site of value that marked the painful history of the stolen generations has been erased. Drawing on the value that so many non-Indigenous peoples attach to war memorials Nyungah elder Robert Bropho asked: 'You only have to look at the war monument in Kings Park to realise that white people pay tribute to their dark time. So why shouldn't we?' (Hillyer 2001: 58).

Multiple meanings

In a country with a population as diverse as that of Australia, some sites of significance may have different meanings for different groups. For example, a railway station may be listed on the heritage register in recognition of its association with an event such as the point of arrival or departure in Australia for particular groups. The same site might have significance to the local Indigenous community. It could also be listed because the buildings are significant in terms of the particular style of architecture or the technology of the station. The multi-layered nature of spaces in the Australian nation needs to be more comprehensively recognised. And, more than this, it needs to be acknowledged that more powerful groups can refuse to recognise other groups' meanings and claims to space. This refusal to see the multi-layered meanings in the landscape or in events can sometimes reflect an anxiety rather than a clear understanding that these other stories are not worthy of a place in the nation.

Rottnest Island, off southern Western Australia, is a popular heritage site that reflects many different communities stories and histories. The island is the country of the Wadjemup Indigenous peoples. In the colonial period, the island was the location for a boys' reformatory and the summer residence for the governor. It was a World War I prisoner-of-war camp, and for almost 100 years (from 1838 to 1931) it was a prison for Indigenous people. The heritage story of the Indigenous prison on a Western Australian government website ends by saying:

> Closure of the Aboriginal prison was recommended in 1902. It officially closed in 1904 although prisoners were used to build roads and other works on the Island until 1931. Closure of the prison turned the attention of the public and the Government to Rottnest Island's possibilities as a recreation destination (Rottnest Island Authority 2005).

One of the key meanings of Rottnest Island is its history as a prison. Perhaps attention needs to turn to the place of prisons in the heritage of the nation. To begin with, Indigenous men have long been over-represented in the nation's prison population. Steve Mickler (1990) points out that if one traces the country origin of the inmates of Western Australian prisons over the life of the prisons, it matches the moving frontier of colonialism. Resistance to dispossession was frequently read as criminality by the authorities. So in the Rottnest Island history to glibly move from the repugnant history of colonialism to the fun recreational facilities that can be initiated when the Indigenous bodies are removed demonstrates a common refusal by many non-Indigenous people to properly acknowledge the cost of colonialism for Indigenous peoples and the role of non-Indigenous peoples in this heritage.

This painful acknowledgement is starting to take place. Massacre has long been denied as an aspect of Australian heritage. In 2001, the descendants of Indigenous peoples who were murdered and the descendants of the perpetrators of one particular massacre, known as the Myall Creek Massacre, came together to produce a memorial to that massacre. In 1838, a group of non-Indigenous men massacred a group of mostly Wirrayaraay people—including many old people, women and children—on the central coast of New South Wales. This is the only massacre of Indigenous peoples in Australia for which non-Indigenous people were convicted and punished. The project to commemorate this difficult part of Australian heritage emerged from Indigenous and non-Indigenous peoples working together as part of a reconciliation group. The central boulder at the commemorative site starts: 'We Remember Them'. Indigenous and non-Indigenous peoples remember from different standpoints, each painful in its own way. It is by bringing difficult aspects of Australian heritage to the fore, rather than erasing it from national stories, that new futures can be imagined for Australia.

Canberra, the nation's capital

Many visitors to Australia do not include a trip to Canberra on their itinerary. They have heard it is a dull public service town, and decide a week in Noosa or Darwin is a better option than a trip to the inland national capital. As a planned city, Canberra not only has a reputation for being dull, but is also seen as not being a real town— more a toy-town. Yet visitors do come to Canberra—500 000 of them every year. Many of them are Australian children who are often brought to the city on school excursions. So what does Canberra present to the visitor? What stories are told about Australia and being Australian in this space?

Those who manage and market Canberra to overseas visitors and Australian citizens know exactly what their story of Canberra is— Canberra embodies Australian-ness. The website for the National Capital Authority (NCA), the group that oversees the development of Canberra, says of the capital:

> In the lead up to Federation and in the decades which followed the Australian people have sought to build a National Capital of which they are proud: a capital which represents our unity as a people; and stands proudly in the ranks of national capitals throughout the world (NCA 2002).

It goes on to suggest that 'the vision of the National Capital Authority is for a national capital, which symbolised Australia's heritage, values and aspirations, is internationally recognised, and of which Australians are proud' (NCA 2002). In this story, Canberra is a place where Australia is produced and exhibited.

Similarly, the Canberra Tourist Authority is quite explicit in linking the idea of visiting Canberra with ideas of being Australian. Spruiking its 2004 advertising campaign for the city, the website states:

> The *See Yourself in Canberra* brand campaign is a long-term project designed to change perceptions of Canberra by communicating that it is the only city that represents and can reflect what it is to be Australian. Canberra represents Australia's history, culture, democracy and identity. The campaign embodies these elements and carries the theme that no matter who we are or where we came from, the only place to see our true reflection as Australians is in the nation's capital (Australian Capital Tourism 2005).

In the television advertisement that accompanies this 'branding campaign', the scene opens with a young boy on the edge of Lake Burley Griffin in central Canberra and the text: 'How do you see yourself as an Australian?' Then three scenarios are put forward. The first shows a young man in a business suit imagining his Australia in terms of government and power, and finishes with the text: 'See our secrets, see our History'. Then a young woman swimmer imagines her Australia in terms of sport and a gold medal performance in an international setting: 'See what makes us proud'. Lastly, an old man in a backyard imagines a scene with young men from World War II working together repairing a plane—the air filled with red poppies; the text exhorts Australians to 'See yourself with some old mates'. The advertisement finishes with the words: 'Come see your nation reflected in its capital'. Not surprisingly, the nation shown so far is about politics, sport and war.

These stories represent Canberra as a microcosm of the nation, and suggest it simply reflects back to the people of the nation their own visions. Obviously a national capital is nothing so simple. The visions of the nation produced in the space of Canberra are more complex. It needs to be stated here that, in analysing Canberra, the focus is not the entire city of Canberra—with all its suburbs, shopping malls, car parks and swimming pools. The capital is home to many people whose back yards and Hills Hoists have the same significance as those located in different areas. It is only some parts of Canberra that are regarded as highly symbolic in terms of nation, and it is these places that are explored. The areas understood to be of high significance and symbolic value for the nation are set out in legislation. The central area of significance is known as the Parliamentary Zone. Within the triangle of this zone lie the Parliament House (at the triangle's apex), the High Court, Old Parliament House, the National Library, the National Gallery, Commonwealth Place, Reconciliation Place, the Gallery of Flags, the Captain Cook Memorial Jet and the Carillon. Across the lake and in a direct line with Parliament House are Anzac Avenue and the Australian War Memorial, lying at the foot of Mount Ainslie (see Figure 12.2).

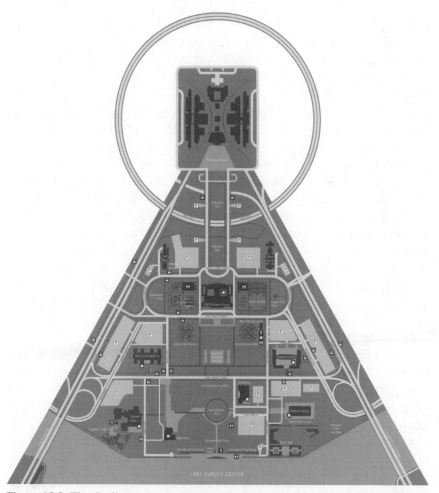

Figure 12.2 The Parliamentary 'triangle' in Canberra is understood as a part of Canberra with significant national meaning. (*Map courtesy of NCA*)

Creating Canberra

Canberra is a planned city. There was no non-Indigenous town in the area of Canberra when it was declared the site for the new capital in 1909. In 1911, an international design competition was launched to find someone to design the new city. The representation of the site for new national capital as blank and awaiting the creation of a 'virgin city' (Duggan 1998: 86) reinforces the idea of Australia as *terra nullius*. As with other areas of Australia, the land was occupied—the Ngun(n)awal peoples are the custodians of the Canberra region. Interestingly, the story that no one would move to Canberra of their own volition has reinforced the emptiness of the place in the face of a significant local Indigenous community and as the site for the growing Indigenous land rights' movements.

American architects Walter Burley Griffin and his wife Marion Griffin won the design competition. Their backgrounds were in the Garden City and City Beautiful movements, whose ideas focused on the desire to build healthy cities unblemished by ghetto and disease. They were also movements linking landscape and the urban setting. Both these notions fitted with ideas prevalent in Australia at the time. The healthy city notion fitted with the eugenic principle of healthy populations and the government ideas of the need to create a fit Anglo–Australian population to fill the nation (Taylor 1996: 3). Peter Proudfoot (1994: 83) argues that in Canberra the dominant motif is landscape rather than monumentalism. It is not buildings that dominate the area, but trees, land and water. This aspect of Griffin's plans fitted with the nostalgic ideas held by many Australians about the place of the bush at the heart of Australia. Having a bush capital built in empathy with the splendour of its surroundings made sense. Further, the prominence of landscape rather than monumental constructions could be translated in terms of the myth of Australian egalitarianism.

In his plans for the capital, Walter Burley Griffin imagined a relationship between the different natural and built aspects of the city. The plan for the city was intricately geometric. There were three centres organised around three axes linking natural objects: a land axis that ran from Mount Ainslie to Capital Hill (where Parliament House sits), a water axis and a municipal axis (Proudfoot 1994: 76). It is perhaps the land axis that most visibly lays out the city for visitors. One of the most majestic views of Canberra is from Mount Ainslie to the New Parliament House or vice versa (see Figure 12.3). In both cases, the viewer is on a hill or rise and sees the long avenue of Anzac

Figure 12.3 The view down Anzac Parade from the Australian War Memorial and
Mount Ainslie—an important axis in Walter Burley Griffin's design of
Canberra. (*Image courtesy of Australian Capital Tourism*)

Parade with either Parliament House or the Australian War Memorial
at the end of the view. War and politics sit at either end of the axis.
As suggested in the 2004 advertising campaign, these two visions
dominate the story of Canberra. The National Capital Authority has
noted that a larger than usual number of the memorial spaces and
objects in Canberra commemorate war. They suggest that this skews
the story of the nation told in the capital. Yet the Australian War
Memorial at one end of Anzac Parade and Parliament House at the
other fit into a very powerful story of Australia forged through a
combination of democracy and individual (military) courage.

Griffin's plan did not site the Parliament on Capital Hill. He
suggested that a national institution such as an archive be built here.
However, the idea of the House on the Hill appealed to many politicians. Interestingly, it is sometimes argued that this high and mighty
position is moderated by the low—in fact, buried—nature of
the parliament. The form of the building moderates ideas of the
parliament as powerful and replaces it with a flatter, more egalitarian

story. This is demonstrated in an oft-quoted line from the architect of the new Parliament House, Romaldo Giurgola:

> According to our design 85% of the site is intended to be devoted to landscape, most of which is available to the public. Rather then being an imposition on the site, the Parliament building is generated by the natural state of the land configurations, just as democratic government is not an imposition on the community but rather originates organically from within the populace (Proudfoot 1994: 82).

The choice of Giurgola's design for the new federal parliament fitted with and reinforced the understanding of Australian-ness being premised on an egalitarian nature. One of the popular understandings of the new Parliament House was that it could be stood on by the people. The 'roof' of the parliament is a lawn. The sense of the people being above the parliamentarians appeals to many as a symbol of the parliamentarians as representatives of the people. Interestingly, since the idea of the war on terror has taken hold, the lawn roof of the parliament is no longer a zone for the people. A permanent concrete waist-high wall now surrounds it.

Other Canberras

Though Canberra is highly regulated by the National Capital Authority and the federal parliament, other stories still exist to disturb the supposedly singular national story. Other stories—the counterpublic, the repressed—always exist in tension with the dominant national story. Given that Canberra is the formal political centre for the vision of Australian nationalism, it is not surprising that these counterpublics are hidden as best they can be or removed as quickly as possible. Further, given the place of Canberra as the site of the coming into being of Australia as a nation, it is not surprising that one of the central points of tension is between Indigenous claims to sovereignty and the non-Indigenous counter-claim of the sovereignty of the colonies that federated to create a nation.

The walk up Anzac Parade towards Mount Ainslie and the Australian War Memorial (initially called Prospect Parkway and destined to lead to a casino) takes the visitor past a pantheon of Australian heroes. On both sides of the road are memorials to Australian military endeavour. There are monuments to the Light Horse, the Vietnam and Korean wars, the Australian army, air force and navy, the Greek campaign of World War II, Turkish and

Australian soldiers in World War I. Recently the first memorial to explicitly honour Australian women in war appeared with a memorial to nurses. At the top of the parade is the Australian War Memorial. As part of the 'See Yourself in Canberra' advertising campaign, a newspaper advertisement exhorted people to 'See yourself among the brave'. In this advertisement, the text was superimposed over a close up of three panels of the Roll of Honour in the Memorial Courtyard (see Figure 12.4). In smaller lettering it said: 'Nothing matches the experience you'll have at the Australian War Memorial.'

Yet, as a number of scholars have noted, not every Australian does see himself or herself 'among the brave' (Inglis 1998, Styles 2000). Not even all those involved in military endeavour see themselves 'among the brave'. Though the Roll of Honour has been updated over time to fill gaps and omissions, for a long time for many

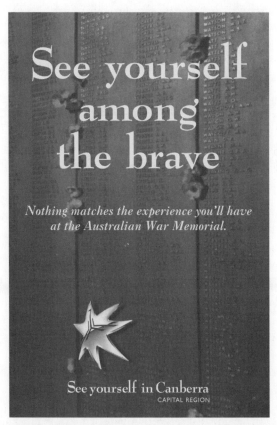

Figure 12.4 Advertisement for Canberra asking visitors to identify themselves with the Roll of Honour at the Australian War Memorial. (*Image courtesy of Australian Capital Tourism*)

Indigenous soldiers to 'see themselves among the brave' they needed to walk up Anzac Parade past all the specific memorials, past the Honour Roll, out the back and into the bush at the base of Mount Ainslie. It was there they would find a plaque specifically honouring their contribution in war. The Australian War Memorial has had temporary exhibits about Indigenous people's participation in Australian wars. In particular, *Too Dark for the Light Horse* was a very successful touring exhibition that recalled the contribution of Indigenous men in World War I (Figure 12.5). However, this type of exhibition works to fit Indigenous military endeavour and love of country within a national context. There is still serious resistance to including in any national war memorial an acknowledgment of the military endeavours of Indigenous peoples to protect their land from invaders.

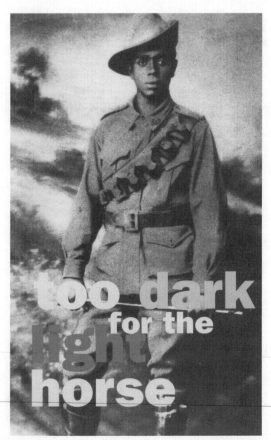

Figure 12.5 Poster for the Australian War Memorial travelling exhibition, *Too Dark for the Light Horse*, 2000/2001. (*AWM P00889.012*)

The Aboriginal Tent Embassy

At the other end of the land axis, just in front of old Parliament House, is another story that irritates the national story of Canberra. This story is embodied in the Aboriginal Tent Embassy, a changing collection of tents, lean-tos and caravans that has been on the lawns in front of old Parliament House, on and off, for 30 years. Though the embassy is on the Register of the National Estate as a place of special significance, it is an unauthorised building within the Parliamentary Zone.

The Aboriginal Tent Embassy first appeared in January 1972 when a group of Koori activists made their way to Canberra to protest a decision made by the conservative federal government watering down earlier promises for national land rights legislation. The protestors, who brought a tent and set it up in front of the parliament, said they were protesting the government's new approach to land rights which 'makes us aliens in our own land' (Dow 2000). Over the next few months, the Tent Embassy grew, with supporters from the local university and other Indigenous peoples coming to Canberra (especially on weekends) to camp and take up space on the lawns in front of the parliament. By late autumn, the Liberal government was so embarrassed and annoyed by the presence of the embassy it passed an ordinance outlawing camping on unleased Commonwealth land, making the presence of the tents on this part of parliament lawns illegal (Harris 2003: 84). As the authorities tried to implement the ordinance, there were violent confrontations between the activists and the police. Many who were there remember these confrontations as some of the fiercest altercations in that turbulent era of protest. The Whitlam government was elected late in 1972 and, in the euphoria of a more sympathetic regime, the embassy disappeared. However, it was not gone for good. Over the next ten years, the embassy would re-emerge and disappear as a reminder to the different governments that took office of the broken promises around land rights. In 1992, the embassy returned once more (20 years after the original protest) and has remained on the lawns ever since.

For many Indigenous peoples, this site is an important symbol of resistance. Kevin Buzzacott said of the sacred fire that burns at the site: 'We will keep this fire burning until the law makers come and talk to us about recognising our sovereignty' (Dow 2000). The meaning of the embassy is not the same for all Indigenous peoples (Moloney 2002). Carol Dow makes this point when she explains how these differences are exploited by non-Indigenous people: 'Senator Macdonald in 1999 appeared to play on perceived differences of local opinion when he claimed "The Ngunnawal people don't want [the embassy] there, they find it embarrassing. They refer to the people who run it as the Redfern mob"' (Dow 2000). Indigenous activist Isobell Coe also makes this point about the exploitation of differences of opinion amongst Indigenous peoples on the embassy: 'how they attack us [the embassy activists] is they usually hand pick one of these so-called local elders around here, the paid ones, and they usually attack us through them' (Watson 2000: 18). As Mark Harris points out, 'any expectation that there should be a consistent voice of resistance . . . merely seeks to resurrect the vision of Indigenous Australians as a homogenous group reified through the projected desires of non-Indigenous spectators' (2003: 86). Yet this natural heterogeneity of opinion can be mobilised to suggest that Indigenous peoples only need one memorial—Reconciliation Place (see next section)—and the eyesore of the embassy can go.

The story of Australian-ness the embassy produces is a striking one. If you visit the embassy, you will find a diverse collection of tents and mobile housing, surrounded by various signs explaining the reason for the presence of the embassy. There is always a fireplace with a slow-burning fire. And, depending on the day, there may be half a dozen or hundreds of people on the site. The physical organi-sation of the Tent Embassy contrasts with the usual stereotype of Canberra—as neat, orderly and perfectly planned. The embassy is opposite the well-manicured rose gardens of the old Parliament House—a striking juxtaposition. Over time, many politicians and media commentators have complained about the 'unsightly' nature of the embassy. It has been called an eyesore, a disgrace and a health danger. Different government ministers over the past 30 years have threatened to remove it.

By contrast, the Embassy is now on the itinerary of some Canberra tourist bus routes. International students studying at Australian universities come to Canberra to visit the embassy and increase their knowledge of Indigenous politics in Australia. In these cases, the embassy is situated in terms of an alternative global cultural tourism that seeks to see beyond the official story of nations. The embassy has become known overseas, through documentaries and news reports—especially from around the time of the 2000 Olympics—and is now part of an international travel route of political sites where the struggle of Indigenous peoples around the globe can be experienced and supported.

As stated above, the Aboriginal Tent Embassy is an unauthorised structure. No planning permission was obtained: a Koori mob simply turned up and set up shop. There are some interesting points to note here. First, the Indigenous people of the embassy have never asked permission for their installation. At some level, there is an assumption by the protesters that they could be there and that they were on Indigenous own land. On the other hand, it is important to note the tenuous existence of the embassy. It is always being threatened with closure. Yet the very precariousness of the rights of the embassy to be where it is reflects the point the Indigenous peoples are making: the guarantee of rights to land for Indigenous people is not automatic— in fact, it is unusual.

Reconciliation Place

One of the reasons given for why the Tent Embassy should close down is that across the road is a new space that does exactly the same job as the embassy. Prime Minister John Howard opened Reconciliation Place in July 2002. It is a site designed:

> for contemplation and the telling and sharing of stories of reconciliation. It recognises the importance of understanding the shared history of Indigenous and non-Indigenous Australians, and reaffirms our commitment to the cause of reconciliation as an important national priority (Headon 2002: 41).

Reconciliation Place is a beautiful site. It includes a walkway divided by a grassy mound. Installations called 'slivers' are being created and placed along a pedestrian walkway over time. The slivers highlight important aspects of Indigenous peoples' experience of colonialism. For many Australians, this beautiful and serene memorial is a far better signifier of Indigenous stories than the Tent Embassy. Since they are quite close together, some argue that the unofficial and eyesore embassy should go. The important question to consider here is why there is such an insistence on only one site and why Reconciliation Place is nominated as that site. Not many Australians would argue that since there were so many war memorials in Anzac Parade they should all be removed except one.

Some Indigenous peoples are involved in both the embassy and Reconciliation Place. Both tell stories of Indigenous survival. One is funded and recognised by the government; the other is not. This is the point of the embassy proponents. As suggested earlier, there have been disagreements between Indigenous members of the embassy and the Reconciliation Place committee. Indeed, playing on such divisions is a well-known ploy used by non-Indigenous peoples to supposedly demonstrate the implausibility of Indigenous political arguments (for example: 'Well if what you say is true then why does this Indigenous person not agree with you?') The issue here is not which story is true, but why non-Indigenous peoples find one story comfortable and the other so noxious it is represented as detrimental to health.

Reconciliation Place encourages non-Indigenous peoples to consider the impact of non-Indigenous colonialism on Indigenous peoples. It also suggests considering what Indigenous peoples have achieved in the face of that impact. The embassy takes this process to its next logical step—asking about how did non-Indigenous peoples come to get Indigenous land. This is the story some politicians hope to erase from the landscape by dismantling the embassy. This is easy to do in stories and sites controlled by non-Indigenous people—non-Indigenous peoples often erase Indigenous peoples' stories and replace them with stories of politicians, sports stars and old diggers. But when Indigenous people turn up unannounced with their Tent Embassy, ready to stay until justice is done, it is mostly understood as a sore that needs to healed. But how is that healing to take place?

Anyone who has been to the National Museum or the War Memorial or Canberra knows how much work goes into keeping these places running. They employ hundreds of people. Part of the work of these people is to help produce for the citizens of Australia a sense of sharing a coherent and stable identity—that is a shared sense of being Australian. Museums, galleries and the national capital draw on historical events and cultural products to create a suite of 'representational codes'—stories of shared emotions, feelings and experiences. These feelings are not innate they need to be produced. For example, at the Australian War Memorial there are guides and guards who are employed to share narratives of Australian war history with visitors. They can also guide visitors in adopting the right demeanour when in the Memorial—so if a visitor is too boisterous in the Hall of Memory they will politely be told to be more quiet. This may be a reasonable request to put to a visitor in a space dedicated to the memory of war dead, but it is still a process of learning how to be Australian. This learning takes place in all sorts of places—most centrally in education, but also in every day living: watching television, going to the cricket or visiting a museum.

FURTHER READING

Attwood, Bain 2005, *Telling the Truth About Aboriginal History*, Allen & Unwin, Sydney.

Council for Aboriginal Reconciliation 1994, *Sharing History: A Sense for All Australians of a Shared Ownership of their History*, Australian Government Publishing Service, Canberra.

Fforde, Cressida, Hubert, Jane and Turnbull, Paul (eds) 2002, *The Dead and their Possessions: Repatriation in Principle, Policy, and Practice*, Routledge, New York.

Headon, David 2002, *The Symbolic Role of the National Capital: From Colonial Argument to Twenty-first Century Ideals*, National Capital Authority, Canberra.

Healy, Chris 1997, *From the Ruins of Colonialism: History as Social Memory*, Cambridge University Press, Cambridge and Melbourne.

Lake, Martin (ed.) 2006, *Memory, Monuments and Museums: The Past in the Present*, Melbourne University Press, Melbourne.

Macintyre, Stuart and Clark, Anna 2003, *The History Wars*, Melbourne University Press, Melbourne.

McIntyre, Darryl and Wehner, Kirsten (eds) 2001, *National Museums: Negotiating Histories*, National Museum of Australia, Canberra.

National Museum of Australia 1999, *National Museum of Australia: A Museum for the New Millennium*, National Museum of Australia, Canberra.

Proudfoot, Peter R. 1994, *The Secret Plan of Canberra*, University of New South Wales Press, Sydney.

Schlunke, Katrina 2005, *Bluff Rock: Autobiography of a Massacre*, Fremantle Arts Centre Press, Fremantle.

CONCLUSION

THE PRODUCTION OF Australian-ness creates the 'in-common community' (Secomb 2003: 9), but it also excludes others from the community called Australia. There are parts of the process of being Australian—both historical and contemporary—that are excluded from the stories. The long discussions about the form of the exhibitions in the National Museum of Australia is an example of this process of exclusion and inclusion. For some Australians stories about the violence of the process of colonisation do not belong in a national story of being Australian. For others the history of the exclusion of this story of violence—and the concomitant exclusion of actual people from Australian citizenship—needs to be challenged and the story made part of national narratives.

In the twenty-first century these discussions about the negative side of Australian-ness can seem worrying even dangerous for many citizens. There is sometimes a sense of anger or sadness about the challenges to the old stories of 'good' Australia: who are we if we are not the proud pioneers who fought fire and flood to make this country great? How can we just be these bad people who did so much wrong? Engaging with the history of nationalism, the history of stories of being Australian, can be painful. National stories are by their very nature exclusionary. They are also by nature mythical—they depend on a phantasm—and invite an intense emotional engagement. So undoing and critiquing these stories is painful for many. For Australians who benefited from the dominant stories—mostly Anglo–Australians—it is often experienced in terms of loss and accusation. For others it can be experienced as a sort of liberation.

These feelings of loss, liberation, anger and sadness are real and in many ways need to be acknowledged. However, it is what Anglo–Australians in particular do with these feelings that is important. As the reconciliation bridge walks and the support for the Australian Capital Territory legislation for civil unions for same sex couples demonstrates some Australians are listening to the stories of citizens who have been excluded from nation and are responding by imagining new ways of building communities. Other citizens are clinging to the phantasm of Australian national identity—the mythical story of Australia as the empty place which over 200 years was filled with an exemplary culture. Australian-ness is just one way of understanding who the 22 million people who occupy the large southern continent are. It will always be an ambivalent identity—one that is desirable and at the same time worrying. It will continually be challenged by other ways of thinking about belonging. What is important is to understand that being Australian is an identity that does work—that is, it is productive—and we need to be aware of what is being produced.

GLOSSARY

ABC—The ABC or Australian Broadcasting Commission is the government owned television and radio network in Australia. Established in 1932, today it includes a national television station, a digital-only free-to-air station and regional radio stations across the country. It also broadcasts in the Asian region. The ABC has been a key producer of original Australian television and radio shows and a vital supporter of the marginal and outrageous in popular culture. In the past few years the ABC has been under scrutiny by more conservative critics who worry it is too 'left-wing' and as a result 'biased'.

ACON—The establishment of the AIDS Council of New South Wales (ACON) was one of a range the early state initiatives to include the gay community in designing and implementing strategies to deal with the HIV/AIDS epidemic from the mid 1980s. Gay community members set up the AIDS Action Committee in Sydney in 1983, in 1994, this committee became the government funded AIDS Council of NSW. ACON is designed to provide health promotion in the gay, lesbian, bisexual and transgender communities with a central focus on HIV/AIDS: 'We provide HIV prevention, health promotion, advocacy, care and support services to members of those communities including Indigenous people, injecting drug users, sex workers and all people living with HIV/AIDS' <http://www.acon.org.au/acon/>.

Anangu—Anangu are the custodians of the area that surrounds Uluru. When visitors enter the Uluru–Kata Tjuta National Park they are in the country of Anangu. The Anangu played a key role in negotiations to have Uluru returned to Indigenous people and they are major players in the ongoing management of the national park.

Anglo–Australian—This is a common term used to describe Australians whose heritage is British. It conflates many different British ethnicities—Anglo and Celtic for example. The popularity of the terms reflects the immigration history of Australia. There were differences in the status of the various groups of Britons and the Irish who arrived in Australia, especially between Catholic and Protestant

354

migrants. However the general focus on other groups as needing to be actively excluded meant Australians with ancestors from the various British and Irish cultural groups came to be placed in the same category.

AnTAR—AnTAR is an acronym standing for Australians for Native Title and Reconciliation. The group emerged in the mid 1990s in response to conservative political and community response to the *Mabo* decision. AnTAR, a coalition of groups mostly made up of non-Indigenous people, supports the recognition of Indigenous native title. One of the most successful AnTAR events was the Sea of Hands. In October 1997, 70 000 plastic hands (in the colours of the Aboriginal and Torres Strait Islander flag) was planted in the lawns of the parliament house in Canberra to signify Australian citizens putting up their hands for Indigenous rights.

Anzac—This is an acronym (ANZAC) of Australian and New Zealand Army Corps. It emerged as a term during World War I to describe the combined military presence of these countries in the British Imperial forces. Today it is used as a term to describe Australian military personnel generally. It is also a word used to describe a particular 'spirit' or ethos of Australian-ness that developed in World War I.

ASEAN—This acronym stands for the Association of South East Asian Nations. ASEAN emerged in 1967 as a body organised to foster economic and social regional co-operation and deal with shared security issues.

ATSIC—The Aboriginal and Torres Strait Islander Commission was inaugurated in 1990 through an act of federal parliament (*Aboriginal and Torres Strait Islander Commission Act* 1989). The commission, which was a commonwealth statutory authority, was designed to provide policy advice to the federal government on Indigenous affairs. What was unique about ATSIC was that the members were elected by Indigenous peoples. ATSIC had a board of commissioners and regional councils. ATSIC was disbanded in 2004 with the prime minister saying 'We believe very strongly that the experiment in separate representation, elected representation for indigenous people has been a failure'.

The Ashes—This is a cricket series played between Australia and England every three years. It originated in 1882. The Ashes refers to a story about England's loss to Australia in England. Someone placed a wry notice in a sports paper noting this cricket had 'died' and that 'the Ashes' had been taken to Australia.

Aussie—This is a shortened form of the word Australian. Many visitors to Australia notice an Australian speech habit of shortening words and adding –ie to the end. For example barbeque becomes 'barbie', present (gift) becomes 'pressie' and football becomes 'footie'. In the world of work the postal worker who delivers the mail becomes the 'postie' and the fire fighter who puts out the bush fires becomes the 'fireie'.

Australian Rules—This is a home-grown code of football. Australian Rules football emerged in Melbourne in the 1850s. For the first few years it was played teams involved in a match would clarify the rules before they commenced. For many years Australian rules was the most popular code of football played in Victoria, South Australia and Western Australia. Australian Rules is a fast running game, played with 18 footballers per side.

Black armband history—The term 'black armband' history was coined by historian Geoffrey Blainey in 1993 to describe, what he considered to be, the unnecessary emphasis in contemporary Australian history on the violence and racism of the Australian past. Blainey considered that where earlier histories of Australia had been too positive contemporary histories were too negative or gloomy.

Bloke—This is a slang word for a man. It has positive and familiar connotations. So a bloke is almost always a good bloke and someone you feel some warmth towards (whether he is known to you or not). The matching word for bloke for women is 'sheila'. This term has however not retained its popularity. It also has more negative connotations.

Bludger—A bludger is Australian slang for someone who lets other people do the work, yet makes sure they benefit from the other person's efforts. Early twentieth-century meanings of bludger focused on men who lived off the earnings of sex workers; by the late twentieth century the meaning was more general. The archetypal bludger was the 'dole bludger', someone who refuses to try and get a job and instead lives on government unemployment benefits.

Bobby Goldsmith Foundation—Bobby Goldsmith was a Sydney gay man who died in 1984 of HIV/AIDS. As Bobby got sicker his friends banded together to provide the care and medical equipment required so he could remain living at home. The Bobby Goldsmith Foundation aims to provide support for people living with HIV/AIDS, enabling them to live lives that are about 'independence and participation'.

Bringing Them Home—This is the title of the Human Rights and Equal Opportunity Commission report on the removal of Aboriginal and Torres Strait Islander children from their families. The report was released in 1997 and, most unusually for a government report, was reprinted many times as members of the public purchased copies to read. The 700-page report was also released in summaries available on the web and on video.

Bush—This is the generic term used to describe land in Australia that is not considered the city or suburbs. It can refer to heavily wooded areas or open country. Bush more signifies the non-city aspect of an area than the type of vegetation.

Bush tucker—This is a popular phrase used to describe what is sometimes called traditional Indigenous food. Bush tucker is increasingly becoming a part of the tourist experience in Australia. Eating bush tucker often involves taking part in an Indigenous-led tour where participants are told about the way flora and fauna are used to prepare meals. This sharing of knowledge often also includes stories of the place of ingredients in the broader life of the community.

Country—In Aboriginal English country is both a common noun and a proper noun. Country refers not just to a geographic space but is a word that refers to people, The Dreaming, animals, plants, soil and water in an area. When an Indigenous person refers to their country they are speaking about a complex living thing to which they belong.

Didjeridu—This is the most well-known of Indigenous musical instruments. It is often represented as a part of all Indigenous communities in Australia, however it is specific to Indigenous communities in northern Australia. Many of the didjeridu on sale to tourists are mass-produced items far removed from the rituals and arts of any specific Indigenous community.

Digger—The term digger first appeared on the colonial goldfields in Australia and referred to the miners. In World War I it came to have broad appeal. A digger was an Australian or New Zealand soldier. The term is sometimes said to have been applied to the Anzac troops at Gallipoli because they were instructed to dig themselves into their trenches. After the war digger was used to refer to returned soldiers. Digger today is a term of affection and to be called digger would mean you were held in high regard.

Dykes on Bikes—Dykes on bikes are a lesbian motorbike group. The idea of dykes on bikes was brought to Australia from New York—where a similar group participated in the Gay Pride March in that city. They have been participating in the Sydney Gay and Lesbian Mardi Gras since 1987 and today are well-known as the leaders of the parade.

Eora—The Eora community was an Indigenous group who lived in the area now known as central Sydney when the First Fleet arrived in 1788. This group was devastated by the smallpox epidemic that spread through the colony soon after the British arrived.

Family First—In the 2004 federal election a new political party emerged—Family First. This small party campaigned on a platform of supporting legislation that will 'result in the health, welfare and unity of families in Australia and to oppose legislation that will be hurtful to families'. The party does not support abortion and does support the rebuttable presumption of joint residency. It understands the family to be a heterosexual unit.

Federation—In 1901 the six colonies of Australia—Queensland, NSW, Victoria, Tasmania, South Australia and Western Australia—federated to form the Australian state. The colonies each retained their own government, the state government, but a new federal level of government was added. Federation was never taken-for-granted. Early discussions included New Zealand and many of the Australian colonies were wary of a federation. One of the key issues that drew the colonies together was a shared desire to keep out non-British migrants, in particular Chinese sojourners.

Gallipoli—This peninsula in Turkey is a key site in Australian national mythology. It was the place where in April 1915 Australian soldiers landed for a long and drawn out campaign with the Turkish enemy. The long and costly year of trench warfare is often represented as the birth of the Australian nation. The campaign has been frequently recorded in history and film. It is by far the most famous military encounter in this country.

Gurindji—The Gurindji people live in the northwest of Australia. They are well-known for their labour strike and land rights protest in the 1960s. Vincent Lingiarri, one of their key spokesmen, led a walk-out from the cattle station where many of the community were working after his demand for better pay and conditions were refused by the manager.

Hills Hoist—This is the name of a brand of rotary clothesline that was ubiquitous in Australian suburbs throughout the twentieth century. As back yards have grown smaller the rotary Hills Hoist has been replaced by smaller more discrete clotheslines.

History Wars—The 'History Wars' were a robust discussion between historians, journalists and politicians about Indigenous history in Australia. The war was based around reactions to Keith Windschuttle's book *The Fabrication of Aboriginal History* (2002). Windschuttle sought to discredit histories of British colonisation of Tasmania, arguing they were poorly researched, incorrect and, as the title suggests, deliberately misleading.

Kata Tjuta—These are ancient rock formations to the west of Uluru. They were called The Olgas by non-Indigenous people for many years. Like Uluru, Kata Tjuta is part of the Dreaming of the Anangu.

Koori—This is the collective name used by Indigenous peoples in southern Australia. An Indigenous person who referred to themselves as Koori would probably also identify with a more specific language group within this large area.

La Perouse—Also referred to by locals as 'LaPa', this is a suburb in eastern Sydney. In 1900 an Aboriginal reserve was set up in the area—the closest reserve to Sydney. It has a large Indigenous community and also large non-Anglo–Australian communities. The La Perouse Aboriginal Community were the hosts for the Sydney Australia Day Survival concerts for many years.

McMansions—The term 'McMansion' is a slightly derogatory term used by detractors to describe a newer style of house being built on the outer fringes of Australian cities. The McMansion is a much larger house fitted onto the traditional sized urban block. It is sometimes environmentally less friendly than earlier housing stock—in particular lacking sufficient natural cooling design and depending on air-conditioning. The McMansion has come to stand for an ethic of over-consumption and increasing household debt.

Mabo—Edward Koiki Mabo was Torres Strait Islander man (from the island of Mer) whose name has become synonymous with a 1992 High Court decision, where in response to Mabo's petition, the court recognised the existence of native title. This meant that the British Crown's declaration of sovereignty over the land of the Australian continent had not automatically extinguished the pre-existing claims of the Indigenous peoples of Australia.

Makarrata—This is a Yolngu word meaning the end of a dispute and the resumption of normal relations. The Makarrata was suggested by the National Aboriginal Conference, a governmental advisory body in the late 1970s. One of the key groups involved in supporting the Makarrata was the Aboriginal Treaty Committee. However, after years of work this group was wound up in 1984, deciding that the political opposition to Makarrata or treaty meant it would never succeed.

Murri—This word is used to describe the various Indigenous communities in northern New South Wales and southern, central and northern Queensland. An Indigenous person who referred to themselves as Murri would probably also identify with a more specific language group within this large area.

Noongar/Nyungar—The Noongar Nation are the Indigenous community of south-west Australia. This is the largest Indigenous group in Western Australia—over 26 000 people are Noongar. In 2006 Noongar people were granted Native Title rights over the city of Perth.

Ocker—The term 'ocker' is slang for a type of Australian male. The term emerged in the 1960s from a character in an Australian television comedy—*The Mavis Bramston Show*. An ocker is an uncouth male, his preferred dress is thongs and stubbies (see below) and he is usually found drinking a beer. An ocker is also profoundly anti-culture—he watches sport but does not attend the theatre.

Pitjantjatjara—The Pitjantjatjara are an Indigenous community from central Australia—an area known as the Western Desert. The Pitjantjatjara received title over their land in 1981.

Pom, Pommie—This is slang for an English person. It can be used affectionately but is mostly used as a derogatory term. For example the term 'whinging pom' was used to describe English people who migrated to Australia only to complain about the inferiority of country.

SBS—SBS or the Special Broadcasting Commission was established in 1991 in response to calls for non-English media in Australia. SBS was part of the multicultural policies pursued by governments in Australian throughout the 1980s and most of the 1990s.

Stolen Generations—Throughout the nineteenth and twentieth centuries Indigenous children were removed from their families and placed in institutions and foster homes to be brought up by non-Indigenous people. The children who were removed have come to be known as the stolen generations. From the late 1800s the process of removal was formalised in most states. Welfare agencies, churches and state governments worked together to remove children. The reasons for removing children were various, but all identified a belief it was in the children's 'best interests' to be raised in non-Indigenous society. The practices of removal have had devastating effects on Indigenous communities even though individual children sometimes benefited from a formal non-Indigenous education, something that has enabled them to work within the non-Indigenous community. But it has also caused untold suffering for the removed children and the families who never knew what happened to them.

Stubbies—A multipurpose word, a stubby is slang for a small bottle or can of beer; however a pair of stubbies can also refer to workmen's shorts.

Swag—A swag is the items, especially the bedroll, carried by a bushman. A swagman is an itinerant worker, someone who carries their belongings with them.

Thongs—What other people call flip flops, Australians call thongs. This form of informal footwear is found all over Australia, especially in summer and at the beach.

Thongs were long understood in other countries as footwear suitable only for public showers, in Australia they were much more widely worn. In the 2000s thongs along with ugg boots became a fashion fad in the USA and they both now have a higher profile as fashion footwear.

Tjukurpa—Tjukurpa is an Indigenous term that appears in a number of languages. It refers to the set of principles Indigenous peoples live by. Tjukurpa is sometimes translated as the Dreaming. It incorporates the laws and beliefs that explain how humans should live together and in harmony with their environment.

Torres Strait Islanders—These are the islands between the northern tip of Queensland and Papua New Guinea, located in the Torres Strait are the home of many Indigenous communities whose collective identity is Torres Strait Islanders. The TSI community has its own flag.

Uluru—Uluru is one of the earth's largest sandstone monoliths. It sits in the 'centre' of the Australian continent. Uluru is of substantial geological significance for many scientists—in terms of its age, the story of how it was formed and its size. Uluru is located in the Anangu people's country and is part of their Dreaming (Tjukurpa). Uluru is very significant in Anangu people's lives. Many aspects of its significance are sacred and cannot be shared with non-Anangu. In the last few decades Uluru has also become a massive tourist attraction for local and international visitors. It is seen as a beautiful natural attraction situated in a gorgeous desert. The different meanings of Uluru—Anangu sacred site and tourist space—sometimes clash as tourists clamber over a rock that for Anangu should not be walked upon.

Walpiri—The Walpiri are the Indigenous people of the area northwest of Alice Springs. Many of them moved to Yuendumu community when the government established a reserve there in the 1940s. Walpiri are known globally through the Walpiri Media Association—one of the early users of satellite technology and video production facilities in remote locations.

Wharfies—This is slang for a maritime worker, a person who works on the docks or wharves.

Wik—The Wik people are an Indigenous community from Cape York in northern Queensland. Their name had become synonymous with a 1996 High Court decision made in response to a claim by the Wik people. The court found in this decision that native title could continue to exist after Crown land had been leased to pastoralist. The *Native Title Act* was later amended to preclude this possibility of co-existing title.

Wog—This is a derogatory term that was used against migrants from non-English speaking countries, in particular Italy and Greece. Until the mid-1980s using the term wog was considered by many Anglo–Australians to be an acceptable form of address. The insulting and racist connotations are now more widely recognised. The term has been taken up by many second or third generation children of migrants as an affectionate form of self-identification.

Women in Black—Women in Black is a feminist activist peace network, that emerged first in Israel, but now exists in cities around the world. Similar to groups such as

Take Back the Night, Women in Black seeks to protest against violence against women, in particular atrocities that take place during war. Women in Black mobilisations involve a silent vigil in a public place by a group of women, dressed in mourning. These protests were at their peak in Australia in the 1990s.

Yobbo—A slang term for an uncouth person. A yobbo is personified in literature and comedy as a bloke wearing thongs, stubbies, and a singlet, drinking a stubby and watching sport.

Yolgnu—Yolngu are the people of northeast Arnhem land in Australia. They have a long history of political activism—they sent the bark petition to the federal parliament—and cultural achievement—the rock band Yothu Yindi are from Arnhem Land. In the 1950s many Yolngu people were settled in the town of Maningrida, but in the 1970s they rejected the assimilation implicit in this move and started to return to their country.

Yuendumu—This is a community 300 kilometres northwest of Alice Springs. It is one of the many remote Northern Territory communities that was created in the twentieth century by government officers bringing many different Indigenous language groups to live in one place as part of assimilation policies. Yuendumu is a large community—the community government area covers over 22 000 square kilometres. It is also one of the famous painting communities of the desert region. It is also one of many remote Indigenous communities that is dry—no alcohol or drugs permitted.

BIBLIOGRAPHY

AAP (Australian Associated Press) 2005, 'Bishop Backs Ban on Muslim Headscarves', Sydney Morning Herald, 28 August.

Ackland, Michael (ed.) 1993, *The Penguin Book of Nineteenth Century Australian Literature*, Penguin Books, Melbourne.

Adams, Phillip 1984, 'Two Views', *Cinema Papers*, vols. 44–45, pp. 70–72.

Adams, Simon and Frances, Rae 2003, 'Lifting the Veil: the Sex Industry Museums and Galleries', *Labour History*, vol. 85, pp. 47–64.

Adelaide Advertiser 2001, 'Hill backs Uluru close', 17 May, p. 7.

——2005, 'Australians Not Racist: PM', 20 December.

Age, The, 'Kimmoy and Co Have a Laugh' 2002, cited at <www.theage.com.au/articles/2002/06/01/1022569844132.html>, accessed on 2 June.

Alach, Felena 1997, 'Youth Subculture and Urban Space', *Studies in Western Australian History*, vol. 17, pp. 116–38.

Allen, Christopher 1997, *Art in Australia: From Colonization to Postmodernism*, Thames and Hudson, London.

Allen, Judith 1990, *Sex and Secrets: Crimes Involving Australian Women Since 1880*, Oxford University Press, Melbourne.

Altman, Dennis 2001, *Global Sex*, Allen & Unwin, Sydney.

Anderson, Benedict 1983, *Imagined Communities: Reflections on the Origin and Spread of Nationalism*, Verso, London.

Andrew, Brook 2001, 'Remembering Jesus', *Artlink*, vol. 21, no. 2, pp. 20–25.

——2004, Interview on 'Message Stick', ABC Television, 12 November, cited at <www.abc.net.au/message/tv/ms/s1242475.htm>.

Anker, Kristen 2005, 'The Truth in Painting: Cultural Artefacts as Proof of Native Title', *Law Text Culture*, vol. 9, pp. 91–124.

Attwood, Bain 2004, 'Whose Dreaming: Reviewing the Review of the National Museum of Australia', *History Australia*, vol. 1, no. 2, pp. 279–292.

——2005, *Telling the Truth About Aboriginal History*, Allen & Unwin, Sydney.

Attwood, Bain and Markus, Andrew 1999, *The Struggle for Aboriginal Rights: A Documentary History*, Allen & Unwin, Sydney.

Australian Broadcasting Corporation (ABC) 2002, 'Farewell to the Last Anzac Digger', *Lateline,* 17 May, cited at <www.abc.net.au/lateline/stories/s558558. htm>, accessed July 2005.

——2003, 'PM Weighs into Gay Marriage Debate', *Lateline,* 6 August, cited at <www.abc.net.au/lateline/content/2003/s918026.htm>, accessed in May 2006.

Australian Capital Tourism 2005, 'Tourism Brand for Canberra', ACT Government, cited at <www.tourism.act.gov.au/CA256E1D0083A261/page/Canberra+brand? OpenDocument&1=70-Canberra+brand~&2=~&3=~>, accessed in December 2005.

Australian Declaration Towards Reconciliation 2000, cited at <www.austlii.edu.au/au/ other/IndigLRes/car/2000/12/pg3.htm>, access on 11 March 2007.

Australian Prospectors and Miners Hall of Fame 2005, 'What is the Mining Hall of Fame?', cited at <www.mininghall.com/about/index.htm>, accessed in December 2005.

Australian Stockman's Hall of Fame and Outback Heritage Centre 2005, 'Gallery One—Discovery', cited at <www.stockmanshalloffame.com.au/display.asp>, accessed December 2005.

Australian Tourism Net 2005, 'The Red Centre Northern Territory (NT)', cited at <www.atn.com.au/nt/south/nt-e.htm>, accessed in December 2005.

Australian War Memorial, pamphlet.

Avram, Elizabeth 2004, '*Finding Nemo:* Australian National Cinema', *Metro Magazine,* no. 142, pp. 22–28.

Ayres, Tony 1998, 'Undesirable Aliens', *HQ,* no. 57, March/April 1998, pp. 110–15.

Bailey, Janis and Iveson, Kurt 2000, '"The Parliament Call Them Thugs": Political/ Industrial Protest and Public Space', *Proceedings of the 14th Annual Association of Industrial Relations Academics of Australia and New Zealand Conference,* 2–4 February.

Baker, David and Oakham, Katrina Mandy 1999, 'Dishing Up the Docks: the MUA Dispute as a Case Study of Successful Agenda Setting', *Australian Journalism Review,* vol. 21, no. 3, pp. 127–49.

Balibar, Etienne 1991, *Race, Nation, Class: Ambiguous Identities,* trans. Chris Turner, Verso, London.

Balint, Ruth 2005, *Troubled Waters: Borders, Boundaries and Possession in the Timor Sea,* Allen & Unwin, Crows Nest.

Bamber, Greg et al. 2005, *Research Evidence About the Effects of the Work Choices Bill: A Submission to the Inquiry into the Workplace Relations Amendment (Work Choices) Bill 2005.*

Barclay, Ryan and West, Peter 2006, 'Racism or Patriotism: An Eyewitness Account of the Cronulla Demonstration of 11 December 2005', *People and Place,* vol. 14, no. 1, pp. 75–85.

Bashford, Alison 2002, 'At the Border: Contagion, Immigration, Nation', *Australian Historical Studies,* vol. 33, pp. 344–58.

Bean, C.E.W. 1910, *On the Wool Track,* Alston Rivers Ltd, London.

——1981, *The Official History of Australia in the War of 1914–1918,* University of Queensland Press, Brisbane.

Behrendt, Larissa 2003, *Achieving Social Justice: Indigenous Rights and Australia's Future,* Federation Press, Sydney.

Bell, Jeanie 1997, *Talking About Celia: Community and Family Memories of Celia Smith,* University of Queensland Press, Brisbane.

Bennett, Gordon 1996, 'The Manifest Toe', in Ian McLean and Gordon Bennett (eds), *The Art of Gordon Bennett,* Craftsman House, Sydney, pp. 9–62.

Bennett, Tony 1995, *The Birth of the Museum: History, Theory, Politics,* Routledge, London.

Bennett, Tony, Buckridge, Pat, Carter, David and Mercer, Colin (eds) 1992, *Celebrating the Nation: A Critical Study of Australia's Bicentenary*, Allen & Unwin, Sydney.

Berry, Chris 1994, *A Bit on the Side: East–West Topographies of Desire*, EMPress, Sydney.

——1996, 'Response to Denis Altman "On Global Queering"', *Australian Humanities Review*, July.

Bertrand, Ina 1984, '"National Identity"/"National History"/"National Film": The Australian Experience', *Historical Journal of Film, Radio and Television*, vol. 4, no. 2, pp. 179–86.

Bhabha, Homi (ed.) 1990, *Nation and Narration*, Routledge, New York and London.

Bhattacharyya, Gargi 2002, *Sexuality and Society: An Introduction*, Routledge, London.

Biber, Katherine 1999, '"Turned Out Real Nice After All": Death and Masculinity in Australian Cinema', in Katherine Biber, Tom Sear and Dave Trudinger (eds), *Playing the Man: New Approaches to Masculinity*, Pluto Press, Sydney.

Birch, Tony 2001, 'The Last Refuge of the "Un-Australian"', *University of Technology Sydney Review*, vol. 7, no. 1, pp. 17–22.

Bone, Pamela 2004, 'How Far Have Women Come?', *The Age*, 12 March.

Boomalli Aboriginal Artists Co-operative Ltd, cited at <www.boomalli.org.au>.

Booth, Douglas and Tatz, Colin 2000, *One-eyed: A View of Australian Sport*, Allen & Unwin, Sydney.

Brett, Judith 2003, *Australian Liberals and the Moral Middle Class: From Alfred Deakin to John Howard*, Cambridge University Press, Melbourne.

Brett, Judith and Smith, Graeme 1998, 'Nation, Authenticity and Social Difference in Australian Popular Music: Folk, Country, Multicultural', *Journal of Australian Studies*, no. 58, pp. 3–17.

Breyley, Gay 2005, 'Unfolding Australia's Fan of Memory: Music in Ruby Langford Ginibi's *Don't Take Your Love to Town*', *Journal of Australian Studies*, no. 84, pp. 11–22.

Brook, Heather 1997, 'Big Boofy Blokes in Frocks: Feminism, Football and Sexuality', *Social Alternatives*, vol. 16, no. 1, pp. 5–9.

Brooks, Geraldine 2003/4, 'The Painted Desert', *Griffith Review*, no. 1, pp. 197–208.

Broome, Richard 1994, *Aboriginal Australians*, 2nd edn, Allen & Unwin, Sydney.

Broome, Richard with Jackomos, Alick 1998, *Sideshow Alley*, Allen & Unwin, Sydney.

Brown, David and Hogg, Russell 1997, 'Violence, Masculinity and Sport: Governance and the Swinging Arm', *University of Technology Sydney Review*, vol. 3, no. 1, pp. 129–41.

Buchanan, Rachel 1999, 'Truth and Valour: Anzac Day, the Myth', *Sydney Morning Herald, Good Weekend*, 24 April, pp. 43–44.

Buckley, Ken and Wheelwright, Ted 1998, *False Paradise: Australian Capitalism Revisited*, Oxford University Press, Melbourne.

Bulbeck, Chilla 1998, *Social Sciences in Australia*, Harcourt Brace, London.

Bullock, Chris 2000, 'South Sydney vs the National Rugby League', *Radio National's Background Briefing*, 30 July, cited at <www.ausport.gov.au/fulltext/2000/bbrief/s159144.htm>, accessed in September 2004.

Burgmann, Verity 2003, *Power, Profit and Protest: Australian Social Movements and Globalization*, Allen & Unwin, Sydney.

Burke, Anthony 2001, *In Fear of Security: Australia's Invasion Anxiety*, Pluto Press, Sydney.

Bury, Robin 2001, 'Adelaide to Alice Springs: The Best of the Red Centre', *The Word: Backpacking Australia*, cited at <www.thewordaustralia.com.au/features.asp?Keywords=FT2002&RegionID=&StateID=&StoryID=195>, accessed in December 2005.

Butcher, Melissa 2003, 'Breaking Away: Youth Culture and Public Space' in Melissa Butcher and Mandy Thomas (eds), *Ingenious: Emerging Youth Cultures in Urban Australia*, Pluto Press, Sydney.

Butcher, Melissa and Thomas, Mandy 2001, *Generate: Youth Culture and Migration Heritage in Western Sydney*, Institute for Cultural Research, University of Western Sydney.

——(eds) 2003, *Ingenious: Emerging Youth Cultures in Urban Australia*, Pluto Press, Melbourne.

Cannon, Michael 1971, *Who's Master? Who's Man: Australia in the Victorian Age*, Thomas Nelson, Sydney.

Carbery, Graham 1995, *A History of the Sydney Gay and Lesbian Mardi Gras*, Australian Lesbian and Gay Archives, Melbourne.

Carbone, Suzanne 2003, 'Trying to be a New Chum Jackeroo', *The Age*, 3 October.

Carmody, Kev 1995, 'An Indigenous Perspective on Our National Day', *Sydney Morning Herald*, 26 January.

Carr, Adam 2000, 'Policing the Abominable Crime in Nineteenth Century Victoria' in David L. Phillips and Graham Willett (eds), *Australia's Homosexual Histories: Gay and Lesbian Perspectives V*, Australian Centre for Gay and Lesbian Archives, Melbourne.

Carroll, Leonardo 2003, 'Mobility of the Vietnam-born in Sydney: A Re-assessment After the 2001 Census', *People and Place*, vol. 11, no. 2, pp. 1–15.

Carter, David 2005, *Dispossession, Dreams and Diversity*, Palgrave Macmillan, Sydney.

Carton, Adrian 1994, 'Symbolic Crossings: Vietnamese Women Enter the Australian Consciousness, 1976–1986' in K. Darian-Smith (ed.), *Working Papers in Australian Studies*, University of London, no. 91, pp. 57–84.

Casey, Dawn 2001, 'The National Museum of Australia: Exploring the Past, Illuminating the Present and Imagining the Future' in Darryl McIntyre and Kirsten Wehner (eds), *National Museums: Negotiating Histories*, National Museum of Australia, Canberra.

Cerwonka, Allaine 2004, *Native to the Nation: Disciplining Landscapes and Bodies in Australia*, University of Minnesota Press, Minneapolis.

Chedgzoy, Kate, Francis, Emma and Pratt, Murray 2002, *In a Queer Place: Sexuality and Belonging in British and European Contexts*, Ashgate, Aldershot.

Clark, Jane 1985, 'Naturalism and Nationalism' in Jane Clark and Bridget Whitelaw (eds), *Golden Summers: Heidelberg and Beyond*, International Cultural Corporation of Australia.

Clarsen, Georgine 1999, 'Tracing the Outline of Nation: Circling Australia by Car', *Continuum*, vol. 13, no. 3, pp. 359–69.

Cliff, Paul (ed.) 1999, *A Sporting Nation: Celebrating Australia's Sporting Life*, National Library of Australia, Canberra.

Collins, Felicity and Davis, Therese 2004, *Australian Cinema After Mabo*, Cambridge University Press, Melbourne.

Collins, Jock, Noble, Greg, Poynting, Scott and Tabar Paul 2000, *Kebabs, Kids, Cops and Crime: Youth Ethnicity and Crime*, Pluto Press, Sydney.

Collis, Christy 1999, 'Mawson's Hut: Emptying Post-Colonial Antarctica', *Journal of Australian Studies*, no. 63, pp. 22–29.

—— 2004, 'Australia's Antarctic Turf', *Journal of Media-Culture*, vol. 7, no. 2, pp. 1–5, cited at <http://journal.media-culture.org.au>.

Congram, Richard 2005, *The Weekend Australian*, Letter to the Editor, 17–18 December, p. 16.

Connell, Robert W. 1995, *Masculinities*, Allen & Unwin, Sydney.

Corn, Aaron 2002, 'Burr-Gi Wargugu ngu-Ninya Rrawa: Expressions of Ancestry and Country in Songs by the Letterstick Band', *Musicology Australia*, vol. 25, pp. 76–101.

Cornford, Phillip, Brown, Malcolm and Allard, Tom 2003, 'Bloody Battle for Qantas Jet', *Sydney Morning Herald*, 30 May, p. 1.

Corroboree Speeches 2000, cited at <www.austlii.edu.au/au/other/IndigLRes/car/2000/14/speeches.htm>, accessed on 11 March 2007.

Coslovich, Gabriella 2004, 'Bennett Puts on Brave Face', *The Age*, 28 April.

Council for Aboriginal Reconciliation Act 1991, Parliament of Australia 1991, No. 127.

Council for Aboriginal Reconciliation 1994, *Sharing History: A Sense for All Australians of a Shared Ownership of Their History*, Australian Government Publishing Service, Canberra.

Cowlishaw, Gillian 2004, *Blackfellas, Whitefellas and the Injuries of Race*, Blackwell, Malden.

Craig, Lyn 2002, *Caring Differently: A Time Use Analysis of the Type of and Social Context of Child Care Performed by Fathers and by Mothers*, Discussion Paper No. 116, Social Policy Research Centre, Sydney.

Crawford, David and MacDonald, John 2002, 'Fathers and the Experience of Family Separation', First National Conference on Mental and Health of Persons Affected by Family Separation, Liverpool Hospital, Liverpool, 10–11 October, cited at <http://menshealth.uws.edu.au/documents/Fathers%20sep%20ment%20hlth.pdf>, accessed in May 2006.

Creagh, Sunanda 2004, 'Random Acts of Silliness', *Sydney Morning Herald*, 6 October.

Creswell, Toby and Fabinyi, Martin 2000, *The Real Thing: Adventures in Australian Rock and Roll, 1957–Now*, Random House, Sydney.

Cubby, Ben 2006, 'The Australian Way', *Griffith Review*, No. 79, pp. 78–87.

Curthoys, Ann 1998, 'National Narratives, War Commemoration and Racial Exclusion' in Richard Nile and Michael Peterson (eds), *Becoming Australia: The Woodford Forum*, University of Queensland Press, Brisbane.

——2002, *Freedom Ride: A Freedom Rider Remembers*, Allen & Unwin, Sydney.

Dalziell, Tanya 2004, *Settler Romances and the Australian Girl*, University of Western Australia Press, Perth.

Davison, Graeme 1982, 'Sydney and the Bush: An Urban Context for the Australian Legend' in John Carroll (ed.), *Intruders in the Bush: The Australian Quest for Identity*, Oxford University Press, Melbourne.

——1994, 'The Past and Future of the Australian Suburb' in Louise Johnson (ed.), *Suburban Dreaming: An Interdisciplinary Approach to Australian Cities*, Deakin University Press, Geelong.

——2001, 'National Museums in a Global Age: Observations Abroad and Reflections at Home' in Darryl McIntyre and Kirsten Wehner (eds), *National Museums: Negotiating Histories*, National Museum of Australia, Canberra.

Dawe, Bruce 2006, 'The Family Man' in *Sometimes Gladness: Collected Poems 1954–1997*, 6th edition, Pearson Education Australia, Sydney.

Dennis, Anthony 2003, 'Bittersweet Replay of Show-stoppers Past', *Sydney Morning Herald*, 1 March.

Dermody, Susan and Jacka, Elizabeth 1988, *The Screening of Australia*, Currency Press, Sydney.

Devine, Miranda 2005, 'Muslim Cleric: Women incite men's lust with "satanic dress"', *The Sun-Herald*, 24 April.

Dixson, Miriam 1999, *The Real Matilda*, 4th edn, Penguin, Melbourne.

Dodson, Pat 1999, *Until the Chains are Broken*, Fourth Vincent Lingiari Lecture, cited at <www.austlii.edu.au/au/other/IndigLRes/car/pubs.html#publish>, accessed on 11 March 2007.

Dow, Coral 2000, *Aboriginal Tent Embassy: Icon or Eyesore?*, Department of the Parliamentary Library, Canberra.

Dowsett, Gary 1997, 'Sexual Conduct, Sexual Culture, Sexual Community: Gay Men's Bodies and AIDS' in Jill Matthews (ed.), *Sex in Public: Australian Sexual Cultures*, Allen & Unwin, Sydney.

D'Souza, Miguel and Iveson, Kurt 1999, 'Homies and Homebrewz: Hip Hop in Sydney' in Rob White (ed.), *Australian Youth Subcultures: On the Margins and in the Mainstream*, Australian Clearinghouse for Youth Studies, Hobart.

Duggan, Laurie 1998, '"A Sort of Mythical Thing": Canberra as an Imaginary Capital', *Journal of Australian Studies*, no. 57, pp. 83–92.

Dunbar-Hall, Peter and Gibson, Chris 2000, 'Singing About Nation Within Nations: Geopolitics and Identity in Australian Indigenous Rock Music', *Popular Music and Society*, vol. 24, no. 2, pp. 45–74.

Edgar, Don and Glezer, Helen 1992, 'A Man's Place . . . ? Reconstructing Family Realities', *Family Matters*, no. 31, pp. 36–39.

Editorial, 2005, 'This is Who We Are: We Have a Problem with Law and Order, Not Race Hate', *The Weekend Australian*, 17–18 December, p. 16.

Elder, Catriona 2003, 'Invaders, Illegals and Aliens: Imagining Exclusion in a "White Australia"', *Law Text Culture*, vol. 7, pp. 221–50.

—— 2005, '"I Spit on Your Stone": National Identity, Women Against Rape and the Cult of Anzac' in Maja Mikula (ed.), *Women, Activism and Social Change*, Routledge, London.

Elder, Catriona, Pratt, Angela and Ellis, Cath 2007, 'Running Race: Reconciliation, Nationalism and the Sydney 2000 Olympic Games', *International Review for the Sociology of Sport*, vol. 41, no. 2, pp. 181–200.

Ellard, Jeanne 1999, 'What's Love Got To Do With It? Male Victims and the Family Court' in Katherine Biber, Tom Sear and Dave Trudinger (eds), *Playing the Man: New Approaches to Masculinity*, Pluto Press, Sydney.

Ellemor, Heidi 2003, 'White Skin, Black Heart? The Politics of Belonging and Native Title in Australia', *Social and Cultural Geography*, vol. 4, no. 2, pp. 233–52.

Ensor, James 1999, 'A Tale of Two Sacred Stones', *Horizons: The Magazine for Supporters of Community Aid Abroad*, vol. 8, no. 2, p. 5.

Evans, Raymond and Saunders, Kaye 1994, *Gender Relations in Australia: Domination and Negotiation*, Harcourt Brace, Sydney.

Evans, Raymond, Saunders, Kaye and Cronin, Kathryn 1993, *Race Relations in Colonial Queensland: A History of Exclusion, Exploitation and Extermination*, University of Queensland Press, Brisbane.

Evans, Vanessa and Sternberg, Jason 1999, 'Young People, Politics and Television Current Affairs in Australia', *Journal of Australian Studies*, no. 63, pp. 103–09.

Everingham, Christine and Bowers, Tarquin 2005, 'Reclaiming or Re-shaping Fatherhood', unpublished paper presented at *Revisioning Institutions: Change in the 21st Century*, The Australian Sociology Association Conference.

Farouque, Farah 2004, 'So will you do it for your country', *The Age*, 12 May.

Farrell, Warren 1994, *The Myth of Male Power: Why Men are the Disposable Sex*, Random House, Sydney.

Fforde, Cressida, Hubert, Jane and Turnbull, Paul (eds) 2002, *The Dead and their Possessions: Repatriation in Principle, Policy, and Practice*, Routledge, New York.

Fiske, John, Hodge, Bob and Turner, Graeme 1987, *Myths of Oz: Reading Australian Popular Culture*, Allen & Unwin, Sydney.

Foucault, Michel 1976, *History of Sexuality*, vol. 1, Gallimard, Paris.

Fox, Charles and Lake, Marilyn 1990, *Australians At Work*, McPhee Gribble, Melbourne.

Frankel, Boris 2004, *Zombies, Lilliputians and Sadists: The Power of the Living Dead and the Future of Australia*, Fremantle Arts Centre Press, Fremantle.

Freeman, Cathy 2000, 'I'm Running for Sport, Not Politics', *Herald Sun*, 2 February, p. 4.

French, Simon 1999, 'Masculinity, Violence and the Playground' in Katherine Biber, Tom Sear and Dave Trudinger (eds), *Playing the Man: New Approaches to Masculinity*, Pluto Press, Sydney.

Garnaut, John 2005, 'Costello Taxes the Point: We're All Working Class', *Sydney Morning Herald*, 17 May.

Garton, Stephen 1996, *The Cost of War: Australians Return*, Oxford University Press, Melbourne.

Gay and Lesbian Rights Lobby 2003, *And then the Brides Changed Nappies: Lesbian Mothers, Gay Fathers and the Legal Recognition of our Relationships with the Children We Raise*, Gay and Lesbian Rights Lobby Inc., Sydney.

Gelder, Ken 1998, 'The Trouble With Australian Literature', *AQ: Journal of Contemporary Analysis*, vol. 70, no. 6, pp. 8–12.

Gellatly, Kelly 1999, 'Showing the Moment to Itself: Indigenous Documentary Practice', *Photofile*, no. 58, pp. 8–11.

Gellner, Ernest 1983, *Nations and Nationalism*, Cornell University Press, Ithaca.

Gerster, Robin 1995, 'A Bit of the Other: Touring Vietnam' in Joy Damousi and Marilyn Lake (eds), *Gender and War: Australians at War in the Twentieth Century*, Cambridge University Press, Melbourne.

Ghosh, Devlena 2003, '"I Can Make Chutney Out of anything": Young Indians Growing Up in Sydney' in Melissa Butcher, and Mandy Thomas (eds), *Ingenious: Emerging Youth Cultures in Urban Australia*, Pluto Press, Sydney.

Gibson, Chris and Connell, John 2003, '"Bongo Fury": Tourism, Music and Cultural Economy at Byron Bay, Australia', *Tijdschrift voor Economische en Sociale Goegrafie*, vol. 94, no. 2, pp. 164–87.

Gifford, Kenneth Harril 1944, *Jindyworobak: Towards an Australian Culture*, Jindyworobak Publications, Melbourne.

Gleeson, Brendan 2003, 'What's Driving Suburban Australia: Fear in the Tank, Hope on the Horizon', *Griffith Review*, no. 1, pp. 57–71.

——2006, *Australian Heartlands: Making Space for Hope in the Suburbs*, Allen & Unwin, Sydney.

Goodall, Heather 1995, 'New South Wales' in Ann McGrath (ed.), *Contested Ground: Australian Aborigines Under the British Crown*, Allen & Unwin, Sydney.

Gora, B. 1999, 'Invaded', *Sunday Telegraph*, 11 April, p. 1.

Goward, Pru 2002, *A Time to Value—Proposal for a Paid Maternity Leave Scheme*, Sex Discrimination Unit, Human Rights and Equal Opportunity Commission, Canberra.

Graham, Helena 2002, 'Stillness and Intrigue in *The North and Sadness* by William Yang', *Journal of Australian Studies*, no. 73, pp. 151–59.

Grant, Col 2003, *Matthew Flinders and the Costal Landforms of South Australia*, cited at <www.vnc.qld.edu.au/enviro/flinders/mflind-lett-a.htm>, accessed in April 2006.

Green, H.M. 1930, *An Outline of Australian Literature*, Whitcombe and Tombs Ltd, Sydney and Melbourne.

Green, Stephanie 2002, 'Wildflowers and Other Landscapes', *Transformations*, no. 5, cited at <http://pandora.nla.gov.au.arc=2450a>.

Griffiths, Tom 2007, *Slicing the Silence: Voyaging to Antarctica*, University of New South Wales Press, Sydney.

Grimshaw Patricia, Lake, Marilyn, McGrath, Ann and Quartly, Marian 1994, *Creating a Nation*, McPhee Gribble, Melbourne.

Guilliatt, Richard 2005, 'Once Were Warriors: The Painful Price of Sporting Glory', *Sydney Morning Herald, Good Weekend*, 17 September, pp. 26–32.

Gunn, Aeneas 1908, *We of the Never-Never*, Hutchinson, London.

Haebich, Anna 2000, *Broken Circles: Fragmenting Indigenous Families 1800–2000*, Fremantle Arts Centre Press, Fremantle.

Hage, Ghassan 1998, *White Nation: Fantasies of White Supremacy in a Multicultural Society*, Pluto Press, Sydney.

——2003, *Against Paranoid Nationalism: Searching for Hope in a Shrinking Society*, Pluto Press, Sydney.

Hains, Brigid 1997, 'Mawson of the Antarctic, Flynn of the Inland: Progressive Heroes on Australia's Ecological Frontiers' in Tom Griffiths and Libby Robin (eds), *Ecology and Empire: Environmental History of Settler Societies*, Melbourne University Press, Melbourne.

——2002, *The Ice and the Inland: Mawson, Flynn, and the Myth of the Frontier*, Melbourne University Press, Melbourne.

Hall, Stuart 1990, 'Cultural Identity and Diaspora' in Jonathan Rutherford (ed.), *Identity: Community, Culture, Difference*, Lawrence and Wishart, London.

Haltof, Marek 1996, *Peter Weir: When Cultures Collide*, Twayne, New York.

Harris, Mark 2003, 'Mapping Australian Postcolonial Landscapes: From Resistance to Reconciliation?', *Law Text Culture*, vol. 7, pp. 71–97.

Hartcher, Peter 2005, 'Now to Bury the Latham Obsession with Class Warfare', *Sydney Morning Herald*, 3 February, p. 9.

Haskins, Victoria and Maynard, John 2005, 'Sex, Race and Power: Aboriginal Men and White Women in Australian History', *Australian Historical Studies*, vol. 37, no. 126, pp. 191–216.

Hassall, Anthony, J. (ed.) 1988, *The Making of Xavier Herbert's* Poor Fellow My Country, Foundation for Australian Literary Studies, Townsville.

Haynes, Roslyn 1998, *Seeking the Centre: The Australian Desert in Literature, Art and Film*, Cambridge University Press, Melbourne.

Haywood, Ben 2004, 'Bid For My Babies', *The Age*, 24 May, p. 3

Headon, David 2002, *The Symbolic Role of the National Capital: From Colonial Argument to Twenty-first Century Ideals*, National Capital Authority, Canberra.

Healy, Chris 1997, *From the Ruins of Colonialism: History as Social Memory*, Cambridge University Press, Cambridge and Melbourne.

Heiss, Anita 1998, *Token Koori*, Curringa Communications, Sydney.

Henderson, Sara 2002, *From Strength to Strength: An Autobiography*, Pan Macmillan Australia, Sydney.

Herbert, Xavier 1938, *Capricornia*, Angus & Robertson, Sydney.

Hess, Michael 1994, 'Black and Red: The Pilbara Pastoral Workers' Strike, 1946', *Aboriginal History*, vol. 18, no. 1, pp. 65–83.

Hicks, Neville 1978, *This Sin and Scandal: Australia's Population Debate*, Australian National University Press, Canberra.

Hill, Barry 1994, *The Rock: Travelling to Uluru*, Allen & Unwin, Sydney.

Hill, Ernestine 1937, *The Great Australian Loneliness*, Robertson and Mullens, Sydney.

——1941, *My Love Must Wait: The Story of Matthew Flinders*, Angus & Robertson, Sydney.

Hillyer, Vivienne 2001 'Bennett House: Aboriginal Heritage as Real Estate in East Perth', *Balayi: Culture, Law and Colonialism*, vol. 2, no. 1, pp. 41–72.

Hinkson, Melinda 2004, 'What's in a Dedication? On being a Walpiri DJ', *The Australian Journal of Anthropology*, vol. 15, no. 2, pp. 143–64.

Hoffie, Pat 2003, 'Next Wave Coming', *Artlink*, vol. 23, no. 2, pp. 46–48.

Hogan, Trevor 2003, '"Nature Strip": Australian Suburbia and the Enculturation of Nature', *Thesis Eleven: Critical Theory and Historical Sociology*, no. 74, pp. 54–75.

Hollier, Nathan (ed.) 2004, *Ruling Australia: The Power, Privilege and Politics of the New Ruling Class*, Australian Scholarly Publishers, Melbourne.

Holmes, Katie 1999, 'Gardens', *Journal of Australian Studies*, vol. 61, pp. 152–62.

Homan, Shane 2003, *The Mayor's a Square: Live Music and Law and Order in Sydney*, Local Consumption Publications, Sydney.

Home, R.W., Maroske, Sara, Lucas, A.M. and Lucas, P.J. 1992, 'Why Explore Antarctica?: Australian Discussions in the 1880s', *Australian Journal of Political History*, vol. 38, no. 4, pp. 386–413.

Hooton, Joy 1995, 'Laurie and Noeline and Sylvania Waters' in David Headon, Joy Hooton and Donald Horne (eds), *The Abundant Culture: Meaning and Significance in Everyday Australia*, Allen & Unwin, Sydney.

Horin, Adele 2004, 'Women Bosses Take Sting Out of Queen Bee', *Sydney Morning Herald*, 3 April, p. 3.

Horne, Donald 1971, 'The Australian in the Mirror', *Australia: This Land, These People*, Reader's Digest, Sydney.

——1990, 'The Stockman's Hall of Fame', *Continuum: the Australian Journal of Media and Culture*, vol. 3, no. 1.

Horne, Julia 2005, *The Pursuit of Wonder: How Australia's Landscape was Explained, Nature Discovered and Tourism Unleashed*, Miegunyah Press, Melbourne.

Howard, John 1997, '7.30 Report', ABC television, cited at <www.pm.gov.au/news/interviews/1997/730wik2.htm>, accessed in January 2005.

——2000, 'Reconciliation Documents', Media Release, 11 May, cited at <www.pm.gov.au>.

Howard, Peter 2003, *Heritage: Management, Interpretation, Identity*, Continuum, London and New York.

Huggins, Jackie 1998, *Sister Girl: The Writings of Aboriginal Activist and Historian*, University of Queensland Press, Brisbane.

Huggins, Jackie and Blake, Thom 1992, 'Protection or Persecution?: Gender Relations in the Era of Racial Segregation' in Raymond Evans and Kaye Saunders (eds), *Gender Relations in Australia: Domination and Negotiation*, Harcourt Brace, Sydney.

Hughes, Helen 1961, 'The Eight Hour Day and the Development of the Labour Movement in Victoria in the Eighteen-Fifties', *Historical Studies*, vol. 9, no. 36.

Hughes, Robert 1970, *The Art of Australia*, Penguin, Melbourne.

——2004, *Isma-Listen: National Consultations on Eliminating Prejudice Against Arab and Muslim Australians*, Human Rights and Equal Opportunity Commission, Canberra.

Human Rights and Equal Opportunity Commission 1997, *Bringing Them Home: Report of the National Inquiry in the Separation of Aboriginal and Torres Strait Islander Children from their Families*, HREOC, Canberra.

Humphries, Barry 1990, *The Life and Death of Sandy Stone*, Macmillan, Sydney.

Huxley, John 2006, 'The Man and the Myth', *Sydney Morning Herald*, 18–19 February, pp. 1, 28.

Huxley, John and Ireland, Judith 2005, 'The Pride is High and There's No Holding Back', *Sydney Morning Herald*, 27 January, p. 1.

Inglis, Ken 1998, *Sacred Places: War Memorials in the Australian Landscape*, The Miegunyah Press, Melbourne.

Ion, Judith 1997, 'Degrees of Separation: Lesbian Separatist Communities in Northern New South Wales, 1974–95' in Jill Matthews (ed.), *Sex in Public: Australian Sexual Cultures*, Allen & Unwin, Sydney.

Isaacs, Jennifer 1992, *Aboriginality: Contemporary Aboriginal Paintings and Prints*, University of Queensland Press, Brisbane.

——1999, 'Indigenous Designs on Australia', *Art and Australia*, vol. 37, no. 1, pp. 66–74.

Iveson, Kurt 1997, 'Partying, Politics and Getting Paid: Hip Hop and National Identity in Australia', *Overland*, no. 147, pp. 39–44.

——2001, 'Counterpublics and Public Space: Comparing Labour Movement and Aboriginal Protest at Parliament House, Canberra' in Raymond Markey (ed.), *Labour and Community: Historical Essays*, University of Wollongong Press, Wollongong.

Johnson, Lesley (ed.) 1994, *Suburban Dreaming: An Interdisciplinary Approach to Australian Cities*, Deakin University Press, Melbourne.

Johnston, Craig and Johnston, Robert 1988, 'The Making of Homosexual Men' in Verity Burgmann and Jenny Lee (eds), *Staining the Wattle: A People's History of Australia*, Penguin, Melbourne.

Jordens, Ann Mari 1995, *Redefining Australians: Immigration, Citizenship, and National Identity*, Hale & Iremonger, Sydney.

Jorgensen, Darren 2004, 'Martian Utopia, Land Rights and Indigenous Desert Painting', *Futures Exchange: Australian Cultural History*, no. 23, pp. 105–19.

Joseph, Nicola 1996, 'Am I Black Enough for You?' in Ross Gibson (ed.), *Exchanges: Cross-cultural Encounters in Australia and the Pacific*, Museum of Sydney, Sydney.

Jupp, James 1991, *Immigration*, Sydney University Press, Sydney.

Kalantzis, Mary and Cope, Bill (eds) 2001, *Reconciliation, Multiculturalism, Identities: Difficult Dialogues, Sensible Solutions*, Common Ground, Australia.

Kell, Peter 2000, *Good Sports: Australian Sport and the Myth of the Fair Go*, Pluto Press, Sydney.

Kelly, Kim 2003, 'Outback South Australia', Youth Hostels Australia, cited at <www.backpackeressentials.com.au/article/feature.cfm?objectID=175>, accessed in January 2006.

Kirby, Joan 1998, 'The Pursuit of Oblivion: in Flight From Suburbia', *Australian Literary Studies*, vol. 8, no. 4, pp. 41–55.

Kirk, Alexandra 2000, 'Ruddock Stresses Need for Dialogue', *The World Today*, 29 May, cited at <www.abc.net.au/worldtoday/stories/s132161.htm>, accessed in May 2006.

Lake, Marilyn 1992, 'Mission Impossible: How Men Gave Birth to the Australian Nation—Nationalism, Gender and Other Seminal Acts', *Gender and History*, vol. 4, pp. 305–22.

——1999, *Getting Equal: The History of Australian Feminism*, Allen & Unwin, Sydney.

Lake, Martin (ed.) 2006, *Memory, Monuments and Museums: The Past in the Present*, Melbourne University Press, Melbourne.

Landes, Joan 2001, *Visualising the Nation: Gender, Representation and Revolution in Eighteenth Century France*, Cornell University Press, Ithaca.

Langton, Marcia 1993, *'Well, I Heard it on the Radio and Saw it on the Television . . .'*, Australian Film Commission, Sydney.

——1998, 'The Valley of the Dolls: Black Humour in the Art of Destiny Deacon', *Art and Australia*, vol. 35, no. 1, pp. 100–07.

——2000, 'Homeland: Sacred Visions and the Settler State', *Artlink*, vol. 20, no. 1, pp. 11–16.

——2006 'Out from the Shadows: The Significance and Development of the Aboriginal Tracker Figure in Australian Film' in *Meanjin*, vol. 65, no. 1, pp. 55–64.

Lawson, Valerie 2003, 'Struggling against the guilt-laden', *Sydney Morning Herald*, 25 August, cited at <www.smh.com.au/articles/2003/08/24/1061663673169.html?>.

Lever, Susan 2000, *Real Relations: Australian Fiction, Realism, Feminism and Form*, Halstead Press, Sydney.

Levis, Ken 1971, 'The Role of *The Bulletin* in Indigenous Short-story Writing During the Eighties and Nineties' in Chris Wallace-Crabbe (ed.), *The Australian Nationalists: Modern Critical Essays*, Oxford University Press, Melbourne.

Lobley, Katrina 2006, 'Rock the Block', *Sydney Morning Herald*, 5 May.

Lockyer, Helen 1993, 'Defiant', *SPAN: Journal of the South Pacific Association for Commonwealth Literature and Language Studies*, no. 37, cited at <www.mcc.murdoch.edu.au/ReadingRoom/litserv/SPAN/37/Lockyer.html>, accessed on 13 March 2007.

Low, Lenny Ann 2005, 'Made in Australia', *Sydney Morning Herald*, 26 January, pp. 17–18.

Lucas, Rose 1995, 'The Gendered Battlefield: Sex and Death in Gallipoli' in Marilyn Lake and Joy Damousi (eds), *Gender and War: Australians at War in the Twentieth Century*, Cambridge University Press, Melbourne.

——1997, 'Ancient Continents', *Southern Review*, vol. 30, no. 2, pp. 159–69.

Luckman, Susan 2001, 'Practise Random Acts: Reclaiming the Streets of Australia' in Graham St John (ed.), *FreeNRG: Notes from the Edge of the Dance Floor*, Common Ground, Melbourne.

Macintyre, Stuart and Clark, Anna 2003, *The History Wars*, Melbourne University Press, Melbourne.

McCauley, Kym 2000, 'From Terror to Terylene and Fit for a Queen: Some Representations of Masculinities in the Outback' in Jeff Dolyle, Bill van der Heide and Susan Cowan (eds), *Our Selection On Writings in Cinema's Histories*, National Film and Sound Archive/Australian Defence Force Academy Book, Canberra.

McCauliffe, Chris (ed.) 1994, *Beasts of Suburbia: Reinterpreting Cultures in Australian Suburbs*, Melbourne University Press, Melbourne.

McClymont, Kate 2006, 'Above All, He Was My Dad, and That's My Greatest Fortune', *Sydney Morning Herald*, 18–19 February, pp. 1, 10.

McGrath, Ann 1987, *Born in the Cattle: Aborigines in Cattle Country*, Allen & Unwin, Sydney.

McGregor, Craig 1966, *Profile of Australia*, Penguin Books, Melbourne.

——2001, *Class in Australia*, Penguin, Melbourne.

McGregor, Russell 1997, *Imagined Destinies: Aboriginal Australians and the Doomed Race Theory, 1880–1939*, Melbourne University Press, Melbourne.

McIntyre, Darryl and Wehner, Kirsten (eds) 2001, *National Museums: Negotiating Histories*, National Museum of Australia, Canberra.

McKee, Alan 1997, '"The Aboriginal Version of Ken Done . . ." Banal Aboriginal Identities in Australia', *Cultural Studies*, vol. 11, no. 2, pp. 191–206.

McKnight, David 2005, *Beyond Right and Left: New Politics and the Culture Wars*, Allen & Unwin, Sydney.

McLean, Ian 1998, 'Gordon Bennett's Home Decor: The Joker in the Pack', *Law Text Culture*, vol. 4, no. 1, pp. 287–307.

McMaster, Don 2001, *Asylum Seekers: Australia's Response to Refugees*, Melbourne University Press, Melbourne.

Maddison, Sarah 1999, 'Private Men, Public Anger: The Men's Rights Movement in Australia', *Journal of Interdisciplinary Gender Studies*, vol. 4, no. 2, pp. 39–51.

Maher, Sid 2004, 'Howard Presses Flesh after Welcome Rain', *The Australian*, 19 August, p. 2.

Main, George 2005, *Heartland*, University of New South Wales Press, Sydney.

Mangan, J.A. and Nauright, John (eds) 2000, *Sport in Australasian Society: Past and Present*, F. Cass, London.

Mann, Leonard 1963, *Venus Half-Caste*, Hodder & Stoughton, London.

Mansell, Michael 2002, 'Finding the Foundation for a Treaty with the Indigenous Peoples of Australia', *Balayi*, vol. 4, pp. 83–89.

Mant, Julia 2002, 'A Casualty of Constructs: Ted Harvey's War', *Journal of Australian Studies*, no. 73, pp. 27–39.

Marchbank, Thomas 2004, 'Intense Flows: Flashmobbing, Rush Capital and the Swarming of Space', *Philament: An Online Journal of Arts and Culture*, no. 4, cited at <www.arts.usyd.edu.au/publications/philament/index.htm>, accessed on 13 March 2007.

Marcus, Julie 1989, 'Prisoner of Discourse: The Dingo, the Dog and the Baby', *Anthropology Today*, vol. 5, no. 3, pp. 15–19.

—— 1997, 'The Journey Out to the Centre: the Cultural Appropriation of Ayers Rock' in Gillian Cowlishaw and Barry Morris (eds), *Race Matters: Indigenous Australians and 'Our' Society*, Aboriginal Studies Press, Canberra.

Mares, Peter 2001, *Borderline*, University of New South Wales Press, Sydney.

Markus, Andrew 1994, *Australian Race Relations 1788–1993*, Allen & Unwin, Sydney.

Marr, David 2005a, 'Alan Jones: I'm the Person That's Led This Charge', *The Age*, 13 December.

——2005b, 'One-way Radio Plays By Its Own Rules', *Sydney Morning Herald*, 13 December.

Marriner, Cosima 2004, 'Play School's Lesbian Tale Sparks Outrage', *Sydney Morning Herald*, 4 July.

Marx, Karl 1962, *Capital: A Critique of Political Economy*, Foreign Languages Publishing House, Moscow.

Matthews, Jill 1984, *Good and Mad Women: The Historical Construction of Femininity in Twentieth Century Australia*, Allen & Unwin, Sydney.

—— 1997, *Sex in Public: Australian Sexual Cultures*, Allen & Unwin, Sydney.

Mawson, Melinda 1999, 'The Boy Who Played the Man: Narratives of Masculinity in the Aftermath of the Port Arthur Massacre' in Katherine Biber, Tom Sear and Dave Trudinger (eds), *Playing the Man: New Approaches to Masculinity*, Pluto Press, Sydney.

Maynard, Sean 1989, 'Black and (White) Images: Aborigines in Film' in Albert Moran and Tom O'Regan (eds), *The Australian Screen*, Penguin, Melbourne.

Mellor, David 2004, 'The Experiences of Vietnamese in Australia: The Racist Tradition Continues', *Journal of Ethnic and Migration Studies*, vol. 30, no. 4, pp. 631–58.

Mendes, Philip 1999, 'From Protest to Acquiescence: Political Movements of the Unemployed', *Social Alternatives*, vol. 18, no. 4, pp. 44–50.

Menzies, Robert 1967, *Afternoon Light: Some Memories of Men and Events*, Cassell, Melbourne.

Metherell, Mark and Kennedy, Les 2001, 'Territory Economy is Mourning Loss of Income, Says MP', *Sydney Morning Herald*, 17 May, p. 11.

Michaels, Eric 1987, 'Western Desert Sandpainting and Post-Modernism' in *Kuruwarri: Yeundumu Doors*, Australian Institute of Aboriginal Studies, Canberra.

Mickler, Steve 1990, 'Curators and the Colony: Managing the Past at Rottnest Island Museum', *Continuum: the Australian Journal of Media and Culture*, vol. 3, no. 1.

Migration Heritage Centre 2003, 'A Multicultural Landscape: National Parks and the Macedonian Experience', Migration Heritage Centre, Powerhouse Museum Sydney, cited at <www.migrationheritage.new.gov.au/docs/npws/nsws-Contents.html>, accessed in May 2006.

Mitchell, Lisa 2003, 'Flashing the e-mob', *The Age*, 2 September.

Mitchell, Tony 2003, 'Australian Hip Hop as a Subculture', *Youth Studies Australia*, vol. 22, no. 2, pp. 40–48.

Moloney, John-Paul 2002, 'Tempers Flare at Reconciliation Place', *The Canberra Times*, 1 August.

Moran, Albert and O'Regan, Tom 1989, *The Australian Screen*, Penguin, Melbourne.

Moran, Anthony 2005, *Australia: Nation, Belonging and Globalization*, Routledge, London.

Moran, Rod 2003, 'Grasping at the Straws of "Evidence"', *Quadrant*, vol. 47, no. 11, pp. 20–24.

Moreton-Robinson, Aileen 1998, 'Witnessing Whiteness in the Wake of Wik', *Social Alternatives*, vol. 17, no. 2, pp. 11–14.

——2000, *Talkin' Up to the White Woman: Aboriginal Women and Feminism*, University of Queensland Press, Brisbane.

——(ed.) 2004, *Whitening Race: Essays in Social and Cultural Criticism*, Aboriginal Studies Press, Canberra.

Morgan, Tony, 2001, 'East Perth has become a "Classy" Urban Village of the Twenty-first Century', *Australian Property Journal*, November, pp. 718–24.

Morris, Meaghan 1998, 'White Panic or Mad Max and the Sublime' in Kuan-Hsing Chen (ed.), *Trajectories: Inter-Asia Cultural Studies*, Routledge, London.

Mosely, Philip 1994, 'Life and Sweaty: Ethnic Communities at Play' in David Headon, Joy Hooton and Donald Horne (eds), *The Abundant Culture: Meaning and Significance in Everyday Australia*, Allen & Unwin, Sydney.

Mosse, George L. 1985, *Nationalism and Sexuality: Respectability and Abnormal Sexuality in Modern Europe*, Howard Fertig, New York.

Mudrooroo 1995, *Us Mob: History, Culture, Struggle—An Introduction to Indigenous Australia*, Angus & Robertson, Sydney.

Muir, Kirsty 2002, '"Idiots, Imbeciles and Moral Defectives": Military and Government Treatment of Mentally Ill Service Personnel and Veterans', *Journal of Australian Studies*, no. 73, pp. 41–47.

Mundine, Djon 2005, 'White Face, Blak Mask (Apologies to Franz Fanon)', *Artlink*, vol. 25, no. 3, pp. 17–22.

Murphy, John 1995, 'Shaping the Cold War Family: Politics, Domesticity and Policy Interventions in the 1950s', *Australian Historical Studies*, vol. 26, no. 105, pp. 544–67.

Murphy, John and Probert, Belinda 2004, '"Anything for the House": Recollections of Post-war Suburban Dreaming', *Australian Historical Studies*, vol. 36, no. 124, pp. 275–93.

Murphy, Peter and Burnley, Ian 2002, 'Change, Continuity or Cycles: The Population Turnaround in New South Wales', *Journal of Population Research*, vol. 19, no. 2, pp. 137–54.

Murray, Scott (ed.) 1994, *Australian Cinema*, Allen & Unwin, Sydney.

Murrie, Linzi 1998, 'The Australian Legend: Writing Australian Masculinity/Writing Australian Masculine', *Journal of Australian Studies*, no. 56, pp. 68–77.

National Capital Authority 2002a, *Canberra: The Nation's Capital*, cited at <www.national capital.gov.au/plan/index/htm>, accessed in December 2005.

——2002b, *Guidelines for Commemorative Works in the National Capital*, NCA, Canberra.

National Museum of Australia 1999, *National Museum of Australia: A Museum for the New Millennium*, National Museum of Australia, Canberra.

——2006, *Many Rhymes One Rhythm: Young Australian Hip Hop From the Bush to the Plains*, cited at <www.nma.gov.au/exhibitions/community/many_rhymes_one_rhythm/>, accessed in May 2006.

Neill, Rosemary 2002, *White Out: How Politics is Killing Black Australia*, Allen & Unwin, Sydney.

New South Wales Parliament 1881, *Parliamentary Debates*, Australian Government Printing Service, Sydney.

New South Wales Rape Crisis Centre, *Information Sheets: Does Anyone Know How I Feel?*, cited at <www.nswrapecrisis.com.au/Information%20Sheets/Does-anyone-know-how-i-feel.htm>, accessed in May 2006.

Nicoll, Fiona 1993, 'The Art of Reconciliation: Art Aboriginality and the State', *Meanjin*, vol. 54, no. 4, pp. 705–18.

——1999, 'Pseudo-hyphens and Barbaric/Binaries: Anglo-Celticity and the Cultural Politics of Tolerance', *Queensland Review*, vol. 6, no. 1, pp. 77–84.

——2001, *From Diggers to Drag Queens: Configurations of Australian National Identity*, Pluto Press, Sydney.

O'Brien, Philippa 1999, 'History and Memory', *Artlink*, vol. 19, no. 1, pp. 56–59.

O'Malley, Nick 2003, 'Carr Savages Puplick's Race Report', *Sydney Morning Herald*, 2 May, p. 7.

O'Regan, Tom 2004, 'Australian Film in the 1970s: The Ocker and the Quality Film', *Oz Film: Australian Film Reading Room*, cited at <www.mcc.murdoch.edu.au/ReadingRoom/film/1970s>, accessed in April 2005.

O'Sullivan, Kimberley 1997, 'Dangerous Desire: Lesbianism and Sex or Politics' in Jill Matthews (ed.), *Sex in Public: Australian Sexual Cultures*, Allen & Unwin, Sydney.

Osuri, Goldie and Banerjee, Bobby 2004, 'White Diasporas: Media Representations of September 11 and the Unbearable Whiteness of Being in Australia', *Social Semiotics*, vol. 14, no. 2, pp. 151–71.

Ozdowski, Sev 2003, 'Long Term Immigration Detention and Mental Health', Diversity in Health Conference Sydney, October, cited at <www.hreoc.gov.au/speeches/human_rights/health_diversity.html>.

Palmer, Vance 1971, 'The Legend' in Chris Wallace-Crabbe (ed.), *The Australian Nationalists: Modern Critical Essays*, Oxford University Press, Melbourne.

Papastergiadis, Nikos 2004, 'The Invasion Complex in Australian Political Culture', *Thesis Eleven*, no. 78, pp. 8–27.

Paterson, Banjo 1992, *Selected Works*, Modern Publishing Group, Australia.

Pearce, Lynne 2000, 'Devolutionary Desires', in Richard Phillips, Diane Watt and David Shuttleton (eds), *De-centring Sexualities Politics and Representations Beyond the Metropolis*, Routledge, London.

Peel, Mark 2003, *The Lowest Rung: Voices of Australian Poverty*, Cambridge University Press, Melbourne.

Peers, Laura 2004, 'Repatriation—A Gain for Science?', *Anthropology Today*, vol. 20, no. 6, pp. 3–4.

Perera, Suvendrini (ed.) 1995, *Asian and Pacific Inscriptions: Identities, Ethnicities, Nationalities*, Meridian, Melbourne and La Trobe University, Melbourne.

——2005, 'Who Will I Become? The Multiple Formations of Australian Whiteness', *Australian Critical Race and Whiteness Studies Association Journal*, vol. 1, pp. 30–39.

——2006, 'Race Terror, Sydney, December 2005', *Borderlands e-journal*, vol. 5, no. 1.

Perkins, Hetti and Fink, Hannah 2000, 'Covering Ground: The Corporeality of Landscape', *Art and Australia*, vol. 38, no. 1, pp. 74–83.

Phillips, David L. and Willett, Graham (eds) 2000, *Australia's Homosexual Histories: Gay and Lesbian Perspectives V*, Australian Centre for Lesbian and Gay Research and the Australian Lesbian and Gay Archives, Melbourne.

Pocock, Barbara 2006, *The Labour Market Ate My Babies: Work, Children and a Sustainable Future*, Federation Press, Sydney.

Poynting, Scott 2004, *Living With Racism: The Experience and Reporting by Arab and Muslim Australians of Discrimination, Abuse and Violence Since 11 September 2001, Report to the Human Rights and Equal Opportunity Commission*, Centre for Cultural Research, University of Western Sydney.

Poynting, Scott, Noble, Greg, Tabar, Paul and Collins, Jock 2005, *Bin Laden in the Suburbs: Criminalising the Arab Other*, Institute of Criminology, Sydney.

Pratt, Angela 2005, *Practising Reconciliation? The Politics of Reconciliation in the Australian Parliament, 1991–2000*, Parliament of Australia, Canberra.

Pratt, Angela, Ellis, Cath and Elder, Catriona 2001, 'Papering Over Differences: Australian Nationhood and the Normative Discourse of Reconciliation' in Mary Kalantzis and Bill Cope (eds), *Reconciliation, Multiculturalism, Identities: Difficult Dialogues, Sensible Solutions*, Common Ground, Melbourne.

Pringle, Rosemary 1973, 'Octavius Beale and the Ideology of the Birth Rate: The Royal Commissions of 1904–1905', *Refractory Girl: A Women's Studies Journal*, vol. 3, pp. 19–27.

Probyn, Fiona 2005, 'An Ethics of Following and the No Road Film: Trackers, Followers and Fanatics' in *Australian Humanities Review*, no. 37.

Proudfoot, Peter R. 1994, *The Secret Plan of Canberra*, University of New South Wales Press, Sydney.

Pryor, Lisa and Lewis, Daniel 2004, 'Sydney It Ain't: and That's Why They Love It', *Sydney Morning Herald*, News Review 14–15 August, pp. 25, 32.

Prystupa, Steve 2001, 'Cross Currents of Change and the Future Role of National Museums' in Darryl McIntyre and Kirsten Wehner (eds), *National Museums: Negotiating Histories Conference Proceedings*, National Museum of Australia, Canberra.

Purcell, Leah 2004, *Black Chicks Talking*, Hodder, Sydney.

Queensland Police Service 2005, *Rape and Sexual Assault*, cited at <www.police.qld.gov.au/pr/program/p_safety/rape/rasa.shtml>, accessed in 2005.

Ramsey, Alan 2004, 'The Search for Wedges of Mass Destruction', *Sydney Morning Herald*, 9–11 April, p. 29.

Read, Charles 2005, *Sydney Morning Herald*, Letter to the Editor, 31 August, p. 12.

Reynolds, Henry 1987a, *Frontier: Aborigines, Settlers and Land*, Allen & Unwin, Sydney.

——1987b, *The Law of the Land*, Penguin, Melbourne.

Reynolds, Robert 2002, *From Camp to Queer: Re-making the Australian Homosexual*, Melbourne University Press, Melbourne.

Rheingold, Howard 2002, *Smart Mobs: The Next Social Revolution*, Perseus Publishing, Cambridge, Massachusetts.

Roach, Neville 2000, 'Reconciliation is a Race All Australians Must Run', *Sydney Morning Herald*, 2 October, p. 10.

Rose, Deborah Bird 1996, *Nourishing Terrains: Australian Aboriginal Views of Landscape and Wilderness*, Australian Heritage Commission, Canberra.

Rottnest Island Authority, 2005 'History and Heritage', cited at <www.rottnestisland.com/rotto/history_and_heritage/penal_aboriginal/>, accessed in December 2005.

Rutherford, Jennifer 2000, *The Gauche Intruder: Freud, Lacan and the White Australia Fantasy*, Melbourne University Press, Melbourne.

Ryan, Edna and Conlon, Anne 1989, *Gentle Invaders: Australian Women at Work*, Penguin, Melbourne.

Ryan, Robin 2001, 'Educational Perspectives on Indigenous Country Music', *The Australian Journal of Indigenous Education*, vol. 29, no. 1, pp. 43–48.

Said, Edward 1978, *Orientalism*, Routledge & Kegan Paul, London.

Salter, David 2006, 'Who's For Breakfast Mr Jones: Sydney's Talkback and its Mythical Power, *The Monthly*, no. 12, pp. 38–47.

Sayers, Andrew 2001, *Australian Art*, Oxford University Press, Oxford.

Scalmer, Sean 2006, *The Little History of Australian Unionism*, Vulgar Press, Melbourne.

Scanlon, Christopher 2004, 'A Touch of Class', *The Age*, 17 April.

Schaffer, Kay 1988, *Women and the Bush: Forces of Desire in the Australian Cultural Tradition*, Cambridge University Press, Melbourne.

Schlunke, Katrina 2005, *Bluff Rock: Autobiography of a Massacre*, Fremantle Arts Centre Press, Fremantle.

Scott, Kim 1999, *Benang*, Fremantle Arts Centre Press, Fremantle.

Scrutiny of Acts and Regulations Committee 2002, *Parliamentary Review of ANZAC Day Laws*, Parliament of Victoria, cited at <www.parliament.vic.gov.au/sarc/Anzac/Anzac%20Report.htm>, accessed in May 2006.

Sculthorpe, Gaye 2001, 'Exhibiting Indigenous Histories in Australian Museums' in Darryl McIntyre and Kirsten Wehner (eds), *National Museums: Negotiating Histories*, National Museum of Australia, Canberra.

Secomb, Linnell 2003, 'Introduction', *Cultural Studies Review*, vol. 9, no. 1, pp. 9–11.

Shapiro, Michael 1999, *Cinematic Political Thought: Narrating Race, Nation and Gender*, Edinburgh University Press, Edinburgh.

Sherwood, Juanita 1999, 'Community What is it?', *Indigenous Law Bulletin*, vol. 4 no. 19, pp. 4–6.

Smith, Anthony 1996, 'Memory and Modernity: Reflections on Ernest Gellner's Theory of Nationalism', *Nations and Nationalism*, vol. 2, no. 3, pp. 371–88.

Smith, Philip and Phillips, Tim 2001, 'Popular Understandings of "UnAustralian": An Investigation of the Un-national', *Journal of Sociology*, vol. 37, no. 4, pp. 323–39.

Smith, Rodney 2001, *Australian Political Culture*, Pearson Education, Sydney.

Smith, Sidonie and Schaffer, Kay 2000, *The Olympics at the Millennium: Power, Politics, and the Games*, Rutgers University Press, New Brunswick.

Spark, Ceridwen 1999, 'Home on "The Block": Rethinking Aboriginal Emplacement', *Journal of Australian Studies*, no. 63, pp. 56–63.

——2003, 'Documenting Redfern: Representing Home and Aboriginality on The Block', *Continuum: Journal of Media and Cultural Studies*, vol. 17, no. 11, pp. 33–51.

Spillman, Lyn 1997, *Nation and Commemoration: Creating National Identities in the United States and Australia*, Cambridge University Press, Cambridge.

Stephenson, Percy Reginald 1935, 'The Foundations of Culture in Australia: An Essay Towards National Self Respect' in John Barnes (ed.), *Writer in Australia*, Oxford University Press, Melbourne, 1969.

Stephenson, Peta 2003, 'New Cultural Scripts: Exploring the Dialogue between Indigenous and "Asian" Australians', *Journal of Australian Studies*, no.77, pp. 57–68.

St John, Graham (ed.) 2001, *FreeNRG: Notes from the Edge of the Dance Floor*, Common Ground, Altona.

Stocks, Jenni (ed.) 1998, *Images and Language '88: Aboriginal Perspectives on a Celebration*, Inner City Education Centre, Sydney.

Stopes, Marie Carmichael 1918, *Married Love: A New Contribution to the Solution of Sex Difficulties*, G.P. Putnam's Sons, London.

Stringer, Chris 2003, 'Bones of Contention', *Telegraph* (United Kingdom), 12 November.

Styles, Catherine Anne 2000, *An Other Place: The Australian War Memorial in a Freirean Framework*, PhD Thesis, Australian National University.

Summers, Anne 1975, *Damned Whores and God's Police: The Colonisation of Women in Australia*, Penguin, Melbourne.

——2003, *The End of Equality: Work, Babies and Women's Choices in Twenty-first Century Australia*, Random House, Sydney.

Sydney Gay and Lesbian Mardi Gras 1997, *Sydney Gay and Lesbian Mardi Gras Festival Program*, Sydney Gay and Lesbian Mardi Gras Inc., Sydney.

Taylor, Ken 1996, 'Anzac Parade: A Landscape of Memory', *Canberra Historical Journal*, no. 38, pp. 2–12.

Taylor, T.D. 1997, *Global Pop*, Routledge, New York.

Teo, Hsu Ming 1999, 'Shanghaied By Sheiks: Orientalism and Hybridity in Women's Romance Writing', *Olive Pink Society Bulletin*, vol. 11, no. 1, pp. 12–21.

Thomas, Mandy 2002, *Moving Landscapes: National Parks and the Vietnamese Experience*, NSW National Parks and Wildlife Service, Sydney.

Thomas, Ray 2002, 'Pride of Anzacs Brace for Raiders of the North', *Daily Telegraph*, 4 November, p. 5.

Thomson, Alistair 1994, *Anzac Memories: Living with the Legend*, Oxford University Press, Melbourne.

Tickner, Robert 2001, *Taking a Stand: Land Rights to Reconciliation*, Allen & Unwin, Sydney.

Tilley, Elspeth, 2002, 'Space, Memory and Power in Australia: The Case for No Nation', Refereed Articles from the Proceedings of the Australian and New Zealand College of Anaesthetists 2002 Conference: *Communication: Reconstructed for the 21st Century*, cited at <www.bond.edu.au/hss/communication/ANZCA/journtp.htm>.

Trinca, Helen 2000, 'The Battle for Australia's Waterfront', *Sydney Papers*, vol. 12, no. 3, pp. 107–10.

Troy, P.N. 2000, *A History of European Housing in Australia*, Cambridge University Press, Melbourne.

Tsiolkas, Christos 1995, *Loaded*, Vintage, Sydney.

Tully, James 1998, 'A Fair and Just Relationship: the Vision of the Canadian Royal Commission on Aboriginal Peoples', *Meanjin*, vol. 57, no. 1, pp. 146–66.

Turner, Graeme 1989, 'Art Directing History: The Period Film' in Albert Moran and Tom O'Regan (eds), *The Australian Screen*, Penguin, Melbourne.

——1993, *National Fictions: Literature, Film and the Construction of Australian Narrative*, 2nd edn, Allen & Unwin, Sydney.

——1994, *Making it National: Nationalism and Australian Popular Culture*, Allen & Unwin, Sydney.

Turrbal Traditional Owners, 'Turrball and Native Title' cited at <www.dakibudtcha.com.au/Turrbal_Native_Title.htm>, accessed in December 2005.

Vacation Australia 2005, 'Adventure Tours departing from Alice Springs', cited at <www.vacationaustralia.com.au/northern-territory/alice-springs.php>, accessed in December 2005.

Valentine, Alana 2004, *Run Rabbit Run*, Currency Press, Sydney.

Vandenberg, Andrew 2001, 'Reappraising the Waterfront Dispute of 1998', *Southern Review*, vol. 34, no. 3, pp. 22–40.

Varadharajan, Asha 1995, *Exotic Parodies: Subjectivity in Adorno, Said and Spivak*, University of Minnesota Press, Minneapolis.

Velayutham, Selvaraj and Wise, Amanda 2001, 'Dancing with Ga(y)nesh: Rethinking Cultural Appropriation in Multicultural Australia', *Postcolonial Studies*, vol. 4, no. 2, pp. 143–60.

Vromen, Ariadne 2004, 'Three Political Myths about Young People', *Australian Review of Public Affairs*, Digest 26.

Walker, Clinton 1996a, *Buried Country: The Story of Aboriginal Country Music*, Pluto Press, Sydney.

——1996b, *Stranded: The Secret History of Australian Independent Music, 1977–1991*, Pan Macmillan, Sydney.

Walker, David 1997, 'Australia as Asia' in Wayne Hudson and Geoffrey Bolton (eds), *Creating Australia: Changing Australian History*, Allen & Unwin, Sydney.

——1999, *Anxious Nation: Australia and the Rise of Asia 1850–1939*, University of Queensland Press, Brisbane.

Walker, Shirley 1988, 'Perceptions of Australia, 1855–1915' in Laurie Hergenhan (ed.), *The Penguin New Literary History of Australia*, Penguin Books, Melbourne.

Wallace, Natasha 2004, 'Short Skirt Questions Put to Rape Accuser', *Sydney Morning Herald*, 1 December.

Walwicz, Ania 1986, 'Australia', *The Penguin Book of Australian Women Poets*, Penguin Books, Melbourne.

Wang, Ning 1999, 'Rethinking Authenticity in Tourism Experience', *Annals of Tourism Research*, vol. 26, no. 2, pp. 349–70.

Ward, Russel 1958, *The Australian Legend*, Oxford University Press, Melbourne.

Waterhouse, Richard 2000, 'Australian Legends: Representations of the Bush, 1813–1913', *Australian Historical Studies*, vol. 31, no. 115, pp. 201–21.

Watson, Irene 2000, 'The Aboriginal Tent Embassy: 28 Years After It was Established: Interview with Isobell Coe', *Indigenous Law Bulletin*, vol. 5, no. 1, pp. 17–18.

Weber, Kimberley 1992, 'Imagining Utopia: The Selling of Suburbia' in *The Lie of the Land*, National Centre for Australian Studies, Monash University, Melbourne.

Welcome to Uluru–Kata Tjuta National Park n.d. (brochure) in *West Australian* 2005, 26–27 July.

Wells, Jeff 1998, *Boxing Day: The Fight that Changed the World*, Harper Sports, Sydney.

White, Richard 1981, *Inventing Australia: Images and Identity 1688–1980*, Allen & Unwin, Sydney.

Willett, Graham 2000, *Living Out Loud: A History of Gay and Lesbian Activism in Australia*, Allen & Unwin, Sydney.

Williams, Deane 1996, *Mapping the Imaginary: Ross Gibson's Camera Natura*, Australian Teachers of Media in association with Australian Film Institute Research and Information Centre, Melbourne.

Williams, Donald 2002, *In Our Own Image: The Story of Australian Art*, McGraw-Hill, Sydney.

Williams, Sue 2005, 'Revealed: Why Many Doubted Joanne Lees', *Sydney Morning Herald*, 18 December.

Willis, Anne-Marie 1993, *Illusions of Identity: The Art of Nation*, Hale & Iremonger, Sydney.

Wills, Sara 2002, 'Unstitching the Lips of the Migrant Nation', *Australian Historical Studies*, vol. 33, no. 118, pp. 71–89.

——2005, 'Passengers of Memory: Constructions of British Immigrants in Post-Imperial Australia', *Australian Journal of Politics and History*, vol. 51, no. 1, pp. 94–107.

Wilson, Jason 2002, 'A Game of Distinction: Football, the World Cup, and the Australian Urbane', *m/c reviews*, cited at <http://reviews.media-culture.org.au/sections.php?op=viewarticle&artid=156>, accessed in September 2004.

Wilson, Shaun 1998, 'Union Mobilisation and the 1998 Maritime Dispute', *Journal of Australian Political Economy*, no. 41, pp. 23–36.

Wilson, Shaun, Meagher, Gabrielle, Gibson, Rachel, Denmark, David and Western, Mark 2005, *Australian Social Attitudes: The First Report*, University of New South Wales Press, Sydney.

Windschuttle, Keith 2001a, 'How Not to Run a Museum: People's History at the Postmodern Museum', *Quadrant*, vol. 45, no. 9, pp. 11–19.

——2001b, 'Why There Should Be No Aboriginal Treaty', *Quadrant*, vol. 45, no. 10, pp. 15–24.

——2002a, *Submission to the Review of the National Museum*, cited at <www.nma.gov.au/libraries/attachments/review_submissions/Mr_Keith_Windshuttle.pdf>, accessed in February 2006.

——2002b, *The Killing of Aboriginal History: How Literary Critics are Murdering Our Past*, Encounter Books, San Francisco.

——2003, 'Doctored Evidence and Invented Incidents in Aboriginal historiography', in Bain Attwood, and S.G. Foster (eds), *Frontier Conflict: The Australian Experience*, National Museum of Australia, Canberra.

Wood, Dennis, 2002, 'Selling the Suburbs: Nature, Landscape, Adverts, Community', *Transformations*, no. 5, cited at <http://pandora.nla.gov.au/pan/24509/20030509/www.ahs.cqu.edu.au/transformations/journal/issue5/articles/text.htm#denniswood>.

Wotherspoon, Garry 1991, *City of the Plain: History of Gay Subculture*, Hale & Iremonger, Sydney.

Yunupingu, Galarrwuy 1997, 'From Bark Petition to Native Title' in Galarrwuy Yunupingu (ed.), *Our Land is Our Life: Land Rights—Past, Present and Future*, University of Queensland Press, Brisbane.

——1998, 'Indigenous Art in the Olympic Age', *Art and Australia*, vol. 35, no. 1, pp. 64–67.

Yunupingu, Mandawuy, Lui, Getanu, Anderson, Ian, Bell, Jeannie, West, Dott and Pearson, Noel 1993, *Voices from the Land*, ABC Books, Sydney.

Yarmirr, Mary Magulagi 1997, 'Women and Land Rights: Past, Present and Futures' in Galarrwuy Yunupingu (ed.), *Our Land is Our Life: Land Rights—Past, Present and Future*, University of Queensland Press, Brisbane.

Zubrzycki, Jerzy 1995, 'Arthur Calwell and the Origin of Post-War Immigration', Bureau of Immigration, Multicultural and Population Research, Canberra, cited at <www.multiculturalaustralia.edu.au/doc/zubrzycki_1.pdf>, accessed in May 2006.

INDEX

Aboriginal Day of Mourning 241–2, 243, 330
Aboriginal Tent Embassy 346–9
Aboriginal Year of Mourning 243–5
Aborigines Protection Act 244
ACTUP (AIDS Coalition to Unleash Power) 112
Adams, Phillip 196
Adams, Simon 330
Adventures of Priscilla, Queen of the Desert, The 69, 315
Alach, Felena 303
alternative lifestylers 313–14
Alvin Purple 195
Anderson, Benedict 25
Anderson, John 91
Ang, Ien 116
Anglo–Australian women 82–4, 97, 117, 120, 197, 306
Antarctica 223–30
Anthony, Larry 91
anxiety (national narrative) 17–18
Anxious Nation 17
Anzac Day 7, 10, 48, 111, 137, 239, 246–52, 260, 264, 278–80, 289
Arab–Australians 2, 135, 144, 208
Armstrong, Gillian 196
art
  and exclusion 187–8
  and gender 184–5, 186–8
  Heidelberg School 182–6, 187, 189

Indigenous 167–72
  parochialism 188–9
  women and the family 186–7
'Asian invasion' 12, 124–5, 127
assimilation
  gay men and women 112
  immigrants 129–31, 136
  Indigenous Australians 150, 159–60
asylum seekers 126, 127, 307, 311
ATSIC (Aboriginal and Torres Strait Islander Commission) 158
Attwood, Bain 255, 325, 326
Auction Squad 302
'Aussie bloke' 4, 5, 8, 26, 40, 47–8, 76, 100–1, 137, 139, 156, 190–1, 197, 198, 217, 303, 312
'Aussie digger' 99–100, 156, 247, 310
Aussie Rules 210
Australia Day 7, 10, 45, 127, 239–41, 244, 245, 260, 264
Australian Capital Territory Law Reform Society 109
Australian Film Commission 195–8
Australian Labor Party 14, 56, 57, 58, 60, 61, 95
Australian Rules football 76–7, 290, 295, 355
Australian War Memorial 323, 327, 341, 342–3, 344–5, 347, 350
Australian-ness
  and art 184–5

the bush 72–4, 137–9, 184–5, 186–7,
190–1, 311–13
and class 53–4
and film 196, 197, 198–200
and larrikin 5, 33–4, 36, 43, 47, 53,
86, 190, 303, 312, 317
and unions 269
and women 47
see also Anzac Day; 'Aussie bloke';
'Aussie digger'
Australians for Native Title and
Reconciliation (AnTAR) 254, 355
Avram, Elizabeth 200
Ayres, Tony 140, 281

Babe 200
Backroads 198
Bailey, Janis 263
Balibar, Etienne 29
ballads and the bush 50, 202
Balint, Ruth 310
Banerjee, Bobby 16
Banks, Joseph 71
Barak, William 173
Bardon, Geoffrey 168–9
beaches 303–7
Bean, C.E.W. 5, 50, 153, 154
Bell, Jeanie 165
Bell, Richard 170
Benang 159
Bennett, Gordon 171
Berry, Chris 112
Bertrand, Ina 195
Bhabha, Homi 30, 38
Biber, Katherine 75, 76, 156
birth rate 84, 90, 92, 96, 112
Bishop, Bronwyn 134
Black and White 210
Blackfellas 156, 200
Blak Like Me 102, 103
Block, The 302
'boat people' 127, 128
Box the Pony 104
Blue Hills 73
Border Protection Act 2001 126
boxing 296–7
Boylan, Patrick 320
Breaker Morant 196, 197
Brett, Judith 58
Breyley, Gay 205
Bringing Them Home report 9, 160, 253,
254

Britain and class 49–53
British immigrants 118–19
Brook, Heather 107
Broome, Richard 296
Bropho, Robert 337
Brown, Bob 3
Brown, David 75
Bryant, Martin 74
Bulbeck, Chilla 55
Bulletin school 42, 43, 99, 190–2
Bullock, Chris 294
Burke's Backyard 302
Burnley, Peter 314
Burns, Tommy 296
Burstall, Tim 198
bush, the
in art 184
ballads 50, 202
and gender 65, 72–4, 184–5, 186–7,
190–1
and literature 190–1
rural life 311–13
Butcher, Melissa 8
Buzzacott, Kevin 347
Byron Bay 313

Caddie 196
Calwell, Arthur 129
CAMP (Campaign Against Moral
Persecution) 109
Campbell, Alec 48
Canberra 339–50
Carey, Gabrielle 303
Carmody, Kev 240–1
Carr, Bob 143, 144, 145
Casey, Dawn 324–326
Castle, The 301–2
Cerwonka, Allaine 15
Chamberlain, Lindy 215, 216
Chant of Jimmie Blacksmith, The 155–6,
198, 199
Chauvel, Charles 194
Chinese 53–4, 122, 127, 137, 139–40
immigrants 119–20, 120–1
cinema *see* film
class 40–64
Australia 53–4
Britain 49–53
definition 41
as 'divisive' 60
inequality 42, 46, 53, 56, 58, 60, 61
and politics 56–7

and professionals 42
and social justice 60–3
and working man 42–9
Coe, Isobell 348
Collis, Christy 228, 229
colonial exploration and gender 69–72
colonisation 13–14, 16, 30, 61, 70, 89,
  103, 127, 148, 150, 164, 166, 168,
  170–1, 175, 182, 199, 220, 243, 323,
  334–5, 352
comedians and racism 142
'commentary' 30, 34, 42, 248
community 28
  and sport 293–5
Conder, Charles 182
Connell, Robert 67
contraception 84, 97
Cook, Hera 97
Cook, Captain James 32, 70, 228, 282
Cook, Kenneth 315
Cooper, Revel 168
Costello, Peter 60
Council for Aboriginal Reconciliation
  254, 255, 256–7
Council for Aboriginal Reconciliation Act
  253–4
country towns 104, 136, 287, 311–12,
  313, 314, 315–18
  see also bush, the; rural life
Coustas, Mary 142
Cowlishaw, Gillian 315–16
Cox, Paul 198
Craig, Lyn 87–8
cricket 6, 10–11, 289–90, 292, 355
Critical Mass 273–4, 275, 286
Cronulla riots 12, 117, 272, 304–7
Cubby, Ben 305
culture
  Australian 47, 50, 160–2, 181–2, 190–3
  global sexual 112–13
  Indigenous 149, 160–7
  and nationalism 24
Curthoys, Ann 246, 249
Curtin, John 97

Davison, David 298, 312, 324
Dawe, Bruce 301
Dead Heart 104–5
Death in Brusnwick 141
Denton, Andrew 294
Desperately Seeking Sheila 73
divorce 87–8

Dixson, Miriam 67
Djakapurra Munyarryun 35, 36
Dow, Carol 347
'Drover's Boy, The' 103
'Drover's Wife, The' 190, 191
Dungar-Hall, Peter 203
Dupain, Max 189

East Timorese 126
Effie 142
egalitarianism
  in Australia 4, 38, 41, 42, 44–6, 49,
    50, 51, 52, 53, 54–6, 61, 62, 64,
    79, 111, 191, 221, 342
  and exclusion 54–6
  and sport 295–8
Egan, Ted 103
eight-hour day 49, 264
Elder, George 43
Ellemor, Heidi 161
empowerment 87
equality 41, 49, 53–4, 55, 59, 61, 77, 80,
    113, 130, 133, 136, 144, 167, 173,
    192, 276, 295, 297
  see also inequality
Eros Foundation 330
ethnic enclaves 136–7
ethnicity
  and nation 115–45
  'typical Australian' 137–9
Everidge, Dame Edna 107
exclusion and egalitarianism 54–6

40,000 Horseman 194
families
  fatherhood 86–9
  gender 90–2
  Indigenous Australians 85–6, 89–90
  motherhood 82–4
  and sexuality 90–2, 96–8
Family Court 78
Family Law Act 78
Family Law Amendment (Shared
    Parental Responsibility) Bill 2005
    88
Family Tax Benefit Part B 82, 86
fatherhood 86–9, 90
  Indigenous 89–90
Federation 42, 43
femininity
  Anglo–Australian 120
  of Indigenous women 69

of women 68–9
  see also women
feminism 18, 26, 38, 69, 79, 86–7, 109, 280
film 104–5, 141, 156, 181–2, 193–200, 315
Finding Nemo 200
First Fleet 182, 239, 243, 244, 245, 328, 331
FJ Holden, The 198
flashmobs 262, 270–3, 274, 275, 285
Flinders, Ann 70–1
Flinders, Matthew 70–1
Flynn, John 335
Foucault, Michel 30, 106, 108
Francis, Rae 330
Franklin, Lady Jane 70
Franklin River 235–6
Franklyn, Lee 277
Fraser, Dawn 295
Freeman, Cathy 3, 257–8
French, Simon 75
Furphy, Joseph 190

Gallipoli 5, 43, 48, 50, 52, 86, 99, 246–52
  see also Anzac Day
Gallipoli 5, 52, 68, 196, 197, 247
gardens, suburban 308
Gauche Intruder, The 142
Gaudron, Mary 81
gay *see* homosexuality; lesbianism
Gelder, Ken 189
Gellatly, Kelly 170
Gellner, Ernest 24
gender
  and art 184–5, 186–8
  and the bush 65, 72–4, 184–5, 186–7, 190–1
  and colonial exploration 69–72
  and families 90–2
  hegemonic stories 67–9
  and the home 77–9
  and labour 185, 187, 190, 197
  and literature 190–3
  and nation 65–92
  and the paid workforce 79–82
  portrayal of men and women 66–7
  and sexuality 90–2, 93, 303
  subversive stories 67–9
  traditional roles 86–90
  and violence 74–7
  and white Australia 120–1

  see also 'Aussie bloke'; 'Aussie digger'; femininity; masculinity; women
Getting of Wisdom, The 196
Gibson, Ross 71
Giurgola, Romaldo 343–4
Goldsmith, Bobby 284, 356
Gleeson, Brendan 302
globalisation 3, 15–17, 41, 62, 270, 312, 313
  and neo-liberalism 57–9
Good and Mad Women 68
Gordon River 235–6
Goward, Pru 82
Gowland, Lance 276–7
Great Australian Loneliness, The 72
Green, Stephanie 72
Griffin, Marion 342
Griffin, Walter Burley 342–3
Grimshaw, Patricia 78
Gunn, Aeneas 73

Hagarty, Myra 294
Hage, Ghassan 116, 117, 129, 137, 141, 144, 149
Hall, Stuart 26
Haltof, Marek 193
Hanson, Pauline 59, 125
Harris, Mark 348
Harris, Max 300
Harvester Judgement 54, 55
Hassall, Anthony 212
Haynes, Roslyn 212
Head On 200
hegemonic masculinity 67–8
Heidelberg School artists 182–6, 187, 189
Heiss, Anita 166
Henderson, Sara 73
heterosexuality 6, 676, 90, 91, 93, 94, 95, 96–8, 99–100, 101–5, 108
heritage 328–31
  suburban 335–7
hijab 28, 134–5, 145
Hill, Ernestine 70, 72
hippies 313–14
HIV/AIDS 110–12, 278, 284, 285, 354
Hobday, Brian 278
Hogan, Paul 47, 137
Hogan, Trevor 298, 301
Hogg, Russell 75
Holmes, Katie 308
Home and Away 303

homosexuality 90–1, 94–5
  communities 108–9, 282–6, 317–18
  country towns 317–18
  HIV/AIDS 110–12, 278, 284, 285, 354
  and homosociality 98–101
  and identity 112–13
  and the law 105–7, 108
  Tasmania 94
  see also lesbianism; Sydney Gay and
    Lesbian Mardi Gras
homosociality 67, 68, 69, 93, 98–101, 197
Hooton, Joy 301
Horne, Donald 44
Howard, John 9, 18, 44, 84, 90–1, 92,
  126, 252, 254, 304, 309, 311–12, 349
Huggins, Jackie 85
Hughes, Robert 185
human rights 16, 56
Human Rights and Equal Opportunity
  Commission 135, 253
Humphries, Barry 107, 300
Hurley, Frank 228

identity
  sexual 90, 93–5, 107, 112–13
  stories 38–9
identity, Australian 40–1, 197, 198,
  259–60, 280
  working-class 48–9, 50, 61
  see also 'Aussie bloke'; 'Aussie digger';
    Australian-ness; masculinity;
    national identity; women
'imagined community' 26, 29, 30, 32,
  33
Imagined Corroborree 168
immigrants 144
  assimilation 129–31, 136
  British 118–19
  Chinese 119–20, 120–1
  ethnic enclaves 136–7
  Vietnamese 123–4, 128, 132, 135, 136
immigration 16, 51, 84, 124
Immigration Restriction Act 120–1
Indigeneity 10, 147–8, 159–63, 165–6,
  172, 217–19, 222, 243, 281
Indigenous Australians
  Aboriginal Day of Mourning 241–2,
    243, 330
  Aboriginal Tent Embassy 346–9
  Aboriginal Year of Mourning 243–5
  art 167–72
  assimilation 150, 159–60

and Australia Day 240–1, 244–5
authenticity 162–4
Bennett House 337
communities and cultures 149, 160–7
dispossession 331–5
Eora community 37, 241, 282, 357
eradication stories 150–5
fatherhood 89–90
and femininity 69
in film 156–7, 194, 198–200
Gurindji people 264–7, 270, 357–8
inter-racial relationships 101–5,
  315–17
and land 30, 147–9, 150–5, 165–71,
  174–6, 188, 244–5, 253, 309
Mabo decision 175, 253, 309
marginalisation 26, 28, 35–7, 89, 147,
  156, 282, 295, 316
men 89–90, 102, 103, 156, 187, 241,
  250, 295, 297, 338, 346
and music 202–6, 209–10
Myall Creek Massacre 339
and national heritage 330–5, 337,
  338–9
and national identity 26
Native Title Act 164, 253, 254
Northern Territory Land Rights Act 1975
  174, 243
parks and wilderness 232–3, 237
protection stories 157–8, 159
reconciliation 9, 18, 252–61, 349–50
right to vote 77
self-determination 148, 158, 172–4,
  256, 259
'stolen generation' 9, 85–6, 159–60,
  254, 257, 337
terra nullius 30, 35, 37, 70, 147–76,
  230, 241, 342
and tourism 151–3, 217–18
Uluru 213, 219–23
violence and eradication 151, 155–7,
  325–7, 338–9
women 69–70, 73, 85–6, 90, 102–4,
  172, 265, 337
and workplace inequality 55
Indigenous sovereignty 30
individual identity 26
Individual Workplace Agreements 89
industrial disputes *see* labour, protests;
  strikes
industrial relations reforms 53–4, 88–9,
  269

inequality
    class 42, 46, 53, 56, 58, 60, 61
    economic 42, 46, 61
    social 38, 46, 47, 48–9, 55, 113, 136,
        144, 210, 259
    workplace 55
inter-racial relationships 101–5, 315–17
Inventing Australia 6
in-vitro fertilisation (IVF) 90–1
Irwin, Steve 5, 33, 48, 65
Isaacs, Jennifer 169, 172
Iveson, Kurt 50, 201, 206, 263, 271, 275

Jackamos, Alick 296
Jackson, Judy 337
Japanese Story 200
Jedda 194
Jindabyne 200
Johnson, Colin 199
Johnson, Jack 296
Jones, Alan 44, 117
Joseph, Nicola 116, 208

Kalgoorlie 330
Kath and Kim 301
Keating, Paul 52
Kell, Peter 289, 295
Kelly, Paul 203, 266

Labour Day 264
labour
    Indigenous Australians 55, 79–82,
        265–7
    manual 42, 185, 190, 217
    masculine 40, 42–9, 185, 187, 190,
        197, 217
    and national identity 49–50, 187
    protests 262, 264, 269, 275, 286
    working man 40, 42–9
    and women 54–6, 79–82
    see also industrial relations reforms;
        strikes
Lake, Marilyn 38, 86, 191–2
land
    Antarctica 223–30
    the 'centre' 212–19
    front and back yards 308–10
    and Indigenous people 150–5,
        165–71, 174–6, 188, 217–19,
        244–5, 253, 309
    multiculturalism and parks 233–4
    parks and wilderness 230–3

suburban subdivision 307–8
    Uluru 213, 219–23
    wilderness 230–3, 234–8
Landes, Joan 99
Langton, Marcia 162–3, 169
Lantana 200
larrikin and Australian-ness 5, 33–4, 36,
    43, 47, 53, 86, 190, 303, 312, 317
Latham, Mark 14–15, 60
Lawson, Henry 42, 190
Lebanese–Australian 12, 117, 306–7
Lees, Joanne 215
Leong, Hou 137–8
lesbianism 90–1, 109, 282–6
    see also homosexuality; Sydney Gay
        and Lesbian Mardi Gras
Lette, Kathy 303
Liberal Party 56, 57, 58
lifestyle 49, 99, 112, 165, 208, 214, 299,
    302, 313
Lingiari, Vincent 265–6
literature 42–3, 189–93
Little Fish 200
Loaded 303
Lonely Hearts 198
Lucas, Rose 68
Lyons, Enid 77, 97

McCauley, Kym 94
McCubbin, Frederick 182, 185, 186,
    196
McGrath, E.C. 80
McGregor, Craig 42, 288, 298
McKee, Alan 155
McMansions 301, 358
McMaster, Don 127
Mabo decision 175, 253, 309
Mad Max 71
Mansell, Michael 163
Marchbank, Thomas 270, 271
Marcus, Julie 160, 215
marginalisation 28, 38, 89, 100, 147,
    156, 263, 282, 295
maritime union strike 267–9, 270, 275
Markus, Andrew 38
Married Love 98
Marshall, James Vance 104
Marx, Karl 41
masculinity
    Australian 156, 185, 190–2, 303
    crisis of 87
    hierarchy of 67–8

and labour 185, 187, 190, 197, 217
and literature 190–2
and violence 315
see also 'Aussie bloke'; 'Aussie digger';
    gender
mateship 100–1
Matrix, The 181
Matthews, Jill 68
Mawson, Douglas 225, 228–9, 230
Mawson, Melinda 75
May, Ngarralja Tommy 167, 168
media and racism 143
men
    fatherhood 86–90
    Indigenous 89–90, 102, 103, 156,
        187, 241, 250, 295, 297, 338, 346
    portrayal of 66–7
    see also 'Aussie bloke'; 'Aussie digger';
        gender; heterosexuality;
        homosexuality; masculinity
Michaels, Eric 167
Mickler, Steve 338
Midikuria, Les 171
Midnight Oil 201, 202, 203
*Migration Amendment (Excision from
    Migration Zone) Act 2001* 126
Mitchell, Thomas 71
modern nation 30
Moffatt, Tracey 170
Moran, Anthony 14, 57
Moreton-Robinson, Aileen 12–13, 38,
    311
Morris, Meaghan 13
Mosely, Philip 290
motherhood 82–4
'motherhood principle' 78
Moulin Rouge 181
multiculturalism 127–9, 131–2, 139–41,
    141–2
    limits of 132–6
    and parks 233–4
    and white Australia 115–18, 142–5
Muriel's Wedding 315
Murphy, Peter 314
Murrie, Linzi 190
museums 320–8
    colonial 321–3
    national 323–8
music
    American cultural imperialism 201–5
    Australian world 209–10
    contemporary 201

country 205–6
    hip hop and rap 206–9
Muslim–Australians 16, 28, 132–3,
    134–5, 144–5, 305
My Brilliant Career 192, 196
My Love Must Wait 70
Myall Creek Massacre 339
Myth of Male Power, The 78

Namatjira, Albert 168
nation 'phantasm' 30, 35–7
nation state 23
nationhood 26
national collectivity 30
national identity 26–8, 29, 38, 40–64,
    259–60
    see also 'Aussie bloke'; 'Aussie digger';
        Australian-ness; identity,
        Australian
national narratives 25
national parks *see* parks and wilderness
National Party 56, 58
national unity 29, 30
nationalism 24–6, 29–31, 36, 62, 144,
    183, 189, 196, 288, 344, 352
Native Title Act 164, 253, 254
neo-liberalism and globalisation 57–9
New South Wales Anti-Discrimination
    Board 143
Nicoll, Fiona 106, 111, 131, 258, 259,
    310
Northern Territory Land Rights Act 1975
    174, 243

O'Brien, Phillipa 168
On the Wool Track 50
One Nation Party 59, 125
One Night the Moon 156
Onus, Lin 172
orientalism 121–2
Osuri, Goldie 16
Outback Jack 73

Packer, Kerry 44
Page, Stephen 37
Palmer, Vance 189
Panopoulos, Sophie 134
Papastergiadis, Nikos 12
parks and wilderness 230–8
Paterson, A.B. 'Banjo' 42, 43, 190, 227
Patten, Jack 241–2
Perera, Suvendrini 11, 135, 306, 311

Perkins, Charles 174
Perkins, Rachel 156
personhood 26
Petersen 198
Picnic at Hanging Rock 195, 196, 197
Pilger, John 332
Pioneer, The 186
Pizza 142
Play School 91–2
politics
  and class 56–7
  and working class 48, 56
'populate or perish' 83
population 82–4
Port Arthur massacre 74–5
Preston, Margaret 169
Price, Steve 117
professionals and class 42
Prospectors and Miners Hall of Fame
  330–2
Proposition, The 200
prostitution 330
protests
  flashmobs 262, 270–3, 274, 275, 285
  labour 262, 264, 269, 275, 286
  smartmobbing 272
  Sydney Gay and Lesbian Mardi Gras
    10, 107, 111, 262, 276–9, 280,
    282–6
  Women in Black protest 270, 272,
    360–1
protection and Indigenous Australians
  157–8, 159
Puberty Blues 303
pubs 44–5, 100–1

Rabbit-Proof Fence 200, 210
Race for the Headlines 143
Racial Discrimination Act 1975 16
racism 36–7, 56, 139–41
  attitudes 116–17
  and comedians 142
  and country living 315–17
  Cronulla riots 12, 117, 272, 304–7
  in the media 143
  is power 117–18
  and sport 295–7
  and white Australia 142–5
Rankin, Annabelle 97
Rankin, Scott 104
rape 117, 132–3, 135, 249, 250, 251,
  306–7, 315, 332

Real Matilda, The 67
Reclaim the Streets 274–6
reconciliation 9, 18, 252–61
Reconciliation Convention 9, 18
refugees 92, 122, 123–4, 126–7, 128,
  133–4, 216–17
'representational code' 25, 26, 31, 33,
  42, 139, 204, 350
Reynolds, Henry 155, 255
Reynolds, Robert 109
Rheingold, Howard 272
Riley, Jack 43
Roach, Neville 258
Robbins, Sally 297–8
Roberts, Ian 76
Roberts, Rhonda 37
Roberts, Tom 182, 185, 196, 197, 199
Rottnest Island 338
Royal Flying Doctor Service 335
Ruddock, Phillip 216
rugby 107, 289, 290, 291, 293–4, 295
rural life 311–18
  see also bush, the; country towns
Russell, Todd 100
Russian Revolution 61
Rutherford, Jennifer 13, 14, 36, 69,
  124, 135, 142–3
Ryan, Lyndall 255

S11 63–4
Said, Edward 121–2
Scanlon, Christopher 59
Scott, Kim 159
Schaffer, Kaye 65
Sculthorpe, Gaye 324
Secomb, Linnell 28
Secret Country, The 332
self-determination 148, 158, 172–4,
  256, 259
sex and sexuality
  assault 117, 132–3, 135, 249, 250,
    251, 306–7, 315, 332
  and families 90–2, 96–8
  and gender 90–2, 93, 303
  global cultures 112–13
  and heritage 330–1
  identity 90, 93–5, 107, 112–13
  inter-racial relationships 101–5
  literature 98
  and nation 93–113
  regulation of 95–6
  and women 96–8, 303

see also heterosexuality;
      homosexuality; lesbianism
Sexy and Dangerous 102
Shame 72
Shearing the Rams 185, 197
Shapiro, Michael 29, 38
Sherwood, Juanita 166
Shiyab, Maha 134
Silver City 200
single mothers 85–6
smartmobbing 272
soccer 290–3, 294, 304
social inequality 38, 46, 47, 48–9, 55,
      113, 136, 144, 210, 259
social justice and class 60–3
Socialist Alternative 270, 272
society, British 49–53
Sons of Matthew, The 71
space and place 7–8
sport 287–8
   and community 293–5
   and egalitarianism 295–8
   national 289–90
   and the suburbs 298–9
   and racism 295–7
   un-national 290–3
   and violence 75–6
Stephenson, Percy 118–19
stereotypes 142
Stockman's Hall of Fame 330–2
'stolen generation' 9, 85–6, 159–60,
      254, 257, 337
Stopes, Marie 98
Stork 52
Story of the Ned Kelly Gang, The 193
street action 262, 271, 272
Streeton, Arthur 182, 183
Strictly Ballroom 141, 200
strikes 10, 56, 62, 262, 264, 265–9, 270,
      275, 286
   Gurindji walkout 264–7, 270, 357–8
   maritime union 267–9, 270, 275
suburban
   beaches 303–7
   front and back yards 308–10
   heritage 335–7
   life 298–308
   McMansions 301, 358
   subdivision of land 307–8
Sum of Us, The 94
Sunday Too Far Away 195, 197
Sunday Telegraph 125

Swan, Robert A. 226
Swan, Wayne 91
Sydney Gay and Lesbian Mardi Gras
      10, 107, 111, 262, 276–9, 280, 282–6
Sydney Gay Liberation 109
Sydney Morning Herald 78
Sydney Olympics 31–8, 287
Sydney Star Observer 110
systemic racism 145

Talking About Celia 165
Tampa incident 126, 310–11
Tangey, Dorothy 77
Tasmania
   gay law reforms 94
   Gordon/Franklin river 235–6
Ten Canoes 200
terra nullius 30, 35, 37, 70, 147–76, 230,
      241, 342
terrorism 135
Thatcher, Margaret 41
They're a Weird Mob 101
Thomas, Rover 169
Thornhill, Michael 198
Tilley, Elspeth 30
Tracker, The 156–7, 200, 210
trade unions 53–4, 57, 61, 63, 119
travel
   campaigns 151–3, 218
   the 'centre' 212–19
   Uluru 213, 219–23
Trinca, Helen 268
Tsiolkas, Christos 303
Turner, Graeme 24, 25, 196, 197
Two Bob Mermaid 316
'typical Australian' 137–9

Uluru 213, 215, 219–23
'un-Australian' 2–3, 5, 10, 12, 17, 27,
      59, 63, 111, 117, 133–4, 136, 267–9,
      298
   mothers 85–6
United Australia Party 57
United Nations
   Committee on the Elimination of all
      Forms of Racial Discrimination
      145
'unity-promoting articulations' 38

Valentine, Alana 294
Varadharajan, Asha 123
Velayutham, Selvaraj 141

violence
  Cronulla riots 12, 117, 272, 304–7
  domestic 249
  and gender 74–7
  and Indigenous people 151, 155–7
  and masculinity 315
  and sport 75–6
Vietnam War 11, 123, 133, 249, 262,
    344
Vietnamese 123–4, 128, 130, 132, 135,
    136
Voss 212

wages
  and Indigenous people 54–5, 265–7
  and women 54, 79, 81
Wake in Fright 71, 315
Walkabout 104
Walker, Clinton 205
Walker, David 17
Walker, Shirley 191
Walwicz, Ania 6, 139
war 249–51
  see also Anzac Day; Gallipoli
Ward, Russel 4, 5, 34, 47, 214
Wave Hill cattle station 265–7
We of the Never Never 73
Webb, Brant 100
Weber, Kimberley 298
Webster, Nikki 35, 37
Weeks, Jeffrey 111
West Australian 133–4
White, Patrick 193, 212
White, Richard 6, 51
white Australia 11–13, 83, 118–20, 147
  and desire 121–2
  and gender 120–1
  and heterosexuality 101–5
  invasion complex 122–7
  and multiculturalism 115–18, 142–5
  and racism 142–5
White Nation 116
wilderness 230–8
'Wildflowers and Other Landscapes'
    72
Willett, Graham 38, 108, 280
Williams, Deane 196, 200
Wills, Sara 126, 127
Wilson, Jason 293
Wilson, Shaun 267, 268
Windshuttle, Keith 255

Wise, Amanda 141
Wogboy 142
Wolf Creek 182, 216
women
  Anglo–Australian 82–4, 97, 117, 120,
      197, 306
  and Australian-ness 18, 26, 47
  and birth rate 84, 90, 92, 96, 112
  and the bush 65, 73, 186–7
  depicted in art 186–7
  depicted in film 197–8
  depicted in literature 191–2
  domestic violence 249
  and femininity 68–9
  and the home 77–8
  Indigenous 69–70, 73, 85–6, 90,
      102–4, 172, 265, 337
  motherhood 82–5
  national identities 26, 37–9
  portrayal of 66–7
  in public life 77–8
  'right to vote' 77
  sex and sexuality 96–8, 303
  and the suburbs 302
  and wages 54, 79, 81
  and war 249–51
  in the workforce 54–5, 79–82, 85
  see also feminism; gender; lesbianism
Women and the Bush 65
Women in Black protest 270, 272,
    360–1
women's movement 86–7
work see labour
Workers' Educational Association
    (WEA) 48
working man 40, 42–9
working-class
  Australian identity 48–9, 50, 61
  culture 44
  politics 48, 56
workplace inequality 55, 79–82
Workplace Relations Amendment (Work
    Choices) Act 2005 269
World Refugee Day 133–4
World War II 79–81
Wright, Tom 62

Yang, William 139–40
Yarmirr, Mary Magulagi 165, 166
Yunupingu, Galarrwuy 167, 172
Yunupingu, Mandawuy 156